Mass Dictatorship in the Twentieth Century

The concept 'mass dictatorship' addresses the (self-)mobilisation of 'the masses' in and for twentieth century dictatorship. In contrast to tyrannies which imposed power from above, mass dictatorships have encouraged multiple forms of active participation of the people. In this highly modern process, distinctions between subjects and citizens are blurred. Through deliberate strategies of political, social, cultural and moral manipulation and persuasion, mass dictatorships tend to represent themselves as, ostensibly, 'dictatorships from below', and are indeed deeply entrenched at a grassroots level. Free of the Manichean dualism which had characterised both the totalitarian and Marxist models of the Cold War era, the series stresses the dialectical interplay between power and people.

Gender politics, modernity, everyday life, memory and the imagination are the themes explored in the individual volumes of the series. What they have in common, and what makes the series unique, is the global scale of the comparativist approach taken throughout. Readers are thus invited to explore and interrelate the pre-World War II dictatorships of Fascism, Nazism, Stalinism and Japanese colonialism with the postwar communist regimes and post-colonial developmental dictatorships in Asia, Africa and Europe.

Series Editor: Jie-Hyun Lim
Professor of Comparative History and Director of the Research Institute for Comparative History and Culture, Hanyang University, Seoul

Editorial Board:

Peter Lambert
Lecturer in Modern European History at Aberystwyth University

Alf Lüdtke
Honorary Professor of Historical Anthropology at the University of Erfurt, and Distinguished Visiting Professor at the Research Institute for Comparative History and Culture Hanyang University, Seoul

Karen Petrone
Professor and Chair, Department of History, University of Kentucky

Michael Schoenhals
Professor of Chinese Studies, Center for Languages and Literature, Lund University

Other titles in this series:

Jie-Hyun Lim and Karen Petrone (*editors*)
GENDER POLITICS AND MASS DICTATORSHIP: GLOBAL PERSPECTIVES

Michael Kim, Michael Schoenhals, and Yong-Woo Kim (*editors*)
MASS DICTATORSHIP AND MODERNITY

Michael Schoenhals and Karin Sarsenov (*editors*)
IMAGINING MASS DICTATORSHIPS: THE INDIVIDUAL AND THE MASSES IN LITERATURE AND CINEMA

Jie-Hyun Lim, Barbara Walker and Peter Lambert (*editors*)
MASS DICTATORSHIP AS EVER PRESENT PAST

Forthcoming titles:

Alf Lüdtke (*editor*)
EVERYDAY LIFE IN 20TH CENTURY MASS DICTATORSHIPS: COLLUSION AND
EVASION

Paul Corner and Jie-Hyun Lim (*editors*)
THE PALGRAVE HANDBOOK OF MASS DICTATORSHIP

Mass Dictatorship in the 20th Century
Series Standing Order ISBN 978–0–230–30072–9 (Hardback)
978–0–230–30073–6 (Paperback)
(*outside North America only*)

You can receive future titles in this series as they are published by placing a
standing order. Please contact your bookseller or, in case of difficulty, write to
us at the address below with your name and address, the title of the series and
the ISBN quoted above.

Customer Services Department, Macmillan Distribution Ltd, Houndmills,
Basingstoke, Hampshire RG21 6XS, England

Gender Politics and Mass Dictatorship

Global Perspectives

Edited by

Jie-Hyun Lim

Professor of Comparative History and Director, Research Institute of Comparative History and Culture, Hanyang University, Seoul

and

Karen Petrone

Associate Professor of History, University of Kentucky, USA

First published 2010 by
PALGRAVE MACMILLAN

Palgrave Macmillan in the UK is an imprint of Macmillan Publishers Limited,
registered in England, company number 785998, of Houndmills, Basingstoke,
Hampshire RG21 6XS.

Palgrave Macmillan in the US is a division of St Martin's Press LLC,
175 Fifth Avenue, New York, NY 10010.

Palgrave Macmillan is the global academic imprint of the above companies
and has companies and representatives throughout the world.

Palgrave® and Macmillan® are registered trademarks in the United States,
the United Kingdom, Europe and other countries.

ISBN-13: 978–0–230–24204–3 hardback

This book is printed on paper suitable for recycling and made from fully
managed and sustained forest sources. Logging, pulping and manufacturing
processes are expected to conform to the environmental regulations of the
country of origin.

A catalogue record for this book is available from the British Library.

A catalog record for this book is available from the Library of Congress.

Transferred to Digital Printing in 2015

Contents

List of Illustrations

Acknowledgements

This book, the first volume of a series on mass dictatorship, was motivated by a conference called 'Mass Dictatorship and Gender Politics' that Jie-Hyun Lim hosted at Hanyang University, Korea in July 2006. The Research Institute of Comparative History and Culture (RICH) at Hanyang University organised six consecutive 'mass dictatorship' conferences between 2003 and 2008. Among themes such as 'coercion and consent', 'political religion and hegemony building', 'everyday lives between desire and delusion', 'gender politics', 'modernity' and 'coming to terms with past', the 4th Conference of Mass Dictatorship addressed the gender issue. The mass dictatorship project was inspired by a scholarly shift from the conception of 'dictatorship from above' to 'dictatorship from below'. This project assembled a trans-atlantic and trans-pacific scholarly constellation with the aim of a global study of dictatorship, without any claim to comprehensiveness.

Without the help of many friends, colleagues, and institutions, this book would have remained only in the realm of ideas. The Korean Research Foundation was the principal sponsor that financed the project and multiple international conferences. The editors would like to express our special thanks to the programme managers and administrative staff of the Humanities and Social Sciences Section of the KRF. Hanyang University and the French Cultural Council in Seoul also contributed funding. Dr Kim Chong Yang, the present Hanyang University president and Dr Pascal Dayez-Burgeon, a diplomat and historian in the French embassy, were very supportive of the project. 'Humanist Books', RICH's publication partner in Korea, made RICH's scholarly materials look virtually and visually rich. More than one hundred scholars from various corners of the world, including the authors of this volume, deserve gratitude as well. We are grateful particularly to Charles Armstrong, Stefan Berger, Paul Corner, Roger Griffin, Minoru Iwasaki, Kyu Hyun Kim, Michael Kim, Claudia Koonz, Volodymyr Kravchenko, Marcin Kula, Peter Lambert, Alf Lüdtke, Robert Mallet, Hiroko Mizuno, Martin Sabrow, Naoki Sakai, Michael Schoenhals, Feliks Tych and Michael Wildt for their multiple commitments. Unfortunately, it would be too long a list to name all of the wonderful colleagues who have participated in the mass dictatorship project, but their professional erudition must be acknowledged.

The research fellows of the mass dictatorship project, research assistants and the administration staff anchored at RICH made it possible for the mass dictatorship project to shift from the realm of ideas into concrete reality. The painstaking work of the staff and fellows at RICH produced the optimal conditions that enabled scholars from dozens of countries to participate in enormously productive scholarly exchanges. Dr Yong Woo Kim has conducted the individual and unique voices of these young scholars in miraculous concert. We are grateful to Choi Chatterjee for her perceptive comments on the manuscript, Peter Lambert for his assistance with editorial work, and Jae Kyom Shim, Matthew Wright and James Bartek for technical assistance. Finally our thanks are extended to Michael Strang and Ruth Ireland at Palgrave for their professional editorial work and friendship.

Jie-Hyun Lim and Karen Petrone, Kyoto and Lexington,
January 2010

Notes on Contributors

Yonson Ahn is a visiting professor in Korean Studies at Goethe University in Frankfurt, Germany, and a former Research Fellow at the East Asian Institute of the University of Leipzig, Germany. She has published on the issues of 'comfort women' during the Asia-Pacific War and on historical controversies in East Asia, such as debates over the ancient kingdom Koguryo/Gaogouli, colonial history in Korea, and historical revisionism in Japan.

Barbara Einhorn is Professor of Gender Studies in the Department of Sociology at the University of Sussex in Brighton, UK. Professor Einhorn's research concerns issues of citizenship, gender and civil society; gender and mass dictatorships; migration and notions of 'home' and belonging; nation and identity; religion, gender and conflict. She is best known for her work on gender and citizenship in Central and Eastern Europe. Her most significant publications include *Cinderella Goes to Market: Citizenship, Gender and Women's Movements in East Central Europe* (1993); 'Gender, Nation, Landscape and Identity in Narratives of Exile and Return', *Women's Studies International Forum*, 23(6) (2000), pp. 701–13; 'Gender and Civil Society in Central and Eastern Europe' (with Charlotte Sever), *International Feminist Journal of Politics*, 5(2) (2003), pp. 163–90; *Citizenship in an Enlarging Europe: From Dream to Awakening* (2006; 2nd edn forthcoming 2010); 'Insiders and Outsiders: Within and Beyond the Gendered Nation', in Mary Evans, Kathy Davis and Judith Lorber (eds), *Handbook of Gender and Women's Studies* (2006), pp. 198–215; *Questioning the Secular: Religion, Gender, Politics*, Special Issue of the *European Journal of Women's Studies*, 15(3) (2008); and (co-authored with Mary Evans) *Religion, Gender, Politics: Questioning the Secular* (2011 forthcoming).

Eun-shil Kim is currently Professor in the Department of Women's Studies at Ewha Womans University in Seoul, Korea. She has published many books and articles, including 'Questioning the Modernity of Rha Hye-Seok's Idea of "Newness" in Colonial/Modern Chosun' in the *Journal of Korean Women's Studies* (2008), 'The Gender Politics of Women's Migration: Focusing on the Discourse of "Women Lost" and Women's Experience of Migration in Korean-Chinese Society' in *Feminist Review* (Korea, 2006) and 'Itaewon as an Alien Space within the Nation-State and a Place in the Globalization Era' in *Korea Journal* (2004). Her research interests include gender politics along with globalisation, transnationalism, migration, emergent Asia and bio-power.

Kyu Hyun Kim is Associate Professor of Japanese and Korean History at the University of California, Davis. He received a PhD in history and East Asian languages at Harvard University specialising in modern Japanese history, and has since been an Edwin O. Reischauer Postdoctoral Fellow and a recipient of the Japan Society for Promotion of Science Grant. He is the author of *The Age of Visions and Arguments: Parliamentarianism and the National Public Sphere in Early Meiji Japan* (2007). He is currently working on his second book project, tentatively entitled 'Treasonous Patriots: Modernity, War Mobilization and the Problem of Identity in Colonial Korea'. Kim's other academic interests include the democratic and liberal traditions in modern Japanese history, Japanese popular culture, Korean cinema, the discourse on 'non-humanity' in Japanese culture, and the rise and decline of the 'moderate' left in immediate post-war Korea.

Michael Kim is Assistant Professor of Korean History at Yonsei University's Graduate School of International Studies in Seoul, Korea. He received his PhD in Korean History from the East Asian Languages and Civilizations Department at Harvard University. His research primarily focuses on colonial Korea, and he has published on urban culture, print culture, collaboration and the wartime mobilisation of Koreans.

Sangsoo Kim is Assistant Professor of the Faculty of English, Hankuk University of Foreign Studies, South Korea. His major publications include 'The Language of Socialism in Public Debate in Britain, 1880–1914' (2005, PhD Dissertation, Cambridge) and 'The Relationship between History and Literature: Intertextuality and Agency', *The Haskins Society Journal* 14 (2007), Kumamoto, Japan. He is interested in political discourses in modern Britain and the relationship between history and literature.

Claudia Koonz has taught courses on genocide and European history at Duke University since 1990. After conducting research on Nazi Germany for years, and writing *Mothers in the Fatherland* (1988) and *The Nazi Conscience* (2005) she shifted her focus to West Europeans' reactions to the Muslim headscarf, or hijab.

Jie-Hyun Lim is Professor of Comparative History at Hanyang University in Seoul, South Korea. He is director of the Research Institute of Comparative History and Culture in Seoul, and has held visiting appointments at Cracow Pedagogical University (Poland), Warsaw University (Poland), Glamorgan (Wales), Nichibunken (Kyoto) and Harvard University (USA). He is the author of numerous books on comparative histories of nationalist movements, the socio-cultural history of Marxism in East Asia and Eastern Europe and issues of memory, colonialism and dictatorship in East Asia (in Korean). He is now writing a monograph on the transnational history of 'victimhood nationalism'.

Alf Lüdtke, born in 1943; after having retired from the Max Planck Society in 2008, he is now Honorarprofessor at the University of Erfurt and co-organiser of the Graduate School on 'Media and History' (University of Erfurt, Weimar and Jena); he also holds a Distinguished Visiting Professorship at Hanyang University, Seoul. His research focus is on the 'field of forces' of domination and violence; practices of work and the emergence of 'modern' forms of the visual. Among his publications are *State and Police in Prussia, 1815–1850* (1989); *Alltagsgeschichte* (1989, French 1993, English 1995, Korean 2002); *Herrschaft als soziale Praxis* (1991); *Eigen-Sinn. Fabrikalltag, Arbeitererfahrungen und Politik* (1993); *Die DDR im Bild* (2004); *The No Man's Land of Violence. Extreme Wars in the 20th Century* (2006); *Staats-Gewalt: Ausnahmezustand und Sicherheitsregimes* (2008); 'Energizing the Everyday: On the Breaking and Making of Social Bonds in Nazism and Stalinism', in M. Geyer and S. Fitzpatrick (eds), *Beyond Totalitarianism: Stalinism and Nazism Compared* (2009), pp. 266–301 (co-authored with S. Fitzpatrick); 'Purification: Pleasure and Pain. The Opening of the East German Stasi Files and the Politics of German History in the 1990s', in Denis Laborde (ed.), *Désirs d'histoire. Politique, mémoire, identité* (2009), pp. 41–68.

Małgorzata Mazurek is a Postdoctoral Fellow at the Center for Contemporary History Potsdam, Germany. She graduated from Warsaw University and the Graduate School for Social Research at the Polish Academy of Sciences. She is the author of *Socialist Factory: Workers in Communist Poland and the GDR on the Eve of the 1960s* (2005) and of several articles on the comparative and social history of post-war Poland in

Polish, German, French and English. Her second book *Society in Waiting Lines: On Experiences of Shortages in Postwar Poland* will be published in 2010 in Polish. She is currently writing a history of Polish intellectuals working on decolonisation, planning and development studies in post-war Warsaw.

Karen Petrone is Associate Professor of History at the University of Kentucky, USA. Her research interest is in twentieth-century Russian (and Soviet) cultural and gender history. She is the author of *Life Has Become More Joyous, Comrades: Celebrations in the Time of Stalin* (2000) and co-editor (with Valerie Kivelson, Michael S. Flier and Nancy Shields Kollmann) of *The New Muscovite Cultural History: A Collection in Honor of Daniel B. Rowland* (2009). Her forthcoming book *The Great War in Russian Memory* will be published in 2011.

Michael Schoenhals is Professor of Chinese at the Centre for Languages and Literature, Lund University, Sweden. He has published on the social and political history of modern China, including a history of the Cultural Revolution entitled *Mao's Last Revolution* (2006) (co-authored with Roderick MacFarquhar). He is co-founder of the Forum för litteraturens offentligheter (FOLIO), a Swedish interdisciplinary academic forum bringing together researchers interested in exploring how writers and constellations of readers emerge as actors in public settings by attempting to employ literature and literary works for non-literary purposes.

Woonok Yeom is Research Professor at the Institute of World and Global History at Ewha Womans University. She has recently published the book *DNA Politics and British Eugenics* (2009) in Korean. She is also co-author of *Memory and Body* (2008) and *Body in Everyday Life* (2009). Her research interests include eugenics, gender studies and migration and ethnicity studies.

Series Introduction: Mapping Mass Dictatorship: Towards a Transnational History of Twentieth-Century Dictatorship

Jie-Hyun Lim

Beyond the history of martyrdom

The idea of 'mass dictatorship' originated in my encounter with the history politics of coming to terms with the past in South Korea and Poland. In the midst of radical democratic transformations sweeping through these two societies at the end of the Cold War, I have lived a complicated present history as a participatory observer wandering over the transnational space between Korea and Poland. In the last two decades, these two post-totalitarian democracies have shared a history of martyrdom supported by twin pillars of memory: of tragic victimhood and of heroic resistance.[1] Any challenge to this dominant memory in the post-totalitarian era would have been dismissed as politically 'incorrect' in both countries. But a history of martyrdom, however popular, was only made possible by ironing out crooked histories and memories, converting them into a neatly lined History. Plural memories betray and rupture such a linear History. As Vaclav Havel constantly stressed, the line did not run clearly between victimisers and victims. Rather, it ran through each individual. Not everyone was an accomplice but everyone was in some measure co-responsible for what had been done.[2] Adam Michnik's stance, represented by his slogan of 'amnesty yes, amnesia no', seems implicitly to allude to this complexity of coming to terms with the past in post-totalitarian Poland.[3] As the *lustracja* controversy shows, coming to terms with the past of communist dictatorship is too complex to accommodate the popular history of martyrdom.

In Korea, the memory war over the past of Park Chung-hee's development dictatorship spawned a new problem set in relation to establishing 'what happened in and to the dictatorship'. The socially widespread nostalgia for Park's era has been extremely embarrassing to left-wing

1

intellectuals, for whom the phenomenon was wholly unexpected in the context of a now democratised Korea. The Korean version of memory war and the *lustracja* controversy has revolved around 'how to read this perplexing nostalgia'. In my essay on 'Reading the Code of Everyday Fascism' which triggered a sharp controversy over the legacy of developmental dictatorship, I raised questions concerning the fascist *habitus* and *mentalité*, and how they have been accommodated in the everyday life of many a Korean since the dictatorship era. Dictatorship as a political regime is long gone, but fascist *habitus* still reigns in everyday practices and influences people's way of thinking. So this nascent political democracy is haunted by the legacy of dictatorship. In a subsequent essay on 'Fascists' War of Position and Dictatorship of Consent', I proposed a transnational history of dictatorship. By reflecting on the history of coming to terms with the past in post-war Germany, Italy and Poland, I tried to suggest that the popular nostalgia for the era of dictatorship is not a Korean peculiarity. Neither is trying to explain that nostalgia by reducing it to a by-product of one's political opponents' propaganda a unique response.[4] Even though memories are often framed according to its precepts, the conspiratorial propaganda theory cannot explain under what circumstances, why and how popular memories are susceptible to this propaganda.

What is most intriguing in the transnational history of dictatorship is the contrast in the political constellations involved in coming to terms with the past. A strange convergence of anti-communist Korean right wingers and old fashioned Polish communists is discernable. They have misused and abused popular nostalgia to excuse the developmental dictatorship and communist regime respectively. Conversely, my essays on 'Everyday Fascism' and 'Fascists' War of Position' have met with vehement opposition from the Korean left-wing intellectual establishment, just as Havel's and Michnik's stance against the *lustracja* provoked angry responses from the anti-communist Right in the Czech Republic and Poland.[5] That bizarre discursive companionship of the political rival camps in a transnational space freed me from demonological discourses, be they right- or left-wing. It put a question mark behind the usefulness of both the totalitarian and Marxist paradigms, obsessed as they are with a simplistic dualism which posits a few vicious perpetrators (the dictator and his cronies) and many innocent victims (the people). The Manichean presentism of the Cold War blinded both camps to the diverse forms of popular support for the dictatorships to which they were politically opposed. A historicisation freed from ideological obsessions casts serious doubt on that moralist and cliché-ridden Cold

War saga of the history of martyrdom. 'Mass dictatorship' is a term designed in the light of this transnational reflection in the post-Cold War era.[6]

Mass dictatorship in post-colonial perspectives

'Mass dictatorship' as a working hypothesis starts from a simple question: what is the difference between pre-modern despotism and modern dictatorship? My tentative answer is that despotism does not need massive backing from below, but modern dictatorship presupposes mass support. The term 'mass dictatorship' implies the attempted mobilisation of the masses by dictatorships, and that these frequently secured voluntary mass participation and support.[7] Once the masses had appeared on the historical scene, voices of ordinary people could no longer be silenced or disregarded by any regime, whether democratic or dictatorial. Rather, the socio-political engineering of the modern state system demanded the recruitment and mobilisation of the masses for the nation-state project, and indeed commanded their enthusiasm and voluntary participation. Two world war experiences demonstrated the vital importance to the total war system of the voluntary mobilisation and participation of the masses. That helps explain why a modern state system whose defining features included 'universal suffrage/plebiscite as a popular endorsement', 'compulsory education/nationalisation of the masses', 'universal conscription/national appellation' and 'social welfare/social bribery' was adopted not only by democracies but also by dictatorships. Mass dictatorship is dictatorship appropriating modern statecraft and egalitarian ideology, and thus its study needs to be situated in a broader transnational context of political modernity understood in relation to territoriality, sovereignty, population and so on. It is at this moment that 'dictatorship from above' transforms itself into 'dictatorship from below'.

Thus, mass dictatorship is far from being an inevitable product of deviation or aberration from a normal path to modernity, or of the dominance of pre-industrial, pre-capitalist and pre-bourgeois authoritarian and feudal traditions. Mass dictatorship argues against the *Sonderweg* thesis which seeks to set Nazism, and perhaps other manifestations of fascism, apart from parliamentary democracies of the 'West' because of the bourgeoisie's alleged lack of 'emancipatory will' and 'sense of citizenship'.[8] The dichotomy of a particular/abnormal path in the 'Rest' – quintessentially represented by Germany – and a universal/normal path in the 'West' presupposes a hierarchical order of comparison in which the 'West' occupies the position of universality. In this dichotomy, the history of the 'West' becomes the hegemonic mirror in which histories of the 'Rest' reflect themselves. In this way the comparison of aberrant dictatorship and normative democracy strengthens a Western/European claim to exceptionalism, according to which democracy, equality, freedom, human rights, rationalism, science and industrialism promulgated by the European Enlightenment are phenomena unique to the 'West'. The normative presupposition inherent in the *Sonderweg* thesis implies Eurocentrism, suggesting that the 'West' has achieved the maturation of the unique historical conditions necessary for democracy and human rights. In the 'Rest', in contrast, these remained un- or underdeveloped. In fact, this sort of Eurocentrism is profoundly misleading, encouraging us to believe that fascism and the Holocaust can be reduced to manifestations of peculiarities of the pre-modern 'Rest'. The argument serves as the historical alibi of the modernist 'West', which is thus exempted from association with a barbarism defined *ab initio* as pre-modern.[9] That is precisely why mass dictatorship should be mapped onto the transnational history of modernity.

Eurocentrism is reinforced by the clichéd, geographically positivistic concept of East and West, and of Asia and Europe. But neither Europe nor Asia is a positivistic concept. Neither is geographically fixed. The 'strategic location' of each is always in flux in historical discourse. Both are relational concepts that have their own significance only when they are co-figured in the discursive context of the 'problem space'. The 'problem space' of mass dictatorship enables us to see the twentieth-century dictatorship not as the end-point of a particular path of the pre-modern, but as one of the normal paths of the modern, and ultimately to displace 'East' and 'West' as usable categories. The strategic location of interwar Germany, Italy and Russia as the 'problem space' of mass dictatorship is equivalent to a semi-periphery or to the 'East in the West'. It is intriguing to remember that Konrad Adenauer, a German politician from the western Rhineland, muttered 'Asia' every time his train crossed the Elbe into Prussia.[10] In short, those countries which experienced mass dictatorship occupied the position of East in an 'imaginative geography'.[11] In so far as each nation-state is essentialised as the basic analytical unit, the hierarchical order of Asia/Europe and East/West remains intact in a comparative framework. A shift from the 'reified geography' of the dichotomy of East and West to the 'problem space' of the co-figuration of East and West would make it possible to see both mass dictatorship and mass democracy as products of processes of transculturation inherent in modernity.[12] The East/West divide does not make any substantial difference since each of its sides belongs to the same 'problem space' of modernity.

It is through a transnational history of mass dictatorship that one can put the dictatorship of the 'East' and democracy of the 'West' together on the global horizon of modernity. Both democracy and dictatorship are located not in some pre-existing spaces but in the 'problem space' of constant becoming. Once conscripted to modernity's project, people were coercively obliged to render themselves simultaneously as objects and agents of modernity.[13] The historical singularity either of a dictatorship or of a democracy can be analysed from global perspectives on the formation of the modern nation-state. Each kind of formation of the nation-state is a result of negotiations among various conscripts of modernity. Viewed from global perspectives, traditionalism as the ideological proponent of mass dictatorship appears not as a product of the pre-modern but as a variant of modernist discourse. Traditionalism is different from traditional paradigms for the very reason that it constitutes traditionalistic counter-movements against the dominant trend of the West.[14] More sophisticated discourses of 'alternative modernity', 'retroactive modernity', 'modernism against modernity', 'capitalism without capitalism' and so on were also rampant in the metaphorical language of mass dictatorship. They reflect a consciousness that 'oscillated furiously between recognising the peril of being overcome by modernity and the impossible imperative of overcoming it' in the latecomers' society.[15]

Zygmunt Bauman's warning that Holocaust-style genocide should be recognised as a logical outcome of the civilising tendency to subordinate the use of violence to a rational calculus echoes through the transnational perspective. He is suspicious of any attempt to attribute the Nazi atrocities either to certain peculiar convolutions of German history or to the moral indifference and latent anti-Semitism of ordinary Germans.[16] To him, the German *Sonderweg* thesis seems to exonerate the modernity and 'West' from the potentiality of the genocide. This is where transnational perspectives meet post-colonial perspectives in understanding mass dictatorship.[17] To say that 'the transnational meets the post-colonial' is not to imply a linear continuity between German colonialism in South-West Africa and the Holocaust. The Holocaust should not be reduced to another peculiarity of German colonialism. Rather, the Holocaust should be seen in the context of the continuity of 'Western' colonialism, as Hannah Arendt suggested when she articulated the concept of 'administered mass killing' (*Verwaltungsmassenmord*) in respect to the British colonial experience.[18] In other words, the German colonialists' genocide as the breaking of a taboo in the Herero and Nama wars in 1904–07 can be better explained from the transnational perspectives of Euro-colonialism than by recourse to German peculiarities deriving from the circumstance of a latecomer's colonialism. More broadly, one cannot miss the history of a primitive accumulation, full of conquest, enslavement, robbery, murder and all forms of violence in the making of the modern nation-state. The emergence of capitalism and democracy in the 'Western' nation-state should be viewed as having taken place, in Marx's terms, 'under circumstances of ruthless terrorism'.[19]

In fact, the Nazi utopia of a racially purified German empire was mimicry of Western colonialism, 'turning imperialism on its head and treating Europeans as Africans'.[20] Nazi Germans must have felt a kind of 'white man's burden' inside Europe as they regarded Slavic people as 'white negroes' and Slavic land as 'Asia'. Hitler did not stick to a reified geography. He stated explicitly that 'the border between Europe and Asia is not the Urals but the place where the settlements of Germanic types of people stop and pure Slavdom begins'. And 'the Slavs would provide the German equivalent of the conquered native populations of India and Africa in the British empire'.[21] Among Germans in the occupied 'East', it was not difficult to find a sense of cultural superiority similar to that associated with a colonial mission. Indeed, 'Western' colonialism provided an important historical precedent for the Nazis' genocidal thinking. A certain historical connection between colonial genocide and Nazi crimes is undeniable. Genocide of the Native Americans in the frontiers, British colonial genocide in India and Africa, Stalinist mass murder of the kulaks and the Holocaust all belong to the same category of the 'categorical murder' spurred by the essentialist tendency to categorise others on the basis of race, ethnicity, class and so on.[22] From the viewpoint of 'colonialism within', this colonial legacy was bequeathed to colonial subjects who were to be reborn as modern subjects of the independent nation-state in the post-colonial era. The post-colonial type of mass dictatorship, such as the developmental dictatorship in South Korea, provides a vivid example.[23] The interaction of colonisers and the colonised is a key to understanding mass dictatorship in the post-colonial era.

Mixed twins: mass dictatorship and mass democracy

Post-colonial, and perhaps also post-structuralist perspectives on the transnational history of mass dictatorship demand a reformulation of the question: what is the difference between mass dictatorship and mass democracy? The answer is not that simple. What if majoritarian democracy in the modern nation-state is based on the categorisation of minorities as 'Others' in terms of nation, class, gender, race, ethnicity and so on? What if the majority tyrannise minorities? Is that democracy or is it dictatorship? Arguably, the cliché that dictatorship was imposed by a wilful minority upon a confused majority cannot withstand historical scrutiny. A history of modern colonies reveals that, in certain contexts, settler democracies have been more murderous than authoritarian colonial governments.[24] It is also intriguing that 'regimes newly embarked upon democratisation are more likely to commit murderous ethnic cleansings than are stable authoritarian regimes'.[25] And much later, the Hutus' slogan of 'majoritarian democracy' in Rwanda expressed their conviction that 'whoever rules in the name of the "majority people" is ontologically democratic'. It opened the road to the massacre of Tutsis.[26] The characterisation of American democracy as a 'tyranny through masses' (Alexis Tocqueville) and the identification of 'totalitarian democracy' among French Jacobins (J. L. Talmon), insinuate 'mass dictatorship' in more telling ways than does Mao Zedong's declaration that 'dictatorship is dictatorship by the masses'.[27] It is very intriguing that socialist regimes used the metaphor of 'people's democracy' in defining themselves as a variant of proletarian dictatorship.

If mass democracy means rule by the ordinary people, mass dictatorship presupposes the transformation of the chaotic crowd of ordinary people into a disciplined uniform mass, a collective characterised by its homogeneous identity, unitary will and common goal. However, a disciplined uniformity and homogeneous collectivity of the masses is imaginary. In so far as the imaginary homogeneous collectivity is perceived among the masses, it remains effective. That collectivity resides not in the 'Real' but in '*perceived* reality'. Ordinary people's reception of and responses to mass dictatorship are bound up with a transformation not only of objective, but also of perceived reality. Very often, it is not the reality itself, but the interpreted reality that shapes the thoughts and practice of the many in their everyday lives. As an imaginary reality, the general will (or people's will, or nation's will) affords a link between mass democracy and mass dictatorship indicating their shared objective: to nationalise the masses. This analysis finds its most eccentric expression in Simon Tormey's statement that 'liberal democracy is the most refined version of totalitarianism'.[28] Synchronic comparisons aside, a diachronic comparison of pre- and post-war Japan shows that post-war democracy and the welfare state in Japan stood in the line of continuity with the systematic social integration and consolidation which had marked the era of mass dictatorship.[29] The upshot is not that mass dictatorship is democratic, but that mass democracy is no less risky than mass dictatorship.

The blurring of demarcations between dictatorship and democracy in a transnational history of mass dictatorship leads us to rethink domination, violence, coercion and other means of repression. The superior efficiency of Britain's total war system by comparison with Germany's suggests that domination is most effective when people do not realise that they are being dominated.[30] The feeling of being dominated may discourage and dampen the enthusiasm of those who might otherwise support a regime. The most virulent and penetrating forms of domination were therefore to be found in those systems where the appearance of freedom and rationality were greatest. The slow but relentless build-up of pressure on the individual to conform is much more efficient and cost-effective than any means of terror. Presumably any regime's most favoured mode of ruling/subjection is the 'internal coercion' produced by structuring thought and feeling.[31] The success of a mass dictatorship would depend on its ability to involve people in the ritual of legitimacy and make them surrender their own identity and subjectivity in favour of conformity to the model of a subject manufactured by the regime. A modern subject, whether in dictatorial or in democratic regimes, has been exposed to the 'controlled and guided massification' in which a notionally inalienable right of individual freedom proves to be legitimately alienable after all.[32] It is not a coincidence that both Italian fascism and Stalinism very loudly proclaimed their intention to create the 'new man', 'homo fascistus' and 'homo sovieticus' respectively, through an anthropological revolution. Neither of these regimes reached perfection, but both had been driven by an unstinting effort to perform that revolution.[33]

Once launched, however, the anthropological revolution shifted from revolutionary mass movements to institutionalised mass politics. If the consent of high Stalinism was fed by the fever of anthropological revolution, post-Stalinist regimes depended on shared guilt or public complicity for mass consent. As a dissident witness, Vaclav Havel adumbrated the peculiar mass psychology of public complicity or shared guilt in his thesis positing 'post-totalitarianism' as a kind of compromised dictatorship.[34] In time, the large scale of public complicity was bound to create conformity, especially in and after the era of de-Stalinisation. When the post-Stalinist regime abandoned the totalitarian anthropological revolutionary effort to create a 'new man', it lost the ambition to dominate private lives and tolerated people's cynicism despite the official media deploring people's passivity and indifference. Generally speaking, East European people in the post-1956 era just adapted themselves to the system without volunteering enthusiasm for the state project, and the regime was obliged to rest content with such merely passive consent. Compromised in their everyday lives, ordinary people fled into various depoliticised 'niches' where 'they could feel themselves'. The result was a 'niche society' (*Nischengesellschaft*).[35] The heritage of Marxist ideas was reduced to a handful of empty and decontextualised slogans and people's passive consent to this fossilised Marxism was compensated for by material rewards. According to Andrzej Walicki, the de-Stalinisation of 1956 marked a turning point from totalitarianism to authoritarianism.[36]

A re-engagement with Antonio Gramsci can complement this analysis, since his conceptualisation of hegemony helps us to problematise the self- or voluntary mobilisation of the masses. Contrary to a common belief that his concept of hegemony is confined to an analysis of liberal democratic regimes, Antonio Gramsci explicitly wrote that fascism represents a 'war of position'.[37] His intuition was that fascism was entrenched solidly at a grassroots level. Gramsci's grave concern about fascist hegemony chimes with Mussolini's keen interest in 'general economic mobilisation of citizens as means and agents of production, real conscription, a real civic and economic recruitment of all Italians'. Under the scrutiny of the concept of hegemony, the organisation of consent cannot be equated simply with the process of moulding public opinion. Popular consent was not just imposed by state terror and all-pervasive propaganda. It was important to inspire self-motivation among the masses. That explains Mussolini's burning concern with building 'a capillary network of associations with vast powers of social and cultural persuasion'.[38] The Japanese 'moral suasion mobilisation campaign (1929–30)' was second to none in its pursuit of total social control through moral suasion (*kyōka*).[39] With its later development into the *kōminka* (colonial nationalisation) campaign, Japanese imperialism undertook the ambitious task of nationalising its colonial subjects in Korea and Taiwan, making them into Japanese citizens. The project of nationalising the masses in the developmental dictatorship in postcolonial Korea and Taiwan can be located in a line of continuity with the Japanese imperial *kōminka* policy. What one cannot fail to note in mass dictatorship is an experiment in plebiscitary democracy which served to legitimise the regime. Hegemony, in Gramscian terms, paves the way to the 'dictatorship of consent'.[40]

Mass dictatorship is not only a 'hard' power utterly dominating the political sphere, but also a 'soft' power, retuning civil society to its own normative key. Fascist hegemony, entrenched in the grassroots, often attempts to penetrate into the private sphere of individuals. As shown in its pursuit of anthropological revolution, it strives to maximise the hegemonic effect by infiltrating the praxis of everyday life and thus moulding people's minds. Along with Gramsci's interpretation, Louis Althusser's concept of 'appellation' and Michel Foucault's analysis of the modern subject as tailor-made can be very suggestive for an understanding of the fascist *habitus* and the internalisation of coercion.[41] Like all other modern regimes, mass dictatorship struggles to legitimise its political application to multiple arrays of medical, legal, administrative and juridical instruments. What distinguishes mass dictatorship from mass democracy is the extreme way in which the former achieves paroxysmal perpetration. Mass dictatorship shares similar mechanisms for constructing the image of a people of unitary will and action with other forms of the modern nation-state. It made the non-conforming insiders into 'Others', and then hegemonically appropriated the rest of the population in the name of 'the nation's will'. The Nazis' slogans of the *Volksgemeinschaft* and *Volksgenosse* are good examples, symbolic of the organic integration which transcended class and political divisions achieved by making 'Others' through anti-Semitism, anti-Bolshevism and anti-Westernism outwardly, and by inventing a new ethnic unity of the Arian race inwardly.[42]

State racism is an effective means of creating 'biologised' internal or international enemies, against whom society must defend itself. Nazi culture as a contemporary allegory of intolerance, existential extremity and radical evil was in a sense the tragic culmination of enlightened science and rationality.[43] Again Michel Foucault's concept of a 'bio-power' based on the triangular relationship between bio-politics, population and race is evocative of that. If disciplinary society constructs a capillary network of apparatuses to produce and regulate customs, habits, *habitus* and practices, bio-power regulates social life from its interior. Power can achieve effective command over the entire life of the population at the birth of bio-power.[44] One cannot say whether mass dictatorship did attain bio-power to perfection, but it might have harnessed the productive dimension of bio-power for the modern disciplinary state. Evidently mass dictatorship did not fulfil the anthropological revolutionary ambition of creating a new man, but it never abandoned the modernist

dream of the 'society of control'. The fascist aesthetics of the beautiful male body may be one indicator of the dimension of bio-politics in
mass dictatorship, as furnishing a bridge between the public and private
sphere. And what the history of sexuality shows is that the masses' men-
talities and behaviour hinged on the means of controlling passions and
ideals of human beauty, love, friendship and sexual *habitus*. In fact mass
dictatorship regimes deployed the bio-politics of sexuality not less than
mass democracy.[45]

People's sovereignty and political religion

Mass dictatorship as a working hypothesis pays due attention to the
intellectual history of popular sovereignty. Carl Schmitt's advocacy of
Nazism as 'an anti-liberal but not necessarily anti-democratic' regime
represented the climax of a 'new politics' based on the idea of popular sovereignty.[46] In other words, mass dictatorship is congruent
with the change from liberalism to democracy, and then from parliamentary democracy to 'decisionist' or plebiscitary democracy. Popular
sovereignty transformed populations from passive subjects into active
citizens and thus paved the way for participatory dictatorship. Once the
'general will' is hoaxed into becoming the will of the nation, nation
as the 'constituent power' is not subject to a constitution. Instead, it
is the nation that now has the legislative power to make constitutions.
This reveals the secret of 'sovereign dictatorship': its justification by the
logical chain of representation with 'the people representing the multitude, the nation representing the people, and the state representing
the nation'. In this way, the multitude is transformed into an ordered
totality.[47] The sovereign dictatorship can enjoy unlimited constitutional
legitimacy in so far as the people's will as the constituent power supports
that dictatorship. In his address to the National Convention (1793),
Barère could justify Jacobin dictatorship on the grounds that the nation
was exercising dictatorship over itself. By the same logic, 'the might of
the dictatorship of the masses knows no bounds' in Maoist China.[48]
Seen in this light, George Mosse's eccentric assumption that Robespierre
would have felt at home at a Nazi mass rally is not groundless at
all.[49] The Nazi *Volksgemeinschaft* was not a bizarre pre-modern political concept but a meta-modern political order in which people regarded
themselves as the real political sovereign. In Eugene Weber's expression,
Nazism looked 'much like the Jacobinism of our time'.[50]
    The idea of sovereign dictatorship also provides a conceptual clue to
understanding the ironic conundrum of an affinity between the rightist

dictatorship/fascism and the allegedly leftist dictatorship/Stalinism. The cliché that 'the two extremes meet' explains nothing. However, Hardt and Negri's suggestion that 'the abstract machine of national sovereignty is at the heart of both' does seem to have a point.[51] Even for the Left, national community meant a working people's unity forged against the people's enemy. As the nationalist discourse in People's Poland and North Korea vividly demonstrates, the socialist ideal of the ethical and political unity of society unintentionally reinforced the pri-mordialist concept of the nation, that is, a way of seeing it as an organic community and even a family community.[52] As a response to the 'West', the nationalist discourse of mass dictatorship inclined towards Occidentalism. What is most remarkable in this regard is the awkward convergence of fascism and socialism in an anti-Western modernisation project. The dichotomy of the 'bourgeois nation' and the 'proletarian nation', shared by Italian fascists and post-war Third World Marxists of the 'dependency theory', implied a shift from class struggle between bourgeoisie and proletariat to national struggle between rich nation and poor nation. Both fascism and Stalinism laid stress on a developmental strategy designed to catch up with and overtake advanced capitalism at all cost, and justified that strategy by invoking the nation's will.[53]

Once situated within a broader socio-cultural history, popular sovereignty ideologically supports 'the nationalisation of the masses'.[54] This kind of massification corresponds to 'equalisation' and 'homogeni-sation' in the realm of perceived reality.[55] The nationalised masses as a tailor-made totality, assisted by fascist spectacles, deny the liberal image of an autonomous modern subject. The proponents of that transforma-tion asserted that the disenchanted modern subject should be tailored to the demands of the nation-state, which they again justified with ref-erence to the nation's will. But ideological justification is not enough to make people internalise norms and disciplines in everyday life. Popu-lar sovereignty is too abstract to discipline people through bio-power. Beyond the abstract level, what is complementarily needed for the emotional reproduction of a tailor-made subject is anthropo-cultural re-enchantment. It is political religion that satisfied the demand for re-enchantment. It did so by conferring a sacred status on earthly enti-ties like nation, state, class, history and race, and by rendering them into absolute principles of collective identity. Incorporated into a code of ethical and social commandments, political religion functions to bind the individual to the sacralised secular entity.[56] If most people embodied the fascist message via fascist aesthetics, it was mostly nationalism that re-enchanted people by transforming politics into a political religion.

The nationalist narrative of a collective life flowing from the immemorial past into an infinite future could turn the mortal life of the individual into the eternal life of the collective, and thus fill the vacuum caused by the extinction of the mythic along with the religious community.[57] But political religion is not peculiar to mass dictatorship. Rather it was a legacy of the French Enlightenment left both to mass dictatorship and to mass democracy. Theoretically, modern political messianism should be traced back to Rousseau who insisted on the necessity of 'civil religion' and national festivals that would infuse the people with a feeling of moral unity and absolute love of the fatherland. It was the American Revolution of 1776 and French Revolution of 1789 that provided the nationalist affirmation of secular religion, and an apocalyptic vision of national regeneration through politics. Political religion can be found in mass democracy no less than in mass dictatorship. In George Bush's address on the day he announced victory in 2003, American troops stopped being terrestrial combatants and became missionaries. They were no longer simply killing enemies: they were casting out demons in Iraq.[58] From the viewpoint of a transnational history of mass dictatorship, Gentile's binary of 'democratic civil religion' and 'totalitarian political religion' seems to miss the point. They are two sides of the same coin of socio-political engineering in the modern nation-state.

A seemingly one-sided emphasis on consent or consensus may give the impression that mass dictatorship causes one to avert one's eyes from the evident terror. That is not the case. The explication of consensus and hegemonic effects in mass dictatorship never denies violence, terror, repression and coercion. Rather, mass dictatorship questions the very distinction between coercion and consent by asking why a large part of the population ignores or even endorses the horrors of extreme coercion employed by repressive regimes such as the Nazis. The upshot is that terror was an indispensable means of creating consent, appealing not only to fear but also to a feeling of relief among 'national comrades'. Terror was used highly selectively and was initially aimed at 'enemies of the people'. Mass dictatorship deployed massive terror in a radicalised version of a strategy of negative integration, provoking violence against 'Others' in order to homogenise a mass into 'our national community'. Terror and coercion created chaos and fear among outcasts, but it never involved danger to faithful insiders. It was not the terror itself, but the fear of being outcast that was the greater threat to the greater number. That explains why ordinary people readily became active perpetrators, or were passive bystanders, and why even extreme terror could count on consent from below.[59] Thus, coercion and consent should be seen not as polar opposites, but as intimately interwoven integral parts of mass dictatorship. Mass dictatorship was indeed Janus-faced: 'Jekyll to insiders and Hyde to outcasts'.

In light of gender history, people's sovereignty meant a unique opportunity for women under mass dictatorship to be mobilised as citizens equal to their male counterparts. Despite its frequently overt patriarchal ideologies, mass dictatorship could even appeal to some feminists due to its imaginary equality among citizens. In order to establish a productive and effective self-mobilisation system, mass dictatorship regimes often appealed to the idea of people's sovereignty regarding women of the same ethnicity and nationality as national comrades-insiders in contrast to men of a different nationality, ethnicity, race or class, who were seen as national/class enemies-outcasts. Viewed from the interplay between the construction of gender identities and the formation of other identities, such as nation, class and race, women in mass dictatorships cease to be passive victims. Contrary to common belief, women were very often invited into the public sphere by mass dictatorships. As shown by Japanese feminist leaders' participation in the total war system and women's agency as perpetrators in Nazi Germany, the self-mobilisation system could be complete only with women's enthusiastic responses to the regime's calls to participate in the public sphere. Women activists in the British Union of Fascists and female leaders of the New Village Movement (Saemaŭl Undong) in South Korea's development dictatorship can be counted as other examples.

Agency in everyday life

Mass dictatorship may look like a behemoth – a perfect, tightly sutured political machine, which does not allow even a tiny space for dissent and resistance. This is partly due to Foucault's account of power and modernity, on which the mass dictatorship leans methodologically. Because of its focus on the microphysics of power to show how power actually functions at the level of everyday life, Foucault's explanation tends to 'reduce the functioning of a whole society to a single, dominant type of procedure', in this case the panoptical or the disciplinary. Behind the dominant panoptical procedures, however, there exist practices disseminated through unofficial realms. These minor practices have remained 'unprivileged by history', but formed tactical 'anti-disciplines' which served to undermine strategies of official power. Thanks to the silent and unacknowledged forms of resistance which 'break through the grid of the established order and accepted disciplines', mass dictatorship ceases to be a perfect, tightly sutured machine.[60] Together, the Foucauldian genealogy of disciplines and Certeau's meandering anti-disciplines make up the topography of mass dictatorship and mass democracy. The crooked lines of history from below, oscillating between optimism and pessimism, are in themselves causes for reflection on the coexistence of disciplines and anti-disciplines.[61]

A question of terminology arises too. In the 'Western' intellectual tradition, the term 'mass' is pregnant with the political implication that masses would be passive objects of manipulation. But that political implication is only partially merited. As the American socialist magazine *The Masses* (1911–17) suggests, masses were regarded by some liberal leftists as the true agents of societal transformation. To bourgeois and aristocratic circles, however, masses appeared merely as the common herd, characterised by irrationality, disorderliness and poverty. But the bourgeois establishment's contempt, which found its classic expression in Gustave LeBon's writings, denotes fear of the chaotic masses' rebellion. It was Jose Ortega y Gasset who straightforwardly confessed that fear of the new situation where masses rule and decide. In the twentieth century, masses stopped being passive subjects and began to compete for power as active agents.[62] The bourgeoisie's very fear of the masses is in fact indicative of their power as agents. The appearance of words denoting 'masses' in East Asian languages – *Daejung* (Korean), *Dazhong* (Chinese), *Taishu* (Japanese) – confirms a recognition of the agency of the masses, with some exceptional usages, however. Often combined with the adjective of 'working', masses in the East Asian usage of 'working masses' (勤勞大衆) connoted historical actors. Because masses are recognised as agents in the East Asian usage, the mass dictatorship approach waives the top-down structuralist approach.

'Historical actors are back on stage' in mass dictatorship discourses. Resting on the 'empirical turn' in particular, or on an 'investigative turn' more broadly, the concept of mass dictatorship calls attention to 'the patchwork of practices and orientations which people co-produce and which they themselves live with and operate in'.[63] Human agents are not predestined politically. Finding themselves between self-empowerment and self-mobilisation, they meander through historical moments. Thus explanation needs to be multilinear rather than unilinear, pluralist rather than dualist, ambiguous rather than unambiguous. The room for manoeuvre open to each single human agent is a niche from which mass dictatorship, and perhaps also mass democracy, can be deconstructed. So dualistic terms of 'coercion and consent' and 'resistance and collaboration' are deconstructed and pluralised. Every single agent – to say nothing of the masses – resists compartmentalisation and is constituted of heterogeneous identities. Agency in its totality cannot be contained within the tightly woven social and cultural matrix. Selfhood is inescapably dual, comprising both object and subject in the relations between the self and the world.[64]

In this dual relationship, the more the mobilisation system develops, the wider the range of non-conformist behaviour among the mobilised. Resistance arises at the very moment when the regime might appear to have erected a total system of domination. For many people, participation in a self-mobilising regime means subjection to the structure *and* an opportunity to appropriate the structured outer world in their own ways. Mobilised to take part in and to support mass dictatorship, both men and women did not simply undergo subjectification from above. Under the facade of voluntary participation and support, they mobilised themselves as active agents and often appropriated the subjectification process on their own for self-empowerment from below. The dialectic of 'internalising the external' and 'externalising the internal' can be caught by every single human agent. What one can find in modes of life among the masses in the mass dictatorship regime are contradictions or dissimilarities in people's practices or mode of conduct. In lieu of the term 'self-mobilising', Alf Lüdtke suggests the expression of 'self-energising'. It captures these contradictory practices of subjection and appropriation in everyday lives.[65]

Self-contradictions in the masses' modes of everyday life cast doubt on the binaries of consent and coercion, desire and repression, and self-mobilisation and forced mobilisation. These are not irreconcilable opposites, but in a sense aspects of the same process. The question is not of a choice – '*either* control *or* consensus producing longevity (of the mass dictatorship regime)'. Instead, we need to consider 'control *and* consensus (or, perhaps better, compliance) – a combination providing ambivalent reactions to the regime'.[66] This insight leads us to postulate that the experience of consent and coercion itself is multi-layered, spanning internalised coercion, forced consent, passive conformity, consensus, self-mobilisation, forced participation and so on. Subjection was not a one-way street either. Very often, people pretended to be servile to the regime in order to find a way of appropriating the outer world for their benefit. Ultimately, then, the tasks awaiting historians of mass dictatorship include the deconstruction and pluralisation of terms such as 'consent', 'coercion', 'conformity', 'adaptation', 'resistance', 'opposition', 'mobilisation' and so on.[67] Similarly, 'resistance' can be pluralised, allowing us to distinguish between *'Resistenz'* ('structural resistance', a term used to define the defence of identities and social practices threatened by a regime) and *'Widerstand'* (organised resistance – Resistance with a capital 'R'), 'ideologically driven resistance' and 'existentialist resistance', 'resistance subject to hegemony' and 'domination pregnant with resistance'.[68]

Agents are not allowed a free ride. Coming to terms with the dictatorial past demands 'thick description' of yesterday's consent and coercion and today's nostalgia *for* and *against* as a multi-layered experience in everyday lives. Historical actors should pay for their agency when they cease to be passive objects.[69] Given its stress on agency, mass dictatorship does not exonerate the ordinary people from historical responsibility and juridical culpability. The dictum of 'structure does not kill but individuals do' points to the culpability of historical actors. The mass dictatorship hypothesis challenges the moralist dualism which insists on there being a few bad perpetrators and many innocent victims since that dualism facilitates the displacement of the historical responsibility of 'ordinary' people by shifting culpability away from them. When Raul Hilberg asked the question 'wouldn't you be happier if I had been able to show you that all perpetrators were crazy', he seemed to imply his own answer, namely that history brings no comfort.[70] Indeed mass killers were not crazy perpetrators but everyday human beings – normal people.[71] The moral comfort that the image of crazy perpetrators brings to us results not only in self-exculpation but also in moral disarmament. As Bauman put it, 'the most frightening news brought about by the Holocaust and by what we learned of its perpetrators was not the likelihood that "this" could be done to us, but the idea that we could do it'.[72] In other words, 'placed in comparable situations and similar social constituencies, you or I might also commit murderous ethnic cleansing'.[73]

In light of this moral reflection, agents come to possess the reflexive dimension of the self. The reflexive self opens up the possibility for historical actors to stand outside the order of external determinations, though 'in a manner limited by their inherence in that order'.[74] In relation to mass dictatorship, these historical actors as reflexive selves will frustrate the regime's ambition to nationalise the masses, and change the uniform mass of a unitary will into a multitude that communicates and acts 'in common while remaining internally different', and transforms themselves from the tailor-made subjects of a single identity to the autonomous individuals of innumerable differences. And finally they will rupture and punch through the seemingly tightly sutured political machine, that is, mass dictatorship. Despite fascism having lost a 'war of manoeuvre', it is still scoring victories in a 'war of position'. Umberto Eco's warning about 'fuzzy totalitarianism and endless fascism', and Felix Guattari's caution against 'recurrent fascism' imply that 'a war of position' against fascism is still in progress.[75] What makes fascism dangerous is 'its molecular or micropolitical power' which spreads like a cancer. Freed from the Manichean moralism which posits a few bad victimisers and many innocent victims, the historicism of mass dictatorship turns itself into a reflexive presentism on this front.

Notes

1. Andrzej Paczkowski, 'Czy historycy dokonali "obrachunku" z PRL?', in *Ofiary czy Współwinni* (Warszawa: Volumen, 1997), pp. 13–29.
2. Timothy Garton Ash, *History of the Present* (New York: Vintage Books, 1999), p. 264. The Polish word *'współwinni'* is better translated as 'co-guilty' than as 'accomplice' in this context.
3. Adam Michnik, 'rozmowa z Vaclavem Havelem', *Gazeta Wyborcza* (30 November 1991).
4. Jie-Hyun Lim, 'Reading the Code of Everyday Fascism (Korean)', *Contemporary Criticism* 8 (Fall, 1999); 'Fascist's War of Position and Dictatorship of Consent (Korean)', *Contemporary Criticism* 12 (Fall, 2000).
5. For *lustracja* controversies in Poland and Korea, see Piotr Grzelak, *Wojna o lustrację* (Warszawa: Trio, 2005); 'Appendices', in Jie-Hyun Lim and Yong-Woo Kim (eds), *Mass Dictatorship II: Political Religion and Hegemony* (Korean) (Seoul: Chaiksesang, 2005), pp. 401–596.
6. Jie-Hyun Lim, 'Mapping Mass Dictatorship', in Jie-Hyun Lim and Yong-Woo Kim (eds), *Mass Dictatorship I: Between Coercion and Consent* (Korean) (Seoul: Chaiksesang, 2004), pp. 17–55.
7. It is noteworthy too that Francoism is often defined as *'despotismo moderno'* (modern despotism) because it constitutes an alliance of conservatives and the military without mass involvement. Modern despotism of this kind differs from mass dictatorship in that it does not rely on the mobilisation of the masses or on intervention in their private lives. See Salvador Giner, 'Political Economy, Legitimacy and the State in Southern Europe', in Ray Hudson and Jim Lewis (eds), *Uneven Developments in Southern Europe* (London: Methuen, 1985), pp. 309–50.
8. See David Blackbourn and Geoff Eley, *The Peculiarities of German History* (Oxford: Oxford University Press, 1984); Ian Kershaw, *The Nazi Dictatorship: Problems and Perspectives of Interpretation* (London: Arnold, 2000), pp. 20–3. From the mass dictatorship viewpoint, Jürgen Kocka's term 'modern dictatorship', which he applies to the German Democratic Republic (GDR), seems a kind of tautology. Mass dictatorship buys rather into the term *'Fuersorgediktatur'* (welfare dictatorship) to characterise the GDR's

dictatorship. See Konrad H. Jarausch, 'Beyond Uniformity' and Jürgen Kocka, 'The GDR: A Special Kind of Modern Dictatorship', in Konrad H. Jarausch (ed.), *Dictatorship as Experience: Towards a Socio-cultural History of the GDR* (New York: Berghahn Books, 1999), pp. 3–26.

9. It should be noted that Germany had to refer to France as its own puta-tive 'West' because it was situated in the 'East' from France's perspective. The co-figuration of French 'civilisation' and German 'culture' in Norbert Elias's analysis shows this succinctly. See Nagao Nishikawa, *Zouho Kokkyou no Koekata* (Tokyo: Heibonsha, 2001), Ch. 6.

10. Ian Buruma and Avishi Margalit, *Occidentalism: The West in the Eyes of Its Enemies* (New York: Penguin Press, 2004), p. 52.

11. For 'East' and 'West' as the imaginative geography and the schema of co-figuration of East and West, see Edward Said, *Orientalism* (New York: Vintage Books, 1979), pp. 49–72; Naoki Sakai, *Translation and Subjectivity* (Minneapolis, MN: University of Minnesota Press, 1997), pp. 40–71.

12. Daniel Schoenpflug's attempt to comprehend François Furet's and Ernst Nolte's comparative history of totalitarian movements within the frame-work of '*histoire croisée*' is suggestive, but its limits are clear. To say nothing of 'linear causality' and 'potential oversimplifications' in Nolte's thesis on 'Bolshevik's challenge and Nazi's response', Furet seemed to stop at the point of making the analogies between French Jacobins of 1793 and Russian Bolsheviks of 1917. Despite Furet's and Nolte's alleged contribution to the '*histoire croisée*' of the totalitarian movements, its scale of comparison remains confined to Europe. See Daniel Schoenpflug, 'Histoires croisées: François Furet, Ernst Nolte and a Comparative History of Totalitarian Movements', *European History Quarterly* 37(2) (2007), pp. 265–90.

13. David Scott, *Conscripts of Modernity: The Tragedy of Colonial Enlightenment* (Durham, NC: Duke University Press, 2004), pp. 4–9.

14. Dominic Sachsenmaier, 'Searching for Alternatives to Western Modernity – Cross-cultural Approaches in the Aftermath of the Great War', unpublished paper.

15. Harry Harootunian, *Overcome by Modernity: History, Culture, and Community in Interwar Japan* (Princeton, NJ: Princeton University Press, 2000), p. x.

16. Zygmunt Bauman, *Modernity and the Holocaust* (Ithaca, NY: Cornell University Press, 2000), pp. xi–xii, 28, 152 and *passim*.

17. For the continuities between colonial genocide and the Holocaust see Juergen Zimmerer, 'Die Geburt des Ostlandes aus dem Geiste des Kolonialismus: Die nationalsozialistische Eroberungs- und Beherrschung-spolitik in (post-)kolonialer Perspektive', *Sozial Geschichte* 19(1) (2004); Benjamin Madley, 'From Africa to Auschwitz: How German South West Africa Incubated Ideas and Methods Adopted and Developed by the Nazis in Eastern Europe?', *European History Quarterly* 35(3) (2005); Sven Lindquist, *Exterminate All the Brutes* (New York: The New Press, 1996); Enzo Traverso, *The Origins of Nazi Violence* (New York: The New Press, 2003).

18. Robert Gerwarth and Stephan Malinowski, 'Der Holocaust als "kolo-nialer Genozid"? Europaeische Kolonialgewalt und nationalsozialistischer Vernichtungskrieg', *Geschichte und Gesellschaft* 33 (2007), p. 445.

19. Karl Marx, *Capital*, Vol. I, translated by Ben Fowkes (London: Penguin Books, 1990), p. 895.

20. Mark Mazower, *Dark Continent: Europe's Twentieth Century* (New York: Vintage Books, 1998), p. xiii.
21. Ian Kershaw, *Hitler, 1936–45: Nemesis* (New York: W. W. Norton & Company, 2001), pp. 400, 405.
22. Bauman, *Modernity and the Holocaust*, pp. 227–8.
23. Byung-Joo Hwang, 'The Discourse of Domination and Nationalisation of the Masses in the Era of Park Chung-hee', in Lim and Kim, *Mass Dictatorship I*, pp. 475–515.
24. Michael Mann, *The Dark Side of Democracy* (Cambridge: Cambridge University Press, 2005), pp. 70–110.
25. Ibid., p. 4.
26. Ibid., pp. 430–4.
27. The security regime in post-9/11 America is not a result of Bush's stupidity but an invention of the masses and by the masses, though perhaps not for the masses.
28. Simon Tormey, *Making Sense of Tyranny: Interpretations of Totalitarianism* (Manchester: Manchester University Press, 1995), p. 115.
29. Toshio Nagano, 'Japanese Total War System', in Lim and Kim, *Mass Dictatorship I*, pp. 517–32; Yasushi Yamanouchi, J. Victor Koschmann and Ryūichi Narita (eds), *Total War and Modernization* (Ithaca, NY: Cornell University East Asia Program, 1998).
30. See Stefan Berger, 'Total War System in Germany and Britain', in Lim and Kim, *Mass Dictatorship I*, pp. 149–74.
31. Patrick Colm Hogan, *The Culture of Conformism: Understanding Social Consent* (Durham, NC: Duke University Press, 2001), p. 58.
32. Georgi Schischkoff, *Die gesteuerte Vermassung* (Meisenheim am Glan: Anton Hain, 1964), pp. 120–1.
33. Leszek Kolakowski, 'Totalitarianism and the Virtue of the Lie', in Irving Howe (ed.), *1984 Revisited: Totalitarianism in Our Century* (New York: HarperCollins, 1983), p. 133.
34. Vaclav Havel, 'The Power of the Powerless', in John Keane (ed.), *The Power of the Powerless: Citizens against the State In Central-Eastern Europe* (London: Hutchinson, 1985), pp. 23–96.
35. Grzegorz Miernik (ed.), *Polacy Wobec PRL: strategie przystosowawcze* (Kielce: Kieleckie Towarzystwo Naukowe, 2003), p. 7; Harald Dehne, 'Satisfying Consumption as a Social Policy Present from the Leadership? Sisyphus between Securing Central Planning and People's Desire', in Jie-Hyun Lim and Yong-Woo Kim (eds), *Mass Dictatorship III: Between Desire and Delusion* (Korean) (Seoul: Chaeksesang, 2007), pp. 304–5.
36. Andrzej Walicki, *Polskie zmagania z wolnością* (Kraków: Universitas, 2000), pp. 102–9.
37. Antonio Gramsci, *Selections from the Prison Notebooks*, edited and translated by Q. Hoare and Geoffrey N. Smith (New York: International Publishers, 1971), p. 120.
38. Victoria de Grazia, *The Culture of Consent: Mass Organization of Leisure in Fascist Italy* (Cambridge: Cambridge University Press, 1981), pp. 12, 21–2 and *passim*.
39. Sheldon Garon, *Molding Japanese Minds: The State in Everyday Life* (Princeton, NJ: Princeton University Press, 1997).

40. The term 'consensus dictatorship' is found in Martin Sabrow, 'Dictatorship as Discourse: Cultural Perspectives on SED Legitimacy', in Jarausch (ed.), *Dictatorship as Experience*, p. 208. But English translation is tricky since the German word of *'Konsens'* implies both 'consent' and 'consensus'.

41. Žižek's suggestion to read Havel with Althusser may be altered to the suggestion that one might read Havel with Althusser, Foucault and Gramsci in the context of mass dictatorship studies. See Slavoj Žižek, *Did Somebody Say Totalitarianism?* (London: Verso, 2001), p. 90.

42. See Michael Wildt, 'The National Socialist *Volksgemeinschaft* – A New Political Order', in Lim and Kim, *Mass Dictatorship I*, pp. 177–207. For its appeal to ordinary people, see Michael Wildt, *Volksgemeinschaft als Selbstermaechtigung: Gewalt gegen Juden in der deutschen Provinz 1919 bis 1939* (Hamburg: Hamburger Edition, 2007).

43. Paul Betts, 'The New Fascination with Fascism: The Case of Nazi Modernism', *Journal of Contemporary History* 37 (October, 2002), p. 544.

44. Michel Foucault, *The History of Sexuality*, translated by Robert Hurley (New York: Vintage, 1978), Vol. I, pp. 135–45; Michel Foucault, 'The Politics of Health in the Eighteenth Century', in Colin Gordon (ed.), *Power/Knowledge* (New York: Pantheon, 1980), pp. 166–82.

45. George L. Mosse, *The Fascist Revolution* (New York: Howard Fetig, 1999), p. 48; George L. Mosse, *Nationalism and Sexuality* (Madison, WI: University of Wisconsin Press, 1985), pp. 21–2.

46. Carl Schmitt, *Der Gegensatz von Parlamentarismus und moderner Massendemokratie*, translated by H. J. Kim (Seoul: Bupmunsa, 1988), p. 102.

47. Michael Hardt and Antonio Negri, *Empire* (Cambridge, MA: Harvard University Press, 2000), pp. 87, 134. It is very intriguing that Hardt's and Negri's sharp criticism of the 'sovereign machine' and Schmitt's ardent advocacy of 'sovereign dictatorship' stand on the same historical ground of the formation of the modern sovereign state.

48. See Michael Schoenhals, Chapter 11, this volume.

49. Mosse, *The Fascist Revolution*, p. 76.

50. Eugene Weber, *Varieties of Fascism* (New York: Van Nostrand, 1964), p. 139.

51. Hardt and Negri, *Empire*, p. 112.

52. See Jie-Hyun Lim, 'The Nationalist Message in Socialist Code: On Court Historiography in People's Poland and North Korea', in Sølvi Sogner (ed.), *Making Sense of Global History* (Oslo: Universitetsforlaget, 2001).

53. Jie-Hyun Lim, 'Befreiung oder Modernisierung? Sozialismus als ein Weg der anti-westlichen Moderniseirung in unterentwickelten Laendern', *Beitraege zur Geschichte der Arbeiter-bewegung* 43(2) (2001), pp. 5–23; 'An Awkward Conversion? Fascism and Socialism as the Anti-Western Modernization Project', paper presented at the 5th International Conference Mass Dictatorship, Hanyang University, Seoul, 25–28 June 2007.

54. George L. Mosse, *The Nationalization of the Masses* (New York: Howard Fertig, 1975).

55. Salvador Giner, *Mass Society* (New York: Academic Press, 1976), p. 127.

56. Emilio Gentile, 'The Sacralisation of Politics: Definitions, Interpretations and Reflections on the Question of Secular Religion and Totalitarianism', *Totalitarian Movements and Political Religions* 1 (Summer, 2000), pp. 18–55.

57. Benedict Anderson, *Imagined Communities* (London: Verso, 1991), pp. 9–19.

58. George Monbiot, 'America Is A Religion', *Guardian* (29 July 2003).
59. See Jarausch (ed.), *Dictatorship as Experience*; Robert Gellately, *Backing Hitler: Consent and Coercion in Nazi Germany* (Oxford: Oxford University Press, 2001); Robert Mallet, 'Consent or Dissent?', *Totalitarian Movements and Political Religions* 1 (Autumn, 2000), pp. 27–46.
60. Michel de Certeau, *Heterologies: Discoure on the Other*, translated by B. Massumi (Minneapolis, MN: Minnesota University Press, 1986), pp. 188–9, 197.
61. Peter Lambert, 'History from Below, Nazism and Third Reich: Paradigm Shift and Problems', in Lim and Kim, *Mass Dictatorship III*, pp. 41–70.
62. Jose Ortega y Gasset, *La rebellion de las masas*, translated by Young-Jo Hwangbo (Seoul: Yoksabipyŏngsa, 2005).
63. Alf Lüdtke, 'Practicing and Meandering', in Lim and Kim, *Mass Dictatorship III*, pp. 13–37.
64. Jerrold Seigel, 'Problematizing the Self', in Victoria E. Bonnell and Lynn Hunt (eds), *Beyond the Cultural Turn: New Directions in the Study of Society and Culture* (Berkeley, CA: University of California Press, 1999), p. 287.
65. Alf Lüdtke, 'Attraction and Power of (Self-)Energizing: National Socialism in Germany, 1933–1945', paper presented at the panel 'A Global History of Mass Dictatorship as the Self-mobilising Regime', 123rd Annual Meeting of AHA, New York, 4 January 2008.
66. Paul Corner, 'Self-mobilisation in Mass Dictatorships – The Italian Example', paper presented at the panel 'A Global History of Mass Dictatorships as Self-Mobilizing Regimes', 23rd Annual Meeting of AHA, New York, 4 January 2008.
67. Jie-Hyun Lim, 'Conference Report. Coercion and Consent: A Comparative Study of "Mass Dictatorship"', *Contemporary European History* 13(2) (2004), pp. 249–52.
68. The academic achievement of *Alltagsgeschichte* is very suggestive in this context. See Alf Lüdtke (ed.), *The History of Everyday Life*, translated by William Templer (Princeton, NJ: Princeton University Press, 1995); Detlev J. K. Peukert, *Inside Nazi Germany*, translated by Richard Deveson (New Haven, CT: Yale University Press, 1987).
69. This task will prove more than unusually complex because it will involve crossing the line between perceived reality and objective reality.
70. Raul Hilberg, 'Significance of the Holocaust', in Henry Friedlander and Sybil Milton (eds), *The Holocaust: Ideology, Bureaucracy, and Genocide* (Millwood, NY: Kraus International Publications, 1980), p. 101.
71. Most recently, war criminals in the former Yugoslavia confirm this once again. See Slavenka Drakulić, *They Would Never Hurt a Fly: War Criminals on Trial in The Hague* (London: Abacus, 2004).
72. Bauman, *Modernity and the Holocaust*, p. 152.
73. Mann, *The Dark Side*, p. 9.
74. Seigel, 'Problematizing the Self', p. 289.
75. Felix Guattari, *Molecular Revolution* (Harmondsworth: Penguin, 1984), p. 229.

Part I
Comparative Contexts

1

Introduction: Meandering between Self-empowerment and Self-mobilisation

Karen Petrone and Jie-Hyun Lim

The main task of the editors of a collection on *Gender Politics and Mass Dictatorship* is to define both of these terms and elucidate how they work together. In his introduction to the mass dictatorship series, Jie-Hyun Lim argues that 'modern dictatorship presupposes mass support. The term "mass dictatorship" implies the attempted mobilisation of the masses by dictatorships, and that these frequently secured voluntary mass participation and support.' The task of this work on *Gender Politics and Mass Dictatorship*, then, is to explore the operation of gender in the attempted (whether successful or unsuccessful) mobilisation of men and women to participate voluntarily in and to support mass dictatorship. But, as Lim points out, both men and women did not simply undergo 'subjectification from above'. Mobilised selves as active agents tried to appropriate the subjectification process and thus build the foundations for 'self-empowerment from below'.

The comparative focus of this volume pushes the boundaries of the scholarship of 'mass dictatorship' in a variety of ways: it considers both 'dictatorships' and 'democracies'; both colonies and metropoles; both pre-World War II and post-World War II governments; and both Europe and Asia. There is much common ground between twentieth-century 'mass dictatorships' and 'mass democracies' in their use of modern mobilisation techniques conscripting people, in Lim's words, 'to render themselves simultaneously as objects and agents of modernity'. The study of gender provides insight into all modern political mobilisations as gendered citizens became agents of the state and the objects of its disciplines in both dictatorships and democracies. This work considers mass mobilisation in a much broader context than the older school of 'totalitarian' scholarship that tended to concentrate on Nazi Germany and Soviet Russia in the interwar period. Although there are chapters by Barbara Einhorn, Claudia Koonz, Alf Lüdtke and Karen Petrone exploring gender relations in this familiar 'totalitarian' territory, these works stand alongside chapters by Sangsoo Kim and Woonok Yeom on the much less familiar comparative terrain of democratic interwar Britain. Einhorn's chapter is a theoretical overview of gender relations under fascism and socialism, and the contributions by Koonz and Petrone are primarily historiographical reviews, examining how scholars have deployed gender in the study of Germany and the Soviet Union. The rest of the chapters in the volume, however, showcase original research on gendered regimes of power in Europe and in Asia.

Another way in which this volume stretches the usual category of dictatorship is by incorporating the colonial dimension of mass dictatorship and mass democracy. The volume explores how empires (both 'dictatorial' and 'democratic') used gender to mobilise support for their imperial projects among their colonial subjects and the citizens of the metropole. Since the modern empire has the form of a nation-state at its core, gender politics vis-à-vis colonial subjects can be located within the historical paradigms of mass dictatorship and mass democracy. Sangsoo Kim considers gendered training for the young boys who would become agents of the British Empire while Kyu Hyun Kim and Michael Kim examine the participation of Korean women in the Japanese imperial project during the occupation of Korea in the Pacific War era (1931–45).

The World War II era looms large in any history of twentieth-century mass dictatorship; war, with its heightened need for mass mobilisation, is also often pivotal in the reinforcement or destabilisation of gender norms. To complement Kyu Hyun Kim's and Michael Kim's focus on female colonial subjects in the Japanese empire, Yonson Ahn considers the male Japanese soldier and the gendered nature of mobilisation in wartime Japan. But the chapters in this volume also push the analysis of mass dictatorship beyond World War II. The chapters by Einhorn and Lüdtke explicitly compare interwar Germany with post-war Germany and Eastern Europe, and the contributions by Małgorzata Mazurek, Eun-shil Kim and Michael Schoenhals consider mass dictatorships in Poland, Korea and China in the 1960s and 1970s.

This volume also encompasses a broad geographic scope. The series subtitle *Global Perspectives* reflects the transnational nature of this scholarly effort to produce sustained historical comparisons of gender and mobilisation in mass dictatorships across the globe. The authors of these chapters hail from seven different countries on four continents, providing an expansive range of comparative analysis; the dictatorships and ideologies they examine include British fascism and colonialism, Nazi Germany, Stalinist Russia, the total war system in Japan, Korea under colonial rule, Maoist China, Communist East Germany and People's Poland, and South Korea's developmental dictatorship. Broad in its apprehension of modern mass mobilisation, consideration of colony and metropole, twentieth-century chronology and global geography, the volume is tied together by the concept of gender.

Our definition of gender draws on the work of Joan Scott who, in her seminal 1986 article 'Gender: A Useful Category of Historical Analysis', defined gender 'as a constitutive element of social relationships based on perceived differences between the sexes'. Scott also theorized that 'gender is a primary way of signifying relationships of power' and this key insight has shaped the field of gender history over the past two decades.[1] The chapters in the volume examine the myriad ways in which gender difference was embodied, experienced, employed and deployed in twentieth-century dictatorships and democracies not only in the construction of social relationships among male and female citizens, but in the symbolic and ideological dimensions of rule, signifying relations of power among various constituencies within the states.

While many of the chapters in this volume deal explicitly with women, this work is not conceived of as women's history, adding women's activities to an already established male historical narrative. On the contrary, it proposes a gender-historical analysis of mass dictatorship that deals with the formation of both men's and women's subjective identities in relation to other social concepts and categories by deconstructing conventional categories such as woman/man, private/public, feminism/anti-feminism, victim/accomplice in the context of historical reality and showing the interplay between the construction of gender identities and the formation of other identities such as race and class. This study suggests that the cliché dichotomies immanent in conventional categories tend to reproduce the subjectification process from above and deprive people of agency. To restore and theorise the subjectivity of citizens under mass dictatorship, it is essential to regard citizens of both genders as agents in their own history, constructing their own categories and conceptual frameworks, and acting as well as being acted upon.

Gender plays a particularly important role in shaping the identities of modern citizens. As dictatorial regimes deployed gender politics both to control citizens and to mobilise them to the state project, women and men tried to appropriate the opportunities of mobilising citizenship to their best advantage. It is essential to remember that not all citizens of mass dictatorships had an equal opportunity to gain power in mass dictatorships and some citizens were far more constrained than others. While 'traditional' ideas about men's and women's roles may have shaped some of the possibilities open to both men and women, these notions operated differently in each state and were only one of many factors that led to the empowerment of some segments of these populations over other groups. These chapters explore a wide variety of social and political relationships that men and women engaged in to complicate understandings of the relation of the gendered individual to state power and to point out the multiple and differentiated ways in which men and women became agents and objects of state power. The chapters in this volume attempt to capture the constantly fluctuating power dynamics among gendered citizens and between gendered citizens and the mobilising state.

The first two chapters in the volume provide broad critical overviews of gender in mass dictatorships. Barbara Einhorn addresses the philosophical issues raised by the comparison of Nazi gender ideology with the state socialist gender ideologies of Central and Eastern Europe. Sceptical of facile comparisons between the two systems, Einhorn sets the stage for the rest of the volume by resisting broad generalisations and insisting on the social, political and cultural contextualisation of each ideology both in its ideal form and in the various circumstances in which it was implemented. Next is Claudia Koonz's historiographical chapter on the writing of the history of women and gender in the Third Reich. By examining the trajectory of this field of study, Koonz alerts readers to the controversies about women's agency as perpetrators rather than merely victims in the Third Reich, points to the significance of race in considering Nazi gender history, and examines consumption practices and their relation to social support for the Nazis. Koonz's case study of one nation's historiography maps out the intellectual antecedents of the contributors' and editors' insistence on exploring the variegated agency of women and men in mass dictatorships.

The chapters on women in this volume demonstrate that the role of women in mass dictatorships should not be reduced to the far too simplistic dichotomy of victim/perpetrator. While some scholars have tended to emphasise how mass dictatorship regimes were anti-feminist patriarchies that regarded women as mere objects of domination or as passive victims who all experienced a similar kind of sexual discrimination and oppression, others have emphasised women's culpability for forwarding the goals of such regimes. Historical questions that arise from gender politics cannot be adequately answered, however, if women under mass dictatorship are forced into a sharp dichotomy of passive victims and demonised perpetrators.

Woonok Yeom seeks to destabilise categories of victim and accomplice by looking at women activists in the British Union of Fascists in the interwar period. By demonstrating the extent to which British Fascist women could be both fascists and feminists in their 'separate sphere', Yeom shows the way in which even 'patriarchal' ideologies allowed space for women's agency and activities that could empower women both to work on behalf of their sisters' welfare and to regulate their sisters' bodies. Through their work, the fascist women carved out spheres of freedom for themselves.

Sharply challenging a historiography that emphasises Korean victimhood, the chapters by Kyu Hyun Kim and Michael Kim point to the paradoxical role of Korean women in the patriarchal power structures of the Japanese empire after the onset of the 'total mobilisation' system in 1938. Kyu Hyun Kim perceptively asks, 'how could the colonial state "confine" women in the private sphere *and* effectively mobilise them for imperialistic wars at the same time?' By examining women's magazines, Kyu Hyun Kim traces the fate of the Korean 'New Woman' as she was incorporated into the Japanese colonial order. Despite the Japanese empire's emphasis on women's place in the domestic sphere, its adherence to modernity provided the space in which the Korean New Woman could defend her ideals of self-determination and rationality and transcend the domestic sphere. Michael Kim's chapter shows that some Korean women were active leaders of patriotic associations, that they supported the conscription of Korean men into the Japanese army, and that they worked toward the 'Japanisation' of Korea. These women gained status in imperial society as they promoted the unification of Japan and Korea and they endorsed the empire's acquisition of power over male bodies in its mobilisation for war. Both of these authors underscore the active participation of Korean women in Japanese colonial society, a highly controversial topic within contemporary Korean historiography. Their work shows how the Japanese nationalisation policy was applied to colonial women as subjects and how colonial subjects responded to this imperial process.

In theory, at least, the roles of women in the Soviet Union in the 1930s should have been dramatically different from those in the British Union of Fascists or in colonial Korea, since the Soviet Union explicitly embraced a doctrine of gender equality. Karen Petrone's chapter on Soviet women under Stalinism demonstrates that the Soviet Union was the mirror image of more explicitly patriarchal regimes. The Soviet Union's egalitarian rhetoric and official state policies gave some women unique opportunities to be mobilised as citizens equal to their male counterparts, yet the state still relied on patriarchal structures that remained powerful in shaping and limiting women's roles. Małgorzata Mazurek explores the status of women under state socialism 40 years later through an examination of Polish women workers' resistance on the shop floor in the 1970s. She demonstrates that women used both their 'traditional' roles as mothers and caregivers and their professional status as workers to demand improvements in their working conditions. The multiple gender identities of state socialism could be used to mobilise against the state as well as for it.

The turn from women's history to gender history has inspired scholars to think about both women and men as embodying gendered norms and enacting particular kinds of femininity and masculinity. Some of this volume's chapters focus on the male gender, probing the relationship between masculinity, men's agency within mass dictatorships, and their active roles as workers, soldiers, colonisers and enactors of state-sponsored violence. Mobilised bodies of men and boys served not only to forward the political and military goals of mass dictatorships but also to symbolise power. Those who participated in the construction of the image of the 'New Man' in Nazi Germany or Soviet Russia, for example, understood him to be both an ideal political actor and a projection of state power. From its very inception, the 'anthropological revolution' as a dictatorial project was very much gendered in its discourse and ideology.

What is striking in the chapters about masculinity in this volume is the close correlation between the operation of state power and the disciplining of the male body by other male agents. Sangsoo Kim explicitly examines the ways in which British elementary school boys (and to a lesser extent girls) were trained to be agents of authority through the prefect system. In this system, they were empowered to police their peers in order to normalise notions of hierarchy and with the expectation that these students would carry future responsibility for ruling others in the empire. Yonson Ahn explores the relationship between national identity, sexuality and soldiering in the Japanese empire by focusing on the process of socialising Japanese male conscripts to be warriors during World War II. The soldiers of the Japanese army were trained to be aggressive towards enemies but submissive toward military authorities and Ahn argues that the system of 'comfort women' or regulated military prostitution enabled soldiers to reconcile their contradictory roles.

Sexuality was thus central to the process of military mobilisation and military effectiveness.

Alf Lüdtke's chapter traces the history of German male bodies, both ideal and real, from Weimar through Nazi Germany and into the German Democratic Republic. He shows the progression of the ideal male body from the youthful athletic ideals of the Weimar and Nazi periods, through the leanness of the war years, and into the more permissive body culture of the 1950s and 1960s where stout men with beer bellies were the norm. Lüdtke emphasises transformations over time as well as the relationship between male bodies and racial as well as gender hierarchies.

As Joan Scott reminds us, gender is not just about the formulation of the identities of those inhabiting bodies defined as male and female, but also about symbolising power. Lüdtke's chapter considers the male body both in terms of the lives of real men and as a symbol of the power of the state or the party. The symbolic dimension of gender relations is also explored by Michael Schoenhals in his chapter on depictions of sex in Chinese 'big-character posters' during the Maoist Cultural Revolution. Schoenhals shows the way in which the authors of big-character posters used charges of sexual abuse, promiscuity and perversion to disgrace both male and female public officials during the Cultural Revolution because these kinds of allegations had potency to define the class enemy more effectively than other charges. In this particular context, the discursive power of sex could even trump class in its ability to destroy the lives of the unfortunate victims of the Cultural Revolution.

The work of Eun-shil Kim examines the role of gender in the discursive construction of modern Korean identity under the developmental dictatorship of Park Chung-hee in the 1960s and 1970s. Eun-shil Kim demonstrates the ways in which women's participation in the Korean public sphere during modernisation was conceived of as an extension of female roles in the patriarchal order with all of the women as part of a collective entity (state, nation, society) that extended or replaced the family. Young women who worked outside of the home were understood to be contributing to this larger 'family' until they got married and had children. Yet the state's desire to limit population also created a new 'modern' role for women as the bearers of fewer well-raised children. Gender was thus central to the construction of citizenship in the new modern nation.

This volume thus explores all facets of gender by focusing on women's roles, men's roles and the symbolic power of gender in mass dictatorship. By bringing together the study of comparative dictatorships, colonialism and gender, this volume challenges fixed notions about dictatorship and democracy, about colony and metropole, about men and women, about public and private, about victims and accomplices. Commonalities across political systems allow for the breaking down of analytical boundaries, and differences stand in sharper relief, permitting a better understanding of the typical ways in which gender systems operate and the particularities of each case due to chronological, ideological and national differences.

In both mass dictatorships and mass democracies, however strongly 'patriarchal', or avowedly egalitarian, the mobilisation of women led to possibilities for individual women to increase their power in society if sometimes at the expense of other women and even in accordance with patriarchalism. But it must not be forgotten that individual men in these societies were also mobilised through the operation of gender and they also gained or lost power relative to women and to one another through the operation of the gender system. Gender also remained in complex interplay with other social determinants such as race, nationality or class in constructing identities and hierarchies.

While most of the chapters in the volume demonstrate the multiple ways that gendered norms were constitutive of state ideologies and facilitated the incorporation of citizens as agents in the state project, the men's beer bellies in the German Democratic Republic, the Polish women's protests on the shop floor and the Chinese students attacking senior officials by accusing them of sexual perversion remind us that citizens could also be mobilised against authority using gendered norms and precepts. This volume highlights the contingency and complexity of gendered mobilisation that makes cross-cultural comparisons difficult but worthwhile.

In modern twentieth-century states, gender was central to mobilisation both in wartime and in peacetime. Through discourses of anxiety about gender such as concern about the activities of the 'modern' new woman, discourses about motherhood that were both empowering and limiting, and the instilling of male norms of obedience through homosocial and sexual activities, both mass democracies and mass dictatorships employed gender difference as a central mobilising strategy. While the degree of state coercion of male and female citizens certainly varied substantially from context to context, the same tropes of gender mobilisation were ubiquitous in modern states as each state shaped and adapted them to fit its needs and each population responded within its own cultural milieu.

A transnational perspective allows us to see how periods of war and rapid social change precipitated the strengthening of particular kinds of gendered discourse as states in peril or upheaval sought to shore up support by appeal to the core subjectivities of citizens to activate them as agents of the state. Sometimes gender discourse worked in concert with class or racial discourse to produce heightened participation in state projects and an intensification of the exclusion of outsiders. Operating within a broad variety of contexts, concepts such as modern womanhood, disciplined manhood, motherhood and sexual propriety have a global resonance that requires recognition of an underlying commonality in the relationship between gender ideology and mass mobilisation in modern states, even as this relationship plays out differently in different global arenas.

Note

1. Joan W. Scott, 'Gender: A Useful Category of Historical Analysis', *American Historical Review* 91(5) (December 1986), pp. 1067, 1069; see also 'AHR Forum: Revisiting "Gender: A Useful Category of Historical Analysis"', *American Historical Review* 113(5) (December 2008), pp. 1344–429.

2
Mass Dictatorship and Gender Politics: Is the Outcome Predictable?

Barbara Einhorn

The temptation to equate fascism and communism is one to which many historians succumb. However, such equations can be facile or misleading and often suffer from retrospective value judgments that tend to produce historical inaccuracies. An analysis of the gender politics of mass dictatorships is prone to the same hazards. The question posed in the title of this chapter about whether the outcome is predictable can be answered by the simple fact that it depends: first, on the ideology and, second, on the implementation of that ideology in the particular social, political, historical and cultural context.

This chapter raises philosophical considerations about gender politics in mass dictatorships within two specific historical contexts: National Socialist Germany and the countries of Central and Eastern Europe under state socialist regimes.[1] The difference in ideologies is striking. In Nazi Germany, the ideological frame was nationalist: individuals were required to subordinate themselves to the exclusionary and expansionist national interest. Women's duty continued to be encapsulated in the traditional phrase *Kinder, Küche, Kirche* (children, kitchen and church; although the Nazis did not emphasise the latter). Of course everything depended on 'which' women, since not all women were deemed worthy of reproducing the pure 'Aryan' nation. Men's supreme duty was to fight and be prepared to die in the name of the 'Fatherland'. State socialist ideology, on the other hand, set out with an emancipatory objective: the full development of the individual was seen to be achieved through their engagement in the collective aspiration for a socially just egalitarian future. Women were prescribed a dual role, as workers and mothers, whilst men could confine themselves to a single one, as workers. Herein lay the seeds of a troubled gender politics. Whilst both ideologies involved duties and responsibilities to the social or the national interest, both the substance and the implementation of those ideologies differed. This chapter discusses the many-layered differences as well as the similarities between the gender politics of these two types of 'mass dictatorship'.

Introduction

There has been much debate about the politics of comparing dictatorships. Ian Kershaw and Moshe Lewin point out that comparative studies of totalitarianism were very much a part of Cold War discourse and confrontation, with the very concept 'totalitarianism' signalling a particular ideological stance. In this context, they point to the salience of 'facing the past' as a relevant point of comparison, involving 'questioning identities with roots extending beyond the era of the two dictatorships themselves'.[2] One stark contrast between Stalinism and National Socialism, they point out, is the Holocaust – 'the only example which history offers to date of a deliberate policy aimed at the total physical destruction of every member of an ethnic group. There is no equivalent of this under Stalinism. Though the waves of terror were massive indeed, and the death-toll immense, no ethnic group was singled out for total physical annihilation.'[3]

It is important to acknowledge both the different ideological starting points and the differing policy effects of the two regime types. National Socialism was fundamentally *exclusive*, discriminatory and inhumane, from its ideology to its murderous practice. Marxist ideology was humane in its agenda of egalitarian and socially just, in other words, *inclusive* societies. In its implementation, nevertheless, state socialist practice represented a travesty of this impulse, to differing degrees in the different countries of Central and Eastern Europe.

Far from producing nuanced accounts of complexity, contradiction, difference and paradox, however, the historiography of dictatorships is still dominated, argues Jie-Hyun Lim, by what he calls 'Cold War presentism'. This results, in his view, in a situation where 'the moral dualism of both totalitarian and Marxist paradigms facilitates the displacement of the historical responsibility of the ordinary people by shifting culpability away from them, and is thus losing a war of memory'.[4]

In the context of gender politics, it could be argued that both National Socialist and state socialist policies ultimately disempowered women. Nevertheless, it is important to deconstruct this assertion in order to discover its complexities and contradictions. At the level of ideology, there is total contrast between the two systems. While National Social-ism was constructed according to a male principle taken to its extreme – the *Führerprinzip* (leadership principle embodied in one man) – Marxist ideology posited an egalitarian principle, admittedly also led by an elite political party, which during the Stalinist era also involved a cult of personality and mandatory hatred of the class enemy. In terms of gen-der, Nazism constructed a politics of separate spheres based on notions of gender difference epitomised in the family, while Marxist ideol-ogy invoked the ideal of gender equality which focused on the labour market and was interpreted in practice – certainly in the retrospective judgement of some analysts – as gender sameness.

This chapter explores the similarities and differences, convergences and dissonances in the gender politics of Nazi Germany and state socialist regimes. Brief discussion of the terms 'mass dictatorship' and 'political religions', and of (the pitfalls of) comparing dictatorships located in different geopolitical and historical contexts is followed by the substantive section on the gender politics of these two regime types, focusing on the public-private divide, with particular reference to the family, sexuality and reproductive rights, and on access to political power. Attention is also paid to the ways that the nationalist discourses deployed by both regime types manipulate issues of class and ethnic-ity as well as gender stereotypes to produce divisive and exclusionary notions of community and social cohesion.

The central thesis of the chapter is that regardless of the parallels or contrasts between different dictatorship types, a gender equitable poli-tics is incompatible with the ideology and the practice of dictatorships as such. This does not guarantee, however, that formally and institution-ally democratic regimes such as *either* the Weimar Republic preceding National Socialist Germany *or* the post-state socialist regimes in Central and Eastern Europe will display gender sensitivity or institute gender equality. This chapter explores some uncomfortable historical continu-ities, as well as conspicuous differences between the two regime types under consideration. In particular, it pinpoints contradictions between the ideologies and discourses employed by each regime and the social realities of their implementation. The question is: how consistently did each political regime apply its principles, and what difference does the ideology make to the outcome?

Debating the term 'mass dictatorship'

The term 'mass dictatorship' raises questions about the actual extent to which different dictatorships have achieved what might be called the 'mobilisation of the willing', and thus the level of active consent or popular support. How many regimes in history actually fit the bill? Recent debates on Nazi Germany have problematised the level of willing participation. Jie-Hyun Lim rightly critiques earlier interpretations of both totalitarian and Marxist paradigms for their acceptance of Cold War dualisms, according to which a few powerful perpetrators coerced and terrorised an unwilling many. Such a perspective reduces the citizens of these regimes to the status of passive victims, thereby depriving them of agency, and indeed of responsibility. In contrast Lim poses a compelling argument for the term 'mass dictatorship', namely for an analysis of both types of dictatorship 'from below' to ascertain the level of voluntary mobilisation and the internalised consent of the population. A more complex and nuanced approach such as Jie-Hyun Lim's acknowledges the coexistence and interaction of coercion and consent in such regimes. This reflects a situation in which fear of the potential consequences produces silent collusion rather than vocal opposition.

Nevertheless, his argument that mass dictatorships – thus by implication both National Socialism in Germany and state socialist or Stalinist regimes in Central and Eastern Europe – relied on popular support is simultaneously compromised by his acknowledgement that in the post-1956 era, 'the regime was obliged to rest content with ... purely passive consent' so that 'while communist regimes continued to involve masses in ritual performances of compliance, they could not and did not expect ideological commitment from the masses'.[5] One might wish to question to what extent 'passive consent' and silent collusion can be regarded as popular support rather than as manifestations of resignation, cynicism or conformity based on fear, to all of which Lim refers.

The 'political religions' approach also fails to depart significantly from the totalitarian paradigm, in that it too depends upon the notion that the ruling ideology, seen as a secular religion, is imposed from above as an instrument of control. In this view, the mass rallies of the Nazis, or the mass 'demonstrations' of the state socialist regimes, are orchestrated rituals designed to foster adherence to the quasi-religious or ideological creed, rather than spontaneous outbursts of 'belief' in the system and/or dedication to its causes.

Richard Evans feels that National Socialist ideology cannot be considered as a 'political religion', since its focus was very much on the social organisation of this life, rather than on some idea of an afterlife, a life beyond our comprehension or beyond our ability to fashion it.[6] Its appeal – and its notion of constructing an ideal world based on racial superiority and exclusivity – was earthly rather than spiritual. In this respect, perhaps Hans Mommsen's use of the term 'racial "political religion" ' can be useful to the discussion.[7]

Arguing a slightly different case, Doris Bergen holds that while there were ideological differences between Christianity as the dominant religion of the time and National Socialism, nevertheless, seen statistically, the majority of Nazis were Christians. Leaving the pagan elements of National Socialist ideology aside, Bergen identifies a 'partnership' in practice between the Nazi regime and the 'German Christian' churches in Germany. This was particularly evident during World War II, when even the dissident Confessing Church 'rallied to the flag and the fighting *Volk'*.[8] While the latter may have rallied to the nation rather than to the National Socialist Party, ultimately they too supported rather than opposed the Nazi war effort.

Whether the concept of 'political religions' is applicable depends not on ideology alone, nor on the existence within it of quasi-religious ritual, but on the level to which the ideology is internalised by the people, and more specifically on the extent of complicity in crimes enacted in the name of that ideology. Missing from discussions of National Socialism as a political religion, for example, in Bergen's view, is 'an extended analysis of Christian anti-Judaism and its links to Nazi anti-semitic ideology and especially practice'. A key question for her, therefore, is 'the role of Christians as perpetrators of Nazi crimes'.[9]

The question of complicity, and indeed responsibility, is one that raged in a debate at the beginning of the 1990s between feminist historians of National Socialism. While there is no denying that some women were militant Nazis and active perpetrators, for example as members of the SS or concentration camp guards, the debate centred precisely on the Nazi-defined separate sphere of femininity and motherhood. The central questions were whether Nazi reproductive politics instrumentalising motherhood had actually been to women's benefit or their detriment and whether the silent collusion of women in Nazi politics made them guilty of active participation. Beyond this 'victim'/'perpetrator' binary, it is important to understand how gender and sexuality articulated with Nazi doctrines of 'race' in the rhetoric of the 'Aryan' nation as well as in the politics of everyday life, and indeed in the experience of the Holocaust. Thus the category of gender is central to our understanding of this particular mass dictatorship.[10]

Comparing dictatorships

This chapter adopts a comparative approach to National Socialism in Germany and state socialist regimes in Central and Eastern Europe.

Some might well argue that such a comparison is untenable. Clearly, it is a risky enterprise.[11] Arguably, National Socialism in Germany was a mass dictatorship in a way that state socialist dictatorships were not, as they did not enjoy broad popular support. National Socialism in contrast was carried, and legitimated, by the masses. The Nazis were voted into power, and the regime was defended 'to the last drop of blood' by its citizens, even when defeat in World War II had long become evident.

The NSDAP (German National Socialist Workers' Party) was a mass political party; the National Socialist Women's Organisation (*Nationalsozialistische Frauenschaft*) had 2.3 million members by the end of 1938 and about 6 million (roughly one in five German women over the age of 18) by 1941. Between them the Hitler Youth (HJ – *Hitlerjugend*) (Illustration 2.1) and the Federation of German Girls (BDM – *Bund deutscher Mädel*) (Illustration 2.2) had captivated the majority of German youth by 1936 on a voluntary basis, long before membership became compulsory in 1939.[12]

Several authors point out that for women as well as young people in rural areas membership in the *NS-Frauenschaft* and the HJ or the BDM could be seen as offering horizon-broadening opportunities and the potential to transcend traditional gender-ascribed role models. Gerhard Wilke points to the way in which the *NS-Frauenschaft* and the BDM 'allowed women to travel beyond the narrow confines of the village, brought them in contact with women from other regions and made them cross social class-boundaries – in short, Nazism brought a certain "liberation" from the traditional confines of village life'. Detlev Peukert too describes how membership of the BDM, at least in the early days, allowed girls to 'escape from the female role-model centred around family and children – a role-model which, for that matter, was also propagated by the National Socialists'.[13]

State socialist regimes attempted to present – and legitimate – themselves as 'dictatorships of the proletariat' and hence as mass dictatorships. Yet none of them in Eastern Europe (with the exception of Czechoslovakia) emerged, as had the National Socialist regime, from popular will expressed through a democratic vote.

Taking the case of Germany, popular and media discourse routinely brackets the two German dictatorships together, as though they were directly comparable. In reality, although there were similarities, it is precisely on the issue of popular support – taken as the defining marker of mass dictatorships – that they differed fundamentally. Not only was the state socialist regime in East Germany not elected. Far from it: it was an import – the direct result, arguably, of the Hitler regime itself in that it was imposed through Soviet occupation; hence it was, one could

Illustration 2.1   'Young People Serve the Führer: All Ten Year-Olds Join the Hitler-Youth Movement'. Picture Database of the Federal German Archives.

almost claim, not a German dictatorship at all. It was plain to all from the outset that the limited power of the regime rested on the support of 'Big Brother', a fact demonstrated daily by the presence throughout the German Democratic Republic's (GDR) history of Soviet troops on its soil. Unlike the Nazi regime, the government of the GDR could never count on support from the majority of its citizens. The Berlin Wall was clear evidence of that fact, as was the collapse of the regime soon after

Illustration 2.2 'All Ten Year-Olds to Us' – Recruitment Drive for the League of Young German Girls (JM – *Jungmädelbund*). Picture database of the Federal German Archives.

it became clear – prompted by the mass exodus of GDR citizens through Austria and Hungary in the summer of 1989 and the mass peaceful demonstrations of the autumn – that the Soviet Union, after the visit of Gorbachev to the GDR's 40th anniversary celebrations in October, was no longer prepared to defend it.

In practice, none of these regimes ever enjoyed much active popular support. They were carried by the dictatorship of the Communist Party, itself an elite and exclusive organisation. Membership of the party had to be earned, and although it was a means of career advancement or status security in a similar way to membership of the German Nationalist Socialist Party, it is striking that large sections of the populations in most Central and Eastern European countries nevertheless chose not to become members. Membership of the Free German Youth (FDJ) was almost mandatory rather than voluntary if one wished, for example, to pursue higher education (Illustration 2.3).

Mass demonstrations in the GDR were highly choreographed, as in Nazi Germany. However, state socialist marches and celebrations pale into insignificance compared with the sheer scale of Nazi pomp and pageantry, the visually and verbally documented ecstatic frenzy and indeed fanatical devotion to Adolf Hitler personally and to the National Socialist regime and its ideology. Nor can state socialist events count as expressions of popular will, since they depended not on voluntary mobilisation but on compulsory participation by the workers of most state enterprises and national organisations.

Gender is a variable of central salience in historical processes of transformation. This is true both for the rise of National Socialism and the emergence and demise of state socialism. Until recently, this key element has been under-researched. Kevin Passmore points out that 'both totalitarianism and its updated political religions approach rely heavily

Illustration 2.3   Free German Youth (*Freie Deutsche Jugend* – FDJ) members at camp, German Democratic Republic (GDR), *Deutsche Demokratische Republik* (DDR). Picture Archive, German Historical Museum, Berlin.

upon a gendered sociology and political science' and have as a result 'been relatively uninterested in gender or women'.[14] Thus a crucial point of enquiry should be the question of how regimes such as National Socialism or state socialism deployed gendered discourses and practices and whether they ultimately empowered or disempowered their citizens and women in particular.

In their still highly pertinent early book *When Biology Became Destiny* covering the Weimar period and Nazi Germany, editors Renate Bridenthal, Atina Grossmann and Marion Kaplan state that 'gender was an extraordinarily salient category throughout the period addressed in this volume. Indeed its significance increased in the Nazi period'.[15] 'Women's emancipation' was a central tenet of state socialist ideology, even though its motivations – and especially its implementation in practice – were ambivalent and problematic.[16]

Despite the central role of gender in shaping as well as reflecting social, economic and political transformation, especially in times of crisis and uncertainty, it would be dangerous to assume that mass dictatorships promote one kind of gender regime, and democratic societies another. Such an assumption would imply continuities between Nazi Germany and state socialism, rather than between either of them and the regimes which preceded and followed them. Thus parallels might be drawn between democracy as practised in Weimar Germany and the post-1989 democratisation process in Central and Eastern Europe. Paradoxically it is the case, in contrast, that some of the most disturbing continuities – which immediately confound the temptation to assume likeness in the gender politics of all mass dictatorships – appear between early statements by Nazi ideologues and the political discourse following the demise of state socialist regimes in Central and Eastern Europe. Clearly it is the case that a somewhat essentialist gender politics – within re-emergent nationalist discourses – has played an important role in shaping the post-1989 transformation process in many of these countries.[17]

Mass dictatorships and gender politics

The National Socialists claimed that they were rescuing women from the 'emancipation' of the Weimar years. Historians of gender have pointed out that this 'emancipation' was more myth and phantasm than reality; nonetheless it contained enough of a grain of truth to be manipulable, providing supposed grounds for claims that feminism bore a large share of responsibility for the decline of the family and the birth rate, and for social and political turmoil. Thus the Nazi ideologue Alfred Rosenberg declared in his *Der Mythus des 20. Jahrhunderts* (*The Myth of the Twentieth Century*) published in 1930: 'Emancipate women from women's emancipation.'

Adolf Hitler followed this in 1934 with the claim that the very term 'women's emancipation' had been invented by Jewish intellectuals, and was essentially 'un-German'. Hitler told a meeting of National Socialist women held on 8 September 1934 that while matters of state should be run by men, a woman's sphere of responsibility was 'her husband, her family, her children and her home', adding: 'We do not consider it correct for the woman to interfere in the world of the man, in his main sphere. We consider it natural if these two worlds remain distinct.'[18]

Any claim to similarity between state socialist and National Socialist gender doctrines would imply confusing the Nazi regime of a clearly demarcated gender hierarchy with an ideology of gender equality. Joseph Goebbels wrote in his diary in 1932: 'Woman is the sexual and working companion of man. She always has been and always will be. Formerly in the fields, today in the office. The man is the organiser of life, the woman his helper and his executive.'[19] While it could be claimed that the veneer of equality in state socialist regimes masked gender-demarcated domestic inequalities, it must be recognised that the Nazis resolutely practised what they preached: woman was to be the subordinate helpmeet of the 'Aryan' man.

In Central and Eastern Europe, voices were raised long before 1989 asserting that many of the social, economic and political problems these countries were encountering could be attributed to 'too much emancipation'. Already during the late 1970s and early 1980s, argues Dimitrina Petrova in relation to Bulgaria, 'emancipation ... started to be seen as an official fabrication of yesterday, but now out of season, something that just made life more difficult'.[20] Women were thus seen as in need of 'rescue' from the impossibility of the triple burden imposed on them by state socialist ideology; a burden that left them carrying multiple identities as workers, mothers and politically engaged citizens.[21]

The uncanny parallels continue. State socialist societies were to some extent inclusive, even if in a paternalistic and authoritarian manner. Yet the forms of nationalism emerging towards the end of these regimes – and during the subsequent democratisation process – have produced discourses of national identity based on exclusionary notions of ethnicity that invoke and depend upon rigid notions of masculinity, femininity and correspondingly 'proper' gender roles.[22] The declining birth rate and a multitude of other social ills were conveniently ascribed to state socialism's policies of involving women in the public spheres of the labour market and politics.

Early on in the post-socialist transformation in Russia, Olga Lipovskaya described a 'patriarchal tradition' deployed via powerful 'propaganda to send women home.... From conservative writers, the Church and the media comes the familiar charge that the high divorce rate, juvenile delinquency and alcoholism can be directly attributed to women's absence from the family.'[23] The solution to society's ills was seen to lie in the rediscovery of 'appropriate' gender roles: newly assertive masculinity formerly supposedly neutralised by gender-equal labour policies but now restored to dominance in the public sphere was to be complemented by caring femininity returned to its proper role in nurturing the family and 'bearing babies for the nation'. Nor has this rhetoric linking the need to reintroduce 'appropriate' gender roles within an independent national identity disappeared. On the contrary, it has re-emerged more recently in many countries in Central and Eastern Europe as an expression of the fear that EU accession could pose a threat to recently re-established national autonomy.[24]

In these uncomfortably similar discourses about 'proper' gender roles holding sway in separate spheres of responsibility, both National Socialist ideology and the politics of post-communist transformation can be seen to be leapfrogging their respective recent histories, resorting to premodern, idealised stereotypes of gender hierarchies in both the family and the wider national community as a panacea for what they perceive as the social disorder and political chaos of the immediately preceding era: Weimar Germany and state socialism, respectively. Claudia Koonz has identified the tendency whereby 'in chaotic political and economic settings, citizens often look hopefully to an authoritarian culture of orderliness and harmony based on clearly demarcated divisions between men and women and between ethnic communities'.[25] Indeed as several authors have pointed out about Nazi Germany, there was in fact a considerable element of continuity with the Weimar Republic in that the National Socialists were able to build on traditional notions of women and gender that had been voiced by several political parties and women's groups during the Weimar period.[26]

The public-private divide

Treatment of the private sphere and the boundary between it and the public sphere differed fundamentally in communist and National Socialist ideologies. This ideological difference became particularly manifest in the material practices of Nazi Germany and state socialist countries.

The male-dominated, conservative view of social relations propagated by the Nazis simply perpetuated and built on traditional notions of the family, the nation and woman's role within it which had in fact – despite the granting of female suffrage and the inclusion of equal rights provisions in the Constitution – remained dominant during the Weimar Republic. In contrast, early Marxist theorists and ideologues Marx, Engels, Bebel, Alexandra Kollontai and Inessa Armand initially set out to liberate women from imprisonment within the petty constraints of the bourgeois family.

Both ideologies constructed the family as the smallest cell of society, with responsibility towards the community as a whole and in particular to its future. In Nazi ideology this responsibility concerned the desired production and reproduction of a racially homogeneous, 'pure Aryan' community. Policies thus focused above all on reproduction (Illustration 2.4). Nazi policies from the beginning intruded into and attempted to regulate the private sphere in the interests of furthering the goal of eugenic social manipulation. Indeed the 1935 Law for the Protection of the Hereditary Health of the German People made marriage 'in contrast to its former character as a private matter, an institution which lies in the public interest'. Dorothee Klinksiek observes that in the Nazi state 'marriage above all serves the preservation and propagation of the Volk'. Richard Bessel points out how the Nazi slogan of *Gemeinnutz vor Eigennutz* ('the common good before individual good') 'was to be applied to intimate relations; marriage, sexual relations and human reproduction were to be harnessed to serve the *Volksgemeinschaft* in the eternal struggle between the races'.[27]

Kate Lacey vividly describes the implications of this for women's position. Women were confined to the heavily ideologically loaded private sphere, where, 'excluded from positions of any real power, they were fed the myth of an alternative power, one based on the permanent sacrifice of public and political agency' in an 'ongoing politicisation of the private sphere'. She analyses the use of radio – 'the most modern apparatus of communication' – for propaganda purposes in the service of an atavistic and nationalist ideology in which 'women's political support was measured by the extent to which they subordinated their individual and familial interests to the interests of the national community', simultaneously acquiescing in their exclusion from the public sphere.[28]

In fact, *völkische* – as well as anti-feminist – notions had been espoused by several political parties during the Weimar Republic – despite the

Illustration 2.4 Nazi population policy: 'Healthy Parents – Healthy Children!'. Image Archive of the Federal German Archives.

advent in 1919 of female suffrage. The idea that woman's 'proper' place was in the home was therefore one which the Nazis simply perpetuated. Restrictions were placed on women's entry to university following Hitler's conviction that 'the main purpose of educating girls should be to train them to be mothers'.[29] A law passed in April 1933 stipulated that the proportion of girls entering university should not exceed 10 per cent of the number of male university entrants. This measure had the effect by 1936 of halving the number of female university students; from 17,000 female university students in 1932–33, numbers had dwindled to 6000 by 1939.[30]

It is evident that this banishment to the circumscribed private sphere did not apply equally to all German women. For working-class women, the necessity of engaging in paid labour had not diminished. The Nazi doctrine of domesticity applied primarily to middle-class women, whose 'primary occupation should be motherhood' in the service of producing 'inherently healthier' and 'racially more valuable' offspring than women from the lower strata.[31] Working-class women could be more 'effectively' deployed in the lowest-paid occupations in the industrial labour force.

German-Jewish women, as Marion Kaplan notes, suffered a 'dual stigmatisation of gender and "race" in a society that became increasingly misogynist and anti-Semitic'. Discrimination and ostracism in public led them to become, by necessity, inventive. Kaplan documents how 'many experimented with new behaviours rarely before attempted by *any* German women', such that 'at a time when Nazi ideology shrilly reaffirmed male privilege, relegating "Aryan" women to "*Kinder, Küche, Kirche*" (children, kitchen, church), Jewish women took on new roles as breadwinners, family protectors and defenders of businesses or practices'. She concludes that paradoxically, even whilst busy establishing the doctrine of separate spheres for 'Aryan' Germans, 'the Nazis essentially destroyed the patriarchal structure of the Jewish family, leaving a void to be filled by women'.[32]

Communist visions of the family stumbled after early visions from Alexandra Kollontai and others of the dissolution of restrictive bourgeois family bonds. Friedrich Engels had written of a future in which 'the individual family ceases to be the economic unit of society. Private housekeeping is transformed into a social industry. The care and education of children becomes a public matter.' Social production was seen by Lenin in 1919 as the appropriate means to liberate women from the status of 'domestic slave' by socialising the 'barbarously unproductive, petty, nerve-wracking, stultifying and crushing drudgery' of housework.[33]

This vision of marriage and the family as no longer primarily the responsibility of women but a matter of public social responsibility was based, in Kollontai's view, on the abolition of marriage as 'a microscopic state where husband ruled wife and children' and family was seen as 'the incubator of future citizens'. In its place 'public upbringing of children would replace its traditional function; equality of sexes would dethrone its traditional ruler'. In a 1920 speech on 'Communism and the Family' Kollontai stated that 'the family is withering away not because it is being forcibly destroyed by the state, but because the family is ceasing to be a necessity'.[34]

Such early Bolshevik ideals of a new form of family which would liberate women from their traditional role soon foundered, both on unfavourable material conditions and on a failure of political will. World War I and the ensuing civil war had created crushing poverty and severe social dislocation, leaving an enormous number of orphans in the Soviet Union. These problems were compounded by the forced pace of industrialisation and the collectivisation of agriculture initiated by Stalin in 1928. The reaction was forceful: new laws stressing family responsibilities were introduced in 1930; at the same time the *zhenotdel*, the women's department of the Communist Party, was abolished. A 1936 law made divorce more difficult to obtain and outlawed abortion.[35] Thus was the nuclear family reborn, simply with a new signifier: as the 'socialist family', in which gender role divisions went unquestioned as worker-mothers were required to bear and rear the socialist citizens of the future. Nevertheless, in contrast to National Socialist population policies, the focus remained on the 'correct' upbringing of the next generation as young socialists rather than on procreation as such.

The sexual politics of the National Socialists were not, however, as Dagmar Herzog argues, confined to a doctrine of purely procreative sex within the Nazi family. Thus she counters the view that the Third Reich was 'at its core "sex-hostile"', noting that the regime encouraged sexual pleasure, albeit within the confines of its eugenicist, racist and homophobic agendas. Thus the Nazis somewhat paradoxically managed to tie a positive attitude towards the free expression of sexuality to racist notions of excessive sexuality and deficient morality as inherently Jewish – and characteristic of the Weimar Republic. 'The aim was to reinvent it [sexuality] as the privilege of non-disabled, heterosexual "Aryans" (all the while claiming to be "cleaning up" sexual morality in Germany and overcoming the "Jewish" legacy).'[36] Thus the free enjoyment of sexuality was, like so much else, restricted to those considered worthy of such liberties. In Herzog's words:

> Nazi policy and practice, for regime-loyal or regime-indifferent non-proletarian heterosexual 'Aryans' was often anything but repressive. Indeed the regime's brutality and the pleasures it promised to those it did not persecute were inextricably connected. The stepped-up persecution of homosexuals provided a crucial context for the injunction to heterosexual activity; the abuse and murder of those deemed unworthy of reproduction and life because of their supposed behavioral or 'racial' characteristics constituted the

background against which those classed as superior were enjoined to enjoy their entitlements.... What was off-limits was not sexual fulfilment; rather, who could have sex and with whom were circum-·scribed in new ways. As Marcuse noted, Nazism encouraged sexual release and license and worked to link that release and license to racism.[37]

Herzog refers to the SS journal *Das schwarze Korps* (*The Black Corps*) which was 'directed explicitly at the nation's self-understood racial and political elite and one of the regime's prime venues for disseminating its policy views to its most devoted followers'. The views published in this journal were 'carefully contradictory, placing defenses of marriage and critiques of "Marxist" free love and "Jewish" attacks on the family side-by-side with amused diatribes against bourgeois prudery'.[38]

In state socialist societies, traditional notions of sexuality and the family tended to prevail, reinforced in Poland and the Soviet Union by Catholic and Orthodox religious doctrine. Tradition favouring marriage and procreation was given a potent impetus by the demographic pressures of the declining birth rate, on the one hand, and perennial housing shortages, on the other. Marriage was often the only way to access an apartment. As a result, the existence of children in the marriage endowed young people with a preferential position on housing waiting lists.

The state socialists, like the Nazis, introduced a series of policies designed to induce an increase in the birth rate. Yet in both cases, these policies were relatively unsuccessful. Interest-free marriage loans of up to 1000 Reichsmark were introduced on 1 June 1933 as an explicit measure to combat unemployment, that is, to 'encourage' women out of the workforce. A supplementary decree issued on 20 June 1933 reduced the amount repayable by a quarter for each child born into the marriage. This meant that if they had four children, couples would not need to repay anything. The loans were, of course, dependent on the couple having established their credentials as pure 'Aryans'.[39] Without the racist proviso, the marriage loan system introduced as part of state policy in Czechoslovakia and the GDR provides yet another uncanny example of continuity. In both countries, young couples were eligible for a substantial interest-free loan, with each additional child born into the family considered as part repayment. In Nazi Germany, the birth of four children erased the debt entirely; in Czechoslovakia, a family with three children could write off one-third of the loan.[40] Despite the inducements, the birthrate in all the state socialist countries remained extremely low.

The issue of reproductive policy more generally was dealt with completely differently by the Nazis and the state socialists. While the Nazis abolished abortion except for 'unfit' mothers, the state socialist regimes largely made it legally available. In the GDR from 1972, abortion was free – and freely available – on the decision of the woman alone. Indeed abortion famously became the single issue that in 1990 held up and indeed threatened to derail the negotiations on the treaty sealing German unification.[41]

The state socialist record on reproductive politics also demonstrated falterings and exceptions. Contraception was only patchily available in Russia and most of the Central and Eastern European countries during the state socialist period, with the result that abortion was widely used as a (sometimes the only available) method of birth control. In Poland, access to legal abortion varied over the years depending on perceptions of the need for increases in the workforce, rather than any notion of women's autonomy or right to choose. In Romania, abortion was outlawed in an ethno-nationalist campaign to force ethnic Romanian women (as opposed to Roma women) to produce large numbers of children for the nation.[42]

One area of commonality between the two regime types could be their mutual insistence on heterosexuality – and procreation – as the desired norm. However, in contrast to Nazi persecution and murder of homosexuals as deviants, state socialist regimes tended to regard homosexuality as an 'unfortunate' affliction. Nevertheless, although the first post-revolutionary Soviet Constitution had offered homosexuals equal rights, Stalinist puritanism in the 1930s criminalised it. Even in the post-1989 period, while gay activist groups have surfaced across Central and Eastern Europe, legislation has been slow to follow and Gay Pride demonstrations have suffered marginalisation, violence and opprobrium.[43]

Far from being known for its doctrine of 'free love', the Soviet system has been pilloried in retrospect as having been prudish about sex. It has become a commonly expressed view that its policies of gender equality in effect favoured gender sameness and thus a process of de-sexualisation. Reaction has been immediate and powerful. Post-1989 marketisation has quickly rectified any such deficiencies, transforming women into objects for sexual consumption, both in terms of media imagery and in the booming prostitution and trafficking industries. It is interesting to note the contrast here with traditional gender hierarchies and the return to conservative 'family values' and 'appropriate' gender roles espoused in post-1989 public discourse. Does the marketisation of sexuality post-1989 contradict the observation of gender historians about the 'ways in which invocations of a notion of "crisis" facilitate efforts to reconstruct social hierarchies'? Whether or not it represents simply the flip side of the traditionalist coin, this wave of sexualisation certainly contrasts markedly with the sexually conservative attitudes revived in post-war West Germany's reaction against Nazism. This resulted in the paradox that 'popular magazines in the first years of the 1960s expressed more conservative views on gender and sex than did those in the late 1940s'.[44] On this aspect at least there is no continuity to be observed between the post-National Socialist and post-communist periods.

During state socialism, the home remained, in both positive and negative senses the one area of life that was out of reach of the long arm of the socialist state. The negative side of the coin was that the traditional gendered division of domestic labour and women's responsibility for childcare were never questioned during the state socialist period, thus confirming women in their triple burden.[45] Women themselves defended the public-private divide, overlooking their own domestic subordination in the name of gender-neutral solidarity in a situation cast as 'us', the people, versus 'them', the state and its over-politicised public sphere, a stand-off characterised by Polish sociologist Mira Marody as the 'authorities vs. society' dichotomy.[46] The positive side of this situation lay in perceptions of the private sphere as the only locus of autonomy, creativity and independence, as Slavenka Drakulić has described it:

> Apartments were for us mythical cult objects.... An apartment, however small, however crowded with people and things, kids and animals, is 'ours'. To survive, we had to divide the territory, to set a border between private and public. The state wants it all public – it can't see into our apartment, but it can tap our telephone, read our mail. We didn't give up: everything beyond the door was considered 'theirs'. They wanted to turn our apartments into public spaces, but we didn't buy that trick. What is public is of the enemy. So we hid in our pigeonholes, leaned on each other in spite of everything, and licked our wounds.[47]

Thus the private sphere embodied the embryo civil society influential in resistance to the communist state and idealised post-1989 in scholarship and by international donors as *'the'* single necessary and sufficient basis for democratisation. A study conducted by UNICEF in the region in 1999, for example, defines women's participation in civil society as 'vital for [their] well-being and, no doubt, for the success of the transition itself' since 'a strong civil society can provide a sound foundation for economic and political development in the transition countries'.[48]

Differential politics in practice

Politically, at the formal level, strong similarities exist in that both Nazi Germany and state socialist regimes were one-party states. However, the differences are striking. By July 1933, the National Socialists had passed a law formally banning all other political parties, and abolishing trade unions. They went further, in that 'every national voluntary associa- tion, and every local club, was brought under Nazi control, ... women's organisations – in short, the whole fabric of associational life was Nazified'.[49]

In contrast, state socialist polities at least maintained a semblance of democratic process with the existence of multiple political parties and national civil society organisations. In practice, however, both parties and civil society organisations were popularly referred to as 'fig- leaves', autonomous civil society organisations were not permitted, and national parliaments were token institutions, so that the high level of female representation in them remained an empty signifier.

In Nazi Germany the racist, nationalist and sexist vision of the nation set out by Hitler in *Mein Kampf* (*My Struggle*) was strongly borne out in the policies actually implemented by the Nazi regime. This situation presents a stark contrast with the record of state socialism, which man- ifests major discrepancies between the egalitarian and gender equitable ideology of Marxism-Leninism and the practices of Central and Eastern European regimes. Despite the obvious contrasts, however, both forms of dictatorship were politically unrepresentative in gender terms.

Women were marginalised and denied leadership positions in the party and mass organisations of Nazi Germany. Even their own women's organisation, the *NS-Frauenschaft*, was disempowered at an early stage and subordinated to the male leadership of the party and the state. While women in state socialist regimes accounted on average for around 30 per cent of parliamentarians, it is now well documented that the par- liaments were not the decision-making bodies. Rather, power lay with the communist parties, and in particular with the Central Committees and Politburos. Although women made up on average between 24 and 30 per cent of ordinary party membership in Eastern Europe and the Soviet Union in 1975, their representation at Central Committee level in 1976 ranged from a low of 3 per cent in the Soviet Union to a high of just 15 per cent in Czechoslovakia. In the ruling Politburos, they were conspicuous by their absence.[50]

The NSDAP and the mass organisations of Nazi Germany were totally male-dominated. There has been much discussion of the extent to which women's organisations in the Weimar period can be considered feminist or not. Many scholars suggest that in fact they drew on and perpetuated rather traditional notions of women's roles. Karen Offen cites anti-feminist organisations such as the *Deutscher Bund zur Bekämpfung der Frauenemanzipation* (German League for the Prevention of Women's Emancipation) which existed from 1912 to 1920 on a platform of 'genuine manliness for men; genuine femininity for women', arguing that 'equal rights would lead to a "feminization and a weakening of the state itself" '.[51] In the wake of a general climate of anti-feminism in the early Weimar Republic, the 'once radical' BDF (*Bund deutscher Frauenvereine* – League of German Women's Associations) in 1919 revised its programme to endorse not women's emancipation at the very moment that female suffrage was granted, but the family and 'appropriate' gender roles, supporting a middle-class platform of charitable work rather than paid labour for women.[52]

Thus was the German women's movement co-opted to a conservative gender regime even prior to the National Socialists' entry into power. Early in the Third Reich, the BDF, which had earlier become 'increasingly nationalistic and chauvinistic' and had ostracised the *Jüdischer Frauenbund* (Jewish Women's Association), was itself disbanded. Those leaders of the Nazi women's organisation (*NS-Frauenschaft*) who manifested too great an eagerness for a politically independent women's sphere were soon relieved of their posts and even expelled from the organisation.[53] National Socialist policies stressed that while women's sphere should indeed remain separate, it must nevertheless be subsumed under male control. Gertrud Scholtz-Klink was chosen by Gregor Strasser as the perfect leader for the *NS-Frauenschaft* (National Socialist Party Women's Wing). She fulfilled traditional feminine stereotypes (as mother of a large family and grieving widow, rather than the much maligned independent career woman of the Weimar Republic) and was prepared to subordinate herself totally to the dictates of the male NSDAP leadership. She was 'reliably racist as well as an advocate of separate (and subordinate) spheres', stating that 'in principle we permit only Germans to be leaders of German women', and stressing that 'we have never demanded, nor shall we ever demand, equal rights for women with the men of our nation'.[54]

The official women's organisations – the only such organisations permitted under state socialist rule – were similarly subordinated to, and in effect mere executive instruments of, government policy. Thus, for example, the DFD (*Demokratischer Frauenbund Deutschlands* – German Women's Democratic League) in the GDR (East Germany) may be regarded as having been part of the extended arm of the state. In a manner not dissimilar to the *NS-Frauenschaft* its policies and activities simply implemented directives from the ruling party.[55]

Moreover, the DFD bore similarities to the earlier Weimar Republic's BDF in a number of its features: its rather older age structure and failure to attract younger women; the focus of its activities on small town and rural areas, highlighting domestic or at best local community-level welfare-oriented activities; its predominantly middle-class membership; and its lack of both any real gender equality programme and any substantial political impact.[56]

In terms of autonomous political agency, there did exist small resistance groups in both regime types. The *Weisse Rose* was formed in opposition to National Socialism by a group of students and maintained a brief existence from June 1942 to February 1943. It was founded by the student siblings Hans and Sophie Scholl, and operated mainly in a university context. Although Sophie has become the iconic figure associated with the group, for example, in the 2005 feature film *Sophie Scholl*, the group was based neither on gender lines nor on issues of gender politics.[57] Ironically, given the passive and compliant status of its ostensibly independent 'mass organisations', the GDR celebrated Hans and Sophie Scholl with a commemorative postage stamp in 1961. Dissident groups existed in state socialist countries too, especially during the 1980s, from the trade union-based Solidarność in Poland to the environmentally concerned Dialogue group in Hungary. However, none of these groups were founded with any gender awareness. Even the *Frauen für den Frieden* (Women for Peace) in the GDR was initially founded – like the other groups – in solidarity with men in the opposition peace, environment and human rights groups.[58]

In terms of political agency and subject status then, both Nazi Germany and state socialist regimes disempowered women. It could be argued that they also disempowered men, despite the heroic, militaristic masculinity propagated by the National Socialists and the idealised male worker (as opposed to the female peasant) of state socialist iconography.

Yet what *is* significant is differences in the rhetoric and the reality of the two regime types. Despite the uncomfortable parallels between them, it is ultimately arguable that the disjunctures between National Socialist Germany and state socialist regimes, in terms of both ideology and practice, outweigh the continuities.

Conclusion

Notwithstanding its internal contradictions and inadequate implementation, Marxist ideology (if not state socialist practice) did hold to a belief in gender equality. Nazi ideology and practice in contrast rested on an unyieldingly difference-based ideology. The commitment to an ideology of separate spheres did not waver, even under conditions of war, economic duress and impending defeat. Women were never conscripted in Nazi Germany – unlike in the Allied nations such as the UK or the USA – neither into the labour force, nor into military service. It was opposition to the introduction of potential conscription for women in times of emergency that resulted in my imprisonment – along with two leading members of the *Frauen für den Frieden*, Bärbel Bohley and Ulrike Poppe – in the GDR in 1983. However, despite the nuclear stand-off during the Cold War, this was peacetime, so the issue of women's conscription never came to be tested. During World War II, the Soviet Union *had* drafted women, sending them to the front alongside their male comrades.

The subordination of individual needs and aspirations to the common good required by both types of mass dictatorship therefore occurred within different ideological frames and material practices. In Nazi Germany, 'Aryan' women were conceived of as nothing more than breeding machines and adornments for their male partners in a society characterised by extreme class, sexual and particularly 'racial' divisions. In state socialist regimes, all women were exhorted to play an equal role with men in building a better future, as mothers *and* workers, as social and political activists (albeit without much real power). They were even cast as defenders of the idea of an egalitarian society, thus – in times of emergency – as potential defenders of the nation, a role identified with militarised masculinity and thus confined to men in the traditional nationalist discourse of National Socialism.

This chapter intends to open a debate rather than providing conclusive arguments. It asserts that mass dictatorships are neither monolithic nor homogeneous. The record of the two dictatorship types examined briefly here demonstrates (unexpected and uncomfortable) similarities but also dissonances. The most striking disparity lies in the relation-ship between ideology and practice. National Socialism in Germany attests to an almost seamless coherence, and consonance, between ide-ology and practice – the racist beliefs of the ideologues became ends in themselves, carried out through indiscriminate terror and violence culminating in industrialised mass murder. State socialism in Central and Eastern Europe in contrast is marked more by dissonance and rup-ture between the liberatory ideals of the founding ideology and the repressive realities of state policies. The central measure, however, on which the differences between the two regime types demonstrably out-weigh the similarities is that of popular support. In this respect it could be argued that while National Socialism certainly was a mass dictator-ship, a regime carried by the overwhelming support of the populace, the state socialist regimes of Central and Eastern Europe cannot, in fact, be so defined at all. These regimes must be categorised differently: they failed in their aspirations to become 'dictatorships of the proletariat', remaining simply repressive one-party states, imposed by an external power rather than elected, which had largely lost their roots in an emancipatory ideology of social justice.

When examined through the lens of gender, the dissonances and internal contradictions of the two dictatorship types are illuminated fur-ther, as this chapter has attempted to demonstrate. In response to the question raised in the title then, as to whether the gender regimes of different mass dictatorships can be regarded as predictable, the answer must be that it depends: on the particular ideology of the mass dictator-ship in question, on the extent to which that ideology is implemented or contradicted by the material practices of the regime, and on the level of popular support these state policies enjoy.

Looking at gender as a measure of the democratic character of a regime gives a further dimension to this question. National Socialism emanated from a doctrine of gender difference and inequality, while state socialism took a rhetoric of gender equality from Marxist theory. Thus National Socialism, true to its guiding principles in relation not only to gen-der but also to class, 'race', sexuality and disability, could never have implemented a socially just or gender equitable society. In contradiction to their underlying ideology and rhetoric, the reality of state socialist regimes too was that despite some progress, particularly in access to the labour market and the facilitation of work-life balance through the pro-vision of childcare facilities and other social supports, they too were unable – because of the fundamental lack of democratic freedoms – to implement gender equitable societies.

Notes

1. At first glance a comparison between the gender politics of Nazi Germany and Stalinist Russia might be more obviously appropriate. However, the sociological differences between Germany and Russia are so substantial that the societies of Central and Eastern Europe provide a better basis for comparison.

2. Ian Kershaw and Moshe Lewin, 'Introduction: The Regimes and Their Dictators: Perspectives of Comparison', in Ian Kershaw and Moshe Lewin (eds), *Stalinism and Nazism: Dictatorships in Comparison* (Cambridge: Cambridge University Press, 1997), pp. 1–25; here pp. 3, 6.

3. Ibid., p. 8.

4. Jie-Hyun Lim, 'Historiographical Perspectives on "Mass Dictatorship"', *Totalitarian Movements and Political Religions* 6(3) (2005), pp. 325–31; here pp. 325, 330.

5. Ibid., p. 326.

6. Richard Evans, 'Nazism, Christianity and Political Religion: A Debate', *Journal of Contemporary History* 42(1) (2007), pp. 5–7.

7. Hans Mommsen, 'Nationalsozialismus als politische Religion', in Hans Maier and Michael Schäfer (eds), *Totalitarismus und Politische Religion: Konzepte des Diktaturvergleichs Vol. II* (Paderborn: Schöningh, 1997), p. 180; cited in Jie-Hyun Lim and Peter Lambert, 'Appendix: Introduction to TMPR special Issue', *Totalitarian Movements and Political Religions* 6(3) (2005), 'Political Religions and the Sacralisation of Politics', *Totalitarian Movements and Political Religions* 8(3–4) (2007), pp. 721–5; here p. 724.

8. Doris L. Bergen, 'Nazism and Christianity: Partners and Rivals?', *Journal of Contemporary History* 42(1) (2007), pp. 25–33; here p. 32.

9. Ibid., pp. 30, 32.

10. Atina Grossmann, 'Feminist Debates about Women and National Socialism', *Gender and History* 3(3) (1991), pp. 350–8; on the compliant, complicit or enthusiastic participation of female camp guards, see Susannah Heschel, 'Does Atrocity Have a Gender? Feminist Interpretations of Women in the SS', in Jeffry M. Diefendorf (ed.), *Lessons and Legacies VI: New Currents in Holocaust Research* (Evanston, IL: Northwestern University Press, 2004), pp. 300–21.

11. Obviously a chapter of this length is reliant on a level of generalisation which is open to question. I am very aware in writing this that the gender politics of both Nazi Germany and state socialist regimes changed over time, and that the latter differed between countries as well as over time. Nor do the findings necessarily apply to all dictatorships. Nevertheless, it is interesting to note the patterns of similarity and difference that can be discerned through comparisons at this level.

12. Richard Bessel, *Nazism and War* (London: Weidenfeld and Nicholson, 2004; Phoenix Books, 2005), pp. 64–5.

13. Gerhard Wilke, 'Village Life in Nazi Germany', in Richard Bessel (ed.), *Life in the Third Reich* (Oxford and New York: Oxford University Press, 1987), pp. 17–24; here p. 23; Detlev Peukert, 'Youth in the Third Reich', in ibid., pp. 25–40; here p. 28; see also Dagmar Reese, 'Emanzipation oder Vergesellschaftung: Mädchen im "Bund Deutscher Mädel"', in Hans-Uwe Otto and Heinz Sünker (eds), *Politische Formierung und soziale Erziehung im Nationalsozialismus* (Frankfurt a.M.: Suhrkamp, 1991), pp. 203–25.

14. Kevin Passmore, 'Women, Gender and the Extreme Right in the French Third Republic', Paper presented at Mass Dictatorship and Gender Politics: The Fourth International Conference of Mass Dictatorship, 5–7 July 2006, Pyeongchang-Gun, Gangwon-Do, Korea.

15. Renate Bridenthal, Atina Grossmann and Marion Kaplan (eds), *When Biology Became Destiny: Women in Weimar and Nazi Germany* (New York: Monthly Review Press, 1984), p. xiv.

16. Barbara Einhorn, *Cinderella Goes to Market: Citizenship, Gender and Women's Movements in East Central Europe* (London and New York: Verso, 1993); see also Maxine Molyneux, 'Mobilisation without Emancipation? Women's Interests, State and Revolution in Nicaragua', *Feminist Studies* 11(2) (1985), pp. 227–54; Maxine Molyneux, 'Some International Influences on Policy-making: Marxism, Feminism and the "Woman Question" in Existing Social-ism', *Millennium – Journal of International Studies* 18(2) (1989), pp. 255–63; here pp. 255–6.

17. Christina Chiva, 'The Nation and Its Pasts: Gender, History and Democrati-sation in Romania', in Vera Tolz and Stephenie Booth (eds), *Nation and Gender in Contemporary Europe* (Manchester and New York: Manchester University Press, 2005), pp. 80–95; Barbara Einhorn, *Citizenship in an Enlarging Europe: From Dream to Awakening* (Basingstoke: Palgrave Macmillan, 2006; paperback edn, 2010); Barbara Einhorn, 'Democratization, Nationalism, and Citizenship: The Challenge of Gender', in Linda Racioppi and Katherine O'Sullivan See (eds), *Gender Politics in Post-Communist Eurasia* (East Lansing, MI: Michigan State University Press, 2009), pp. 47–66; Susan Gal and Gail Kligman, *The Politics of Gender after Socialism* (Princeton, NJ: Princeton University Press, 2000); Jacqueline Heinen, 'Clashes and Ordeals of Women's Cit-izenship in Central and Eastern Europe', in Jasmina Lukić, Joanna Regulska and Darja Zaviršek (eds), *Women and Citizenship in Central and Eastern Europe* (Aldershot, UK and Burlington, VT: Ashgate, 2006), pp. 81–100; here pp. 83–4.

18. The Rosenberg quotation is reproduced from Ute Frevert, *Women in German History: From Bourgeois Emancipation to Sexual Liberation*, English edition (Oxford and New York: Berg Publishers, 1989), p. 207; for the Hitler speech, see Richard J. Evans, *The Third Reich in Power, 1933–1939* (London, New York and Toronto: Allen Lane, 2005; Penguin Books, 2006), pp. 331–2.

19. Kirsten Heinsohn, 'Germany', in Kevin Passmore (ed.), *Women, Gender and Fascism in Europe, 1919–45* (Manchester: Manchester University Press, 2003), pp. 33–56; here p. 54.

20. Dimitrina Petrova, 'The Farewell Dance: Women in the Bulgarian Transi-tion', in Eileen Janes Yeo (ed.), *Mary Wollstonecraft and 200 Years of Femi-nism* (London and New York: Rivers Oram Press, 1997), pp. 180–92; here p. 187.

21. Einhorn, *Cinderella Goes to Market*, p. 47 and *passim*; see also Chris Corrin (ed.), *Superwoman and the Double Burden: Women's Experience of Change in Central and Eastern Europe and the Former Soviet Union* (London: Scarlet Press, 1992).

22. See note 16 above. On ethno-nationalism see also Maja Korać, 'Under-standing Ethnic-National Identity and its Meaning: Questions from a Woman's Experience', *Women's Studies International Forum* 19(1–2)

(1996), pp. 133–44; Enikö Magyari-Vincze, 'Romanian Gender Regimes and Women's Citizenship', in Jasmina Lukić, Joanna Regulska and Darja Zaviršek (eds), *Women and Citizenship in Central and Eastern Europe*, pp. 21–38; here pp. 28–32.

23. Olga Lipovskaya, 'New Women's Organizations', in Mary Buckley (ed.), *Perestroika and Soviet Women* (Cambridge: Cambridge University Press, 1992), p. 72.

24. On the salience of this argument in the 2004 run-up to EU accession in Poland, see Agnieszka Graff, 'The Land of Real Men and Real Women: Gender and EU Accession in Three Polish Weeklies', in Carolyn M. Elliott (ed.), *Global Empowerment of Women: Responses to Globalization and Politicized Religions* (New York and London: Routledge, 2008), pp. 191–212.

25. Claudia Koonz, 'The "Woman Question" in Authoritarian Regimes', in Renate Bridenthal, Susan Mosher Stuard and Merry E. Wiesner (eds), *Becoming Visible: Women in European History* (Boston, MA and New York: Houghton Mifflin Company, 3rd edn, 1998), pp. 463–92; here p. 484.

26. See, for example, Renate Bridenthal and Claudia Koonz, 'Beyond *Kinder, Küche, Kirche*: Weimar Women in Politics and Work', in Bridenthal, Grossmann and Kaplan (eds), *When Biology Became Destiny*, pp. 33–65; Frevert, *Women in German History*, pp. 168–204; Kirsten Heinsohn, 'Germany', in Passmore (ed.), *Women, Gender and Fascism in Europe, 1919–45*, pp. 33–56; Claudia Koonz, *Mothers in the Fatherland: Women, the Family and Nazi Politics* (London: Methuen, 1988), pp. 19–50; Mary Nolan, 'Work, Gender and Everyday Life: Reflections on Continuity, Normality and Agency in Twentieth-Century Germany', in Kershaw and Lewin (eds), *Stalinism and Nazism: Dictatorships in Comparison*, pp. 311–42.

27. Bessel, *Nazism and War*, pp. 62–3; also citing Dorothee Klinksiek, *Die Frau im NS-Staat* (Stuttgart: Deutsche Verlags-Anstalt, 1982), pp. 80–1.

28. Kate Lacey, 'Driving the Message Home: Nazi Propaganda in the Private Sphere', in Lynn Abrams and Elizabeth Harvey (eds), *Gender Relations in German History: Power, Agency and Experience from the Sixteenth to the Twentieth Century* (Durham, NC: Duke University Press, 1997), pp. 189–210; here pp. 203–4.

29. Evans, *The Third Reich in Power, 1933–1939*, p. 297.

30. Ibid., p. 298.

31. Annemarie Tröger, 'The Creation of a Female Assembly-Line Proletariat', in Bridenthal, Grossmann and Kaplan (eds), *When Biology Became Destiny*, pp. 237–70; here p. 246.

32. Marion A. Kaplan, 'Sisterhood under Siege: Feminism and Anti-Semitism in Germany, 1904–1938', in ibid., p. 174; Marion A. Kaplan, *Between Dignity and Despair: Jewish Life in Nazi Germany* (Oxford and New York: Oxford University Press, 1998), pp. 8, 59.

33. For the quotes from August Bebel, *Woman and Socialism* (1879; Eng. tr. 1910), and Lenin, 'On the Emancipation of Women' (1919), see Richard Stites, *The Women's Liberation Movement in Russia: Feminism, Nihilism, and Bolshevism 1860–1930* (Princeton, NJ: Princeton University Press, 1978), pp. 265, 378.

34. Alexandra Kollontai, speech on 'The Family and the Communist State' (1918), cited in Stites, *The Women's Liberation Movement in Russia*, p. 351;

speech on 'Communism and the Family' (1920), cited from Alix Holt, *Selected Writings of Alexandra Kollontai* (London: Allison and Busby, 1977), p. 258.

35. Wendy Zeva Goldman, 'Women, the Family, and the New Revolutionary Order in the Soviet Union', in Sonia Kruks, Rayna Rapp and Marilyn B. Young (eds), *Promissory Notes: Women in the Transition to Socialism* (New York: Monthly Review Press, 1989), pp. 59–81; here p. 61.

36. Dagmar Herzog, *Sex after Fascism: Memory and Morality in Twentieth Century Germany* (Princeton, NJ and Oxford: Princeton University Press, 2005), p. 4.

37. Dagmar Herzog, 'Desperately Seeking Normality: Sex and Marriage in the Wake of the War', in Richard Bessel and Dirk Schumann (eds), *Life after Death: Approaches to a Cultural and Social History of Europe during the 1940s and 1950s* (Cambridge: Cambridge University Press, 2003), pp. 161–92; here pp. 165–6, 169.

38. Ibid., p. 170.

39. Evans, *The Third Reich in Power, 1933–1939*, pp. 330–2.

40. For Nazi Germany, see, for example, ibid., and Koonz, *Mothers in the Fatherland*, pp. 149–50; for the GDR, see Gunnar Winkler (ed.), *Frauenreport 90* (Berlin: Verlag die Wirtschaft, 1990), p. 149; for Czechoslovakia, see Mita Castle-Kanerová, 'A Culture of Strong Women in the Making?', in Corrin (ed.), *Superwoman and the Double Burden*, p. 119.

41. Brigitte Young, *Triumph of the Fatherland: German Unification and the Marginalization of Women* (Ann Arbor, MI: University of Michigan Press, 1999), pp. 6–7.

42. On reproductive politics in Romania before and after 1989, see Gail Kligman, *The Politics of Duplicity: Controlling Reproduction in Ceausescu's Romania* (Berkeley, CA: University of California Press, 1998); Enikö Magyari-Vincze, 'Public Policies as Vehicles of Social Exclusion: The Case of Romani Women's Access to Reproductive Health in Romania', in Linda Racioppi and Katherine O'Sullivan See (eds), *Gender Politics in Post-Communist Eurasia*, pp. 87–118; on the use of nationalist discourse to restrict access to reproductive health choices after 1989 in Poland, see Anne-Marie Kramer, 'The Polish Parliament and the Making of Politics through Abortion: Nation, Gender and Democracy in the 1996 Liberalization Amendment Debate', *International Feminist Journal of Politics* 11(1) (2009), pp. 83–101.

43. Einhorn, *Cinderella Goes to Market*, pp. 80–2; Agnieszka Graff, 'Gender, Sexuality and Nation – Here and Now: Reflections on the Gendered and Sexualized Aspects of Contemporary Polish Nationalism', in Elżbieta H. Oleksy (ed.), *Intimate Citizenships: Gender, Sexualities, Politics* (London: Routledge, 2009), pp. 133–146.

44. On the post-1989 commercialization of sexualised stereotypes of femininity, see Kristen Ghodsee, 'Potions, Lotions and Lipstick: The Gendered Consumption of Cosmetics and Perfumery in Socialist and Post-Socialist Urban Bulgaria', *Women's Studies International Forum* 30 (2007), pp. 26–39; Svitlana Taraban, 'Birthday Girls, Russian Dolls, and Others: Internet Bride as the Emerging Global Identity of Post-Soviet Women', in Janet Elise Johnson and Jean C. Robinson (eds), *Living Gender after Communism* (Bloomington and Indianapolis, IN: Indiana University Press, 2007), pp. 105–27; for one of a plethora of articles on trafficking, specifically relating to the post-1989 sexualised constructions of femininity, see Rutvica Andrijasevic, 'Beautiful

Dead Bodies: Gender, Migration and Representation in Anti-Trafficking Campaigns', *Feminist Review* 86 (2007), pp. 24–44; on post-National Socialist attempts to 'normalise' gender and sexuality, see Herzog, 'Desperately Seeking Normality', p. 175.

45. Einhorn, *Cinderella goes to Market*, p. 23; Jacqueline Heinen and Stéphane Portet, 'Political and Social Citizenship: An Examination of the Case of Poland', in Maxine Molyneux and Shahra Razavi (eds), *Gender Justice, Development, and Rights* (Oxford: Oxford University Press, 2002), pp. 141–69; here p. 145.

46. Mira Marody, 'Perception of Politics in Polish Society', *Social Research* 57(2) (1990), p. 268; Mira Marody, 'On Polish Political Attitudes', *Telos* 89 (1991), pp. 112–3; see also Heinen, 'Clashes and Ordeals of Women's Citizenship in Central and Eastern Europe', pp. 88–9.

47. Slavenka Drakulić, *How We Survived Communism and Even Laughed* (London: Hutchinson, 1992), pp. 91–2.

48. Barbara Einhorn, 'Where Have all the Women Gone? Women and the Women's Movement in East Central Europe', *Feminist Review* 39, Special Issue on *Shifting Territories: Feminism and Europe*, Winter, 1991), pp. 16–36, and *Cinderella Goes to Market*, pp. 59–62. On the idealisation of civil society in the post-1989 democratisation period, see Barbara Einhorn and Charlotte Sever, 'Gender and Civil Society in Central and Eastern Europe', *International Journal of Feminist Politics* 5(2) (2003), pp. 163–90; Barbara Einhorn, *Citizenship in an Enlarging Europe*, p. 65; UNICEF, *Women in Transition: the MONEE Project – CEE/CIS/Baltics*, Regional Monitoring Report no. 6 (Florence: UNICEF, 1999), p. 100.

49. Evans, *The Third Reich in Power, 1933–1939*, p. 14.

50. Einhorn, *Cinderella goes to Market*, p. 178.

51. Karen Offen, *European Feminisms, 1700–1950: A Political History* (Stanford, CA: Stanford University Press, 2000), p. 297.

52. Ibid., p. 299.

53. Ibid.; see also Kaplan, 'Sisterhood under Siege'; Koonz, 'The "Woman Question" in Authoritarian Regimes'.

54. Offen, *European Feminisms, 1700–1950*, p. 308.

55. Barbara Einhorn, 'Socialist Emancipation: The Women's Movement in the German Democratic Republic', in Kruks, Rapp and Young (eds), *Promissory Notes*, pp. 282–305.

56. Ibid.

57. Sybil Oldfield, 'German Women in the Resistance to Hitler', in Sian Reynolds (ed.), *Women, State and Revolution: Essays on Power and Gender in Europe Since 1789* (Brighton: Wheatsheaf Books, 1986), pp. 81–100.

58. Einhorn, 'Where Have All the Women Gone?', p. 25; Einhorn, *Cinderella Goes to Market*, pp. 2–4, 161, 188, 206–9; see also Mary Kaldor, 'After the Cold War', in Mary Kaldor (ed.), *Europe from Below: An East-West Dialogue* (London and New York: Verso, 1991), pp. 27–42; here pp. 36–8.

3
A Tributary and a Mainstream: Gender, Public Memory and the Historiography of Nazi Germany

Claudia Koonz

For decades after 1945, mainstream historians overlooked the existence of women in the Third Reich. In the totalitarian paradigms that framed their research questions, coercion from 'above' all but obscured consent from 'below'. Since women occupied no positions of authority in the Nazi hierarchy, it seemed to follow that they had exerted no agency. Perhaps most scholars implicitly agreed with a Nazi saying, 'The soil provides food, women provide population, and men make history.' During the last decade of the Cold War, however, historians of women and gender joined with social historians in thinking outside totalitarian frameworks. In this chapter, I use research on women in two very different sub-fields, the Holocaust and consumerism, to examine the connections between transformations in post-Cold War public memory and historical scholarship.

The *Wende*, public memory and the history of women

During the Cold War, historians of Nazism in Germany, Britain and the USA engaged in rancorous debates between 'intentionalists', who emphasised biography and located agency within the elite circle around Hitler, and 'functionalists', who adapted social science methods and attributed causality to large-scale bureaucratic and economic structures.[1] Countering wartime stereotypes of Nazi perpetrators as power-crazed deviants, these scholars either wrote sober biographies of powerful leaders or organisational studies of the government, the military or the party. Both groups thought of Nazi Germany as 'totalitarian' – a term coined by Benito Mussolini and popularised by Peter Drucker on the eve of World War II. In totalitarian states, most scholars assumed, propaganda ('brain washing' in Cold War parlance) had drained ordinary citizens of autonomy and, hence, of agency. It is hardly surprising that women vanished as historical subjects because ordinary men did too. During the 1950s, 1960s and 1970s, few historians thought much about wartime atrocities, and those who did attributed responsibility either to a small number of direct perpetrators who had been hardened sadists or millions of indirect collaborators who had been mere 'cogs' in a totalitarian system.

In the late 1970s, however, at the margins of the profession, historians of women wrote biographies of women resisters who provided role models of civil courage. The very few histories dedicated to 'unsung' heroes included women as well as men who had aided endangered friends and colleagues. During the 1970s and 1980s women survivors and resisters wrote memoirs.[2] A few social historians studied women's mobilisation in Nazi mass organisations and their participation in the labour market. Often they interpreted their findings within the paradigm of myth versus reality.

Feminists approached women's 'brown' past with a special set of concerns. If Nazi Germany represented an extreme case of patriarchy that victimised all women, it seemed logical to conclude that women could not have been implicated in Nazi crimes. Psychologist Christina Thürmer-Rohr, however, caused an uproar when she suggested women had not been only victims, or *Opfer*, but also perpetrators, or *TäterInnen*. Both terms lack exact equivalents in English. '*Opfer*' does not translate smoothly into English because it connotes 'sacrifice' as well as 'victim'. Because '*Täter*', like 'perpetrator', implies criminality, it does not convey the meaning of value-free 'agency'. In 1983, Thürmer-Rohr urged historians to drop their search for inspiring role models and to relinquish an 'a-historical, presentist and episodic consciousness of their past'. Women's agency had to be acknowledged, even if it meant connecting women to the 'lethal heritage of the concentration camp'. Feminist historians could not, in the words of Karin Walser-Windaus, claim innocence simply because they had been born female. Women who displayed subservience to their male superiors in exchange for power over less influential women under them had exercised agency. Like millions of German men, they had participated in state-sanctioned crimes.

Angelika Ebbinghaus captured the ambiguities associated both with women's historical agency and ordinary periodisation in her anthology, *Opfer und Täterinnen*, which documented women's roles in state-sanctioned crimes and identified continuities that linked Weimar, Nazi and West German history. In other anthologies, notably *Daughters' Questions*, feminists reported on their research on women's participation in National Socialism and arrived at different understandings of women's complicity.[3] Particularly in Anglo-American contexts, many historians found post-structural approaches useful for examining identity formation and subjectivity as well as for analysing the subtle gradations in power across ethnic, age and gender (as well as class) lines that had been obscured by both *Opfer-Täter* polemics and by hegemonic history with its focus either on elites or on large-scale state and economic structures.[4]

In the late 1970s and 1980s social historians, oral historians and scholars of everyday life (*Alltagsgeschichte*) included studies of women in many economic and social roles. Thanks to the presses that published books on women's history and the readers who purchased them, the history of women in Nazi Germany also became a lively sub-field. A few scholars began to document women concentration camp survivors' experiences, and some suggested that women's 'feminine' socialisation had enabled them to survive in distinctive ways.[5] Empirical research explored women's roles as workers, mothers, wives, religious activists and Nazi Party members. As studies proliferated, so too did debates about German women's agency. The moral conundrums raised in this debate among feminists continue to provoke debate.[6]

Agency, atrocity and gender in perpetrator studies

Although transformations within an academic field are often traced to theoretical turns (initiated by, for example, Michel Foucault, Judith Butler and Pierre Bourdieu), historians also react to transformations in the public culture they inhabit. Theoretical developments like the 'linguistic turn' and the demise of totalitarian-based conceptual frameworks coincided with the collapse of Soviet rule. At a material level, budget-priced air fares, the Internet and a proliferation of specialised journals facilitated scholarly exchange across national borders. The 50th year anniversaries of turning points in World War II provoked disagreements among veterans, citizens and scholars that attracted media attention. As the general public clamoured for information about previously taboo topics connected to National Socialism, the market for research expanded. Vigorous debates about responsibility, guilt, reparations and justice inspired new research. Dozens of memorials to victims of the Holocaust appeared throughout Germany. Besides this 'memory boom' in popular culture, sensational legal battles about looted property, restitution, victims' bank accounts, unpaid insurance benefits and corporate profiteering under the Nazis called attention to widespread grassroots complicity with crimes within and outside Nazi Germany. Although earlier and far more significant trials of perpetrators had generated relatively little media attention, the last of the war crimes trials in the 1990s brought culpable individuals into the spotlight. Testimonials by Korean 'comfort women' and statements by victims of rape in the Balkan wars prompted historians not to disregard wartime sexual atrocities as merely collateral damage. Helke Sander's film *BeFreier und Befreite* (1992) shattered the silence about German women raped by Soviet soldiers. Historians Christa Paul, Cristl Wickert and David Snyder documented the forced prostitution organised by the German military on the Eastern Front.[7]

In the context of public curiosity about ordinary perpetrators, the sudden availability of vast collections of primary sources in previously Soviet-dominated Europe created a veritable archive rush. Historians perused previously ignored diaries and letters and collected empirical evidence about genocidal processes at the micro-level, within particular offices, camps, military units, ghettos and towns under German occupation. Banks and corporations opened up their archives to scrutiny. Ulrich Herbert signalled the advent of a new era when he challenged researchers to 'leave behind the stale and rigid terms of Holocaust scholarship' and 'plunge afresh into the archives'.[8] Herbert's own research reminds us, however, that this new empiricism did not necessarily mean that all historians would examine women or gender. For those who did, Gudrun Schwarz's pathbreaking history of women in the SS 'clan' (*Sippengemeinschaft*) provided a conceptual framework for interpreting archival records.[9]

Besides these accelerators of conceptual change, an ephemeral cultural shift increased the general public's tolerance of ambiguity. Günther Grass described this sensibility in his Nobel speech. Germans who had been born just before the war, he said, 'were the ones to repudiate the absolutes, the ideological black or white. Doubt and scepticism were our god-parents.'[10] And he captured the gradations along the victim-perpetrator divide in his novel, *Crabwalk*, the account of a glorious low budget Nazi cruise ship and its calamitous sinking at the end of the war. Several films during the 1990s broke public amnesia about the Third Reich by focusing on female characters, among them Michael Verhoeven's *Nasty Girl* (1992) about a teenager who exposes the Nazi collaboration of virtually every adult in her home town. Max Färberböck's *Aimée and Jaguar* (1999) portrays the love between a Nazi officer's wife and a Jewish woman fleeing deportation. Danny Kauntz's *Blind Spot*

(2003) highlights Hitler's private secretary's reflections on Nazism. Like *Schindler's List* and *The Pianist*, these films captured the 'greys' of everyday life in a mass dictatorship. Victim and perpetrator, they suggested, could coexist, often in a single person. 'Structures do not kill. Individuals do.'[11] This simple statement epitomised the interpretative turn of the 1990s. The macro-level totalitarianism-based analyses, once admired as elegant, now seemed simplistic. As the scholar's gaze shifts from powerful elites and impersonal institutional structures, ordinary Germans, male and female, come into focus. Close readings of visual and verbal texts enable historians of gender to discern the workings of power in relationship to identity and popular culture. Concentrating on a single town, workplace or organisation, oral historians viewed history and memory as mutually constitutive. Collaboration among archivists, civic leaders and historians has produced a wealth of information about individual memory, as suggested by book titles based on informants' words, such as 'Finally I have a place to put my Memory' and 'Did something actually happen back then?' Working within a tight focus allows authors to capture nuance and vivid detail in books that range from a study of women composers in Nazi Germany to a history of women in the Nazi Party before 1933.[12]

Rather than searching for contradictions between Nazi doctrine and a stable 'reality', which was a common endeavour in the 1980s, historians are more concerned with understanding how gender-specific social norms and cultural expectations constructed identity and experience. Instead of taking racial and gendered hierarchies for granted, historians ask how 'Aryan' arrogance and gender-specific norms deepened the phobic racism that shaped ethnic Germans' as well as persecuted minorities' experiences of daily life, particularly in relationship to sexuality and violence.

Investigating what Michel Foucault termed 'bio-power', historians identify the operations of gender within state-directed health care, data collection, behavioural regulation and surveillance.[13] They discovered how porous the borders of the so-called private sphere were and realised that vulnerability to intrusive state policies varied widely according to gender, ethnicity and generation. Gabriele Czarnowsky documents the ways that laws, state surveillance and public scrutiny affected ordinary citizens, as well as people designated as 'dangerous'. Using records of public health campaigns against venereal disease, Annette Timm identifies the mechanisms that constrained women's and men's personal choices in the name of collective good.[14] Claudia Schoppmann and

Günther Grau trace the impact of repression on lesbians and homosexuals. Petra Fuchs analyses the fates of physically handicapped people under policy guidelines of Weimar as well as Nazi regimes. Lisa Pine synthesised the extensive literature on 'undesirable' people and propaganda in her *Hitler's National Community*. Petra Kannappel's and Bettina Bab's histories of individual women who had been sterilised add to our understandings of individual 'Aryans' classed as 'unworthy'.[15] Histories of Germans with African origins revealed previously ignored contradictions within Nazi race policy.[16]

Social histories of gender reconstruct cultural milieus within which racial crimes occurred. Kundrus interprets the records of the women accused of having forbidden sexual relationships in the context of prescriptive literature that exhorted soldiers' wives to chastity. Understanding how vital morale was to German military force, some historians use the term 'informed bystanders' to describe the women who facilitated the enforcement of racial regulations on the home front. Alexandra Przyrembel analyses the police records of 2000 Jewish men convicted of having sexual relations with non-Jewish women; Patricia Szobar examines officials' voyeuristic investigations of *Rassenschande*; and both analyse the Nazi media that created panic about the supposedly hyper-sexual Jewish male and shaped 'modes of perception and legitimisation' among average Germans. According to the double standard, when ethnic German males had sexual relations with so-called inferior women, their act was seen as a conquest; but a woman's sexual contact with a so-called inferior male was treason to the race. During the war, when 7 million foreign workers inhabited the Reich, civilian authorities' exhortations against liaisons or even friendships with foreigners proved largely ineffective. The wives of Jewish husbands rounded up for deportation in the Rosenstrasse who demonstrated for their husbands' release generated heated disagreement about the relative importance of gender- and race-based slave labour. Gender certainly mattered in relationship to surveillance of ethnic Germans' sexual activity; but it counted for nothing on killing fields and in camps. 'We shot women as if they were cattle', declared Major General Friedrich von Broich when he described the slaughter at Zhitomir.[17]

As Susanne Heim, Henry Friedlander and others have noted, the extermination facilities constructed during World War II employed personnel from prior eugenic programmes that targeted 'unproductive elements' in the *Volksgemeinschaft*. Although no woman directed any institution, women in the helping professions performed crucial work when they reported potentially 'defective' students and clients to public health authorities and (after 1939) gave the lethal injections that most physicians preferred to avoid. Through individual biographies, Lilo Haag traces social workers' responses to Nazism within specific institutions. In *Women in a Dark Time*, an authors' collective portrays the wide variety of responses to Nazi goals among women social workers in the Confessing Church. In the archives of two 'euthanasia' centres, Bronwyn McFarland-Icke chronicles nurses' 'moral realignment' as they accommodated themselves to a daily routine of quiet murder. She also observes that the very few women who dissented were not punished overtly, but quietly transferred, much as in Battalion 101 which was examined by Christopher Browning. Official rebuke, McFarland-Icke suggests, could have made their opposition a question of conscience. By not calling attention to dissent, authorities framed nurses' civil courage as a personal failure.[18]

Women volunteered for service within other Nazi settings in ways that might seem unconnected with extermination. Adventurous German women made newly conquered territory in the East fit for new ethnically 'Aryan' settlement by redecorating houses whose 'subhuman' Polish owners had been expelled, cleaning public buildings, promoting 'Aryan' folk crafts, establishing schools and organising local residents who appeared 'Aryan'. Elizabeth Harvey incorporates archival research and her interviews with women occupiers and women whose homes were confiscated.[19] Women living near military installations were charged to maintain the morale of soldiers on leave. These oases of *Heimat* (hominess) were designed to revive soldiers' morale and remind them of the higher ethnic values for which they sacrificed. Even though these women performed typically feminine tasks, they exercised agency in social as well as cultural realms.

To a greater extent than Anglophone historians, historians who write in German have explored the construction of masculine as well as feminine subjectivities in their research on the morale, unit cohesion and heroic righteousness that eased whatever doubts soldiers may have had about their filthy 'work'. It becomes clear that masculine identity can only be constructed in relationship to an imagined feminine – a concept that originated in the 1980s with Karin Hausen's scholarship on gendered spheres and my account of perpetrators' wives who preserved husbands' mental stability by creating the home as sanctuary. More recently, Hannes Heer notes that soldiers' vision of their wives and families enhanced their self-image as 'quiet heroes', which in turn facilitated the 'moralisation of crime'.[20] In soldiers' letters, Inge Marssolek discovers a doubled moral self that cordoned off a harmonious 'feminine' home front from a brutal 'masculine' eastern front. As Thomas Kühne puts it, 'constructs of femininity made this world tolerable for both men and women'. In her study of frontline soldiers, Susanne zur Nieden hypothesised that soldiers' motivation shifted away from racial conquest of inferior peoples early in the war to defence of virtuous wives and families when defeat became inevitable. Sybille Steinbach describes the role of domesticity in sustaining the mental stability of the SS personnel at Auschwitz. 'Mass murder and domesticity were not, therefore, the poles of an opposition but instead tightly interwoven.'[21]

What about women's participation in deportations, concentration camp administration and denunciations which unambiguously made them perpetrators? Between 1945 and 1949, Allied courts found 5025 defendants guilty of war crimes. Of this total, 22 were women. These figures illustrate Allies' tendency to understate women's direct participation in war crimes. But the low proportion of women also resulted from the overwhelmingly masculine upper echelons in the killing process. Women served as clerical workers, census takers, cataloguers of Jewish-owned property, neighbourhood spies, shoppers who boycotted Jewish-owned businesses, educators, nurses, social workers, laboratory technicians and camp guards. Women performed relatively minor, but essential, tasks.

Besides well over a dozen archival studies of women's roles in persecution, historians of gender inquire into the particular cultural milieus that framed these women's guilt in post-1945 trials. Anyone who studies individual female perpetrators on the basis of trial records, they note, does so in the context of a culture that has sensationalised Nazism by locating evil in eroticised women (from Lina Wertmuller's 1975 film *Seven Beauties* through Bernard Schlink's 2001 novel *The Reader*). Historians of gender do not dismiss these depictions as fiction, but rather make media-generated contexts central to their research on memory. Approaching the eroticisation of Nazi brutality from very different standpoints, Silke Wenk and Carolyn Dean have historicised the ways particular narratives of masculine/feminine and perpetrator/victim stabilise our knowledge about unspeakable atrocity.[22] The strength of much new research lies in its careful attention not simply to the accuracy of memory, but to its construction (*Gedächtniskonstruktion*).

Despite dozens of outstanding archive-based research projects that examine women as direct and indirect perpetrators, however, some historians appear not to have noticed. 'The history of National Socialism has long been reduced to one that blamed men for everything', announces Kathrin Kompisch in her 2008 book, and a reviewer of the

English translation echoes her claim, praising the book as 'the first German post-war analysis of the role of women in the crimes of the Nazis'.[23] Kompisch ignores three decades of meticulous archival research and thoughtful interpretations that disprove the myth that German women were 'innocent by female birth'.

Consensus, consumerism and gender

According to canonical Cold War history, Nazism was barbaric-part of what Norbert Elias called a 'de-civilising' process that had browbeaten ordinary Germans into obedience. During the collapse of Soviet power in the 1980s, this assumption came under attack. A counter narrative traced the Holocaust to the ravages of a rationality that began with Enlightenment thinkers' hubris about the perfectibility of human society.[24] Far from being barbaric, Nazi race policy epitomised modernity and depended on virtually all citizens' collaboration. Besides exterminating 'undesirables', the Nazi regime maintained levels of consumption that gratified ethnic Germans' expectations for 'the good life'. The proliferation of state-funded media productions, leisure activities, festivals, sports and entertainment mobilised broad-based support for Nazi rule. Even though in the last free election of Weimar Germany, only 33 per cent of all Germans voted for Nazi candidates (compared to a combined vote for Marxist parties of 37 per cent), there is no doubt that Hitler was immensely popular until the very last days of the war.[25] Despite single-issue disillusionment with, for example, local party bosses' nepotism and flagrant corruption in the highest echelons of the Party, ordinary Germans could still remain loyal to Nazi rule in general. 'If Hitler only knew', they could tell themselves, then this or that flaw would be removed.

While the totalitarian 'cog' paradigm faded, post-Cold War historians discovered how popular Nazi rule had been. Attention shifted away from the actions of powerful men and direct perpetrators and focused on the techniques that won the allegiance of ordinary Germans, who appeared hardly to notice as ruthless censorship destroyed the free market of ideas that had flourished during the Weimar Republic. Although historians of other nations began to explore consumerism, marketing and leisure during the 1980s, historians of Nazi Germany neglected these topics (although they did study film). The concept of a totalitarian consumer society may have seemed oxymoronic for two reasons: first, because Cold War historians believed Nazi propaganda deprived individuals of choice, which was a precondition of a consumer society;

and second, because consumer goods had a lower priority than military production. Neither assumption was accurate. Disputing images of an austere anti-consumer Nazi culture, Hartmut Berghoff contends that 'official regulation and the inherent dynamics of consumerism' were evenly balanced. Advertisers incited consumerist desires, despite official admonitions to live frugally.[26] Nancy Reagin and Renate Harter-Meyer examine the impact of housewife education and consumer culture that motivated women shoppers to contribute to meeting the quotas of the first Four Year plan for economic growth.[27] Innovative studies of working-class life barely mention the standard topics of earlier social history, such as police terror and the decline in real wages. Instead, they explore subjects like family consumption patterns, budgets, volunteerism, contraception and leisure activities. New research dispels other stereotypes as well. Hitler's charisma, long treated as if it were innate, comes under the scrutiny of feminists who analyse its foundation in the construction of masculinity. At the dawn of celebrity journalism, Hitler and his private photographer Hans Hoffmann produced a version of *der Führer*'s private life that was designed for public consumption. Hitler's star appeal combined stridently masculine attributes with tiny self-abnegating gestures that suggested feminine vulnerability. The word 'Kitsch' vanishes in art historical studies that scrutinise the gendered and racial cultural production of National Socialist Realism. Christina von Braun draws on Otto Weiniger in exploring the affinities between misogyny and anti-Semitism. Adelheid von Saldern shows how cultural feminism could reinforce the masculinity of Nazi art forms (particularly sculpture). Uli Linke juxtaposes 'the feminine' against 'the Jew' and examines the operations of collective representation in the 'feminisation of the racial subaltern' in the aesthetic of the *Volksgemeinschaft*.[28]

Building on Walter Benjamin's concept of the 'aestheticisation of politics', historians of material culture describe the aestheticisation of everyday life. What Peter Reichel called the 'beautiful glow' (*schöne Schein*) of the Third Reich was not merely a simulacrum of wellbeing that masked a grim reality, but a reflection of most 'Aryan' Germans' experience. Shelley Baranowski, Kristin Semmens and Christine Keitz describe workers' gratitude for the first paid vacations of their lives.[29] Histories of cabaret, jazz, sports and the 1936 Olympics create a portrait of German spectators who behaved much like other West Europeans despite the tightly monitored public sphere in which they lived. Jo Fox, Jana Burns and Angela Vaupel analyse gender in feature films that appeared to be devoid of ideology. Gloria Sultano integrates her own family history into a nuanced account of the expulsion of Jews from the clothing industry, and then analyses the discursive strategies that simultaneously rationalised theft of Jews' property and celebrated Nazi style. Refusing an either/or paradigm, Irene Guenther highlights the ways in which prudery and sexual enticement functioned in tandem in women's fashion.[30] In these works, the gendered, 'Aryan' consumer displaces 'mass man' as an icon of mass marketing.

Attention to the role of gender and generation in shaping women's subjectivity provides a complex account of growing up in both gender integrated and gender segregated contexts in Nazi Germany. Dagmar Reese analyses the paradoxes faced by adolescent girls who learned to both be fiercely independent of parental authority and yet subservient to male superiors. Two collections of documents, edited by Sabine Hering, Kurt Schilde and Gisela Miller-Kipp, give readers direct access to a wealth of primary sources. Specialised studies of socialisation in the Third Reich abound, among which are Angela Vogel's and Susanne Watzke-Otte's histories of state-sponsored youth work programmes, Alexander Shuck's analysis of school books and Haide Manns's history of university women.[31] By emphasising putative biological contrasts between male and female, racial educators naturalised culturally inscribed distinctions.

Because they sideline high politics, historians of women escape from the chronological straightjacket of 1933–45. As the Third Reich settles into *la longue durée*, 1929, 1934, 1939, 1942 and 1948 also emerge as key turning points. Lora Wildenthal, like Martha Mamozai 20 years earlier, continues her history of women and colonialism into Weimar democracy and Nazi dictatorship. Katharina von Kellenbach, Ljiljana Radonic, Ilse Korotin and Charlotte Kohn-Ley discover a tradition of anti-Semitism in women's rights organisations. Contributors to the anthology *Verdeckte Überlieferungen: Weiblichkeitsbilder zwischen Weimarer Republik, Nationalsozialismus und Fünfziger Jahren* follow continuities among Protestant women's lives across temporal divides.[32] Studies by Andrea Süchting-Hänger, Raphael Scheck, Johanna Gehmacher, Elizabeth Harvey, Sophia Kemlein and Julia Seeinger trace ultra-conservative women's contribution to National Socialism within a broad chronological span.[33] Under Angelika Schaser's gaze, women's rights campaigner Gertrud Bäumer becomes at best an ambivalent role model.[34] Thanks to conferences, websites and anthologies, the authors of many specialised studies think comparatively about gender-specific experiences in mass dictatorships as well as about masculine and feminine subjectivities in German-Austrian contexts. In, for example, her magisterial *Warriors' Wives*, Birthe Kundrus makes World War I fundamental to her interpretation of World War II. In a study of ethnic German diasporas, contributors to the anthology *The Heimat Abroad* follow ethnic Germans (*Volksdeutsche*) across time and geography. Christine Eckelmann's study of women in health care and Geraldine Horan's account of the concept of the feminine in Nazi discourse make continuities with Weimar a central theme.

Research in archival sources related to women's lives expands earlier definitions of 'resistance', most of which denoted ideologically oriented, male-directed opposition groups. Conventional women without strong political allegiances, like Protestant theologian Elisabeth Schmitz and Auschwitz prisoner Orli Wald-Reichert, acted without a militant support group when they opposed Nazi rule. Archives have yielded information about hundreds of women labour organisers who quietly resisted racism before and after the Third Reich.[35] Nechama Tec uses gender to understand people who risked their lives to rescue Jews. Generation-based comparisons almost inevitably raise gender-specific issues. In researching the wartime conscription of men and women, Elizabeth Heineman distinguishes between mothers past childbearing age and younger mothers with children at home as a way of identifying the generation- and gender-specific claims to entitlement for state-funded benefits. Dorothee Wierling's description of post-war public memory in the Federal Republic of Germany explores the interaction between gender and generation. Dagmar Herzog discovered that the fictive conceptions of Nazi prudishness had been created by parents who had been adults in Nazi Germany and their 1968-er offspring. Sexuality in the Third Reich actually had been far more permissive than in repressive post-war West Germany.[36] This sampling of research projects illustrates the ways that attention to women and gender can revise stereotypes created by the political and sociological models so common in totalitarian analytic paradigms.

Conclusions

While mainstream historians concentrated on political elites and faceless mass organisations during the Cold War, historians of women wrote accounts of ordinary Germans. This perspective undercuts two notions of uniqueness. The first to crumble was the German *Sonderweg*, the idea that German history had followed a unique path to modernity that predisposed the political system to dictatorship. Doing research on local organisations, events, individuals and leisure activities, historians of women discovered commonalities that spanned the lives of women in liberal democracies and dictatorships. Looking beyond powerful elites, we see women as consumers, audiences, wives, mothers, health care providers, local organisers and government employees who faced the challenges of modernity in similar ways during two world wars and the interwar decades. Transnational continuities, not singularity, frame histories of gender and women. Hitler's deputies did not destroy but rather redeployed the pre-existing institutions of the democracy they had vanquished. In Communist dictatorships such as Mao's China, Soviet Russia and Pol Pot's Cambodia, dictators did their best to obliterate *ancien regimes*. Mass dictatorships, however, appropriated them. Whereas totalitarian interpretive matrices had emphasised repression, post-Cold War approaches investigate persuasion.

Historians of women and gender contributed to the demise of a second assumption of historians writing during the Cold War, the belief that the Third Reich represented a radical rupture with German history. The year 1933 did not constitute a break for the vast majority of women as long as they did not belong to the minority of citizens who were suspected of political opposition or Jewish ancestry. Hitler's rule did obliterate constitutional rights and render elections meaningless, but studies of gender document the importance of other kinds of choices that opened up with economic recovery: where to take a paid vacation, what film or exhibit to see, which organisation to join or whether to participate in a rally, for example. In mass dictatorships, spectators and consumers can experience a sense of autonomy even as they watch their freedoms vanish. Individuals could (and many did) quietly ignore particular commands that violated their moral or pragmatic sensibilities. But their single-issue dissent did not undercut state efficiency and may even have enhanced it by providing them with an emotional safety valve. As in any society, male and female opportunists, careerists, cowards, silent doubters and true believers complied in different degrees with state and party mandates. Far from being hollow men on the model of dystopian novels, such as Evgenii Zamatian's *We* or George Orwell's *1984*, most women and men living in the Third Reich participated in a lively civil society and surrendered civil liberties that few of them had had occasion to exercise.

Obeying what they considered to be a legitimate government, untold numbers of Germans defrauded, tormented and murdered people they believed threatened their *Volksgemeinschaft*. Widespread participation in state-sponsored, bureaucratically organised crimes was facilitated by a division of labour that relieved individuals of thinking morally about the ultimate outcomes of their actions. Imagined identities based on biological distinctions between masculine and feminine, and 'Aryan' and 'Jew' stabilised peer group solidarity as well as individual self-esteem. How different this culture was from wartime Soviet society in which women joined the military as snipers, pilots and machine gunners or from China during the Cultural Revolution when male and female Red Guards joined forces to wipe out suspected class enemies. A society structured by so-called biological traits reassures most people who are considered racially 'fit' that terror would not touch them, whereas in communist regimes no one could be sure whether they might be charged with a 'thought crime'. Consequently, most purge victims were male; but race-based extermination struck male and female alike.

Historians attentive to gender embed the Third Reich within studies of modernity, and eschew paradigms based on political regime typologies.[37] Mass dictatorships like Hirohito's Japan, Horthy's Hungary, Metaxas's Greece, Pilsudski's Poland, King Michael's Yugoslavia, Mussolini's Italy and Pétain's France mobilised women's grassroots support.[38] Emphasising the role of gender in the superficially non-violent, incremental transformation of mass democracies into mass dictatorships opens up transnational perspectives that include post-industrial West Europe and North America. Seeing mass dictatorships as successors to collapsed democracies reminds us of the susceptibility of liberal democratic nations to gradual takeover by powerful men.

Notes

An earlier version of this chapter appeared in Karen Hagemann and Jean Quataert (eds), *Gendering Modern German History* (New York: Berghahn Books, 2007), pp. 147–68.

1. Significantly, refugee historians (George Mosse, Fritz Stern and Peter Gay chief among them) and survivor scholars (Joseph Wulf, Léon Poliakov, Max Weinreich and H. A. Adler) avoided the intentionalist versus functionalist trap and emphasised the role of culture in shaping willing subjects.

2. Among the earliest resisters' memoirs published during the Cold War are Lina Haag, Lore Wolf, Anni Wadle, Simone Saint-Clair, *Ravensbrück: l'enfer des femmes* (1945); Rosane (pseudonym) *Terre de cendres, Ravensbrück et Belsen, 1943–1945* (1946); Gisella Perl, *I was a Doctor in Auschwitz* (1947); Ella Lingens-Reiner, *Prisoners of Fear* (1949); Hanna Lévy-Hass, *Inside Belsen* (1982); and Lisa Scheuer, *Vom Tode, der nicht stattfand: Theresienstadt, Auschwitz, Freiberg, Mauthausen: eine Frau überlebt* (1983). Early accounts by Jewish women survivors include Mary Berg, *Warsaw Ghetto* (1945); Anne Frank, *Het achterhuis; dagboekbrieven van 12 Juni 1942–1 Augustus 1944* (1947); Else R. Behrend-Rosenfeld, *Ich stand nicht allein, Erlebnisse einer Jüdin in*

Deutschland, 1933–1944 (1949); Gerda Klein, *All But My Life* (1957); Charlotte Delbo, *Aucun de nous ne reviendra* (1965); Fania Fenelon, *Playing for Time* (1977); and Isabella Leitner, *Fragments of Isabella* (1978).

3. Angelika Ebbinghaus (ed.), *Opfer und Täterinnen* (Nördlingen: Greno, 1987); Lerke Gravenhorst and Carmen Tatschmurat (eds), *Töchter-Fragen* (Freiburg i.Br.: Kore, 1990); Uta Schmidt, 'Wohin mit unserer gemeinsamen Betroffenheit?', in Ursula Becher and Jörn Büsen (eds), *Weiblichkeit in geschichtler Perspektive* (Frankfurt a.M.: Suhrkamp,1988), pp. 502–16.

4. Jane Caplan, 'Post Modernism, Poststructuralism', and Isabel V. Hull, 'Feminist and Gender History', *Central European History* 22(3–4) (1989), pp. 260–301; Hannah Schissler, *Geschlechterverhältnisse im historischen Wandel* (Frankfurt a.M.: Campus, 1993); Ute Daniel, 'Clio unter Kulturschock', *Geschichte in Wissenschaft und Unterricht* 48 (1997), pp. 195–217.

5. Joan Ringelheim, 'The Split between Gender and the Holocaust', in Lenore Weitzman and Dalia Ofer (eds), *Women in the Holocaust* (New Haven, CT: Yale University Press, 1998); Christa Schikorra, *Kontinuitäten der Ausgrenzung. 'Asoziale' Häftlinge im Frauen-Konzentrationslager Ravensbrück*, TU Berlin Zentrum für Antisemitismusforschung, Vol. 41, Dokumente – Texte – Materialien (Berlin: Metropol, 2001).

6. Karin Windaus-Walser, 'Gnade der weiblichen Geburt?', *Feministische Studien* 6 (1988), pp. 12–31; Christina Thürmer-Rohr, 'Aus der Täuschung in die Ent-Täuschung', *Beiträge zur Feministischen Theorie und Praxis* 8 (1983), pp. 11–26; Claudia Card, 'Women, Evil, and Grey Zones', *Metaphilosophy* 31(5) (2000), pp. 11–23. For an overview in English, see Christina Thürmer-Rohr, *Vagabonding: Feminist Thinking Cut Loose*, translated by Lise Weil (Boston, MA: Beacon Press, 1991).

7. In their film, *Das Grosse Schweigen* (1995), Caroline von der Tann and Maren Niemeyer also called attention to rape. Christa Paul, 'Zwangsprostitution: staatlich errichtete Bordelle im Nationalsozialismus', *Reihe deutsche Vergangenheit* 115 (Berlin: 1994); Christl Wickert, 'Tabu Lagerbordell: vom Umgang mit der Zwangsprostitution nach 1945', in Insa Eschebach, Sigrid Jacobeit and Silke Wenk (eds), *Gedächtnis und Geschlecht: Deutungsmuster in Darstellungen des nationalsozialistischen Genozids* (Frankfurt a.M: Campus, 2002); Annette F. Timm, 'Sex with a Purpose: Prostitution: Venereal Disease, and Militarized Masculinity in the Third Reich', in Dagmar Herzog (ed.), *Sexuality and German Fascism* (Oxford: Berghahn, 2005), pp. 223–55; Christa Schikorra, *Kontinuitäten der Ausgrenzung*; David Snyder, *Sex Crimes under the Wehrmacht* (Lincoln, NE: University of Nebraska Press, 2007).

8. 'Foreword', in Ulrich Herbert (ed.), *National Socialist Extermination Policies* (New York: Berghahn, 2000), p. vii.

9. Gudrun Schwarz, in Karin Hausen (ed.), *Frauen suchen ihre Geschichte: historische Studien zum 19. und 20. Jahrhundert* (Munich: C. H. Beck, 1983); Gudrun Schwarz, *Eine Frau an seiner Seite: Ehefrauen in der 'SS-Sippengemeinschaft'* (Hamburg: Hamburger Edition, 1997); Ursula Nienhaus, 'Himmlers willige Komplizinnen – Weibliche Polizei im Nationalsozialismus', in Michael Grüttner, Rüdiger Hachtmann and Heinz-Gerhard Haupt (eds), *Geschichte und Emanzipation* (Frankfurt a.M.: Campus, 1999), pp. 517–39.

10. Günter Grass, 'Nobel Lecture', http://nobelprize.org/nobel_prizes/literature/laureates/1999/grass-lecture.html (accessed 1 May 2010).

11. Klaus-Michael Mallmann, 'Die Sicherheitspolizei', in Gerhard Paul (ed.), *Täter der Shoah* (Göttingen: Wallstein, 2002), pp. 109–31; here p. 125.

12. Bea Dörr, Gerrit Kaschuba and Susanne Maurer (eds), *Endlich habe ich einen Platz für meine Erinnerungen gefunden* (Herbolzheim: Centaurus, 2000); Ursula Bernhold, Almut Setje-Eilers and Uta Fleischmann, *'Ist denn da was gewesen'?* (Oldenbourg: Isensee, 1996); Claudia Friedel, (Münster: LIT, 1995); Hans-Jürgen Arendt, Sabine Hering and Leonie Wagner (eds), *Nationalsozialistische Frauenpolitik* (Frankfurt a.M: Dipa, 1995); Andrew Bergerson, *Ordinary Germans* (Bloomington, IN: Indiana University Press, 2004).

13. Edward Ross Dickinson, 'Biopolitics, Fascism, Democracy', *Central European History* 37(1) (2004), pp. 1–48; Kathleen Canning, 'The Body as Method?', *Gender and History* 11(3) (1999), pp. 499–513; Marius Turda and Paul Weindling (eds), *'Blood and Homeland': Eugenics and Racial Nationalism in Central and Southeast Europe, 1900–1940* (Budapest and New York: Central European University Press, 2007).

14. Gabriele Czarnowski, *Das kontrollierte Paar* (Weinheim: Deutscher Studien Verlag, 1991); Annette F. Timm, 'Sex with a Purpose', in Herzog (ed.), *Sexuality and German Fascism*, pp. 223–55.

15. Claudia Schoppmann and Günther Grau (eds), *Hidden Holocaust?* (London: Cassell, 1995); Petra Fuchs, *'Körperbehinderte' zwischen Selbstaufgabe und Emanzipation* (Neuwied: Luchterhand, 2001); Petra Kannappel, *Die Behandlung von Frauen im nationalsozialistischen Familienrecht* (Darmstadt: Selbstverlag der HHK, 1999); Bettina Bab, 'Im falschen Moment laut gelacht', *Beiträge Zur feministischen Theorie und Praxis* 18 (1995), pp. 33–42; Lisa Pine, *Hitler's 'National Community': Society and Culture in Nazi Germany* (London: Hodder Arnold, 2007).

16. Tina M. Campt, *Other Germans: Black Germans and the Politics of Race, Gender, and Memory in the Third Reich* (Ann Arbor, MI: University of Michigan Press, 2004); Heide Fehrenbach, *Race after Hitler: Black Occupation Children in Postwar Germany and America* (Princeton, NJ: Princeton University Press, 2005); Clarence Lusane, *Hitler's Black Victims: The Historical Experiences of Afro-Germans, European Blacks, Africans, and African Americans in the Nazi Era (Crosscurrents in African American History)* (New York: Routledge, 2003); Patricia M. Mazón and Reinhild Steingröver (eds), *Not so Plain as Black and White: Afro-German Culture and History, 1890–2000 (Rochester Studies in African History and the Diaspora)* (Rochester: New York University of Rochester Press, 2005).

17. Miriam Enzweiler, *Fremdarbeiterinnen und Fremdarbeiter* (Krefeld: Edition Bilstein, 1994); Birthe Kundrus, 'Forbidden Company' and Patricia Szobar, 'Race Defilement in Germany', in Herzog (ed.), *Sexuality and German Fascism*, pp. 201–22, 142; Kundrus, ' "Die Unmoral deutscher Soldatenfrauen" ', in Kirsten Heinsohn, Barbara Vogel and Ulrike Weckel (eds), *Zwischen Karriere und Verfolgung: Handlungsräume von Frauen im nationalsozialistischen Deutschland* (Frankfurt a.M.: Campus, 1997), pp. 96–110; Alexandra Przyrembel, *Rassenschande* (Göttingen, 2003); Doris Bergen, 'Sex, Blood, and Vulnerability' and Annette Timm, 'The Ambivalent Outsider', in Robert Gellately and Nathan Stoltzfus (eds), *Social Outsiders* (Princeton,

NJ: Princeton University Press, 2000), pp. 192–211 and 273–293. Nathan Stoltzfus, *Resistance of the Heart: Intermarriage and the Rosenstrasse Protest in Nazi Germany* (New York: W. W. Norton, 1996) and the trenchant criticism by Wolf Gruner and Ursula Marcum, 'The Factory Action and the Events at the Rosenstrasse in Berlin: Facts and Fictions', *Central European History* 36(2) (2003); Stephen Tyas, 'Allied Intelligence Agencies and the Holocaust: Information Acquired from German Prisoners of War', *Journal of Holocaust and Genocide Studies* 22(1) (2008).

18. Lilo Haag, *Berufsbiographische Erinnerungen von Fürsorgerinnen* (Freiburg i.Br.: Lambertus, 2000); Bronwyn McFarland-Icke, *Nurses in Nazi Germany* (Princeton, NJ: Princeton University Press, 1999), p. 248; Uta Cornelia Schmatzler, *Verstrickung, Mitverantwortung und Täterschaft* (Kiel: L & F, 1994), pp. 241–87; Susi Hausammann, Nicole Kuropka and Heike Scherer, *Frauen in dunkler Zeit: Schicksal und Arbeit von Frauen in der Kirche zwischen 1933 und 1945* (Cologne: Rheinland-Verlag, 1996); Claus Füllberg-Stollberg (ed.), *Frauen in Konzentrationslagern: Bergen-Belsen, Ravensbrück* (Bremen: Temmen, 1994).

19. Doris L. Bergen, 'The *Volksdeutsche* of Eastern Europe and the Collapse of the Nazi Empire, 1944–1945', in Allen E. Steinweis and Daniel E. Rogers (eds), *The Impact of Nazism. New Perspectives on the Third Reich and its Legacy* (Lincoln, NE: University of Nebraska Press, 2003); Elizabeth Harvey, *Women and the Nazi East: Agents and Witnesses of Germanization* (New Haven, CT: Yale University Press, 2003).

20. Klara Löffler, *Aufgehoben: Soldatenbriefe* (Bamberg: VWB, 1992), pp. 87–116, 125–48; Wolfram Wette (ed.), *Der Krieg des kleinen Mannes* (Munich: Piper, 1992); Ingrid Hammer and Susanne zur Nieden, (eds), *'Sehr selten habe ich geweint'* (Zurich: Schweizer Verlagshaus, 1992); Detlef Bald and Wolfram Wette (eds), *Zivilcourage: Empörte, Helfer und Retter aus Wehrmacht, Polizei und SS* (Frankfurt a.M.: Fischer, 2004).

21. Claudia Koonz, *Mothers in the Fatherland: Women, the Family, and Nazi Politics* (New York: St Martin's Press, 1987), pp. 408–18; Karin Hausen, 'Frauenräume', in Karin Hausen and Heide Wunder (eds), *Frauengeschichte-Geschlectergeschichte* (Frankfurt am Main: Campus, 1992), pp. 21–3; Hans Heer, 'Bittere Pflicht, Der Rassenkrieg', in Walter Manoschek and Reinhold Gärtner (eds), *Die Wehrmacht im Rassenkrieg* (Vienna: Picus, 1996), pp. 116–36; Inge Marssolek, 'Ich möchte Dich zu gern mal in Uniform sehen', *Werkstattgeschichte* 22 (1999), pp. 41–59; Thomas Kühne, 'Comradeship', in Karen Hagemann and Stefanie Schüler-Springorum (eds), *Home/Front: The Military, War and Gender in Twentieth Century Germany* (Oxford: Berg, 2002), pp. 233–54; Susanne zur Nieden, 'Erotic Fraternization', in Hagemann et al. (eds), *Home/Front*, pp. 303–6; Sybille Steinbacher, *'Musterstadt' Auschwitz: Germanisierungspolitik und Judenmord in Ostoberschlesien* (Munich: G.K. Saur, 2000), p. 187.

22. Silke Wenk, 'Rhetoriken der Pornografisierung', in Eschebach, Jacobeit and Wenk (eds), *Gedächtnis und Geschlecht*, pp. 285–90; Carolyn Dean, 'Empathy, Pornography, and Suffering', *Differences* (Spring 2003), pp. 88–125.

23. Kathrin Kompisch, *Täterinnen: Frauen im Nationalsozialismus* (Köln: Böhlau, 2008). According to one reviewer, Kathrin Kompisch 'documents the shameful truth about her sex in the war, which until now has been a taboo

subject in her homeland', uncritically accepting the author's claim, 'The participation of women in the crimes of the Nazis has been blended out of the collective conscious of the Germans for a long time', she writes.

24. Enzo Traverso, *Origins of Nazi Violence* (New York: New Press, 2003), pp. 35–45.
25. Helen Boak, 'Mobilizing Women for Hitler: The Female Nazi Voter', in Tim Kirk and Anthony McElligott (eds), *Working Towards the Führer: Essays in Honour of Sir Ian Kershaw* (Manchester: Manchester University Press, 2004), pp. 68–92; Evan Burr Bukey, *Hitler's Austria: Popular Sentiment in the Nazi Era 1938–1945* (Chapel Hill, NC: University of North Carolina Press, 2000).
26. Hartmut Berghoff, 'Enticement and deprivation', in Martin Daunton and Matthew Hilton (eds), *The Politics of Consumption* (Oxford: Berg, 2001), pp. 166–77; Pamela Swett, Jonathan Zatlin and Jonathan Wiener (eds), *Selling Modernity* (Durham: Duke University Press, 2006); Alon Confino and Rudy Koshar, 'Régimes of Consumer Culture', *German History* 19(2) (2001), pp. 135–61; Paul Betts, *The Authority of Everyday Objects* (Berkeley, CA,: University of California Press, 2004), pp. 21–34. See also Ulrich Heinemann, 'Krieg und Frieden an der "inneren Front"', in Christoph Klessmann and Ute Frevert (eds), *Nicht nur Hitlers Krieg* (Düsseldorf: Droste, 1989); Cornelie Usborne, 'Body Biological to Body Politics: Women's Demands for Reproductive Self-Determination in World War I and Early Weimar Germany', in Geoff Eley and Jan Palmowski (eds), *Citizenship and National Identity in Twentieth-Century Germany* (Stanford, CA: Stanford University Press, 2008), pp. 129–45.
27. Nancy Reagin, '*Marktordnung* and Autarkic Housekeeping', *German History* 19(2) (2001), pp. 162–84; Renate Harter-Meyer, *Der Kochlöffel ist unsere Waffe* (Baltmannsweiler: Schneider, 1999), pp. 74–81, 84–107.
28. Uta Gerhardt, 'Charismatische Herrschaft', *Geschichte und Gesellschaft* 24(4) (1998), pp. 503–38; Cristina von Braun, ' "Der Jude" und "Das Weib" ', *Metis* 1(2) (1992), pp. 6–28; Adelheid von Saldern, *The Challenge of Modernity* (Ann Arbor, MI: University of Michigan Press, 2002), pp. 313–5, 337. Other works on popular culture include Barbara Determann, Ulrike Hammer and Doron Kiesel (eds), *Verdeckte Überlieferungen* (Frankfurt a.M.: Haag + Herchen, 1991); Andrew Bergerson, 'Listening to the Radio', *German Studies Review* 24(1) (2001), pp. 83–113; Kate Lacey, *Feminine Frequencies* (Ann Arbor, MI: University of Michigan Press, 1996); Barbara Schrödl, *Das Bild des Künstlers und seiner Frauen* (Marburg: Jonas, 2004); Inge Marssolek, Adelheid von Saldern, and Daniela Münkel (eds), *Radio im Nationalsozialismus* (Tübingen: Diskord, 1998). Uli Linke, 'The Violence of Difference', in Marcus Funck, Greg Eghigian and Paul Matthew (eds), *Sacrifice and National Belonging* (College Station, TX Texas A&M Press, 2002), pp. 156, 179–87.
29. Shelley Baranowski, *Strength through Joy: Consumerism and Mass Tourism in the Third Reich* (Cambridge: Cambridge University Press, 2004); Kristin Semmens, *Seeing Hitler's Germany: Tourism in the Third Reich* (Houndmills, Baskingstoke: Palgrave Macmillan, 2005). For continuities with Weimar tourism, see Cristine Keitz, *Reisen als Leitbild: die Entstehung des modernen Massentourismus in Deutschland* (Munich: DTV, 1997).
30. Angela Vaupel, *Frauen im NS-Film* (Hamburg: Kovac, 2002); Jo Fox, *Filming Women in the Third Reich* (Oxford: Berg, 2000); Jana Francesca Bruns,

Nazi Cinema's New Women: Twenty Years of Trial and Error (Cambridge and New York: Cambridge University Press, 2009); Gloria Sultano, *Wie Geistiges Kokain* (Vienna: Verlag für Gesellschaftskritik, 1995); Irene Guenther, *Nazi chic?* (Oxford: Berg, 2004).

31. Dagmar Reese, *Growing up Female in Nazi Germany* (Ann Arbor, MI: University of Michigan Press, 2006); Sabine Hering and Kurt Schilde, *Das BDM-Werk 'Glaube und Schönheit': die Organisation junger Frauen im Nationalsozialismus* (Berlin: Metropol, 2000); Elisabeth Perchinig, *Zur Einübung von Weiblichkeit im Terrorzusammenhang: Mädchenadoleszenz in der NS-Gesellschaft* (Munich: Profil, 1998); Gisela Miller-Kipp, *Auch Du gehörst dem Führer* (Weinheim: Juventa, 2001); Ursula R. Mahlendorf, *The Shame of Survival: Working through a Nazi Childhood* (University Park, PA: Pennsylvania State University Press, 2009); Angela Vogel, *Das Pflichtjahr für Mädchen* (Frankfurt a.M: P. Lang., 1997); Haide Manns, *Frauen für den Nationalsozialismus* (Opladen: Leske + Budrich, 1997).

32. Birthe Kundrus, *Kriegerfrauen: Familienpolitik und Geschlechterverhältnisse im Ersten und Zweiten Weltkrieg* (Hamburg: Christians, 1995); Martha Mamozai (ed.), *Herrenmenschen, Frauen im deutschen Kolonialismus* (Reinbek: Rowohlt, 1982); Lora Wildenthal, *German Women for Empire, 1884–1945* (Durham, NC: Duke University Press, 2001); Lisa Pine, *Hitler's 'National Community'*; Krista O'Donnell, Nancy Ruth Reagin and Renate Bridenthal, *The Heimat Abroad: The Boundaries of Germanness* (Ann Arbor, MI: University of Michigan Press, 2005); Emily Turner-Graham, ' "The German Woman has the Inner Energy to Work for Germanness": Race, Gender and National Socialism in Interwar Australia', *Lilith: A Feminist History Journal* 15 (2006); Christine Eckelmann, *Ärztinnen in der Weimarer Zeit und im Nationalsozialismus: eine Untersuchung über den Bund Deutscher Ärztinnen* (Wermelskirchen WFT: Verlag för Wissenschaft, Forschung und Technik, 1992); Geraldine Horan, *Mothers, Warriors, Guardians of the Soul: Female Discourse in National Socialism, 1924–1934* (Berlin: W. de Gruyter, 2003); Michelle Mouton, *From Nurturing the Nation to Purifying the Volk: Weimar and Nazi Family Policy, 1918–1945* (Cambridge: Cambridge University Press, 2007); Ursula Flossmann, *Nationalsozialistische Spuren im Recht: Ausgewählte Stolpersteine für ein selbstbestimmtes Frauenleben* (Linz: Rudolf Trauner, 1999); Barbara Determann, Ulrike Hammer and Doron Kiesel, *Verdeckte Überlieferungen: Weiblichkeitsbilder zwischen Weimarer Republik, Nationalsozialismus und Fünfziger Jahren* (Frankfurt a.M.: Haag and Herchen, 1991).

33. Andrea Süchting-Hänger, *Das 'Gewissen der Nation': nationales Engagement und politisches Handeln konservativer Frauenorganisationen 1900 bis 1937* (Düsseldorf: Droste, 2002); Raffael Scheck, *Mothers of the Nation: Right-Wing Women in Weimar Germany* (New York: Berg, 2003); Ute Planert (ed.), *Nation, Politik und Geschlecht: Frauenbewegungen und Nationalismus in der Moderne* (Frankfurt a.M.: Campus, 2000); Johanna Gehmacher, Elizabeth Harvey and Sophia Kemlein, *Zwischen Kriegen: Nationen, Nationalismen und Geschlechterverhältnisse in Mittel- und Osteuropa, 1918–1939* (Osnabrück: Fibre, 2004); Ralph Leck, 'Conservative Empowerment', *Journal of Women's History* 12(2) (2003), pp. 147–69.

34. Martha Mamozai (ed.), *Herrenmenschen, Frauen im deutschen Kolonialismus* (Reinbeck: Rowohlt, 1982); Wildenthal, *German Women for Empire*,

1884–1945 (Durham, NC: Duke University Press, 2001); Johanna Gehmacher, *Völkische Frauenbewegung* (Vienna: Döcker, 1998); Charlotte Kohn-Ley, Ilse Korotin and Johanna Gehmacher (eds), *Der feministische 'Sundenfall'?* (Vienna: Picus, 1994); Ilse Korotin and Barbara Serlot (eds), *Gebrochene Kontinuitäten zur Rolle und Bedeutung des Geschlechterverhältnisses in der Entwicklung des Nationalsozialismus* (Innsbruck: StudienVerlag, 2000); Katharina von Kellenbach, *Anti-Judaism in Feminist Religious Writings* (Atlanta, GA: Scholars, 1994); Susanne Omran, *Frauenbewegung und 'Judenfrage'* (Frankfurt a.M.: Campus, 2000), pp. 405–35; Ljiljana Radonić, *Die friedfertige Antisemitin?* (Frankfurt a.M.: P. Lang, 2004); Angelika Schaser, 'Gertrud Bäumer', in Heinsohn, Vogel and Weckel (eds), *Zwischen Karriere und Verfolgung*, pp. 24–43.

35. Manfred Gailus, *Elisabeth Schmitz und ihre Denkschrift gegen die Judenverfolgung: Konturen einer vergessenen Biografie (1893–1977)* (Berlin: Wichern-Verlag, 2008); Nechama Tec, *Resilience and Courage: Women, and Men, and the Holocaust* (New Haven, CT: Yale University Press, 2003); Siegfried Mielke (ed.), *Gewerkschafterinnen im NS-Staat: Verfolgung, Widerstand, Emigration* (Essen: Klartext, 2008); Bernd Steger and Peter Wald, *Hinter der grünen Pappe: Orli Wald im Schatten von Auschwitz: Leben und Erinnerungen* (Hamburg: VSA-Verlag, 2008); Heimo Halbrainer and Maria Cäsar, *'Ich bin immer schon eine politische Frau gewesen': Maria Cäsar, Widerstandskämpferin und Zeitzeugin: eine Würdigung aus Anlass ihres 86. Geburtstags* (Graz: Clio, 2006).

36. Elizabeth Heineman, 'Age and Generation', *Journal of Women's History* 12(4) (2001), pp. 139–64; Dorothee Wierling, 'Generations', in Christoph Klessmann, *The Divided Past: Rewriting Post-War German History* (Oxford: Berg, 2001), pp. 69–90; Mark Roseman (ed.), *Generations in Conflict: Youth Revolt and Generation Formation in Germany, 1770–1968* (Cambridge: Cambridge University Press, 1995); Joyce Marie Mushaben, 'Collective Memory Divided: and Reunited: Mothers, Daughters and the Fascist Experience in Germany', *History and Memory* 11(1) (1999); Caroline Schaumann, *Memory Matters: Generational Responses to Germany's Nazi Past in Recent Women's Literature* (Berlin: de Gruyter, 2008).

37. Volker Rolf Berghahn and Simone Lässig (eds), *Biography Between Structure and Agency: Central European Lives in International Historiography* (New York: Berghahn Books, 2008); Eley and Palmowski (eds), *Citizenship and National Identity in Twentieth-Century Germany*; Martin O. Heisler (ed.), *The Politics of History in Comparative Perspective* (Los Angeles, CA: Sage, 2008); Dagmar Herzog (ed.), *Brutality and Desire: War and Sexuality in Europe's Twentieth Century* (Basingstoke and New York: Palgrave Macmillan, 2009).

38. Jie-Hyun Lim, 'Conference Report Coercion and Consent: A Comparative Study of "Mass Dictatorship"', *Contemporary European History* 13(2) (2004), pp. 249–52.

Part II
Interwar Gender Negotiations

4
Little Prefects: The Embodiment of Masculinity in Interwar Britain

Sangsoo Kim

> But is it not exclusively to the Public Schools that one must go to find boys who know what honour and duty mean. Birth and breeding count for much but they are not everything. Nature's gentlemen are to be found in all ranks and conditions.
>
> (W. Jewsbury, Headmaster of Glascote Boys' School)[1]

Introduction: mass dictatorship and mass democracy

At first glance, Britain and its liberal parliamentary democracy are not natural companions for the project of analysing mass dictatorship. This is not least because the major themes of the project have been the dictatorial regimes in the West such as Nazi Germany, Fascist Italy, Franco's Spain and Stalinist Russia. Even when other political forms are mentioned as their counterparts, dictatorships in non-Western countries such as Park Chung-hee's in South Korea, Kim Il-sung's in North Korea and Mao Zedong's in China usually take the spotlight, with the democratic polities such as the USA and the UK slipping into oblivion.

There might be two ways that Britain can draw attention from those interested in mass dictatorship. To take a more feasible option, one can focus on the Fascist movements in Britain such as Oswald Mosley's BUF (British Union of Fascists). It can be argued that the British indirectly experienced dictatorship, as British Fascists succeeded to a degree in propagating some of their ideas (eugenics, for example) during the interwar period though they failed to set up a regime. The second option might be less intriguing to the core supporters of mass dictatorship but could nevertheless broaden their perspectives: it deals with the question of why Britain never experienced a dictatorial regime and makes comparisons between dictatorship and democracy.

The conventional answers to this question are quite simplistic, while providing a clear picture of why Britain has been so different from its neighbouring countries on the Continent. The well-known story goes: Britain, as the first industrial country in the world, did not have to go through a rapid industrialisation and modernisation led by the state; the long-lived Parliament, established political parties and liberal parliamentary democracy made it impossible for extreme forms of political ideas and activities to appeal to the whole nation. This account is certainly based on historical facts and thus quite persuasive, but has some serious problems in that it regards Britain as a role model rather than as an exception and it tends to divide democracy and dictatorship by the simplistic good/evil line. In other words, this account implies that the British would never fall into the Fascist trap, as they were born with an inclination to liberal democratic values and with better moral qualities than Germans or Italians. More seriously, it is suggested that democracy is the legitimate child of modernity and dictatorship is either a deviation from the normal process of modernisation or something miserably stuck in the mire of pre-modernity.

The primary purpose of this chapter is to deconstruct this kind of epistemological dichotomy. One of the most powerful merits of the mass dictatorship project is that it seeks to compare various historical cases throughout the world, often drawing upon interdisciplinary works. And yet, the project has not paid due attention to non-dictatorial regimes, while focusing on comparisons between various dictatorships. The reason why this chapter deals with Britain is that it is urgent to reveal the subtle linkage between democracy and dictatorship. The prefect system, the main topic of this chapter, is a peephole through which we can take a glimpse of such a linkage. As a matter of fact, the concept of mass dictatorship has already opened the possibility that this task might be well worth pursuing. In order to understand better how this topic can contribute to the project, it is highly relevant to look briefly at the path the project has travelled up until now.

The original aim of the mass dictatorship project was to historically analyse not only how dictatorial regimes succeeded in gaining the consent of the masses, but also why the masses gave consent to the regimes. This was not to argue that the masses never resisted against dictators but rather that responses from the masses took various forms, spreading through a broad grey area between absolute consent to dictators at the one end and fierce resistance against them at the other. It is true that the project often faced severe criticisms because it tended to focus on the 'consent' side.[2] A great number of Korean scholars participated in, or observed at least, a series of fierce debates on the nature of

Park's military dictatorship in South Korea, many of whom regarded the project as a defence for the dictatorship. However, one of the reasons why the project had to draw attention to 'consent' was that it tried to show that the conventional accounts were too simplistic to explain why the masses would be nostalgic about dictatorial regimes even after their collapse.

With such misunderstandings mostly resolved after several years' debate, mass dictatorship is now facing a new question. It seems almost natural that those who discovered the masses giving consent even to dictatorship are now turning their eyes to democracy. If both democracy and dictatorship are underpinned by the consent of the masses and thus the definition of the former cannot be based on 'consent', the line between the two political systems should be blurred. It is time to draw attention to the affinity, rather than difference, between the two systems. Both democracy and dictatorship are the by-products of creating modern nation-states. The process by which nation-states were created was based on artificial groupings such as classes, races and nations, blurring the differences among individualities. The ruling classes of the ever-expanding Western powers in the late nineteenth and early twentieth centuries relied with few exceptions on the discourse of 'otherisation' in order to retain superiority over other classes and nations. The belief that such groupings were possible was one of the main characteristics of modernity. In this sense, both dictatorship and democracy should be posited in the domain of modernity. They are the two faces of a coin: they look different, but share the same root. It thus becomes difficult to divide the two by the line of modern/pre-modern or normal/abnormal, leaving aside that of good/evil.

If the focus is laid upon 'artificial categorisation', a shared characteristic of democracy and dictatorship, the theme of mass dictatorship becomes entangled with the question of imperialism, or colonialism in a broader sense. The reason why the two systems took different paths, while sharing the same root, can be found in the degrees of colonial expansion of the Western powers. For the process of categorisation, countries with more colonies like Britain could easily find 'others' in their colonies, while those with fewer like Nazi Germany had to create 'others' among themselves – their neighbour Jews. Britain tried to consolidate its own people by categorising them into a group of the superior 'rulers' while putting the colonised of its Empire into the category of the inferior 'ruled'. The sensibility of being the rulers of the British Empire often blinded the British to their internal problems such as class conflicts and gender inequalities. It follows that the British could retain liberal democratic values while avoiding the advent of a dictatorial regime, less because they were morally superior than because they possessed a vast Empire.

It must also be remembered that even the countries that secured a path toward liberal democracy often committed violence against the 'others' – the ruled in their colonies in particular. Violence and extremism were not monopolised by dictatorship. In the British Empire, the colonised were often denied basic rights. Even Niall Ferguson, one of the most famous admirers of the British Empire, admits that many of those who were governed by the British colonisers were discriminated against and forced to live under often violent and reckless oppression.[3] Thus the historical fact that Britain, thanks to the largest Empire ever, was most successful in safeguarding liberal parliamentary democracy cannot be easily attributed to its superior moral quality. Rather, it should be noted that at the core of the British Empire lay artificial categorisations and blatant discrimination. This is where the British case could provide the mass dictatorship project with renewed insights, because the ultimate goal of the project is to deconstruct the epistemological dichotomies between consent and resistance, dictatorship and democracy, and the modern and the pre-modern, rather than to merely insist that the masses gave consent to dictatorships or to apply the term 'mass dictatorship' to as many historical cases as possible. Both censure of dictatorship and praise of liberal democracy must now be replaced by the deconstruction of modernity.

With this question in mind, the next part of this chapter explores how the discourse of gender served to maintain and expand the British Empire, and vice versa. By looking at how the discourses of masculinity/femininity were applied differently to various groups, it will be revealed how the experience of ruling the Empire influenced the identity of the British.

British Empire and gender discourse

Most dictatorial regimes of the twentieth century drew upon the discourses of masculinity/femininity in order to control the masses efficiently. These regimes were inclined to foster patriarchal values and strict gender roles, by which men were endowed with the right to rule while women were discriminated against in almost all domains of life. Under such circumstances, it has been argued, women had no other options but either to reluctantly accept the situation or to become brainwashed to worship the dictators: to be victims or accomplices.[4] The mass dictatorship project has, however, observed that it was not uncommon for women to empower themselves by actively participating in and thus propping up the dictatorships. Subsequently, the project is now making an attempt to analyse how women liberated themselves from the private sphere and reconstructed their subjectivity in the public sphere either through participating in state projects for modernisation or through helping its war efforts.

In the case of Britain, a discriminatory gender discourse had already begun to appear by the mid nineteenth century. It is widely known that gender discourse played a crucial role in the growth of the British Empire.[5] While recent research has pointed out that some women actively contributed to the expansion of the Empire, most historical accounts focus on the fact that the Empire basically belonged to the domain of men and thus women had few roles to play in it.[6] The role of women became increasingly confined to that of 'guardian of the family' as the gender discourse that legitimised British rule abroad by endowing British men with masculinity and British women and the colonised with femininity began to spread out across the Empire in the second half of the century. The discourse of imperialism justified the inequitable relationship between men and women as well as between the British and the colonised.

It was white middle-class British men who took the initiative in developing the discourse of masculinity/femininity in Britain.[7] By the late eighteenth century, the middle classes had already grown up to compete with the nobility in national politics. They disparaged the nobility as a weak and old class that was not able to pursue the interests of their nation and Empire due to a lack of masculine attributes. It was insisted that Britain and its overseas territories could be ruled only by those with masculine power and strength, that is, the middle classes. By this process, middle-class men began to monopolise genuine masculinity, describing other groups such as the aristocrats, the working class and women as weak and feminine.[8]

In the context of the British Empire, the major targets of this discriminatory gender discourse were categorised into three groups: British women, colonised males and colonised females. After the Indian Rebellion of 1857, the informal rule of India by the East India Company was replaced by direct rule from London. It was at this moment that the 'physically strong and mentally rational' masculinity of the British men became essential in ruling the Empire. Increasing the number of British troops in India was not enough to impose their superiority. In order to constantly remind the Indians that there was an intrinsic difference between the rulers and the ruled, the British drew upon the discourse of masculinity, the virtues of which could be held up only by those who benefited from a proper British education.[9]

It must be noted that masculinity was always constructed against femininity. The reason why middle-class British men put so much emphasis on masculinity was that they wanted to distinguish themselves from others. For this purpose, they described all the other groups as feminine. However, there was a hierarchy of femininities among these groups: the femininity of the British women was considered different from that of the male/female colonised. While the femininity of the British women was considered natural and desirable, the femininity of the Indian men, for instance, was regarded as an abnormality or a disease that should be cured. At the same time, the British were expected to liberate Indian women from the barbaric rule of their male compatriots and help them acquire genuine femininity.

It is interesting to observe that female missionaries, whose aim was to liberate the female inhabitants of colonies, were actually also trying to liberate themselves. While regarding the women of Asia or Africa as victims of the cruel rule of their barbarian male counterparts, and trying to liberate them, these missionaries considered themselves superior to their miserable sisters. They acted as mothers, teachers and nurses of Indian or Afro-Caribbean daughters, teaching them how to manage their households.[10] By these acts, some of them tried to prove that they were able to hold up femininity even though they were unmarried and independent.[11] Femininity lay at the core of British women's superiority over the colonised women.

The colonised elites, for their part, seem to have accepted, or at least adapted themselves to, the British version of gender discourse. The leading groups in India, for example, tried to distinguish themselves from other classes by imitating the British rulers. Now the elites of India began to enjoy British sport, looking down upon those who were not able to understand or follow its rules. Acting like a British man became an essential mark of one's superiority in their own country. It was thought that the Indians must be ruled by the British until they had learned to be truly masculine, which was not likely to happen in the near future. India as a whole was now described as feminine. Here, racism was expressed through the discourse of gender. This is not to say that the Indians never resisted British rule or that they did not possess their own cultural assets. Nevertheless, the way they perceived themselves was increasingly under the control of the British rulers.

The feminine image of India was sometimes utilised to criticise British women. The Conservatives of Britain, who were facing challenges from feminists in the late nineteenth and early twentieth centuries, insisted that Indian women, being devoted wives and mothers, were far more feminine than their British sisters. Not least because the British women had to be the mainstay of femininity, they should not lag behind in the race for femininity. In this way, the British women were required to be the 'angel in the house'.

However, as the British Empire kept on extending its boundaries during the late nineteenth century, the relationship between these four groups became more complicated. This was primarily because the meanings of masculinity/femininity were always defined against each other. The way the colonisers defined the colonised often influenced the way the colonisers defined themselves. The British men not only created the discourses of masculinity/femininity but also had to *perform* masculinity. In order to distinguish themselves from the colonised, they had to constantly discipline themselves as the masculine rulers of the Empire, while repressing any feminine attributes.[12] In other words, they had to become actors to perform a masquerade of masculinity in everyday life.

Although gender discourse functioned to sustain the British Empire, distinguishing the rulers from the ruled, the rulers were also influenced by it. Not least because the gender discourse involved 'otherisation', even those who invented it had to define themselves as the 'others' of their 'others'. As the presence of the Empire provided the British with various 'others', the identity of the British was formed and changed by how the others were defined, and gender discourse was integral to this process. In this sense, gender discourse should not be regarded merely as a tool by which the British ruled their Empire, but as a prerequisite for its very existence. Gender discourse ruled even the rulers of the Empire.

The last part of this chapter thus looks at the rulers' side, focusing on how the discourse of masculinity gained ground across the British nation as a whole. Education played an essential role in spreading the idea across the country that British men, regardless of their social status, should acquire the proper masculinity required for the rulers of the Empire. This process seems to have been finalised by the interwar period when the elementary schools also adopted the public school virtues of manliness.

Embodiment of masculinity: prefect system

Of course, not only education but many other aspects of British society also deserve due attention, as they also played an important role in dispersing public school virtues. Sport, for instance, played a major role in this process. As the working classes began to enjoy various kinds of sports such as football, rugby and boxing, they became familiar with the rules originally set by the public school boys, sharing the virtues of vigour and willingness to win, as well as fair play and respect for losers. Not least because these virtues were thought to be exclusively enjoyed by those who had acquired true masculine attributes, the British working classes increasingly felt that they were superior to any other people in the world. They saw themselves as the rulers of the Empire, although it was rare for them to actually participate in governing its affairs. In this way, the discourse of masculinity gave priority to the identity of ruler of the Empire, while diminishing, though not extinguishing, the internal conflicts between classes or races in Britain, and thus minimising the possibility of the advent of a Fascist regime.

Literature also played its own part in disseminating the discourse of masculinity. In the late nineteenth and early twentieth centuries, a large number of adventure stories were published. The most popular plot lines were that the heroes came across barbarians in Africa or Asia, conquered and ruled over them. Rudyard Kipling's fiction like *The Jungle Book* and poems like 'The White Man's Burden' were, needless to say, the best examples. In many cases, the main characters of the stories were described as strong, unmarried, neatly dressed and respectable men. There was no place for women in these stories. The ideal type of colonial administrator or merchant in this fiction was a role model for public school boys. By the 1920s, even working-class children, in England and Wales at least, seemed to have shared this increasingly common aspiration, due mainly to the extension of the public school style of education to the level of the elementary school, which had been set up in these regions to give working-class children the opportunity to get basic practical training and elementary instruction.

Prefects in the public schools

Before dealing with the elementary school, however, it will be helpful to briefly look at the way the public schools nurtured their students' masculinity. According to Paul Nash, 'the stability, order and good administration which has obtained both at home and throughout the British Empire has been due in no small part to the excellent training in leadership and responsibility which the upper-class youth received as a prefect in a Public School'.[13] The public schools had, by the mid nineteenth century at least, begun to put emphasis upon sport, courage, self-discipline and self-reliance in order to prepare their students to become successful rulers of the Empire. 'The young Earl of Meath had brushed snow from his knees on the playing fields of Eton; a master snarled at him that if his forbears had minded a little snow, there would have been no British Canada, and if they had minded heat, no British India – "so never let me see you shrink from heat or cold." '[14] Educated in this way, the future rulers of the British Empire became increasingly obsessed with acquiring genuine masculinity.

One of the most popular tools for this purpose was the prefect system, which was remodelled into a modern form by Thomas Arnold at Rugby School in the early nineteenth century.[15] The main purpose of this system was to provide the students with the opportunity to exercise self-governing leadership. The students offered obedience to a worthy authority and embodied masculine character during the six years of school life. The prefects, chosen in most cases by the headmasters from among the members of the sixth form, were given important tasks such as 'governing the school, wielding discipline and carrying responsibility'.[16] They were expected to be physically and intellectually superior to their peers, and above all had to possess a suitable character to perform these tasks.

In the eighteenth century, the role of the prefects, or of their equivalents such as monitors or preposters, had been restricted to relatively trivial duties such as reporting offenders to the masters or taking the roll and recording absences. At the turn of the century, however, as increasing numbers of young aristocrats from a homogeneous social background entered the schools, the authority of the masters was challenged by the aristocrats' often rebellious defiance. As the number or authority of the masters did not increase, there were no better options but to accept the reality and let the student leaders take control of their peers. Under these circumstances, the 'fags', the new boys entering the schools, had to do whatever they were told to do by their seniors. In many schools, the prefects even used corporal punishment on younger students.

It was Arnold who refashioned this system into a more manageable one. His motto was the *esprit de corps* of the students, and in order to put it into practice he conferred as much authority as possible on his prefects, asking the masters to treat them and the members of the sixth form as a whole with due respect. By this process, 'the corps of prefects became the commissioned officers in "General" Arnold's crusading army'.[17] The prefects constantly received their instruction from Arnold, internalising aristocratic responsibility, which soon became one of the most important aims of a public school education. According to contemporary observers, the effect of this system was to 'suppress eccentricity and individuality; to foster the worship of "good form"; to idealise boy values like physical strength and athletic prowess; and to help shape the Public School product as a respectable, conventional, conservative fellow'.[18] It is not difficult to find the discourse of masculinity and aspirations for modernity in these observations. During the course of the nineteenth century, along with the expansion of the British Empire, this trend continued to spread among the public schools and established itself as the norm for secondary education in Britain.

Prefects in the elementary schools

By the 1920s, a number of the elementary schools, particularly in England and Wales, seemed to have adopted the prefect system. A pamphlet of educational essays on the introduction of the prefect system to the elementary schools, edited in 1921 by the Education Committee of the Warwickshire County Council, included a 'Summary of Head Teachers' reports on Prefect Systems in Warwickshire Elementary Schools, by the Director of Education for Warwickshire (March 1913)':[19]

> In the Autumn of 1911, as an outcome of Sir Robert Baden-Powell's address to Warwickshire teachers, a Conference of Head Teachers was held on Prefect Systems in Elementary Schools. It was then decided that all the Head Teachers present should try the system for a year, each one on his or her own lines, and then report as to its working. Nearly all have now made reports, one only having failed without good cause. Reports have come in from 6 large or middling boys' schools, 3 large girls' schools, 2 large mixed schools, 11 middling and small schools mostly in villages, and 1 infants' school, 23 in all, embracing schools of practically every type.

According to the Director of Education, 'the record, with one exception, is a story of success, in most cases of extraordinary success, so much so as to put the possibility and value of the system beyond a doubt'.

Such conviction can also be found both in Jewsbury's article in the pamphlet on the prefect system in elementary schools and in the 'Introduction' contributed by Robert Baden-Powell. On the page of the pamphlet previous to the 'Introduction', Bolton King from the 'Education Office, Warwick, February 1921' wrote, 'This Pamphlet was originally published in 1903. Experience has only strengthened the belief in the value of the Prefect System. During the past 8 years it has spread far and wide.' The 'Pamphlet' clearly refers to Baden-Powell's Introduction, Jewsbury's article and the Director's Summary on the following pages, but why it was 'the past 8 years', not '18', is not clear. As the Addenda to Jewsbury's article and 'Summary of Head Teachers' reports' dealt with cases after 1911, as shown in the text quoted above, there is little possibility that 'February 1921' was actually 'February 1911'. It can thus be supposed that the error occurred either in the phrases 'the past 8 years' or in 'originally published in 1903': they should be corrected to '18' or, more likely, '1913'. Whatever was the case, it is certain that the prefect system in elementary schools was still broadening its supporting base in the 1920s, when the pamphlet in question was printed.

Baden-Powell's 'Introduction' clearly demonstrates the ideal purpose of elementary education:[20]

On visiting a great Agricultural School in Australia recently I asked the Principal to tell me briefly what was the general trend of his training.

'Character first, then Agriculture,' was his reply. I should like to hear a similar answer in any school where such a question was asked.

Character is essential to a successful career in whatever line of life – more so than 'the three R's.' And yet, though these are now taught by most enlightened methods, there is so far no practical training in character in the elementary schools. It will assuredly have to come, but at present the formation of a child's character is left to its home environment, which is generally not of the best.

Character-training to be effective must begin early in the child's life – in the elementary school in fact.

Two important points to aim for in such training are the development of

Sense of Duty,

Sense of Responsibility,

as bases for the many other qualities necessary to good citizenship.

Baden-Powell saw the elementary school as the starting point for 'character-training'. At first glance, its purpose may seem to be purely educational or ethical. However, character training had long been the motto for training young elites at the public schools, the men who would rule the British colonies in the future. With the fact in mind that elementary schools were mainly for working-class children, it is not difficult to deduce that elementary education began to tune itself to the rhythm and harmony of the Imperial Symphony, conducted by the public schools.

This picture becomes even clearer if we look at the latter half of Baden-Powell's 'Introduction'. He continued to praise the introduction of the prefect system into the elementary schools, comparing it with his Boy Scout movement:

> It is generally acknowledged that the supremacy of a nation does not lie in its arrangements but in its character, and a nation can only have character where the individuals composing it are trained men of character.
>
> In the Boy Scout movement therefore we have always had as our aim the development of character in each boy. Our system for inculcating this is, inter alia, to put responsibility on to the shoulders of the boy, to take him seriously and to expect a great deal of him.
>
> We effect this by making the 'Patrol,' of six boys, our unit for work, under the permanent command of one boy with the rank and badge of 'Patrol Leader,' assisted by a 'Second' of his own selection. The Patrol Leader is held responsible for all that goes on in his Patrol. The results have been successful beyond expectation.
>
> A scheme somewhat similar in principle is now being tried in the Elementary Schools in Warwickshire, in 'the Prefect System': it is giving most encouraging results, as will be seen from the following interesting reports; and I believe that it may prove a solution of the question 'How can Character be taught in our Elementary Schools?'
>
> If from this beginning a general method of character-education comes to be adopted by teachers, I am convinced it will be a move forward that may be of the highest value to our nation.

It is not surprising to see Baden-Powell link the prefect system with the supremacy of the British nation, not least because he began the Scout movement as military training, based on his own experiences in South Africa. He juxtaposed 'little' prefects with the 'Patrol Leader'. It should also be noted that he confined his views strictly to boys, though the girls' schools and mixed elementary schools were also adopting the prefect system. The character he referred to as the essence of the supremacy of the British was an exclusively masculine trait.

Jewsbury's article, which constituted the centre of the pamphlet, proposed the ideal type of prefect system, which seems to have later been adopted by many Warwickshire elementary schools, according to Bolton King's assessment in 1921.[21] Jewsbury began his article by summarising and praising Thomas Arnold's prefect system, but his major aim was to 'review the objects and methods of the Prefect System, and to consider the introduction of similar methods based on the same principles into Elementary Schools'. Having observed that 'Grammar and Secondary Schools (non-boarding)' adopted this system, he argued that it was time for elementary schools to adopt it.

Jewsbury's idealised prefect system consisted of 'Head Prefect, District Prefects, School Prefects, Class Prefects and Reserve Prefects'. The head prefect had the most power and authority. He or she 'presides at Prefects' meetings in absence of Head Teachers, receives reports from other Prefects, takes minutes of meetings, writes weekly report for the Head, acts as intermediary between the Head and the Prefects as a body or any particular class, receives and transmits to the Head any personal complaints if desirable or necessary'. District prefects were in charge of the districts in which they lived, watching and influencing 'the behaviour of the school children on their way to and from School, in the evenings or whenever and wherever they can'. School prefects were assigned various activities: playground prefects; gate prefects; sports prefects; corridor prefects; cloakroom prefect; lavatory prefect; latrines prefects; late prefect; woodwork, cookery, swimming, garden prefects; dinner room prefects; and needlework prefects. Each class has class prefects, and 'A list is kept of pupils from which new Prefects are elected as vacancies occur.' They were called reserve prefects.

Who made good candidates for the prefects? 'The Prefects will be those who can set the example', Jewsbury emphasised, 'exert the influence, and give a lead in the paths which the Head has indicated'. The most important thing they should possess was 'sound character':

> Truthfulness is essential above all things; one must be able to rely on the word of a Prefect. He should be thoughtful and able to act on his own initiative, self-reliant and reliable. In the playground and on the sports field and wherever children act as their nature dictates, opportunities will occur for noting those pupils whose tendencies are in the right direction. Here also it will be easy to note those who take a natural lead and evidently influence the conduct of their associates. If their influence is for good, so much the better; if not, all the more necessary is it that we should get hold of them, and use them for the good of the school. Such pupils, of strong character, but unruly and often worse, make good prefects. As such, they not only shed their own defects but exert an enormous influence on others .... Character before brains.[22]

It is not difficult to imagine who was regarded as the ideal candidate for the prefects and what 'sound character' meant among students and teachers under these circumstances. Sound character was a synonym for strong character.

Unlike the public schools, the prefects in elementary schools were often elected 'by pupils', who would 'back up and obey one chosen by themselves more readily than one appointed by someone else and put in authority over them'. In most cases, 'the fear that they will choose an unworthy candidate is not verified by experience', because 'boys were always right, masters sometimes, parents never'. In addition, the prefects were given privileges as well as duties:

1. Special badges to be worn on caps or coats (rosettes or badges on breast or shoulder for girls). Metal or cloth badges bearing the County Arms and also the word Prefect or Monitor are supplied by the Warwickshire Education Committee.
2. Head prefect's name emblazed on Honours Board.
3. Certificates on appointment to be completed on leaving.
4. Prefects could enter school before the rest, stay in when they please (if their duties permit), have free access to cupboards and library for books.
5. Not fall in lines *or* have special places.
6. Special places in school assembly.

The prefect system reproduced hierarchical social relations in miniature! Although the students might have learned democracy through the election of prefects, they also experienced everyday life in which there was a marked discrepancy between ordinary students and the prefects, and between the prefects and the head prefect. This also reminds us of the British political system, in which democracy, aristocracy and monarchy are jumbled together.

The Addenda to Jewsbury's article, 'Copies of Reports and Minutes of Meetings made by Prefects at Various Elementary Schools', demonstrates in more detail how the prefects exerted their influence upon ordinary students:[23]

At a meeting of the Prefects on Wed., Oct. 30, at 12–5, the headmaster being present, the conduct of J. B—, a Prefect was brought forward. It appears that B— began fighting. The Prefects who saw the quarrel gave accounts. After a short discussion, the Headmaster asked B— what he had to say for himself. He gave no answer, showing he was in the wrong. Then the master asked him to retire. It was then decided to put him on the reserve List till after Christmas.

In this particular case, it seems that the authority of the prefects was not as great as that in the public schools, as they just reported the student's conduct to the headmaster instead of punishing him on their own authority. However, the accounts by the prefects were respected by both J. B— and the headmaster, so they played the most important role in deciding his punishment. As prefects' meetings were usually held once a week, the everyday life of the students was under constant control of the prefects.

The students were living in a strictly hierarchical order, which reflected the real social relations outside their schools. While ordinary students learned how to obey authority, the prefects learned to discharge their authority through their own responsibility. They tried at least, as the following incident shows:

A short Meeting of the Monitors was held in Standard IA room on Thursday dinner time, April 18th, 1912. The chief question to be discussed was the punishment to be inflicted on several boys who had not shewn the true monitorial spirit in front of younger boys. It was agreed that they should be suspended until the 22nd. A new Secretary was wanted. B— was proposed by A— and seconded by G—, and was unanimously elected.[24]

This record shows that the prefects, called monitors in this case, did make important decisions such as inflicting punishment on their peers. In this sense, the prefects did practice self-government.

The Director of Education for Warwickshire also approved of the authority exerted by the prefects in his Summary by arguing that the essential part of the prefects' work is 'to lead, to influence for good, to uphold the school's honour, if necessary to punish'. According to a headmaster, the prefects of 12 or 13 years of age 'value their position highly and are very careful to do nothing to imperil it'. Another headmaster reported, 'the prefects view their position and authority with pride, and are careful by their actions, speech and manners to be a pattern to the other children'. The Director felt proud that 'from one school the only two prefects who have joined the army became full sergeants in three years', alluding to the military implications of the prefect system.

The Director, believing that the prefect system was 'of immense value to the school in creating a tone which it would have been difficult to obtain in any other way', was still more impressed by the conduct of younger students:

> Equally remarkable is the effect on the other children. They have quickly learnt to respect and obey, especially where they themselves elect the prefects; they regard them as the guardians of the school honour, and come to share their care for that honour; the weaker ones look to them for protection; and every boy with ambition looks to the day when he will be a prefect himself and honours the post accordingly. That wholesome deference to older boys, the embryo hero-worship, which is thought to be the slow product of Public School tradition, shows itself suddenly and without effort in schools without a past and where the heroes are children of 12 and 13 only. The authority of the prefects is undisputed, their punishments are accepted.[25]

He was sure that such an effect would not be confined to the elementary schools. 'Where the system is properly developed', he observed, 'the prefect's influence is felt in streets or roads, and especially on the way to and from school.' Even an infant school adopted the system, having children of six and seven with 'a monitor's bow of ribbon', 'take care of the younger children and remove the dust which has escaped the caretaker's eye'. The Head Mistress of the infant school was reported to say that the system 'encourages those dull children whose character is in advance of their intellect, and gives them new confidence and interest'.

Jewsbury was also interested in expanding the benefits of the prefect system. Although this system was also being adopted by some girls' elementary schools, he concentrated on boys, only intermittently including girls in his story. 'The system of boy government and control', he said, 'as carried on in the great schools of this country is, one may say without fear of contradiction, a most potent instrument in producing those fine qualities of character which we are proud to call English.' He wanted to share the benefits of this system with ordinary people:

> But is it not exclusively to the Public Schools that one must go to find boys who know what honour and duty mean. Birth and breeding count for much but they are not everything. Nature's gentlemen are to be found in all ranks and conditions.... Let it be our ambition to bring down from the schools and colleges to the schools of the people those methods and aims of school boy training which are admitted to have had so great and so ennobling an influence on our national character.[26]

Led by these teachers, British boys of ordinary backgrounds were encouraged to internalise public school virtues in their everyday life. Consequently, the prefect system was at the core of character training, itself at the core of education in Britain. Certainly, the procedures of selecting the prefects and organising their meetings in the elementary schools were far more democratic than those in the Hitler Youth (1922–45) and its junior branch, the Socialist Schoolchildren's League (*c.* 1929–33) in Nazi Germany. In addition, the development of this system was not initiated or led by the government, whereas its German counterparts developed into a paramilitary organisation of the Nazi Party. Indeed, these German organisations were under direct control of the Nazi leadership and closer to political movements than educational institutions. The Hitler Youth, for instance, 'rejected the authority and competence of all teachers who failed to act as "real youth leaders" '.[27] This makes a good contrast with the British prefect system in which students learned deference to existing authority. In this sense, there seems to be a remarkable difference between Britain and Nazi Germany. However, just as the German youth movements were mobilised to promote hatred towards the social order in the Weimar Republic and the financial capitalism allegedly controlled by Jews, so did the prefect system play an important role in sustaining a discriminatory political system: the British Empire. Jewsbury also invoked Kipling to stress such a linkage:

> Kipling has told us in many stirring passage of the youthful middies and officers and their shrill unbroken voices; how, at an unforeseen difficulty they have jumped into a breach and magnificently led bodies of men in positions of great danger. What is the secret of the power of these boys to act like real men? They have learned at school young as they are to govern and lead others, young as they are they have learned to bear and to assume responsibility; they have learned to recognise duty and to do it, and the bearded veteran or hoarse-throated tar eagerly follows to the sabre's point or the cannon's mouth the piping treble of the erst-while school Prefect.[28]

The British, regardless of their social status, were forced to accept public school virtues through the prefect system and were constantly reminded of their superiority as rulers of the Empire. In other words, the government did not have to use coercive methods to encourage national pride or to artificially redefine the existing social order to find 'others' against whom to discriminate. To the British, the status quo was a synonym of superiority. The masses were aware that in order to maintain the status quo, all they had to do was respect the existing systems constructed by the elites, whether political, economic or social. The adoption of the prefect system by the elementary schools was a good example of this tendency.

Girls' elementary schools

What happened to girls then? It seems that Jewsbury's perception of gender roles was typical of British men in this period. He argued that girls were, by their nature, 'more inclined to a regime of law and order, to the side of decent and considerable conduct'. He believed that as girls were more easily influenced by personal example and advice, they would adopt the views of the head mistress and follow her suggestions 'with unbound confidence' and 'their loyalty is a thing to marvel at'. Based upon his own experience at a rural mixed school, he concluded that girls did 'exceedingly well as District Prefects, especially in watching over the conduct of pupils on the way to and from school and in taking care of little ones whose homes are a good distance from the school'. He added that girls were generally more punctilious than boys. In this way, Jewsbury made a clear distinction between the aptitudes of boys and girls. It seems that he was following the classic dichotomy of public/private spheres.

Geraldine Coster, Principal of Wychwood School, Oxford, wrote a pamphlet entitled 'Self-Government in Schools'.[29] According to this pamphlet, it seems that the prefect system, or its equivalent, was accepted by elementary schools of regions other than Warwickshire: 'A very few years ago self-government was the watchword of a small handful of experimental or "freak" schools in America and Europe. At the present day the idea is everywhere, and a considerable percentage of English schools have accepted the theory, and in some form or other the practice, of self-government.' The major purpose of Coster's pamphlet was to explain the school's self-government system to the parents. Although this school also adopted the prefect system, Coster took a slightly different attitude towards it:

> In some schools the term self-government is used to describe a slightly modified form of the prefect system, and it is supposed that if you adopt the innovation of having your prefects elected by the pupils instead of appointed by the head, you have done the trick. A much more dangerous misapprehension of the idea is to take the dictum that 'the child knows best' quite literally, and suddenly and incontinently to leave it to him to do what he can or what he chooses about the discipline of the school, while the staff is bidden to desist

from interference, but to continue to teach as best it may. Teachers and parents who have suffered from this particular form of travesty are naturally bitter opponents of the system.[30]

If Coster was opposed to the idea of allowing the students to make their own decisions, what did 'self-government' mean? 'What it properly means', she stressed, 'is that staff and children combine to manage school affairs on a basis of co-operative amity, and thus the "self" of self-government is neither the staff nor the pupils, but the school as a whole.' In addition, it was always the teacher that 'actually does the governing', and the children's governing was mainly through 'suggestion'.

Compared with the prefect system of boys' elementary schools, idealised by Jewsbury, the modified 'self-government' system of Wychwood School put more weight on the authority of the teachers than of the prefects, who were alternatively called 'Head Girl' and 'Representatives' (that is, councillors, deputies and so on) to avoid a masculine impression, and on virtues such as justice, equity, the 'inward meaning of law and order' and 'a realisation that anarchy is slavery'. Girls were taught to be more cautious than boys in exerting authority upon students:

To be given a certain amount of power and responsibility between twelve and fourteen, when your class-mates will fall upon you tooth and nail if you show any symptoms of being 'bossy,' is an invaluable training, and is very different from being given large powers at a later age, when class-mates will resent your behaviour in silence, and even teachers will think twice before humiliating you.[31]

The Head Girl's motto was 'He that is greatest among you shall be your servant.' As such, girls were expected to learn through the often modified prefect system how to conform to the existing hierarchies. It seems that Coster also was aware of the national interest of her 'self-government' system, boasting that 'the countries where Bolshevism works havoc are those where the people have had least experience in self-government'.

Conclusion

Although the prefect system in the public schools has tended to be regarded simply as a tool for leadership training, it was actually where masculinity was embodied by the public school boys. The masculine virtues they acquired were essential to become the ruling elites of the

British Empire, which provided a number of 'others' to be discriminated against as abnormally feminine and thus inferior groups. The fact that the prefect system began to be extended to the elementary schools in the early twentieth century shows that these virtues were now embraced not only by the elites but also by segments of the larger population. The 'self-government' of the elementary schools might look at first glance democratic and thus very different from its Nazi counterpart. This system, however, put much emphasis upon the deference to the privileged and their authority, preserving the imperial implications of the prefect system in the public schools.

By the interwar period, virtually all the British had been imbued with a strong sense of duty, responsibility, honour, hierarchy and superiority, all of which were vital to the maintenance of order both in domestic and colonial society. The prefect system, adopted by increasing numbers of elementary schools in the preceding years, played an essential role in this process. The embodiment and performance of masculinity from the early stages of life must have exerted a heavy influence upon the identity of British men. The belief that the British retained a strong and rational masculinity regardless of which class they belonged to was shared by more and more Britons, and this belief was complemented by a complex set of gender discourses. It might well be said that the well-known phenomenon of social imperialism was stimulated by the embodiment of masculinity. British women were also expected to share this view.

The fact that the British exported their educational system, often with the prefect system, to their colonies implies that this kind of gender discourse and social hierarchy was increasingly regarded as an ideal type of social relations even among the colonised. For example, according to Rennie Smith, who travelled to East Africa in the late 1920s and early 1930s, some schools such as the Native Industrial Training Depot on the outskirts of Nairobi with 600 pupils for three years of practical education, or Makerere College at Kampla, 'destined to be the first university in Africa', adopted the prefect system. The prefects were usually in charge of dormitories or Houses and had to report to their European instructors or lecturers. Even here, the education of girls was usually confined to 'the development of new pride in personality and diversion of sexual energy through gymnastics, sports, etc.' as in the case of the Evans Schools at Khartoum.[32] Consequently, the most significant effect of the prefect system in the context of colonialism was to perpetuate a discriminatory gender discourse.

In this sense, the British were not very different from their Fascist neighbours. Both of them drew upon gender discourse to uphold their regimes. Only their targets of discrimination were different: European Jews or non-European colonised. It is interesting to observe that the British have not yet broken away from this perception. While other Western European countries came to realise after World War II, or the fall of the Cold War at least, that modern ideologies such as nationalism and racism could lead to catastrophic consequences, Britain still seems to cherish the idea of nation-state, as shown in their sceptical attitude toward the European Union. Ironically, the British who led the modernisation of the world two and a half centuries ago are nowadays lagging far behind in the competition in this post-modern, transnational era.

Notes

1. W. Jewsbury, 'The Prefect System in Elementary Schools', *Educational Essays* 8 (Warwick: The Robert Spennell Press, 1921), p. 19.
2. How to define 'the masses' was another target of criticism.
3. Niall Ferguson, *Empire: How Britain Made the Modern World* (London: Allan Lane, 2003), pp. xvii–ix.
4. This simplistic account was criticised in Claudia Koonz, *Mothers in the Fatherland: Women, the Family and Nazi Politics* (London: Methuen, 1988).
5. Clare Midgley, 'Gender and Imperialism: Mapping the Connection', in Clare Midgley (ed.), *Gender and Imperialism* (Manchester: Manchester University Press, 1998), p. 6.
6. N. Chaudhuri and M. Strobel (eds), *Western Women and Imperialism* (Bloomington, IN: Indiana University Press, 1992), pp. 57–9; Sara Mills, *Discourses of Difference: An Analysis of Women's Travel Writing and Colonialism* (London: Routledge, 1993), p. 3. On the contrary, some research focuses on the roles played by males in the private sphere: Martin Francis, 'The Domestication of the Male? Recent Research on Nineteenth- and Twentieth-Century British Masculinity', *The Historical Journal* 45(3) (2002), pp. 637–52; John Tosh, *A Man's Place: Masculinity and the Middle-Class Home in Victorian England* (New Haven, CT: Yale University Press, 2007).
7. Although it is the English rather than the British males that took the initiative in this process, the distinction between them is less important than the fact that both of them referred to the ruling groups of the British Empire and that they were usually categorised into one group within the gender discourse.
8. Kathleen Wilson, *The Sense of the People* (Cambridge: Cambridge University Press, 1995), pp. 202–3.
9. Mrinalini Sinha, *Colonial Masculinity* (Manchester: Manchester University Press, 1995).
10. Although from a different perspective, the life of missionary wives in Jamaica is well portrayed in Catherine Hall, *Civilising Subjects* (Chicago, IL: University of Chicago Press, 2002), pp. 91–2, 95–6.
11. Jane Haggis, 'White Women and Colonialism: Towards a Non-Recuperative History', *Gender and Imperialism* (1998), pp. 45–75.

12. Kenneth Ballhatchet, *Race, Sex, and Class under the Raj: Imperial Attitudes and Policies and their Critics* (New York: St Martin's Press, 1980), p. 1.
13. Paul Nash, 'Training an Elite', *History of Education Quarterly* 1(1) (1961), pp. 14–21. Nash's statement was based on other materials: C. R. Allison, 'The Future of the Public School', *Journal of Education* 523 (1924); Gerard Fiennes, 'Public School Boys in Industry', *The English Review* 810 (1924); Ronald Gurner, 'The Public School System', *Journal of Education* 645 (1926).
14. Quoted in Brian Moynahan, *The British Century: A Photographic History of the Last Hundred Years* (London: Endeavor, 1997), p. 31. The Earl of Meath refers to Reginald Brabazon, 12th Earl of Meath, 1841–1929.
15. It was also called 'prefect-fagging' or 'prefectorial' system.
16. Nash, 'Training an Elite', p. 14.
17. Ibid., p. 17.
18. All quoted in ibid., p. 17.
19. Director of Education for Warwickshire, 'Summary of Head Teachers Reports on Prefect Systems in Warwickshire Elementary Schools', *Educational Essays* 8 (1913), p. 22.
20. Lieutenant-General Sir Robert Baden-Powell, K. C. B., 'Introduction', *Educational Essays* 8, 3rd edn. The year of publication is not certain. It must have been written sometime between 1903 and 1921.
21. W. Jewsbury, 'The Prefect System in Elementary Schools', *Educational Essays* 8 (1921), pp. 1–19.
22. W. Jewsbury, 'The Prefect System in Elementary Schools', *Educational Essays* 8 (1921), pp. 10–11.
23. 'Addenda: Copies of Reports and Minutes of Meetings Made by Prefects at Various Elementary Schools', *Educational Essays* 8, pp. 20–1.
24. 'Addenda: Copies of Reports and Minutes of Meetings Made by Prefects at Various Elementary Schools', *Educational Essays* 8 (1921), p. 21.
25. Director of Education for Warwickshire, 'Summary of Head Teachers Reports on Prefect Systems in Warwickshire Elementary Schools', *Educational Essays* 8 (1913), p. 23.
26. W. Jewsbury, 'The Prefect System in Elementary Schools', *Educational Essays* 8 (1921), p. 19.
27. Daniel Horn, 'The Hitler Youth and Decline of Education in the Third Reich', *History of Education Society* 45(3) (1976), p. 429.
28. W. Jewsbury, 'The Prefect System in Elementary Schools', *Educational Essays* 8 (1921), p. 18.
29. Geraldine Coster, *Self-Government in Schools: A Pamphlet for Parents, with an Appendix Containing the System in Use at Wychwood School* (Oxford: Basil Blackwell, 1923).
30. Geraldine Coster, *Self-Government in Schools: A Pamphlet for Parents, with an Appendix Containing the System in Use at Wychwood School* (1923), p. 1.
31. Geraldine Coster, *Self-Government in Schools: A Pamphlet for Parents, with an Appendix Containing the System in Use at Wychwood School* (1923), p. 9.
32. Rennie Smith, 'Education in British Africa. Part IV: Report on Visit to East Africa (Continued)', *Journal of the Royal African Society* 31 (1932), pp. 31–124, 255–281.

5
Between Fascism and Feminism: Women Activists of the British Union of Fascists

Woonok Yeom

Introduction

British fascism, in contrast to fascist movements on the Continent, in Germany and Italy, never acquired state power. The British movement failed to get any parliamentary seats in national elections, and British fascists never enjoyed the same status as their fascist colleagues in other European countries. The influence of British fascism in the political arena was relatively limited. The most important fascist organisation, Oswald Mosely's British Union of Fascists (BUF), even at its height in 1934, only had between 40,000 and 50,000 members. The BUF received little support in elections, gaining at best about a fifth of the vote in local elections in 1937, in East London. Shortly after the outbreak of World War II, 747 leading British fascist activists, including Oswald and Diana Mosely, were interned under Defence Regulation 18B 1(a).

However, British fascism's failure to gain power does not mean that it had no effect on British politics. Recent studies reveal that fascism was immanent in British political culture, and there was a rich soil in which fascism in Britain could develop.[1] Alan Sykes interprets Mosley's fascism as the 'radical right' together with Social Imperialism, Race Regeneration, the Union Movement and the National Front. It was not just a variant of the 'far right', but a 'third alternative', a 'third way' or a 'third position', 'beyond' or 'transcending' liberalism and the liberal political spectrum.[2] The nation was the main focus of fascism's political thinking, and the fascist individual considered himself a part of the national organic body. Seeking the regeneration of existing society through transformation of its political and socio-economic structure, British fascism required a new 'higher type of man'.[3]

Stefan Berger's comparative analysis has properly shown that Britain was not a totalitarian country, but Britain's total war system based on voluntary mobilisation and participation of the masses was far more centralised and effective than Germany's in World War II.[4] A state power based on spontaneity could show more powerful national unity than one that relied on compulsory mobilisation. The 'mass dictatorship' paradigm[5] suggested by Jie-Hyun Lim pays attention to the voluntarism of the masses. Given the existence of the 'radical right' tradition in British political culture and the affinity between mass democracy and fascism, the 'mass dictatorship' paradigm is useful not only in Germany and Italy but also in Britain.

Two remarkable studies on the history of women in interwar British fascism, Martin Durham's *Women and Fascism* and Julie Gottlieb's *Feminine Fascism: Women in Britain's Fascist Movement 1923–1945*, have been published in recent years.[6] Not only the release of official documents – the collection of Mosely family papers and the publication of new biographies of leading figures such as Diana Mosely – but also the theoretical development of gender history have stimulated historical research on women's agency in British fascism.

Julie Gottlieb's pioneering book provides exhaustively collected data about the lives, ideologies and motivations of the women who took part in British fascist organisations in the 1920s and 1930s, such as the British Fascists and the BUF. Focusing on the active participation of women in the fascist movement, she dispels any illusions that fascism was to be identified with the traditional conservative assumption that women's natural place was confined to the home. In particular, she deals with fascist women who fought as the vanguard of the Edwardian suffragette movement, reminding us that there existed more complexity in the women's suffrage movement than is often supposed.

As Roger Griffin rightly argues, however, Gottlieb ignores the recent 'new consensus' on the definition of fascism among scholars like Stanley Payne, Roger Eatwell and George Mosse. As a result, she fails to fully recognise that the momentum of fascism devoted itself to the creation of a new type of human being, or 'new man', and the fascist movement was an 'anthropological revolution' and 'cultural revolution'. Therefore even if her approach to gender history is advanced, 'the conceptual framework that she applies to generic fascism is disappointingly retrograde'.[7]

Prior to Gottlieb's work, Claudia Koonz deconstructed the dichotomy of victim or accomplice in her book, *Mothers in the Fatherland: Women, the Family and Nazi Politics*. Koonz's book and her subsequent debate with Gisela Bock revealed that women under the Nazi regime were not helpless victims but appropriated Nazi ideologies for their own sake as active agents.[8] The main concern of the mass dictatorship paradigm is to revive the masses as agents. The masses under dictatorship tried to satisfy their desires by negotiating with the fascist regime. The fascist revolution was not confined to men, and it attempted to forge not only 'new men' but also 'new women'. Therefore the gender politics of fascism provided women with a space in which women agents intervened.

I examine the women activists of the BUF and ask the questions: *how did women's agency operate in British fascism?* And *did they succeed in empowering themselves within fascist gender politics?* Koonz's thesis and the paradigm of mass dictatorship open the way for transcending 'the dichotomy of victim or perpetrator'. By deconstructing the conventional categories such as woman/man, private/public, feminism/antifeminism, this chapter aims to take a more nuanced approach to the history of fascism. In order to restore and theorise the subjectivity of women, it is essential to regard the woman as an agent, not as an object.

In particular, this chapter examines the relationship between feminism and fascism. How did the women's movement change after women's suffrage in 1918? How did this change influence fascism? And how did fascist women respond to the transformed feminist agenda after 1918? The first section of this chapter deals with the legacy of the suffrage movement. The second section addresses the conflicting politics of separate spheres based on the notion of gender differences in the Women's Section of the BUF. And the third section deals with fascist women's self-empowerment under 'new' feminism.

The legacy of the suffrage movement and women fascists

As Kevin Passmore points out, the emergence of women's responsibility is the current trend in the historiography of fascism not only for Britain but also for other European countries. The high proportion of women among fascist elites was not only a British phenomenon. The position of women in fascist movements requires that the main concepts that constitute generic fascism be reconsidered. Passmore says that the absence of gender in a theorisation of fascism 'in turn exposes inherent weaknesses in those theories, not just in terms of their exclusion of women, but of their very assumptions about the nature of society and of the methods of the human sciences'.[9]

In Britain there was no 'big name' woman fascist leader such as Gertrud Scholtz-Klink in Nazi Germany or Teresa Labriola in Mussolini's Italy. But women constituted 24 per cent of the BUF membership. There were 'many little' women activists in the BUF. For Gottlieb, considering the tradition of the Edwardian suffrage movement, the most striking cases were the suffragettes who converted to fascists. With Mary Richardson, Norah Elam and Mary Allen, the legacy of militant feminist struggle was imported into the fascist movement. They revived the extra-parliamentary methods and militancy of their earlier suffragette struggle, while deploring that the vote was an 'empty vessel' and democracy a 'sinking ship'.[10]

The eventual conversion of Richardson, Elam and Allen cannot be seen as an aberration or treachery to feminism when we recall that traces of proto-fascism have been identified in the suffragette movement. The Pankhursts' rule over the Women's Social and Political Union (WSPU) has been characterised as dictatorship. Both movements had the characteristics of nationalist chauvinism, strong leadership, hero-worship, palingenetic imagery and romantic longings for national regeneration. The suffragist Cecily Hamilton argued that the WSPU was 'the first indication of the dictatorship' and that Emmeline Pankhurst 'was a forerunner of Lenin, Hitler and Mussolini – the leader whose fiat must go unquestioned, the leader who could do no wrong'.[11]

The existence of ex-suffragette women in the BUF might seem ironic as the 'masculine spirit' of British fascism is usually considered hostile to militant feminism. However, the ex-suffragettes were welcomed by male fascist colleagues. They held prominent posts and organised the Women's Section within the movement. For Oswald Mosely himself, the suffragette heritage was not to be refused. Introducing Norah Elam to prospective constituents in 1936, Mosely declared that her candidacy 'killed for all time the suggestion that National Socialism proposed putting British women back in the home'.[12] On the one hand, the ideological role that women were expected to play was to construct a discourse in which the suffrage movement was the precursor of fascism. On the other hand, the BUF's ex-suffragettes themselves maintained that their claims went beyond the suffragette movement. It might be said that they tried to construct 'fascist feminism'.

In her article 'Fascism, Women and Democracy', Norah Elam recalled that the first woman to be elected to the House of Commons was the Sinn Fein Countess Markievicz and that the American Lady Astor became the first woman to take a parliamentary seat. She questioned whether women's representation was actually realised with women's suffrage in 1918 (for women over 30 years of age[13]) and universal suffrage in 1928. She said that both the Irish Markievicz and the American Astor could not represent real British women.[14] Elam's attitude was different from other feminists who were disappointed by the election of Lady Astor but warmly welcomed her, an American millionairess who had no previous connection with organised feminism, in the spirit of sisterhood.[15]

Elam said her candidacy in the 1918 election as an Independent, not Labour or Conservative, came from her own distrust of party politics that was in reality manipulated by wealthy financiers.[16] Her disappointment with politics and the gap between democracy in name and democracy in reality after women's suffrage drove Elam to find an alternative solution in fascism. For Elam, even after women's suffrage was granted, parliamentary democracy could not advance the feminist agenda of women's social and economic liberation or solve social problems such as unemployment and poverty.

The BUF attacked democracy as having fallen into the hands of financial elites, 'old gangs'. The deteriorated party politics could not represent the voices of the masses and it even systematically excluded extra-parliamentary politics. British fascism criticised the idea that 'one could make the House of Commons an exact replica of opinion outside ... and if it were possible it would be undesirable'.[17] In order to break away from parliamentary democracy and adopt the principle of direct representation, the BUF advocated vocational representation under the corporate state depicted by Mosely. With 'a vocational franchise, there would be an exact replica of opinion outside'.[18]

Mary Richardson's case is more dramatic than Elam's. In March 1914, Richardson slashed Velasquez's *Rokeby Venus* in the National Gallery as a protest against the arrest of Emmeline Pankhurst in Glasgow. Richardson joined the Labour Party in 1916. In 1922 and 1924, she ran respectively as a Labour and then as an Independent Labour candidate in Acton, on both occasions losing to the Conservative candidate. Before the outbreak of World War I she knew Mussolini well, when he was a prominent Italian socialist and the editor of *Avanti*. When the Italian fascists marched on Rome in 1922, she sent a letter accusing him of betrayal of the socialist principle.[19]

The conversion of the most infamous ex-suffragette to fascism was also highly welcomed, and Richardson rose to the position of Chief Propaganda Officer for the Women's Section of the BUF. In December 1933 it was announced that she had joined the BUF. Richardson explained that the reason was 'its policy of imperialism. ... I feel certain that woman will play a large part in establishing fascism in this country.'[20] She was well aware of her dual identities as a feminist and a fascist. When communist-feminist Sylvia Pankhurst attacked fascism, Richardson replied angrily. She could not understand why Pankhurst attacked British fascism in reference to Italian fascism. Pankhurst criticised fascism because Italian wives and children were subordinate to their husbands as the head of the household under fascist law.[21] Richardson went on to say that 'the position of women in Italy has never been on a par with that of British women.... As for pretending that fascism has degraded women by lowering their status in the eye of the law, this is unjust and utterly false.'[22] Unlike the women in Germany and Britain, Italian women did not yet have the right to vote (they received it only in 1945). Richardson thus argued that it was unfair to compare British women to Latin women.

As one of the outstanding ex-suffragette women, Mary Richardson felt pride in the militant suffragette heritage, and desired to fulfil the feminist agenda such as 'equal pay for equal work' in the fascist movement. But her commitment to fascism did not last long. By November 1935, Richardson had already disappeared from the fascist movement in Britain. She was expelled from the BUF for having organised a meeting to protest against the unequal pay of women employed by the movement. Richardson claimed, in a letter to a trade union official, that 'I had been expelled for daring to put forward demands to the great Mosely, whereby women would receive some measure of fair play. All the best women left when I was expelled.'[23] Two months after she left the BUF, it was reported that she spoke at a meeting of the radical feminist organisation, the Six Point Group.[24] Among the ex-suffragettes, she was the only one who questioned the sincerity of the BUF's policy on women.[25] The breakaway of Richardson and her followers may have been connected with plans to reorganise the fascist movement, as it coincided with other changes in the BUF's policy on women.

After the failed attempt of Mary Richardson's 'fascist feminism', how did women engage in fascist gender politics as agents? Before analysing mechanisms for the empowerment of women in the BUF, I examine the conflicting politics of separate spheres based on the notion of gender difference in the Women's Section of the BUF.

The Women's Section in the BUF: separate spheres and patriarchy

Women activists and supporters recalled their participation in the BUF as a conversion. Fascist women's self-fashioning took on a kind of pseudo-religious form. Fascism was a secular religion, and Mosely was adored as the Messiah saving British civilisation from degeneration. Some have argued that women found the Leader's Blackshirt uniform and his well-trained body sexually attractive and that sublimated sex appeal created their sense of unity with him. As Wilhelm Reich stated in *The Mass Psychology of Fascism*,

> The effect of militarism is based essentially on a libidinous mechanism. The sexual effect of a uniform, the erotically provocative effect of rhythmically executed goose-stepping, the exhibitionistic nature of militaristic procedure, have been more politically comprehended by a salesgirl or an average secretary than by our more erudite politicians.[26]

However, leader-worship, the mechanism of libido and Reich's 'sex-economic psychology' do not satisfactorily explain women's devotion to fascism. Even though young girls threw flowers from windows and gave fascist salutes when a Blackshirt procession passed by, they did not remain in a state of mysterious emotion and blind acceptance. In an issue of the British fascist periodical *Action*, a woman reporter interviewed members of the BUF about why they joined the movement and what policies of the movement particularly appealed to them. Concerned about her children's unemployment and precarious future, a working-class mother said 'The most important one concern (is) my children.... They're all hard working lads, but I never know from week to week whether they'll be in work.... There's no security anywhere. My youngest boy, Bill, he's out of work at this moment.'[27] In another issue, *Action* featured the voice of Josephine Bradley, a journalist who had worked for over 15 years in Fleet Street, London. She contended that 'in Germany and Italy the Press was controlled in the interests of the State, whereas in Britain the control is exercised in favour of a certain section of the community, the advertisers' and she was 'absolutely disgusted at the Press of this country'.[28] That was why she joined the BUF.

In March 1933, the BUF institutionalised women's support and desires through the establishment of the Women's Section under the leadership of Maud Lady Mosely. Ann Page, who joined the Women's Section in 1933, recalled,

> believing as we did in the equality of the sexes, we took part in the same political activities as the men: sales drives, leaflet distribution, whitewashing slogans on walls, door to door canvassing, meetings

and marches, and in much the same leisure activities too: cycling, cricket, swimming, athletics, fencing and judo, even football and flying.[29]

Women who transcended separate spheres were chosen as role models for the BUF women. In particular, contemporary women pilots were selected as heroines. In 1934 the BUF established a special Flying Club for women in Gloucestershire.[30] *Action* reviewed two books written by women aviators, *Last Flight* by Amelia Earhart[31] and *My Life* by Jean Batten.[32] In both cases, the reporter emphasised their accomplishments in breaking records in flying and praised their bravery and adventurous spirit. Together with science and technology, speed is one of the most outstanding symbols of modernity. During the interwar years, aviation was the new technology that showed modernity in a dramatic way. It was logical and natural that the aviatrix emerged as the most suitable metaphor for women's liberation from all restraints of life on the ground.

Yet, while mixed-sex political and physical activities seemed prevalent in the BUF, it was also true that there existed a separate-sphere ideology that split men from women. A blurred dividing line was drawn between men's and women's spheres. There was antipathy toward the interests of feminists in the BUF, and some members of the BUF called for the cessation of sex war and sex antagonism in the name of national community. The ambiguous roles of women in the movement ranged from stereotypical traditionalism to the 'fascist feminism' seen above. The way the members understood womanhood varied.

A conventional separate-sphere ideology was frequently expressed in the pages of BUF periodicals such as *The Blackshirt*, *Action*, *The Fascist Week* and *The Woman Fascist*. In 1938, for instance, a woman fascist named Dinah Parkinson noted that 'to say a woman is equal or superior to a man is as ridiculous as to declare that bread is equal or superior to water. Both are vitally necessary in their own sphere.'[33] Acquiescence to separate spheres was also visible in the pages of *The Woman Fascist*, a short-lived fortnightly newspaper published by women fascists themselves.[34] It urged women who were not breadwinners to serve as volunteer canteen workers.[35] Unpaid charity work belonged to the traditional women's sphere in the Victorian and Edwardian periods, and charity work imposed upon women was a kind of labour exploitation that saved on social welfare expenses. Even though fascist 'women in blackblouses' marched arm in arm with 'men in blackshirts', it is undeniable that there existed a gendered division of labour between them.

Olive Hawks who joined the BUF in 1933 was one of the most frequent contributors to BUF publications such as *The Blackshirt, Action* and *The Fascist Week*. She became a member of the next generation of women fascist leaders, together with Ann Brock Griggs, after the ex-suffragettes departed from the BUF. In her articles about such themes as women's access to the labour market, the low wage labour of factory girls, unemployment and poverty, Hawks revealed the troubled gender politics of fascism. She published four novels between 1945 and 1952. *What Hope for Green Street?*, written during her internment throughout World War II, was the only one with a political theme.[36] In the novel, we can read not only her belief and disbelief in the masses but also her difficulty in positioning women's place within patriarchal structures.

In *What Hope for Green Street?* Hawks felt sympathy for the desires of the masses, but at the same time expressed despair at those who were not fascinated by 'fascinating fascism'.[37] One of the novel's characters, Peter, a clerk working at a clothing warehouse, says that he had hoped 'when I was older, I'd get moved to one of our grand West End branches'.[38] He reveals the unrelenting aspiration for upward social mobility. While feeling sympathetic to the desire of the masses to go up the social ladder, Hawks was disappointed that the masses did not seem interested in what fascism or communism stood for. Instead they were just busy chatting with one another on the sidelines of public rallies.[39]

A remarkable element in the novel pertinent to women is the story of an illegitimate child born of the heroine, Lilly and the hero, Charlie. The existence of illegitimate children might symbolise sexual freedom that could destroy the established family system, as the early feminist Mary Wollstonecraft had shown in the eighteenth century. There are no concerns, however, about the emancipation of women's sexuality in the novel. There are no narratives about the life of the unmarried mother and what she did for a living. Charlie neglects paternal duty and disappears, but Lilly's baby is warmly welcomed by Charlie's family. Despite his unemployment, Charlie's father accepts the baby, saying 'unless father does, grandfather must do'.[40]

Why does an illegitimate child appear in Olive Hawks's novel and why is the baby accepted by the paternal grandfather? The narrative of Hawks's novel reflects the troubles of British women fascists who struggled with the tantalising question of women's proper place in fascism. The story of an illegitimate child is a device that expressed the conciliation between a daughter once fallen and a benevolent father. Thus, the deviation from a monogamous family was resolved, and patriarchy remained safe against women's challenge.

British fascism continuously talked about national regeneration through 'fascist cultural revolution'. As a result these discourses were greatly concerned with women's bodies and womanhood as an instrument for the regeneration of the British race. In fact, racial discourse had the possibility to transcend patriarchy and monogamy, for racial thinking could advocate the necessity of care for unmarried mothers and illegitimate children. Considering the discourse of eugenics, a monogamous family might be an obstacle against 'better breeding'. Even if they were born outside of monogamous marriage, 'healthy and superior' children could contribute to race regeneration and thus they should be cared for. Another woman fascist Rosalind Raby, reporting on welfare policies in Italian fascism and the policy on illegitimate children in Nazi Germany, maintained that tolerance and better care for illegitimate children in Britain were necessary.[41] However, Olive Hawks cut off this potentiality in her novel and rushed into the arms of patriarchy. Therefore she seemed to block a way to subvert patriarchy. One may think that this development within the BUF meant that women's agency was ultimately subordinated to patriarchy. However, in the next section I try to show how this was not always the case.

Maternalist feminism and fascism

The women activists of the BUF tried to adjust their policies to align them with 'new' feminism or 'maternalist' feminism. After 1918, Eleanor Rathbone, a long-time member of Millicent Fawcett's National Union of Suffrage Societies (NUWSS), launched the National Union of Societies for Equal Citizenship (NUSEC). The NUSEC presented 'new' feminist issues in order to appeal to a much larger and broader mass of women. 'New' feminism focused on married women, not single women, as agents and objects of the women's emancipation movement. Eva Hubback who was inaugurated as the president of the NUSEC in 1933 proclaimed that feminists should pursue family allowance, birth control and maternal welfare legislation through state intervention. What was crucial for Hubback was to make motherhood attractive to women. For the eugenicist Hubback, 'new' feminism must include all reforms affecting human reproduction. Thus the NUSEC emphasised its activity as a pressure group for governmental support for welfare services supporting maternity and child rearing.[42]

One may easily find 'new' feminist agendas in the pages of *The Blackshirt*, *Action* and *The Fascist Week*. The Women's Section column dealt with issues such as the declining birth rate, the population question, hygiene, maternal mortality and child welfare. Olive Hawks and Ann Brock-Griggs contributed many articles to BUF publications on race regeneration through healthy childbearing and child rearing. However, it is noteworthy that these two women fascists kept silent on birth control while promoting race regeneration.

Why did they not talk about birth control? One answer can be found in Leader Mosely's view on birth control. Mosely addressed the questions of birth control and compulsory sterilisation of the 'unfit':

> Knowledge of birth control, like all knowledge which modern science affords, should be available to all who desire it. But again the new social sense of Fascism will secure the production of children of the fit, and the raising of the standard of life will further encourage it. At present, birth control is known and practised by the relatively well off. It is largely unknown and less practised by the very poor. The result is exactly the reverse of national interest. The patriotism which Fascism will awaken, coupled with a greater economic security, will lead to larger families among those who at present practise restriction. We will not deny knowledge to the people, for if they do not get good knowledge they are bound to get bad knowledge. But the new values of Fascist civilisation and the new social sense will prevent knowledge being hurtful. Those who rightly oppose present tendencies of birth control can alone secure the result they desire in the national awakening of Fascism.

> The unfit will be offered the alternatives of segregation sufficient to prevent the production of unfit children, or voluntary sterilisation – none will be sterilised against their will.[43]

Mosely approved birth control in principle, but his emphasis was put on pro-natalism among the affluent. Does the silence of women fascists on birth control mean that they followed the Leader's opinion? If this were true, it would be difficult to find evidence of women's agency regarding this issue. I would like to suggest another interpretation. In fact, not only Mosely but also almost all other male elite politicians advocated pro-natalism for the middle and upper classes and the restriction of births among the lower class. Women's main concern was not pronatal policy but practical information about birth control, and there was a gap between the government's policy and the needs of women.[44] British society saw a decline in the birth rate from the late nineteenth-century, and the concern about an aging population reached a peak in the 1930s.[45] In the years of demographic transformation, women who practised birth control were likely to be criticised as selfish. Women searched for more flexible and persuasive rhetoric in trying to negotiate the choice between birth control and motherhood.

It seems that what happened was that new feminist and fascist women sought to connect women's private bodies to the public sphere for the sake of the sacred national community. The BUF women activists mentioned only the high maternal mortality rate in their writings. In an article contributed to *Fascist Quarterly*, Ann Brock-Griggs shared that language with the new feminists. She expressed great concern about the rise of the maternal death rate, which was even higher than 20 years before. She blamed 'the lack of enough skilled ante-natal care, the shortage of beds in maternity and lack of supervision before and after birth'[46] for the rise in maternal mortality. However, she did not advocate for the necessity of birth control to protect women's bodies from frequent pregnancy. For Brock-Griggs, the existing governmental system could not ensure maternity and child welfare to the fullest extent. She rushed to the conclusion that the ultimate solution for this problem depended on the success of fascism and anticipated that 'fascism would restore the prosperity and importance of life'.[47]

In fact, the high maternal mortality could be a way of indirectly talking about the necessity of birth control. While infant mortality decreased remarkably thanks to sanitary reforms and rising wages after World War I, maternal mortality still remained high even in the 1930s. The various campaign groups for birth control, ranging from the pro-eugenicist Marie Stopes's Society for Constructive Birth Control and Racial Progress (SCBCRP) to the anti-eugenicist Worker's Birth Control Group (WBCG) founded by Dora Russell and Stella Browne, used the same argument of the high maternal mortality rate to justify their causes.[48] In short, maternal mortality was a prudent strategy for speaking about birth control both for birth control advocates and for women fascists.

After the Maternal and Child Welfare Act was passed in 1918, local authorities set up committees and provided welfare services, including salaried midwives, health visitors, infant welfare centres, antenatal clinics and food for mothers and infants in need. Those services were welcomed by women. The number of antenatal clinics run by local authorities rose from 995 in 1931 to 1307 in 1937 and the percentage of women attending from 33 per cent to 54 per cent.[49] Despite the discontent of Ann Brock-Griggs, more and more women were benefiting from maternal and child welfare services. However, by the mid

1930s, the case for birth control as a means to further the welfare of the individual woman was outweighed by fears of a declining population and by the growth of pro-natalism. By 1937, only 95 local authorities out of 423 maternal and child welfare authorities had established birth control clinics.[50] The 1920s witnessed the active development of birth control groups such as the SCBCRP, the WBCG and the National Birth Control Association, but the Ministry of Health did not abandon the policy of prohibiting the circulation of birth control and contraception information. It was as late as 1930 that the Ministry of Health issued Memorandum 153/MCW, reluctantly authorising local authorities to permit birth control advice '[i]n cases where further pregnancy would be detrimental to health'.[51]

The ideal representative of womanhood in a fascist corporate state was the 'mother' who took the holy responsibility of race regeneration as her biological destiny. Ann Brock-Griggs and other women fascists seem to have been prudent and strategic in promoting the cause of birth control through the issue of maternal mortality. As activists of the BUF, they wanted to become militant warriors, but simultaneously they did not reject women's duty to reproduce. The contradiction between warrior and mother could be solved in the utopia of the fascist corporate state. On the question of whether women would be eligible as representatives of corporations, Mosely answered,

> They will be eligible on all Corporations representing their industry or profession. In addition the great majority of women who are wives and mothers will for the first time be given effective representation by Fascism. A special Corporation will be created for them, which will have special standing in the State. That Corporation will deal with outstanding women's questions such as mother and child welfare. In addition, it will assist Government in such matters as food prices, housing, education and other subjects, in which the opinion of a practical housewife is often worth more than that of a Socialist professor or spinster politician.[52]

Mosely proudly talked about the harmony of woman's identity as worker, housewife and mother in the fascist corporate state, but it was hard for a woman to perform these roles at once in the real world. It was easier to confine women to limited spaces like the home. The ideal fascist womanhood was motherhood, 'mother of the race' in short, but it is important to recognise the differences between the traditional mother image and the modern fascist mother image. Unlike the highly moral and spiritual image of the traditional Victorian mother, the imagery of an ideal mother in fascism emphasised the virtues of vigour, health, charm and intelligence. Mothers and housewives, as consumers and designers of the home, were interested in the modernisation of the domestic sphere. Along with the fascist movement, the 1920s and 1930s saw the development of a consumer society in Britain. Fascist gender politics resonated with mass consumption. Reports on the annual 'Ideal Home Exhibition' sponsored by the *Daily Mail*, for example, were found in the columns of *The Blackshirt*.[53] The exhibition as well as women's magazines educated the housewives on ways of saving labour-time and the application of American scientific home management techniques. A report in *The Blackshirt* also emphasised the importance of proper diet and connected the health of the British race with the role of women in the kitchen.[54] The home became a laboratory of modernisation and national health.

The women fascists in the BUF employed such a maternalist discourse and thereby intensified patriarchy. Maternalism is not an antithesis to but a complement to paternalism. If patriarchy is a socio-symbolic culture, then both men and women may fortify or resist it. Women can and do support patriarchal culture as a means of empowerment. Women have never been merely victims of patriarchy, for they were the agents of conservative empowerment.[55] If we remember that in the interwar period, except for small groups of radical feminists, maternalist feminists and other women's organisations supported race discourses and eugenics, it is unfair to suggest that only fascism was 'anti-feminist'.

Conclusion

The Nazis' election proclamation for the presidential election of 1932 – *Adolf Hitler: Mein Programm* – states that 'work honours both man and woman. But the child exalts the woman'.[56] The idealisation of motherhood under fascism and maternalism was liable to produce reactionary gender politics. 'Old' feminists, or egalitarian feminists like Cicely Hamilton, criticised 'new' feminism and the institutionalisation of maternity because they demanded that women's bodies should 'always prepare to be pregnant'.[57] Another interwar feminist who attacked 'new' feminism saw the ideology of the BUF as a warning to those who valorised maternity and the domesticity of women, and quoted Mosely's declaration that 'we want men who are men and women who are women'.[58] However, the antagonism between 'equality' and 'difference' in feminism is a false dichotomy. What matters is the subjectivity and agency of women. In this sense, maternalism, like egalitarian feminism, could contribute to women's empowerment.

The participation of women activists in the BUF was a realistic choice for empowerment and enhancing women's agency, although it was a double-edged sword that blunted women's egalitarian demands. The ex-suffragettes Mary Richardson and Norah Elam tried to import the legacy of militant feminist struggle into the fascist movement. After the failed attempt of Richardson's 'fascist feminism', the women activists in the BUF like Olive Hawks and Ann Brock-Griggs adopted and reiterated the discourses of maternalist feminism and, as a result, incorporated the desires of a broad range of British women into the movement. The welfare services requested by maternalist feminism such as maternal and child welfare centres, antenatal clinics and family allowances were gradually realised through a series of new laws only after World War II. Because fascism failed to gain power, there was no space for fascism to implement its own policies on women. The process by which welfare services developed not only shows the flexibility of mass democracy in Britain, but also suggests that British women fascists negotiated between fascism and feminism.

Notes

1. Tony Kushner and Kenneth Lunn, 'Introduction', in Tony Kushner and Kenneth Lunn (eds), *Traditions of Intolerance: Historical Perspectives on Fascism and Race Discourse in Britain* (Manchester: Manchester University Press, 1989), p. 8; Kenneth Lunn, 'British Fascism Revisited: A Failure of Imagination?', in Michael Cronin (ed.), *The Failure of British Fascism: The Far Right and the Fight for Political Recognition* (London: Palgrave Macmillan, 1996), p. 174. For proto-fascism and racial theory, see also Dane Stone, *Breeding Superman: Nietzsche, Race and Eugenics in Edwardian and Interwar Britain* (Liverpool: Liverpool University Press, 2002).
2. Alan Sykes, *The Radical Right in Britain* (London: Palgrave Macmillan, 2005), p. 2.
3. Ibid., p. 63.
4. Stefan Berger, 'The Total War System in Germany and Britain', in Jie-Hyun Lim and Yong-Woo Kim (eds), *Daejung Dokjae: Gangjewa Dongui Saieso* (Mass Dictatorship Between Coercion and Consensus) (Seoul: Chaiksesang, 2004), pp. 149–74.
5. Jie-Hyun Lim, 'Historical Perspectives on "Mass Dictatorship"', paper presented at the RICH International Conference Mass Dictatorship between Desire and Delusion, Hanyang University, 17–19 June 2005.
6. Martin Durham, *Women and Fascism* (London: Routledge, 1998); Julie Gottlieb, *Feminine Fascism. Women in Britain's Fascist Movement 1923–1945* (London: I.B. Tauris, 2000).

7. Roger Griffin, 'Book Review: Julie Gottlieb, *Feminine Fascism*', *European History Quarterly* 32(4) (October 2002), p. 615.

8. Claudia Koonz, *Mothers in the Fatherland: Women, the Family and Nazi Politics* (New York: St Martin's Press, 1987); Gisela Bock, 'Die Frauen und der Nationalsozialismus: Bemerkungen zu einem Buch von Claudia Koonz', *Geschichte und Gesellschaft* 15 (1989), pp. 563–79.

9. Kevin Passmore, 'Theories of Fascism: A View from the Perspective of Women's and Gender History', paper presented at the RICH International Conference Mass Dictatorship and Gender Politics, Pyeongchang, Korea, 5–7 July 2006.

10. Gottlieb, *Feminine Fascism*, p. 147.

11. Cecily Hamilton, *Life Errant* (London: JM Dent and Sons, 1935), p. 68, quoted in Gottlieb, *Feminine Fascism*, p. 159.

12. *Action* 28 (November 1936).

13. The vote was partially granted in 1918 to women over 30 years of age who were householders, wives of householders, occupiers of property with an annual rent of 5 pounds or more or graduates of British universities.

14. Norah Elam, 'Fascism, Women and Democracy', *Fascist Quarterly* 1(3) (1935), p. 293.

15. Barbara Caine, *English Feminism 1780–1980* (Oxford: Oxford University Press, 1997), p. 205.

16. Elam, 'Fascism, Women and Democracy', p. 293.

17. The statement of Mr. Atlee, 6 December 1933, reported in the *New Chronicle*; 'Democracy Speaks Out', *The Fascist Week* 6 (15–21 December 1933).

18. 'Democracy Speaks Out', *The Fascist Week*.

19. Gottlieb, *Feminine Fascism*, pp. 75, 335–6.

20. 'Ex-Suffragette joins the BUF: Mussolini's Prediction', *The Fascist Week* 7 (22–28 December 1933).

21. Sylvia Pankhurst was one of the early and continuous critics of fascism. When she participated in an international communist conference held in Bologna, Italy in 1920, Pankhurst got an early glimpse of fascism when the British delegates, on entering a town hall reception at the mayor's invitation, were attacked by the Arditi, a group of thugs, the forerunners of the Blackshirts. The Arditi were inspired by Mussolini. Barbara Winslow, *Sylvia Pankhurst: Sexual Politics and Political Activism* (London: UCL Press, 1996), pp. 144–5.

22. Mary Richardson, 'My Reply to Sylvia Pankhurst', *The Blackshirt* 62 (29 June 1934).

23. Durham, *Women and Fascism*, p. 63.

24. Ibid., p. 65.

25. Gottlieb, *Feminine Fascism*, p. 152.

26. Wilhelm Reich, *The Mass Psychology of Fascism* (New York: Farrar, Straus and Giroux, 1970), p. 32.

27. *Action* 179 (29 July 1939).

28. *Action* 182 (19 August 1939).

29. Ann Page, 'The Suburban Housewife', in J. Christian (ed.), *Mosely's Blackshirts: The Inside Story of the British Union of Fascists* (London: Sanctuary, 1986), p. 16, quoted in Julie Gottlieb, 'Women and British Fascism

Revisited: Gender, the Far-Right, and Resistance', *Journal of Women's History* 16(3) (2004), p. 110.

30. Gottlieb, *Feminine Fascism*, p. 97.
31. Amelia Earhart, born in the USA, became the first aviatrix who succeeded in a solo flight across the Atlantic Ocean in 1932, but during an attempt to make an around-the-world flight in 1937 she disappeared over the central Pacific Ocean.
32. Jean Batten flew solo from England to Australia in 1934 and she became the best-known New Zealander.
33. Dinah Parkinson, 'Ideals of Womanhood', *Action* 109 (19 March 1938).
34. *The Woman Fascist* was a fortnightly duplicated typescript newsletter circulated to members of the Women's Section during 1934.
35. *The Woman Fascist* 6 (10 May 1934). *The Woman Fascist* was then incorporated into the 'Women's Section' column in *The Blackshirt* and *Action*.
36. Gottlieb, 'Women and British Fascism Revisited', p. 111.
37. The phrase 'fascinating fascism' is the title of an essay written by Susan Sontag on Leni Riefenstahl's *The Last of the Nuva*, photography of the Nuva tribes in Africa.
38. Olive Hawks, *What Hope for Green Street?* (London: Jarrolds, 1945), p. 21.
39. Ibid., p. 19.
40. Ibid., p. 50.
41. Rosalind Raby, 'Daughters of Martha', *The Fascist Quarterly* 2(1) (January 1936), pp. 47–57.
42. Women's Library: Hubback Papers, 'The Women's Movement – Has It a Future?', pp. 6–7; 'Obituary, Eva Hubback (Goldman, P) (1888–1949)', *Eugenics Review* 41 (1949–50), p. 141; Diana Hopkinson, *Family Inheritance: A Life of Eva Hubback* (London: Staples, 1954); Brian Harrison, *Prudent Revolutionaries: Portrait of British Feminism Between the Wars* (Oxford: Clarendon Press, 1987).
43. Oswald Mosely, *Fascism: 100 Questions Asked and Answered* (London: BUF publication, 1939), p. 4.
44. For the discrepancy and interaction between policy makers and female clients of maternal welfare services, see Jane Lewis, *The Politics of Motherhood: Child and Maternal Welfare in England, 1900–1939* (London: Croom Helm, 1980).
45. Pat Thane, 'The Debate on the Declining Birth-rate in Britain: The "Menace" of an Ageing Population, 1920s–1950s', *Continuity and Change* 5(2) (1990), p. 283.
46. Ann Brock-Griggs, 'The Real Wealth of the Nation', *The Fascist Quarterly* 1(4) (October 1935), pp. 436–7.
47. Ibid., p. 436.
48. For various birth control campaign groups, see Lesley Hoggart, 'The Campaign for Birth Control in Britain in the 1920s', in Anne Digby and John Stewart (eds), *Gender, Health and Welfare* (London: Routledge, 1996), pp. 143–88.
49. Lewis, *The Politics of Motherhood*, pp. 34–5, 152.
50. Ibid., p. 212.

51. Ministry of Health Memorandum, 'Birth Control', Memo 153/MCW, July 1930, quoted in Audrey Leathard, *The Fight for Family Planning: The Development of Family Planning Services in Britain 1921–74* (London: Macmillan, 1980), p. 49.
52. Mosely, *Fascism: 100 Questions Asked and Answered*, p. 2.
53. 'Ideal Home Exhibition: Olympia until April 24th', *The Blackshirt* 208 (17 April 1937).
54. 'Fascism and the Kitchen: The Importance of Proper Diet', *The Blackshirt* 79 (26 October 1934).
55. Ralph M. Leck, 'Theoretical Issues: Conservative Empowerment and the Gender of Nazism. Paradigms of Power and Complicity in German Women's History', *Journal of Women's History* 12(2) (Summer 2000), p. 157.
56. Reich, *The Mass Psychology of Fascism*, pp. 60–1.
57. Susan K. Kent, 'The Politics of Sexual Difference: World War I and the Demise of British Feminism', *Journal of British Studies* 27 (July 1988), pp. 243–4.
58. Susan K. Kent, *Making Peace: The Reconstruction of Gender in Interwar Britain* (Princeton, NJ: Princeton University Press, 1993), p. 142.

6
Between Exploitation and Empowerment: Soviet Women Negotiate Stalinism

Karen Petrone

The Soviet Union was distinct from other mass dictatorships in the interwar period in that early Soviet family policy was the most liberal the world had ever seen. In the 1920s, the Soviet state squarely attacked patriarchal familial relations and destabilized marriage and the family. Soviet feminist thinkers such as Aleksandra Kollontai argued that 'the family is ceasing to be necessary either to its members or to the nation as a whole',[1] and the Soviet government enacted progressive legislation that allowed abortion, made divorce easy and broadened the definition of marriage to recognize 'unregistered' unions. This remarkably progressive attitude towards women's equality did not last however. Some scholars trace the Soviet impulse to control sexuality back to the early Soviet period and suggest that the liberatory impact of Soviet policies was always limited by the leadership's puritanical views of sexuality and their understanding of gender roles as strictly circumscribed by biology.[2] Other analysts suggest that the key turning point away from feminism was the 1930 closure of the *Zhenotdel* or Women's Department of the Communist Party. Still others posit that women's liberation was never a part of the Soviet program. Sarah Ashwin argues that 'the policy of the Bolshevik state was never directed at the liberation of women from men, it was directed at breaking the subordination of women to the patriarchal family in order to "free" both women and men to serve the communist cause.'[3]

Despite their disagreements on the degree of continuity and the timing of the changes, all scholars acknowledge that under Stalin, the state became simultaneously more authoritarian and more patriarchal. In 1936, abortion was criminalized and divorce laws were tightened;

women were encouraged to become mothers, and received special premiums for large families.[4] In the midst of World War II (1944) family laws became even more restrictive and pro-natalist policies even more extreme. While some view Stalinist policy towards women in the 1930s in terms of 'retreat' from earlier feminist aims because of lack of social support from the population, others view it in terms of a deepening of the authoritarianism already extant in the 1920s.[5] A third group of scholars suggests that Stalin's so-called 'great retreat' to patriarchy was contradictory and partial. They demonstrate that women's equality remained a central tenet of Soviet ideology and public representations of women throughout the Stalin era. Women were indeed encouraged to become mothers, but they were also encouraged to move into previously all-male spheres, to become tractor drivers, industrial workers, aviators, athletes, sharpshooters and defenders of the country.[6] Women were never enjoined to stay at home and housewives were systematically mobilized for community service outside of the home.

Analysts of women's agency in the Stalin period can be divided into those who frame their arguments as 'glass half empty' or 'glass half full'. Both sides of the debate recognize that Stalinist ideology about women and the realities that women faced diverged sharply from one another. Yet they interpret this divergence in significantly different ways and disagree about the extent to which Soviet discourse could effect change. Those seeing the 'glass half empty' interpret Soviet ideology as a façade that hid the systematic exploitation of women. Often emphasizing social and economic history, these scholars see the Soviet discourse of women's liberation as powerless to change the realities of exploitation. They argue that the unprecedented commitment to women's personal freedom of the early Soviet period had disappeared, and rather than as 'liberation', women's diverse social roles could be viewed merely as an expansion of 'the spheres in which women could be exploited.'[7] The industrial achievements of the First Five Year Plan were carried out on the backs of urban women who streamed into factories in order to ensure the economic survival of their families. Despite women's crucial economic roles and their entrance into a variety of new fields, notions of women's inferiority persisted. Many parts of the new socialist economy were gender-segregated by design with women being channelled into lower paying and less prestigious work.[8] In state planning, heavy industry took priority over services (such as nurseries, laundries and restaurants) that would have eased the domestic burdens of working mothers, leaving women responsible for both production and reproduction.

Some cultural historians have also pointed to the conceptual limitations on women's equality that were visible within Soviet discourse. While women who took part in socialist construction were often heroized in the Soviet media, the celebration of women's achievements often subtly implied that however heroic women were, men would always be one measure more heroic.[9] Women in non-traditional roles in World War II were depicted as 'girlish' and 'gentle and domestic.'[10] Like the 'double helix' model of women in the twentieth-century wartime economy, women moved up only in hierarchical relationship to men who always ascended higher up the spiral ladder than did women.[11] Thus the Soviet state exploited women and cast them permanently in a secondary and supporting role.

Those seeing the glass half full point to the ways in which Soviet discourse valourised women as equal participants in socialist construction, opening up new possibilities for women's self-definition and women's action. These scholars see Soviet discourse as playing a powerful role in shaping women's life choices and possibilities. Historian Choi Chatterjee asks that we keep in mind that 'the precise non-correspondence of ideology and reality constituted an important element of the Soviet experience.' She goes on to suggest that 'the capacity to articulate scenarios of radical change in women's lives was not merely a substitute for concrete action, but was itself a form of political practice.'[12] Some women were able to take action to bring about the radical changes envisioned by official discourse. 'Official' scenarios could transform real lives as the women deployed the state's enduring public rhetoric of equality to advance their personal goals.

Historian Anna Krylova, following Chatterjee, emphasizes the power of Soviet discourse about women in the World War II era; she argues that the hundreds of thousands of women who volunteered to go to the front in response to the German invasion in 1941 demonstrate the construction of an alternate femininity in the 1930s that 'encompassed and redefined the traditionally incompatible qualities: maternal love and military violence, feminine charm and military discipline, military excellence, professionalism, physical endurance, courage.' Krylova grants this new discourse about women enormous power, arguing that because of this new conception of femininity, 'the ultimate expansion of women's social space for self-realization took place in Stalinist Russia.'[13]

Those who see Soviet policy primarily in terms of exploitation tend to discount the power of ideology or to emphasize the contradictions in that ideology. Those who see Soviet policy as empowering tend to grant the ideology a significant amount of power in shaping the minds and lives of Soviet citizens. Before examining women's words about work and family, this chapter will address general notions of agency and subjectivity in the Stalin era in relation to Soviet ideology, the dilemmas of trying to define 'public' and 'private' in a Soviet context and the insights that might be gained from the study of Soviet everyday life. There is a thriving ongoing debate about the nature of 'public' and 'private' in Stalin's Soviet Union. Scholars such as Jochen Hellbeck and Anna Krylova have criticized Western liberal scholars (myself included) for our assumption that the Soviet citizen is a 'Western liberal subject' who conforms to Soviet state ideology in public life but is able to resist this ideology 'by retreating into private spheres unaffected by "official" ideology' or by maintaining a critical stance on this ideology from a subject position outside of it.[14] In his scholarship on Stalin-era diaries, Hellbeck suggests that the diarists' desires to perfect their revolutionary selves were not imposed from without but were evidence of 'individual agency, agency that is not autonomous in nature but is produced by, and dynamically interacts with, ideology.'[15]

Rather than being repressive of individual subjectivity, Hellbeck sees the Soviet state as productive of subjectivities, 'making Soviet citizens think of themselves and act as conscious historical subjects.' In this process, 'Soviet revolutionaries sought to remove all mediation between the individual citizen and the larger community so that the consciousness of the individual and the revolutionary goals of the state would merge.'[16] The ultimate goal of the revolutionary state, therefore, was to dismantle the notion of 'the private' altogether and to circumscribe the possibility of subject positions outside of the collective. Hellbeck suggests that the state, in part because of its 'totalizing insistence on universal self-transformation and self-disclosure', was largely successful in its goal of redefining the private, as diarists described private life outside of the collective as 'inferior' and 'unfulfilled.'[17] A successful redefinition of the private in Hellbeck's terms would necessarily have significant impact on recasting women's social roles and identities. This analyst remains wary, however, of the enormous influence that Hellbeck has granted to state ideology in the construction of the Soviet self.[18]

In a recent article comparing everyday life in the Soviet Union and Nazi Germany, Sheila Fitzpatrick and Alf Lüdtke define everyday life without rigid distinctions into spheres. They analyze both bonding (and exclusion) from the 'state project' and 'the process of *creation or renewal* of bonds' in the family and workplace 'which, while consonant with the state project, also constitutes an effort to carve out social and emotional space for a sphere of one's own.'[19] This formulation offers flexibility by acknowledging the mutual reinforcement of state ideology and the creative power of the individual to define him or herself, without overemphasizing the power of state ideology. Choi Chatterjee and I have elsewhere suggested that it would be productive to situate the Soviet self 'along a continuum of the domestic setting, the intimate collective, the larger socially imagined realities of class, ethnicity, gender, religious affiliations, and nationality and explore how it intersects with the discourses and practices of the state' in order to understand the range of actions within an individual's 'complex and multiple subject positions.'[20]

Can attention to the self and to the everyday help to reconcile the polarities of 'exploitation' and 'empowerment' and reveal the extent to which the state was successful in incorporating women into the state project? Using interviews and memoirs about women's lives between 1917–1953, many recorded or discovered after the fall of the Soviet Union, the rest of this chapter analyzes how Soviet women described their agency in the workplace, social organizations, school, family and home under Lenin and Stalin, in order to document the particular ways in which Soviet ideology and Soviet reality affected the life trajectories of Soviet women. This chapter will focus on women's self-representations and how they envisioned themselves interacting with the wider Soviet society and with their close friends and family. In discussing women's attitudes toward society and family, this chapter will pay particular attention to the women's relationships with the men in their lives, be they family members, mentors or co-workers. For as the Soviet state redefined the parameters of selfhood for women, it also had to redefine the parameters of acceptable masculine selfhood. The story of Soviet gender roles is the story of the clash of new and old, as enduring traditions and beliefs met with revolutionary and utopian visions of equality. The words of individual women demonstrate the complexity of identity and the constant negotiation and contestation of family ideology and gender roles in the Stalinist era. This complexity forces us to 'muddy the waters' and recognize the complex coexistence of 'exploitation' and 'empowerment' not only among Soviet women as a group but sometimes within the life experience of an individual woman.[21]

Women define their social roles

In his discussion of the merging of 'the public' and 'the private', Jochen Hellbeck features the diary of Galina Shtange, the 51 year old wife of a professor of the Moscow Electromechanical Institute of Railroad

Engineers, who was an *obshchestvennitsa* or wife-activist in the 1930s. Shtange's journal is an excellent jumping off point for a discussion of the status of women in the 1930s and the dilemmas facing them. Hellbeck argues that Shtange's definition of self was shaped by her participation in the collective and not by her role in the family. Shtange loved her volunteer social work at her husband's institute and did not want to give it up because of her conflicting domestic responsibilities. Hellbeck quotes Shtange's diary (with his emphasis added): 'The family is upset that I spend so little time at home.... I'm not old yet, I still want to have a personal life. Now that I've fulfilled my obligations to my family, in the few years that remain to me *I want to live for myself.*'[22] Clearly, Hellbeck is right that Shtange's definitions of 'public' and 'private' are not consistent with the standard bourgeois liberal model and Hellbeck's approach of historicizing and contextualizing the 'public' and the 'private' in the 1930s is an extremely fruitful one.

But how do we understand Shtange's definition of self? The first complication in trying to understand Shtange's social role is her membership in the *obshchestvennitsa* movement. The gender implications of this strangely hybrid 'social movement of the middle and late 1930s, which mobilized housewives for voluntary social service work while encouraging their domestic endeavors'[23] have been difficult to determine. On the one hand, these women were mobilized into public life to aid in socialist construction and some of them carved out active social roles and new identities for themselves. On the other hand, these identities were primarily as wives, and therefore they gained status only in relation to their husbands' roles. When Shtange gave her name at one of the wives' meetings, the political officer said to her, 'But Shtange! You really have to make a contribution, since your husband is such an important person.'[24] Shtange was delighted when the political officer recognized the merits of her husband. She was simultaneously a new Soviet women and a woman defined by her role in her family. There is no easy correlation between empowerment and women's equality.

Hellbeck's emphasis on revolutionary subjectivity tends to minimize the impact of the pre-revolutionary forces that shaped personality and life-goals. Forming a revolutionary self did not necessarily mean erasure or the reforging of all previous beliefs. Soviet subjectivity was not written on a *tabula rasa* population and Soviet ideology interacted in complex ways with existing beliefs. However subjectivising the Soviet state was, and however much it tried to reconfigure gender roles, it nonetheless had to contend with strong traditions and deeply imbedded beliefs about the proper relations between men and women and their proper social roles. These earlier beliefs also continued to interact dynamically with individual agency to shape subjectivity.

Shtange was over 30 years old when the revolution began and surely these 30 years had some impact on her formation of definitions of public and private. Although her diary is not published in its entirety, the editors of the collection give us some background on Shtange's pre-revolutionary life. They note that 'under the special heading of "community work" Shtange mentions a series of personal contributions to society that she had made since 1905, including the organization of amateur performances for school children and warm meals for students of the railway school, as well as nursing in a hospital during World War I.'[25] Although Hellbeck attributes Shtange's conflation of 'personal life' with community work to the influence of Soviet ideology, she had been actively participating in very similar volunteer activities as a 'bourgeois' wife before the revolution, and clearly was strongly inclined to the social before 1917. Her efforts to participate in such activities during the 1920s were limited by class antagonisms in the place where she lived. She resigned from the Village Council in Udelnaya because 'there was a blatant campaign to rid the Council of an "aristocrat," which was how they viewed me at the time. It was very insulting, and I turned in my resignation.'[26] Shtange's subject position was shaped not only by her gender but also by her status as a member of the pre-revolutionary bourgeoisie and then the Soviet elite.

Her choices were conditioned by her social position and gender norms as much as by Soviet ideology. Shtange's family was resentful of her social work only because there was a strong expectation that she would help her daughters-in-law take care of the grandchildren. She complained about having 'to give up her personal life just so my son's wife can live the way she pleases.'[27] Never was there any suggestion that her son might interrupt his work to assist with domestic duties. Shtange had to quit her social work because there was not enough living space or enough money for her sons and their wives to hire a maid. Once they were able to do so, Shtange was free to return to social work while a subordinate female took over the domestic work. Shtange's story of involvement in the community is thus as much a one of privilege as it is of empowerment. And while she may have crossed the boundaries from domestic to community work, she did so in a way that was consistent with a pre-revolutionary pattern and because of the assistance of other females who were confined to the domestic. Neither exploitation nor empowerment is adequate to fully capture the complex contexts and choices that women faced in the 1930s. While the *obshchestvennitsa* movement was not precisely a retreat from Soviet ideology of women's equality, it did provide conditions for the empowerment of women only within a context limited by social hierarchies and gendered social roles.

Those scholars who argue that Soviet ideological pronouncements about gender had the power to transform women's aspirations and shape their life choices often focus on the generation of women who grew up in the post-revolutionary years in particular. The life of Nina Raspopova provides one concrete example of Soviet ideology facilitating a radical change in a girl's life course. In a 1990 interview, Raspopova told of her difficult life growing up in the Soviet Far East. In 1926, when Raspopova was 13, she had to go to work as a cook in a gold mine to help support her nine brothers and sisters. When she was 15, the *Komsomol* sent her to the town of Blagoveshchensk to go to mining technical school. However, she was initially denied entrance to the mining school and told that girls were not accepted. Rather than returning home, she persisted and she sat for two months 'on the stairs of the technical school in hope that I would be admitted.'[28] Because of the official government policy of gender equality and the arrival of eight other girls who hoped to become mining engineers, Raspopova's determination paid off and she was eventually admitted to the school. Soviet ideology was crucial for Raspopova; her firm beliefs that girls had an equal right to enter the school and that mining engineering was a career appropriate for women led to her perseverance. She noted that 'We girls proved to be as well-trained and industrious as the boys.'[29] She was then recommended to the Irkutsk Mining Engineering College without entrance examinations.

Later, she was chosen to train as a pilot in one of the civil pilots' schools. When she and another girl arrived at the school, 'The commander of the school said he wouldn't admit us because we were girls, but the government said they must admit us, so I was enrolled.'[30] She eventually trained as a pilot, was a flight commander during World War II and was awarded the most prestigious Soviet honour, Hero of the Soviet Union. Despite her belief in women's equality and the right to equal access, her story is notable in that at every step of the way lower level male officials sought to prevent girls from studying and barred their path. Only through the intervention of mid- and upper-level government and *Komsomol* officials were girls' rights to enroll in technical schools enforced. Raspopova's struggle for admission demonstrates that those who see the Stalinist state's commitment to women's equality as only empty rhetoric are mistaken. In the early 1930s, Soviet officials often supported women's access to education and jobs. Yet the attitudes of lower level officials are also telling. Access for women was a struggle because many of the rank and file male officials did not believe that women belonged in their institutions and it is likely that sometimes they won their battles and succeeded in keeping women out. The 'collective', as imagined by these officials, privileged male membership.

The attitudes of some officials towards women applicants reveal that Soviet ideology did not automatically erase pre-existing ideas about the roles of women and Soviet males continued to articulate hierarchies of males over females. These existing beliefs as well as other cultural conventions that shaped Soviet male subjectivities provide a point of view separate from official Soviet ideology from which it was possible to assess, react to and, in this particular case, undermine Soviet official policy. Hellbeck is correct to point out that the evaluative stance of Soviet citizens in the 1930s is not the same as the twenty-first century Western liberal stance, but it is a mistake to suggest that all who challenged the collective vision saw themselves as outside of it. These male actors challenged the gender tenets of collective ideology as they affirmed their belonging to the 'collective body of the Soviet people.'[31] It is thus necessary to trace the complex interplay between Soviet ideology and pre-revolutionary gender traditions, as Soviet men and women interacted with all of these ideas in the writing of their identities.

Scholars' arguments about the redefinition of femininity do shed light on a critical part of the story of women's lives in the Stalin period. The transformation in Soviet discourses about women's roles emboldened some women to define themselves in new ways; yet as they did so, there was a constant struggle with the males in their school or workplace who were often slower than government officials to embrace the notion of women's equality. Women's self-definitions were shaped in the clash of new and old discourses about women and the persistence of the old discourses tempered the efficacy of the new ones. Furthermore, these ideologies of liberation and equality coexisted with ambiguous programs such as the *obshchestvennitsa* movement that framed women's participation in a much more limited way. And all of these ideas coexisted with pro-natalist aspects of 1930s culture that defined motherhood as a crucial occupation for women. Ultimately, it would be a mistake to view the ideologies shaping the formation of women's identities in the 1930s as a coherent whole. It is only by understanding the variability and fragmentation of the many competing ideologies that we can analyze the kinds of choices that were available to Soviet women.

Relationships and work in the home

Thus far, this chapter has considered the roles of women who moved into the public sphere as social workers and Soviet professionals. It is much more difficult to discuss women's relationships with the men in their own families, particularly husbands and lovers. Many diarists and memoirists were reticent about issues of love and sex. They tended to write about the ways in which their lives intersected with the 'broader sphere of public life' and did not focus on their intimate relationships.[32] While evidence of women's fight for equality is evident in the memoirs about school and work, it is much harder to find in memoirs about home life.

The diary of women's activist Agrippina Korevanova offers some insight into one of the many problems facing Soviet women: in the late 1920s and early 1930s, projects to create a new communal life through cafeterias, nurseries and laundries that would free women from housework failed because there was simply no money to pay for such facilities. Korevanova's record of a women's meeting that she organized reveals some of the dynamics of the home lives of women in the city of Sverdlovsk. Women at the meeting declared in turn:

'We need freedom from pots and pans! We need a cafeteria and a laundry!'

'In the summer we've got to open a children's playground and a laundry. We're sick of washing men's pants. Every time my husband goes anywhere on business, he comes back so dirty I never stop washing his clothes. I've got too many kids to bother with his pants.'

'Everyone has problems. This one is sick of washing her husband's pants!'[33]

Both the complaint itself and the less than sympathetic response from another of the women reveal that women's subservience in the domestic sphere was so pervasive that despite Soviet rhetoric, many women had trouble imagining themselves escaping from domestic tasks. And while the state surely contributed to women's exploitation by not providing the funding for communal facilities, the non-state familial bonds that included husbands' expectations that it was their wives' job to launder their work pants also contributed to women's plight. Clearly, the never-ending demands of domestic life impinged upon women's relationships with their husbands and their senses of self, even if it is difficult to document these struggles.

One diary that is unusually open in discussing power relations between sexual partners is that of Mary Leder, an American teenager whose family moved to Stalin's Russia in the early 1930s. By the mid 1930s, she had left her family in Birobidzhan and moved to Moscow on her own as a Soviet factory apprentice. While she was not a product of the Soviet Union and therefore was more forthcoming about love and sex than many of the Russian women, the men with whom she had relations were products of the Soviet era. She candidly described losing her virginity to one of the other workers living in her factory commune in Moscow, although her friends warned her that the man in question was an unreliable character who was 'sexually experienced beyond his years.'[34] Mary and her boyfriend Haitin did not discuss 'marriage' but instead considered applying for a room together because, Leder noted, 'If a couple set up housekeeping together, they were considered to be married – in the eyes of the law as well as society. Formalization of the relationship was not important.'[35] Leder explained how difficult it was to find any place to be alone with her lover: 'Like courting couples all over the city, we would embrace in dimly lit doorways of the building before going upstairs, jumping apart when we heard footsteps. We snatched moments when there was no one home in the apartment or when we thought (or hoped) everyone else was sound asleep.[36] Leder's description of her relationship suggests that she believed her behaviour to be typical for her milieu.

Unfortunately for Leder, this first love affair was not long lasting and the worker unceremoniously jilted her. She went away to a sanitorium after an illness and when she returned, 'he greeted me politely and asked how I was, behaving as if there had never been anything between us.'[37] Her youth and inexperience no doubt put her in a vulnerable position in relation to this man. While she took the break-up hard at first, she was resilient and eventually recovered. While memoirs written by Russian women tend to be silent about broken love affairs, the warnings of Leder's friends and the Soviet legal preoccupation with the payment of child support suggest that Leder's experience of being deserted by a sexual partner was fairly typical.[38] It is hard to fit this kind of relationship into rubrics such as 'liberation' or 'exploitation.' Relationships seemed to be as much shaped by the constraints of living space as by any ideology about marriage or about sexual liberation.[39] Given the context of housing shortages all across the Soviet Union, looking at new definitions of the 'private' in the 1930s in ideology alone is insufficient.

Mary Leder later married Abram Leder and discussed their domestic arrangements in some detail. There was some tension in their marriage because she was not a good housekeeper and he was a perfectionist.

As a result, he took over some of the housework but only in private, and some chores, such as cooking, he refused to do altogether. He would not sweep the floor in the kitchen and the hall of the communal apartment because 'he did not want to be seen doing "women's work," '[40] and he camouflaged the trash before he took it out by making neat packages 'tying strings or even ribbons around them.'[41] This memoir demonstrated that there was no new ideology of men's work in the domestic sphere corresponding to the new ideology of women's role in the workplace. Sweeping, cooking, washing dishes and taking out the trash were still women's work, no matter the occupation of the woman outside of the house. Mary Leder noted, 'I know of no other couple, then or later, in which the wife did not do all the washing, mending, cooking, laying out of her husband's clothes for the day, and even the packing of his bags when he went on a business trip.'[42] Like Shtange, the only alternatives Mary had were to do the domestic labour that Abram would not do herself, or hire a female domestic.

Throughout their relationship, Abram did not limit Mary's social participation in work or at school. The couple was childless, however, losing their only daughter during the evacuation from Moscow during World War II. It is likely that Mary's career would have been more constrained had her child lived. Without male participation in domestic labour, Soviet women who did not have help from a female relative or who could not afford to hire a maid struggled to achieve their social goals while performing all of the family's domestic labour. In this regard, the historians who emphasized Soviet exploitation of women are at least partly right. Despite grand ideologies of equality, without significant government resources invested in communal dining, laundries and childcare, Soviet women's ambitions were severely constrained by the realities of domestic life whatever their definitions of femininity were. Both practical obstacles and unchanging male attitudes could and did interfere with self-realization. The more privileged one was in the Soviet system, however, the more 'self-realisation' was likely to occur, especially for women with children.

Post-war women

Soviet redefinitions of femininity were also time sensitive. The height of egalitarian rhetoric was in the pre-war period. After World War II, in the Soviet Union as in the USA and many other countries around the world, there was a renewed emphasis on women's domestic and maternal roles and a devaluation of women's participation in the war effort. In theory, at least, Soviet men's rewards for defeating the Germans included an idealised domestic life surrounded by an adoring wife and children.[43] In these circumstances, new definitions of military femininity met with even more resistance than they had in the 1930s.

One former fighter pilot, Valentina Petrochenkova-Neminushaya recalled that at the end of the war her mother asked her 'to come home and not to fly any longer', because her brother had been killed in the war. In 1946, Petrochenkova-Neminushaya married a pilot she had met during the war. Her new husband gave her an ultimatum about her life choices: 'You choose – aviation or me.'[44] Petrochenkova-Neminushaya chose to stop flying. In this brief interchange we get a glimpse both at the way in which wartime losses and family grief shaped gender identities and at power relations within post-war marriages. While it is not clear why Petrochenkova-Neminushaya's husband wanted her to stop flying, he, too, was a test pilot engaged in dangerous work. Although she did not have the power to make him give up his perilous profession, he, along with her mother, was able to force her to leave flying. The chronology is not entirely clear, but it seems as though Petrochenkova-Neminushaya later was able to work as a senior test technician at a parachute centre. Her days in the air, however, were over because of familial restraints on her career. Now that the national emergency had passed, husbands (and families in general) had more power to dominate the life courses of their female members.

Post-war memory also dramatically recast women's participation in the war effort by suggesting that women at the front were 'loose' and received their medals not for heroism but for sexual favours to army elites. Front-line doctor Vera Malakhova wrote movingly of her own experiences after World War II. She had saved lives under fire at the front and participated in the battle of Stalingrad. Yet, after the war, she was ashamed to put on her medals because many considered the women who had been on the front lines to be little better than prostitutes. Her husband encouraged her to wear her medals to a May Day parade a few years after the war, saying 'Put them on. You're going with me, you earned them. I know everything there is about you, and you earned them honestly.' Nevertheless, when her husband lagged behind, a man accosted her, saying 'Here comes a frontline W[hore], and her husband punched him in the face.'[45] Ironically, Malakhova could only celebrate her wartime valour and independence under masculine protection. Her husband was supportive of her wartime efforts and wanted her to receive recognition for them, but the social milieu of the post-war Soviet Union was not receptive to the definition of women as war heroes. The ideology of empowerment that motivated some Soviet women in the pre-war years seems to have been greatly weakened in the post-war era.[46]

Conclusions

This chapter has examined the status of women at work and in the home in Stalin's Soviet Union and has endeavoured to complicate the concepts of 'exploitation' and 'empowerment' by showing the intricacies of women's lives and their variegated relationships with men, work and family. Furthermore, this chapter has tried to show that Stalinist discourses and subjectivities were powerful and could change the lives of women and men. Soviet men and women made their decisions and choices based on the ways that they interacted with Soviet ideologies and other ideological forces such as previous life experiences and pre-revolutionary and traditional beliefs. Soviet ideologies were in constant tension with previously held notions that often provided actors with multiple vantage points from which to critique, resist and also support Soviet ideologies in the making of their own subjectivities.

Soviet commanders who did not want to let girls into pilot school, women who used their pre-revolutionary volunteer experience to improve their Soviet social work, men who refused to sweep the floor in public and men who called women soldiers 'whores' were all drawing on experiences outside of official Soviet ideology either to critique that ideology or to reinforce selected aspects of it while downplaying others. Furthermore, the efficacy of Soviet gender ideology was contingent on status hierarchies, time and place. These varying conditions led to moments when Soviet ideology could empower women and times when it constrained them. Attention to context and to the multiplicity of ideological forces enables us to draw a variegated picture of Soviet gender relations in the Stalin period.

To what extent, then, were women (to use Fitzpatrick and Lüdtke's terminology) 'energized' to participate in the state project of socialist construction? Women's memoirs suggest that state ideology was extremely appealing to many women and that many gained some kind of 'empowerment' by enthusiastically embracing identities that were supportive of state goals. But the realities of life in the Soviet Union often undercut the potential for overlapping women's identities and state goals. Resurgent interwar pro-natalism and the state's priorities on heavy industry and defense caused it to renege on many of the central promises made to women. Furthermore, the state also needed to 'energize' heroic Soviet male identities, and they often did so at the expense of women. While in many ways the Soviet Union remained unique in terms of its potential for women's emancipation and its transformation of the lives of some individual women, much of this potential was squandered through skewed economic priorities, the refusal to transform male identities in ways that reinforced female emancipation and the pervasive oppression of both men and women in the Soviet system.

Notes

I would like to thank Jie-Hyun Lim, all of the organisers of the 'Mass Dictatorship' project at the Research Institute of Comparative History and Culture (RICH), Hanyang University, and the participants of the Fourth International Conference of Mass Dictatorship (Gender Politics) for their helpful comments. Thanks also to Choi Chatterjee whose insights have fundamentally informed my views on gender and ideology.

1. Aleksandra Kollontai, 'Communism and the Family', in *Selected Writings of Alexandra Kollontai*, translated by Alix Holt (London: Allison and Busby, 1977), p. 253.
2. Frances Lee Bernstein, *The Dictatorship of Sex: Lifestyle Advice for the Soviet Masses* (DeKalb, IL: Northern Illinois University Press, 2007), p. 50.
3. Sarah Ashwin, 'Introduction', in Sarah Ashwin (ed.), *Gender, State, and Society in Soviet and Post-Soviet Russia* (London: Routledge, 2000), p. 5. See also Elizabeth Wood, *The Baba and the Comrade: Gender and Politics in Revolutionary Russia* (Bloomington, IN: Indiana University Press, 1997).
4. For a discussion of Soviet family legislation, see Wendy Goldman, *Women and the Soviet State: Soviet Family Policy and Social Life, 1917–1936* (Cambridge: Cambridge University Press, 1993).
5. The term 'great retreat' was coined in 1946 by sociologist Nicholas Timasheff who argued that Stalin's Soviet Union made a systematic retreat from communist ideology in the 1930s. Nicholas S. Timasheff, *The Great Retreat: The Growth and Decline of Communism in Russia* (New York: E. P. Dutton and Co., 1946). For a critique of the 'great retreat' and a reading of Stalinist gender policy as consistent with that of all modernizing states in the interwar period, see David L. Hoffmann, *Stalinist Values: The Cultural Norms of Soviet Modernity (1917–1941)* (Ithaca, NY: Cornell University Press, 2003), especially pp. 88–117.
6. For a discussion of women's military roles in Soviet interwar media, see Alison Rowley, 'Ready for Work and Defense: Visual Propaganda and Soviet Women's Visual Preparedness in the 1930s', *Minerva: Women and War* 18(3–4) (2000), pp. 3–15; John P. Davis, 'Soviet Women, Militarization, and Modernity in the 1930s', MA Thesis, University of Kentucky (2005).
7. Melanie Ilič (ed.), *Women in the Stalin Era* (Houndsmills, Hampshire: Palgrave, 2001), p. 6.
8. See Wendy Goldman, *Women at the Gates: Gender and Industry in Stalin's Russia* (Cambridge: Cambridge University Press, 2002).

9. See Karen Petrone, *Life Has Become More Joyous, Comrades: Celebrations in the Time of Stalin* (Bloomington, IN: Indiana University Press, 2000), pp. 59–65.

10. Barbara Alpern Engel, 'Women Remember World War II', in Nurit Schleifman (ed.), *Russia at a Crossroads* (London: Frank Cass, 1998), p. 129.

11. Margaret R. Higgonet and Patrice L.-R. Higgonet, 'The Double Helix', in Margaret R. Higgonet, Jane Jenson, Sonya Michel and Margaret Collins Weitz (eds), *Behind the Lines: Gender and the Two World Wars* (New Haven, CT: Yale University Press, 1989, reprint edn), pp. 31–50.

12. Choi Chatterjee, *Celebrating Women: Gender, Festival Culture, and Bolshevik Ideology, 1910–1939* (Pittsburgh, PA: University of Pittsburgh Press, 2002), p. 6.

13. Anna Krylova, 'Stalinist Identity from the Viewpoint of Gender: Rearing a Generation of Professionally Violent Women-Fighters in 1930s Stalinist Russia', *Gender and History* 16(3) (November 2004), pp. 628–9.

14. Jochen Hellbeck, 'Working, Struggling, Becoming: Stalin-era Autobiographical Texts', *Russian Review* 60(3) (July 2001), p. 340. See also Anna Krylova, 'The Tenacious Liberal Subject in Soviet Studies', *Kritika* 1(1) (Winter 2000), pp. 119–46.

15. Jochen Hellbeck, *Revolution On My Mind: Writing a Diary under Stalin* (Cambridge, MA: Harvard University Press, 2006), p. 12.

16. Hellbeck, 'Working, Struggling, Becoming', pp. 341–2.

17. Ibid., pp. 345, 357–8.

18. For a critique of Hellbeck, see Choi Chatterjee and Karen Petrone, 'Models of Selfhood and Subjectivity: The Soviet Case in Historical Perspective', *Slavic Review* 67(4) (Winter 2008), pp. 977–80.

19. Sheila Fitzpatrick and Alf Lüdtke, 'Energizing the Everyday: On the Breaking and Making of Social Bonds in Nazism and Stalinism', in Michael Geyer and Sheila Fitzpatrick (eds), *Beyond Totalitarianism: Stalinism and Nazism Compared* (Cambridge: Cambridge University Press, 2009), p. 267.

20. Chatterjee and Petrone, 'Models of Selfhood and Subjectivity', p. 986.

21. Fitzpatrick and Lüdtke also point to how 'individual practices' are 'complex and sometimes contradictory.' Fitzpatrick and Lüdtke, 'Energizing the Everyday', p. 267.

22. Quoted in Hellbeck, 'Working, Struggling, Becoming', p. 356.

23. Rebecca Balmas Neary, 'Mothering Socialist Society: The Wife-Activists' Movement and the Soviet Culture of Daily Life, 1934–41', *Russian Review* 58(3) (July 1999), p. 396. See also Mary Buckley, 'The Untold Story of the *Obshchestvennitsa* in the 1930s', in Ilič, *Women in the Stalin Era*, pp. 151–72.

24. Galina Vladimirovna Shtange, 'Diary of Galina Vladimirovna Shtange', in Veronique Garros, Natalia Korenevskaya and Thomas Lahusen (eds), *Intimacy and Terror: Soviet Diaries of the 1930s* (New York: The New Press, 1995), p. 172.

25. Ibid., p. 167.

26. Ibid., p. 170.

27. Ibid., p. 189.

28. Anne Noggle, *A Dance with Death: Soviet Airwomen in World War II* (College Station, TX: Texas A&M University Press, 1994), pp. 21–2.

29. Ibid., p. 21.

30. Ibid., p. 22.

31. Hellbeck, *Revolution On My Mind*, p. 114. Hellbeck suggests that individuals who struggled with Soviet ideology tended to be 'atomised selves in crisis.' Here the officials' struggle against ideology strengthened their own sense of collective belonging.

32. Cynthia Simmons and Nina Perlina, 'Introduction', in Cynthia Simmons and Nina Perlina (eds), *Writing the Siege of Leningrad: Women's Diaries, Memoirs, and Documentary Prose* (Pittsburgh, PA: University of Pittsburgh Press, 2002), p. 16.

33. Agrippina Korevanova, 'My Life', in Sheila Fitzpatrick and Yuri Slezkine (eds), *In the Shadow of Revolution: Life Stories of Russian Women from 1917 to the Second World War* (Princeton, NJ: Princeton University Press, 2000), p. 201.

34. Mary M. Leder, *My Life in Stalinist Russia: An American Woman Looks Back* (Bloomington, IN: Indiana University Press, 2002), p. 59.

35. Ibid., p. 58.

36. Ibid.

37. Ibid., p. 67.

38. Hoffmann, *Stalinist Values*, p. 105.

39. Living space played a role in Leder's next two relationships. She claimed she would have married her next boyfriend Izzy, 'if either one of us had had a permanent room.' She married Abram Leder when her roommate moved out and the housing committee chair told him that he'd better hurry and propose marriage to be registered in her room (Leder, *My Life in Stalinist Russia*, pp. 108, 164).

40. Ibid., p. 166.

41. Ibid., p. 167.

42. Ibid., p. 168.

43. See Vera S. Dunham, *In Stalin's Time: Middleclass Values in Soviet Fiction* (Durham, NC: Duke University Press, 1990).

44. Noggle, *A Dance with Death*, p. 178.

45. Vera Ivanovna Malakhova, 'Four Years as a Front-line Physician', in Barbara Alpern Engel and Anastasia Posadskaya-Vanderbeck (eds), *A Revolution of Their Own: Voices of Women in Soviet History* (Boulder, CO: Westview Press, 1997), p. 215.

46. See Engel, 'Women Remember World War II' for further discussion of women's reputations after the war.

7
Male Bodies: Well-Trained Muscles or Beer Bellies? From the 'Master Race' in Nazism to the Ruling Class in East Germany

Alf Lüdtke

The following explorations address gender in terms of masculinity. Their particular focus is on body images and body practices. Scrutiny of the views and visions of contemporary intellectuals and (medical) experts shall provide insights into their assessments of the body; at the same time these explorations ought to reveal the body practices that the 'many' employed and privileged.

The starting point for contemporary representations of the body consists of pleas for the 'new man' as they were increasingly published around 1900, in both the European and North American contexts. Against this background, this chapter traces the emerging prominence of the 'slim' athletic body in public arenas in Germany, from the late Wilhelmine Empire and the Weimar Republic to its rather unfettered popularity during Nazi rule. Body practices and related policies were not simply discarded with the defeat of racist Nazism in 1945. How did the activists for a socialist 'new Germany' in the Eastern part of the country deal with the legacy of Nazism and war? In East Germany, acceptance of the new regime by the 'many' never turned into that active support Nazi leaders could draw on. Still, did the imaginaries of the proletarian male body and its conspicuous muscular strength in East Germany overrule the former ideal of a slim body? The 'many' readily shifted from visions of slenderness to those featuring an opulent, stout and even fat male body. To the increasing chagrin of physicians, the latter rapidly became popular in East Germany (and to a certain extent in West Germany), to some degree articulating people's self-willed stubbornness (*'Eigensinn'*) to keep to preferences of their own choosing.

The icon of the 'new man'

In Nazi Germany, males with slender but still muscular bodies appeared in posters and films, on book covers and in reports of mass rallies carried by the illustrated newspapers. Both their very physicality and posture alluded to discipline and focus. These mostly young men thus radiated energy and devotion.

This iconography resonated with self-presentations of the 'new man' as envisioned in the wake of 'reform' and youth movements that had gained momentum in Germany around 1900. Central to their demands was to liberate everyone's body from external restrictions and pollution and, as importantly, from internal poisoning. Thus, a cleansing programme focused on dress or more precisely on undressing and thus removing external impacts on one's body as much as possible. At the same time, such programmes emphasised the proper intake: food and drink that should not contaminate people. The main goal was to achieve and then to keep a healthy body. Such effort would bring people into concordance with the 'laws' of biology.

An icon of this view swiftly emerged: the drawing of Fidus, the 'Lichtgebet' (1922, the Adoration of Light) (Illustration 7.1). This picture became a preferred decoration in the rooms of high school and university students; reports also mention it hanging in offices of high-ranking National Socialist functionaries.[1] Visual representations in particular depicted the body as the actual vessel of the 'new man'. His body would actually resemble and thus 'embody' the aspired – far 'better'... These images displayed a slender male body that showed a lean physique with well-trained muscles indicating both athletic stamina and gymnastic flexibility. It was this combination that indicated a merging of health and good prospects based on an intricate interconnection of creativity and productivity.

The imagery: *longue durée* and counter-images

The striking power of this pictorialisation operated on several registers at the same time. One was the continuation of envisioning the victorious and, ultimately, invincible redeemer. In its secular version Albrecht Dürer had visualised this figure in several drawings and etchings (in the early sixteenth century) that were widely circulated during his lifetime. Since then both the population and artists or experts referred to and invoked this figuration of the male hero who overcame the forces of evil and darkness.

Illustration 7.1 '*Lichtgebet*' by Fidus. Verwertungsgesellschaft (VG) Kunst, Bonn, Germany.

Secondly, such pictorialisation derived its power from constant references to counter-images that depicted the 'other' as embodying evil or sin. This figure represented those times and settings and, in particular, people whom one sought to overcome and, ultimately, make invisible. This 'other' showed all the signs of being an alien creature, and thus was potentially dangerous. Still, the specific features could change and were malleable. Thus, in the course of the nineteenth century the spectrum of the presumably dangerous 'others' increasingly ranged beyond the confines of Europe, more precisely beyond physiognomies and skin colours that were commonly understood as European. Accordingly, the unspoiled native who represented paradise lost disappeared.[2] Now, pictorial representations and, presumably, popular imagination revolved around and were populated with coloured people. And these representations portrayed people in need of control and discipline. They, however, were the token of that 'civilising mission' that Europeans of all denominations and political orientations openly claimed or implicitly pursued.

The rapidly spreading beliefs in the ultimate truth of science massively bolstered such perceptions and evaluations. In their wake the craze for biologically defined distinctions between 'us' and 'them' gained ever more momentum. It was primarily the impact of Charles Darwin's *On the Origin of Species* (1859) and the emergence of Social Darwinism that fuelled visions of the progress of man, not merely in terms of moral improvement or social reorganisation but in terms of his (or her) physical perfection.

However, in the Central European context it was not only and perhaps not even primarily Africans who figured as the primary embodiment of those at the margins of humanity, if not as 'sub-humans'. Here, Jews, or more precisely, those stereotyped as Jews appeared with particular prominence.[3] These pictorial representations also targeted other peoples from the margins of those Central European societies and settings, among them Poles, but people from the Southeast like the Bosnians even more so. Pictorial features included stereotypes that were commonly taken as indicators of stupidity and childishness but also of filth and laziness – more generally, they represented 'mean' ways of conduct.[4] Such images were common in illustrated newspapers and on posters and they all revolved around the effort to demarcate the gap between 'us' and 'them'. During and after World War I this imagery was amply used in the respective war efforts. In Germany, the occupying Allied forces after 1918 were targeted by this very iconography. In particular the French and their colonial troops, that is, the black soldiers, were put on centre stage in these pictures. And even the limited emphasis of some physiognomic features like lips made amply clear the message that these were barbarians and those who had sent them were even more barbarous.[5]

Masculinity–femininity

Notions and images of masculinity referred to and resonated with icons that represented femininity. In the emergence of what people claimed as European modernity, males especially had appropriated the public domain to the male folk; accordingly, the females would tend to home and hearth – or care for the private.[6] According to this separation of spheres, in pictorial as in verbal representations, all of the potential for good developments and actual accomplishments that would spring from production and demand productivity henceforth appeared as male. The rise of industry and commerce as it shattered but also transformed Western and Central European societies reaffirmed such notions. In particular, this process emphasised the stereotypes of mutually exclusive and – rigidly – unequal spheres of males and females. Thus, productivity outside of household and 'home' appeared as a pivotal feature of the male who would struggle for survival in an alien and rather hostile environment. The women would, in turn, keep the hearth glowing and tend to the personal relationships among spouses and the household and family but also among the wider kin. Above all, women were the immediate bearers of the next generation; thus they would physically 'produce' the future, at least the future generation.

The actual interrelationships of males and females, however, by no means followed such stereotypes. Not least, the scheme of the tough and outgoing male who physically and mentally would withstand every onslaught while the females provided for relationships and shelter never withstood the test of everyday life, in particular among people of lesser means who were immersed in respective 'makeshift-economies'.[7] Also in the relative quiet of bourgeois house holding, these demarcations were either overstepped or never taken too seriously.[8] Moreover, these stereotypes collapsed in times of emergency and, especially, war. Feminist research has amply shown the multiple female engagements in spheres conventionally deemed as 'public', from warfare to proto-industrial production to trading.

Still, even if the distance of gender inequality was part of the everyday of males and females alike, interrelationships between both developed in the realms of dreams or longings but also in people's anxieties. In fact, the regulations for separation may have enhanced efforts to get across boundaries mentally if not physically. It was against this background that Detlev von Liliencron portrayed '*Mine, Trine, Stine*' shortly after 1900. The three were obviously young teenage women who the author showed as thrilled by an approaching military unit and its band. '*Wenn die Musike kommt*' (if the band comes), then these young women would look out of 'door and gate' and even step out of 'house and yard' to get closer to the young men. In this case, marching by was a company of infantry comprising ordinary soldiers almost the age of '*Mine, Trine,*

Stine' but also several petty-officers and a few officers, all of them shining and in their physical and bodily presence demonstrating energy and determination: the epitome of that maleness prescribed in the scheme of patriarchal rule *modo militare*.[9] In his song, Liliencron alluded to the attraction of the scene to both males and females. In particular, however, his song captured the appeal of the military formation to females – and perhaps the awareness of the soldiers that they received the fond looks of *'Mine, Trine, Stine'*. And even if this attraction and related admiration was influenced if not manipulated in various ways, there seems to have been heartfelt and intense feelings cutting across the boundaries of gender.

However, at the same time women of this very segment of society repeatedly if not regularly suffered sexual violence. Husbands raped their wives but obviously also daughters, sometimes in weekly turns according to the recollections of women.[10] They had to cope with the brute force of those males who were (or who claimed to be) dear to their victims, who demanded not only control but possession of the body. One may speculate whether these males sought compensation for the rigid limits of power most of them were facing in, for instance, their sphere of production, that is, in their industrial, commercial or clerical jobs.

'New man': eugenics and racism

Around 1900 and even more in the 1920s the drive to aspire for and actively contribute to a better future was cultivated in different if not antagonistic political camps. Eugenics and, in particular, plans for actively inhibiting the procreation of those considered mentally disabled received applause amongst activists from the political left (see, for instance, the physician Alfred Grotjahn of the Social Democratic Party), at the same time that such projects were acclaimed in conservative and liberal camps.[11]

It cannot come as a surprise that Fidus's depiction of the *'Lichtgebet'* became so popular almost over night. This 'persona' of a healthy and fit body visualised longings for the future that would put to rest the distress, pain or shortcomings of people's actual everyday lives – and also the horrors of war and their repercussions. In the wake of war, the socialist or communist projects of a 'new man' presented a body similar to the one that aspired to the 'rebirth' 'of a nation' or 'race': a muscular young male. And in the cases where females appeared, they were accompanied by small children – and if they were on their own, they appeared smaller and were set behind the male(s).

All those pictured were young adults and even parents in these pictures appeared as being not much older than perhaps 30 years of age. As in commercial advertisements, males and females in these presentations were never shown as 'old' or aging, nor did they ever show any ailments. Only rarely did someone or some organisation deviate. A case in point was the aggressive, though marginal in its range, anti-war propaganda that employed pictures of mutilated bodies and, in particular, destroyed faces.[12] Generally, not least in the political arena, bodies had to resemble and actually show potential for a better future. And in politics (and related spheres like union activities and professional associations) the male body figured stronger than the female.

Across the board, aspiration and planning for a 'better future' employed images focusing on similar if not almost identical bodies that would symbolise the 'better future' of the society or polity. In this respect, socialist (or social democratic) and communist organisations did not principally differ from those on the right side of the political (and cultural) spectrum. Still, important differences remained. The nationalist-racist case of biologically grounded images was explicitly related to and based on notions of racial priority, if not domination, especially of the 'Nordic' and 'Aryan' peoples that the authors and sponsors deemed as superior by, as was the claim, biological law. One of the most active and, increasingly, prominent authors of such propaganda tracts and books was Hans F. K. Günther. Beginning in the early 1920s, he published his *Rassenkunde des deutschen Volkes* in ever newer versions.[13] He restlessly put the 'Nordic race' at the centre of his reiterated calls for stemming what he portrayed as the biological decay of the German people by more and more losing their supposed 'Nordic' traits. However, at the same time, he considered six modulations of the 'Nordic race' ('Westphalian', 'Eastern' and others). Again, pictures were pivotal: Günther prominently displayed photographs of people that he considered 'typical' for these respective modulations. Especially after the Nazis seized power in 1933, the gist of his scheme resonated strongly with the line of prevalent school books for biology such as the one authored by Otto Schmeil and revised by Paul Eichler.[14]

Certainly, in contrast to Fidus's imagination of the '*Lichtgebet*', even males who shared one or the other of the projects for betterment went naked only in the carefully selected and restricted settings of the 'cult of nudity' (*Freikörperkultur*, or in its popular abbreviation: *FKK!*). Nevertheless, muscular arms and bare breasts adorned many political posters; they also appeared in illustrated newspapers after 1900, and again from the mid and later 1920s onward in works issued by both commercial publishers and political organisations (Illustration 7.2). In contrast, women appeared as mothers and housewives. If the setting of the picture had women on the job, they appeared in contexts of teaching or advertising the prevention of accidents in images issued by

Illustration 7.2 'My System: 15 Minutes of Daily Work for Your Health!'. Joergen Peter Müller, *Mein System*, 3rd edn (Copenhagen: Tillge's Boghandel, 1905), cover.

social insurance companies, employers and unions as well. Here women were shown as acting naively and, thus, causing accidents; such portrayals were to alert people to behave 'more rationally' and, thus, to avoid or prevent painful and costly injuries to themselves and to their colleagues.

The lean well-trained male body referred also to the standard iconographic codes for depicting aristocratic and military figures or leaders in contrast to figures representing academics, priests or pastors, and, in particular, shopkeepers and tradespeople: the latter figures sported bellies, fat faces and double chins.

Lean and athletic

References to the 'young' as guarantors of a better future to come had become part of both political rhetoric and education since the late nineteenth century. In verbal and visual presentations these 'young folks' appeared in their corporeality as young bodies. Of course, they had lean bodies and males also displayed muscles. Either way, these bodies would show their potential for individual betterment and progress for all[15] (Illustrations 7.3 and 7.4). By the same token it was these bodies that appeared as authentic proof that health was available (as well as happiness and productivity) for everybody that takes care of his or her body. At the same time beauty was at least hinted at if not directly invoked. One can only speculate about the extent to which such pictorial claims and visual demonstrations caused chagrin among those deemed less fit if not unfit in the terms that were displayed in these presentations. Without much speculation, however, it is obvious that the segments of society beyond the age of 30 or 35 were excluded from the bracket of promising young males and females.

The booming popularity of mass and spectator sports since the 1920s has added to the imagery of the well-proportioned and healthy but also productive body. In sports, people wanted and had to bend and move their bodies easily and without pain. Participation in competitions and training was crucial for getting one's body into that very shape that not only allowed for easy movement but made it a pleasure.

Still, displays of sports in the Weimar Republic and in the Nazi era after 1933 did not feature free-roaming movement but the rigid discipline of parading and demonstrating in well-ordered 'masses' of bodies. Whether it was the '*Deutsche Turnfest*' or other shows in front of large audiences, the actors moved their bodies in a well-coordinated fashion and at a simultaneous speed and rhythm. Thus, these shows invoked the

SPIEL- UND BODENGYMNASTIK

Illustration 7.3 'Play and Gymnastics'. Hans W. Fischer, *Körperschönheit und Körperkultur* (Berlin: Deutsche Buchgemeinschaft, 1928), p. 154.

military model that most participants executed willy-nilly if not with enthusiasm.

Membership in sports associations in Germany in the later 1920s and the 1930s ranged between 15 per cent and 18 per cent among teenagers and young adults. In the late 1930s, these people were between 25 and 35 years of age. Whether or not they had actively participated in sports activities and recognised their increasing prominence, they were exposed to a body profile that connected flexibility with the stamina to withstand physical (and mental) hardship and that closely resembled the standard image of the proper soldier. Still, sports demanded not the regular and strict discipline of marching columns but the agility that made possible an optimal usage of one's mental and physical energies. Again, in terms of images of sports, there were no visible differences between the ideas and their visual representations in leftist, right-wing or other conceptions of actual politics or future developments.

Phot. Atlantic

Motorradfahrer bei einer Rekordfahrt

Illustration 7.4 'Motorcyclist – Riding for a Record'. Hans W. Fischer, *Körper-schönheit und Körperkultur* (Berlin: Deutsche Buchgemeinschaft, 1928), plate 79.

Body images – in Nazism

The presence of young muscular men and physically fit and 'proper' women was ubiquitous in the media worlds of the Third Reich. The military model of body discipline permeated particularly the official youth organisations of the Nazi regime and the state. The Hitler Youth and the League of German Girls time and again enforced the paradigm – which also indicates that such a policy met with a certain degree (and perhaps conjunctures) of scepticism if not indolence. As far as autobiographical material goes, children and especially teenagers and young adults seemed to have been attracted or at least impressed by both the depicted corporeality but also by many if not most of the underlying assumptions on the future of the German *Volk* as well as of its individual members.

Such images appeared in the context of Nazi efforts to occupy not only the physical terrain of streets and squares but also the cultural and mental spaces provided by posters and films, the latter ranging from newsreels to documentaries to, not least, feature films (Illustration 7.5).

Illustration 7.5   SA-Trooper. Section from a drawing in *Der Stürmer*, 14 April 1935.

How far-ranging were the films of, for instance, Leni Riefenstahl and other less talented directors in the realm of documentary cum propaganda is still an open question. It seems clear, however, that 'Ufa-Stars' such as Zarah Leander or Marianne Hoppe captured the imaginations of both males and females.[16] Thus, it is perhaps even more important that similar images dominated in other kinds of visual public culture, for instance, stamps and materials used as textbooks and folding '*Wandbilder*' (murals) in schools of all levels, including those for the training of apprentices in industrial and artisanal occupations. Moreover, these images structured the aesthetics and visual arrangements of feature films and their popularity can hardly be exaggerated.

The range of such images, of course, cannot be discerned precisely. Still, resonances and reverberations resound in diaries and autobiographies – from Victor Klemperer to lesser known contemporaries such as Hermann Stresau.[17] The latter moved to Göttingen in the late 1930s where he survived in various occasional and intermittent occupations. Females recall in autobiographical writings the concern that they were not like the projected 'Aryan' model[18] but had rounder heads, were small and not blond. Charlotte Beradt's treatment of dreams in the Third Reich recalls a dream where someone finds himself in an all-blond company and a little child of two years of age who is not yet speaking still speaks to him and tells him 'but you do not belong here'. The dreamer is someone who does not fit the projected stereotype of the proper German.[19]

Paula Diehl has recently investigated the images and imaginaries related to the body in Nazi ideology and politics. Her particular emphasis is on the SS – that is the self-declared guarding order of the Third Reich – a declaration that was well received and accepted by the Reich's very leaders. The discrepancy between the posturing of the SS males and the immense effort and practice of bringing the bodies of the SS into this shape cannot be taken as a direct model for, for instance, ordinary Hitler Youth or League of German Girls' groups whether in an urban, small town or village context. Still notions like '*straffe Körperhaltung*' (rigid posture), or the emphasis on controlling one's body ('*Körperbeherrschung*') was to be found in almost every pamphlet or speech of these respective organisations.[20] In fact, the difference between the elite (especially the '*Leibstandarte* Adolf Hitler') and one's own unit 'on the ground' was part of the display but also the rallying effect of the respective arrangements – employing differentiation in order to enhance both cooperation and subordination of the 'masses'.

War times – or: the increasing appeal of lean bodies and physiognomies

Visual and pictorial representations of the lean but presumably healthy body, whether male or female, had been a recurrent part of people's everyday life since the infamous 'hunger winter' during World War I in 1916/17. Scarcity of food if not hunger had also been recurrent. And hunger hit the urban poor and unemployed again after 1929 and never faded from people's imagination until the late 1930s. Certainly, such experiences among most city dwellers reverberated with notions of deprivation and feelings of desperation. Shortages of butter, eggs or meat (such as pork or bacon) were felt and angrily criticised with different emphases in all regions of Germany during the mid 1930s.[21] Recurrent if not permanent food shortages severely limited people's strivings for taking a break from the chores of the everyday if not for tasting the sweetness of better times. At least in the semi-public milieu of neighbourhood shops or pubs many people frankly complained that dire straits had come again, notwithstanding the grand perspectives of the 'new era' that Nazism would provide.[22]

At the same time, however, the vast majority of Germans seemed to draw a positive overall picture of Nazism with regard to the economic upswing and general improvements in the society and polity.[23] The point, however, is whether and to what extent did people consider or even welcome food shortages as a chance to improve one's body shape and body feel? Did people detect that very flip-side: the chance to acquire a new fitness and reshape their body in ways that otherwise did not seem available?

Lean and athletic bodies occupied centre stage during World War II, in feature films and elsewhere in public displays. Such was the image of the soldier of the *Wehrmacht* conquering much of Europe and, thus, 'cleansing' the continent from 'plutocrats' and, more explicitly, Jews. Movie actresses and stars sported the yet even slimmer female edition of that active persona.[24] Also after the obvious turn of the tide in early 1943 (defeat at Stalingrad), this set of images kept its valence but now it represented the heroes who would stem the tide of 'Bolshevik aggression'. Similar images stood for those who manned the 'home front' of the respective hinterlands. A fat face or belly appeared, in turn, as the visible mark of those who shied away and did not pitch in to help the *Volk*'s efforts – more generally, the fat belly and chin marked the appearance of the enemy whether he operated internally or externally.

Thus, the slogan of the last feature film the Nazis started to produce in 1945 *'Der Alltag geht weiter'* (the everyday is going to go on) not the least alluded to people's longing for a body that would be healthy amidst the rubble of German towns and cities. To present on screen bodies at the limits of being emaciated would, then, be a plea that relied on its demonstrative realism. Thereby, this visualisation might encourage that sort of activity or, at least, alertness that was so in demand in times of warfare – in times of risking and of destroying human lives.

Occupied Germany after 1945: from lean to emaciated bodies

Visual documentation from all zones of Allied occupation showed what data on food production (if not distribution) and nutrition confirm for most of the first three years after 1945: hunger became a widespread experience, once again primarily among city dwellers. Generally, in the first years after 1945 the scarcity of food that had hit German towns and cities during the last two years of the war[25] turned into the long-term absence of food and, thus, almost permanent hunger. Now, people did not focus anymore on 'as much as you want' of cigarettes and coffee, butter or cake. Instead, the struggle for the very basics ruled people's days and nights. Only those who by themselves or via kin had access to a plot of land that allowed the growing of some potatoes, cabbage and tobacco were better off; the ultimate was if such a plot would feed even one or two rabbits. By this token, only farmers and peasants lived on the other side of the hunger line.[26]

To feed themselves or loved ones, some people hunted for remnants from Allied canteens and kitchens. Almost everyone turned to foraging for potatoes, beans or cabbage and minimal portions of milk and bacon, not even to mention butter or eggs.[27] Not all had sufficient bargaining power for such activity or for the flourishing black markets: both activities, illegal as they were, stood for the intensity of people's efforts to acquire at least small quantities of basic food stuffs that would provide a meal or, rarely enough, a momentary treat. In that context socio-economic distinctions revolved primarily around people's bartering power embodied in their practical abilities (or lack thereof) or in symbols of affluence old and new, from carpets or jewellery to cigarettes, chocolate or nylons – items hopefully worth at least five or six pounds of potatoes plus a small chunk of bacon. Thus, this *'society in a state of emergency'* rapidly developed distinctions of its own, making visible the differences between the happy few who were rather well fed and the vast majority of those who suffered from hunger, partly bordering on starvation, particularly the young and the elderly whether male or female.

Scarcity and hunger determined body shapes, body weights and body experiences. Photographs show male and female bodies in need. The slender appearances almost never hid that this was not a well-trained, fit and healthy body but a body that operated at the limits of survival. These bodies were prone to picking up colds, indigestion and any other ailments or illnesses that, given the fatigued bodies and minds, could endanger survival. Faces and bodies, as far as they can be seen under coats or skirts that are mostly too wide and do not fit, appear in these pictures almost always as emaciated.

'Satisfactory meal': for men only

The rationing system in all zones of occupation pursued a line that had been in effect during the Nazi period; in fact, it continued the distribution system introduced in World War I. Accordingly, the best rations were reserved for 'hard-working' people; in the queue were to follow wage workers in general, and only at the end of the line the 'unemployed' and the house wives supposedly got their even more limited ration. In fact, this system inherently privileged the male part of the workforce since they held most of the jobs that were registered as strenuous and, thus, 'hard'. By this token, the system totally ignored the stress and strain of house and family work. Housework was still and continued to be, after the gradual return of POWs, the domain of women. In this very vein, wage work that was primarily performed by women such as textile manufacture or dairy production was not considered 'hard work'.

The 'satisfactory meal' or, what appeared to most as the most nutritious diet, included meat (mostly pork but also ham or bacon), eggs, butter, cheese and cream; these foods were desired by all but particularly demanded by men. Women almost always agreed and granted men at least the bigger share. Thus, after the gradual return of the POWs, there was not much dispute that males were again to be 'bread-winners' and that they should go hungry last.

Back to the working man: the East German version

Immediately after the military defeat of Nazi Germany women were both actors and icons of recovery. They cleared streets and towns from rubble. These so-called 'rubble women' (*Trümmerfrauen*) received attention more in hindsight. Still, when the men returned home from the war and POW camps, public attention focused again on the productivity and energy that was traditionally attributed to males.

When in East Germany the political authorities emphasised the need for that productivity that especially male workers would provide, they could rely on views of industry as a gender hierarchy that had been beyond question across the board of organised politics for decades – including in the political left, and not least the communist labour movement of the 1920s.

Thus it did not come as a surprise that in the Soviet zone, the public eye of the German authorities focused on men as the main performers at the various fronts of the new and better future. For example, the miner Adolf Hennecke, in a carefully staged action, set a record breaking norm in October 1948, thus stimulating a constant competition for titles and medals (and bonuses!) as an 'activist' and 'a hero of work'. It was only several years later, in December 1953, when the female weaver Frida Hockauf entered this male bracket – not in the realm of heavy industry though. Not merely in the arena of work but similarly in politics the officials of the German Democratic Republic (GDR), which was founded in October 1949, put male figures on centre stage. Thus, the propaganda film for the celebration of the 60th birthday of Walter Ulbricht, the actual leader of both the Socialist Unity Party (SED) and the state, on 30 June 1953 merely followed suit.[28] Here, his long-standing companion Lotte appeared only briefly as his 'cheerful companion'. Her own active role as amply documented in archival material is never even hinted at.[29]

This focus on masculinity and its assumed 'productiveness' showed stark resonances with and similarities to Nazi presentations of the male body. In both contexts, men who relied on muscular bodies that allowed for determination if not self-will had been at the centre of representation. However, East German authorities and common people alike claimed a fundamental difference; 'heroes of socialist labour' did not pride themselves on nor were they shown producing weapons. To the contrary, they were presented as guarantors of the economy and the whole society who would devote all their energies to peace. Whatever their products were, from generators to kitchen knives, from water reservoirs to marine vessels or tractors, it was the male workers who stood guard so that such products would only serve peaceful tasks. The females appeared in cooperating and supporting roles. However, in contrast to earlier pictorial conventions, women now also appeared in action at industrial worksites and at the very point of production, such as moving soil in the construction of roads. They even seized the heights of heavy industry, at least in one spot: women operating cranes in steel mills rapidly became one of the iconic images of production, too.

Of course, the Soviet example had a major influence on the imagery of male and female labour, at least during the first years of occupation. However, whether and to what extent women were recognised and respected among their male colleagues remained a difficult story; only in the worlds of literary or journalistic accounts did things look generally positive.[30]

Interestingly, the frames and profiles of male and female bodies presented in such pictures showed them closer to stout than to lean and athletic. The men could rely on well-developed muscles on their arms, neck and legs and did not appear hampered by extra body fat; the women did not deviate although their 'energy' was not embodied in similar detail. These images emphasised the body as a source of endurance and the potential for good and proper work. It was the masculine body that provided the model; only he seemed capable of mastering adverse and difficult circumstances.

'As much as you want . . . ': a boost for stout men in the 1950s and 1960s

After the currency reform in East Germany of June 1948 (and the respective political consolidation of October 1949, including the founding of the East German state, GDR) production went up and distribution improved, though rather slowly and irregularly.[31] While this is part and parcel of the standard narrative for West Germany and its focus on the market, such an account also captures principal features of the East German planned economy. In both economies and societies people's desire for unlimited consumption was for years to come a longing for a future only barely visible at the distant horizon.

In the late 1950s, production in East Germany not only stabilised but increased, as did the buying power of consumers. Although the majority of consumers in West Germany were far from overcoming scarcity, for instance, in their diet, the tendency was 'upward'.[32] In fact, people even started to bemoan the eagerness of many fellow citizens to 'make good' for the previous years of direness and to 'fill up to the brim' (*Fresswelle*). East Germans did not show different desires. Meat, bacon and sausages, but also cream, cake and pastries rich with sugar, chocolate and fat were, again, popular symbols and desired for delights. While men unpacked sausages and bacon at their lunch break, they rarely hesitated to consume tortes and cakes when they were offered at company or 'brigade' outings and at the coffee table on Sunday.

These were the same males who basked in the reputation of devotion to their task and openness to cooperation on the job. Their partners in cooperation were, again, males; females could be accepted if the males recognised them as operating and acting like males. The males treated their colleagues with a mixture of curiosity and respect, while superiors were viewed with scepticism. In contrast, newcomers on the shop floor regularly had to face a certain and persistent condescension from the old hands.

To others and to themselves, these male workers appeared as rather versatile: not only could they adapt to changing demands but they were also able to master them. The 'Brigadier' in the popular novel by Erik Neutsch *Spur der Steine* (The Trace of the Stones)[33] is a case in point. The widely admired 'Manne Krug' (Manfred Krug) gave a perfect personification of this character in the 1965 film that was censored and rereleased only in the mid 1980s.[34] This 'Brigadier' is not only someone in command of his tools and his task; at the same time he is good natured and even in his pranks never hurt anybody seriously. Also his regular boisterousness provides a certain kind of cheerfulness, perhaps as a precursor to the happy times of socialism.

Sexuality – some aspects

The 1950s and early 1960s were also years of rather unregulated sexuality cutting across marital bonds and the norms of the bourgeois family.[35] Those engaging in such relationships in the late 1940s and early 1950s sought to master the daily chores as well as the demands of reconstruction. They sought to win the future for themselves, and also for East German society and state if not for socialism in general. Their sexual encounters were, however, strictly confined to the realm of privacy. In public, any hint was castigated by rhetorical and pictorial means (and also within the SED members employed such hints as a 'dirty' means of control, thus denunciations flourished). Only since the 1960s, have activities of *'Freikörperkultur'* step by step attained recognition and a muffled publicity, even if the printed media or newsreels and television, controlled by party and state, mostly ignored it.

Liberated sexual relations contradicted in interesting, but rather subdued ways, the ambivalent anti-militaristic stance of the state and the party (SED). Condemnation of weapons remained curtailed:

already in 1947 semi-military units and related training were introduced and advertised. One of the slogans was to 'defend socialism'. Thus, the weapon or gun was restored as a well-respected 'tool' of the proper socialist male[36] and to a much lesser extent also of females. Still, liberation and sexual relationships resonated with the anti-militaristic practices of clothing and of keeping and presenting one's body that were cherished among West German peers. The presence of the Western media but also personal contacts in the 1950s made this 'unofficial' knowledge public and helped to turn it into an ideal for teenagers and young adults in East Germany as well.

Stout or fat? Beer bellies under attack

Since the mid 1960s, the attention to body shape has changed: the belly of males appears more conspicuously displayed. This goes in parallel with a relaxed attitude among many, if not most, of these men: to them, their visible belly seems nothing to be embarrassed about. It may be that they, in a literal sense, built up a corporeal shield against those disappointments that came with the 'hardship of the everyday' (referring to a popular quote from Bertolt Brecht on the '*Mühen in unserer Ebene*'[37]) as they became more imminent at that time. In this view, the bellies stood for an increase of 'normalisation'[38] allowing an increase in self-assurance. However, the question has to be left open if, and to what extent, these bellies also embodied people's awareness of impinging failure – of the GDR, of their individual life course. Still, such representations alluded to a masculinity that privileged and was symbolised in stout bodies, certainly not in slender or lean ones. Here, athletes could and did link up too. In their realm of sports, muscles remained both functional and popular.

Such imagery reflected a development that was criticised, at least internally, by physicians since the mid 1960s: about 40 per cent of the females and 20 per cent of the males showed definite signs of obesity.[39] While this was discussed from different angles including the surplus costs it generated for the society as a whole, publications addressing the wider public refrained from such debates or visual representations. In contrast, pictures that were published in illustrated newspapers like *Neue Berliner Illustrierte* and other official or licensed publications, in celebration of the 20th and then 25th anniversary of the GDR, did show well fed but not 'fat' people. And athletes did not deviate much; here muscles appeared rather conspicuously.

The debates about obesity reflected the perception of specialists. They also referred to and recognised direct similarities with other 'developed industrial countries'; a mixture of irritation and pride dominated their references to the latter. According to these experts on health issues, about one-third of the populations of such societies showed similar signs and indicators of being overweight. Ironically, the achievement of being among the leading industrial societies brought about a problem that increasingly occupied the specialists in the field: how to entice at least one-third of the population to reduce its weight?

Slender types, on the other hand, sat in offices or laboratories. The open-air settings in front of a furnace, at a construction site or in a ship building yard receded from public attention and appreciation. Illustrated news like *Neue Berliner Illustrierte* turned to clean and well-lit indoor offices and laboratories. Here, one could observe males and females again cooperating without recognisable differences or distinctions. Such pictures, however, leave open whether male types of conduct still prevailed.

Sportive bodies: a possible alternative?

Since the 1970s the intensive support of those sports disciplines that would yield positive results in terms of world records and international gold medals developed a specific cult of particularly trained bodies for this task. It was no longer the persons but the bodies that occupied centre stage.

Accordingly, the training and accompanying treatments totally ignored any possible intentions of the athletes: their bodies had to 'work' in perfect rhythm to the calendar of events. In due course, doping was practised but never ever mentioned, and in many cases obviously not even disclosed to those concerned, the athletes themselves. In this sphere, aspirations for ultimately producing the 'new man' seem to having gained momentum among those involved and acting as 'experts'. At first glance, short-term results in competitions seemed to prove them right. But the long-term results in human costs were and are abominable. Such interventions betrayed the individual athletes and inflicted harm on many of them. It also betrayed those many young males and perhaps females who took these athletes as 'models' for perceiving and shaping their own bodies.

In the end: beer bellies as symbol – men's claim for their own bodies

The loosening up of body postures among those who determinedly acted as 'working men' in East Germany peaked in conspicuous displays

Lohnende Arbeit, gesellschaftliches Anse-
hen, gute Stimmung – das ist für die Werktätigen unserer Landwirtschaft seit vielen
Jahren ein Teil der großen und der schein-
bar kleinen Errungenschaften, die auch auf
dem Lande zu ganz neuen, höchst mensch-
lichen gesellschaftlichen Verhältnissen ge-
führt haben.

Illustration 7.6 An official anniversary volume celebrating 25 years of the German Democratic Republic (GDR) showed among its more than 300 photographs only one depicting stout men: 'Rewarding Work, Social Respectability, Good Humor: For many years, these have been for our agricultural workers a part of the great and even seemingly small accomplishments, that have brought about more humane social relations even in the countryside.' Institut für Gesellschaftswissenschaften beim ZK der SED, *Mit dem Sozialismus gewachsen. 25 Jahre DDR* (Berlin: Verlag Die Wirtschaft, 1974), p. 162.

of one's body hair and one's beer belly (Illustration 7.6). Such appearances offended every sense of bourgeois decency and orderliness. And oftentimes they were meant to do so. Primarily, however, such loosening up was both an expression and symbol of the wellbeing of the 'ruling class' in a very literal sense, especially of its male pivot, as proclaimed by East German authorities. By not hiding but displaying body hair and belly the members of this class demonstrated at home, on the job and in the semi-public locations of pubs or social associations how they cared for nothing but for having a 'good time' – a 'good time' politics as defined with the party and state left out (Illustration 7.7)!

Ergebnisreiche Arbeit und ein glückliches Leben gehören im Sozialismus zusammen. Die Werktätigen unserer Republik können stolz auf ihre Leistungen in zweieinhalb Jahrzehnten sein und die Früchte ihres Schaffens genießen.

Illustration 7.7 The final image of the GDR's anniversary volume showed a young couple on the beach – both lean but not athletic. The caption reads: 'Productive work and a happy life are connected in socialism. The laboring people of our Republic can be proud of their accomplishments during two and a half decades and should savor the fruits of their pursuit.' Institut für Gesellschaftswissenschaften beim ZK der SED, *Mit dem Sozialismus gewachsen. 25 Jahre DDR* (Berlin: Verlag Die Wirtschaft, 1974), p. 247.

Notes

1. Paula Diehl, *Macht – Mythos – Utopie. Die Körperbilder der NS-Männer* (Berlin: Akademie, 2005), p. 51; Fidus's picture on p. 101; cf. Paula Diehl (ed.), *Körper im Nationalsozialismus: Bilder und Praxen* (Munich: Fink, 2006); on the cult of nakedness and the respective socio-cultural movements in Germany, see Maren Möhring, *Marmorleiber. Körperbildung in der deutschen Nacktkultur (1890–1930)* (Cologne: Böhlau Verlag, 2004), Chs. 7–10, pp. 261–377).
2. See, however, on various features and dynamics of 'orientalising' the other, Edward Said, *Orientalism* (New York: Random House, 1978).
3. Sander L. Gilman, Robert Jütte, Gabriele Kohlbauer-Fritz, *Der 'schejne Jid': das Bild des 'jüdischen Körpers'*, in Sander L. Gilman, *Mythos und Ritual* (Wien: Picus Verlag, 1998); for contrasting images, see Möring, *Marmorleiber* and Heiko Stoff, *Ewige Jugend. Konzepte der Verjüngung* (Cologne: Böhlau Verlag, 2004), esp. Ch. 3, pp. 269–375.
4. Special edition of *Simplicissimus* 13(32) (9 November 1908); the entire issue in many variations depicting Bosnians as 'lice' – in the wake of imminent war between Austria-Hungary and the Bosnians.
5. Gisela Lebzelter, 'Die "Schwarze Schmach". Vorurteile-Propaganda-Mythos', *Geschichte und Gesellschaft* 11(1) (1985), pp. 37–58; Alexandra Przyrembel, *'Rassenschande': Reinheitsmythos und Vernichtungslegitimation im Nationalsozialismus* (Göttingen: Vandenhoeck Verlag, 2003), pp. 56–62.
6. Karin Hausen's notion of *'Geschlechtsrollenstereotype'* (stereotypical gender roles) has had a wide impact, at least among social historians since the early 1970s; see her self-reflexive account, 'Die Nicht-Einheit der Geschichte als historiographische Herausforderung. Zur historischen Relevanz und Anstößigkeit der Geschlechtergeschichte', in Hans Medick and Anne-Charlott Trepp (eds), *Geschlechtergeschichte und Allgemeine Geschichte* (Göttingen: Wallstein Verlag, 1998), pp. 15–50, especially pp. 42ff.
7. See on this notion Olwen H. Hufton, *The Poor of Eighteenth-Century France, 1750–1789* (Oxford: Clarendon, 1974).
8. See the detailed analysis of one Hamburg example by Anne-Charlott Trepp, *Sanfte Männlichkeit und selbständige Weiblichkeit: Frauen und Männer im Hamburger Bürgertum zwischen 1770 und 1840* (Göttingen: Vandenhoeck Verlag, 1996); on her main point see also her article, 'The Emotional Side of Men in Late Eighteenth-Century Germany (Theory and Example)', *Central European History* 27(2) (1994), pp. 127–52.
9. This refers to military conduct and demeanour as the ultimate standard of maleness among large segments of German society since the later nineteenth century. However, such exposure would resonate with rigid disciplinary codes increasingly impregnating the style of domination in Western and Central Europe since the early eighteenth century. See on the related 'microphysics' of power, Michel Foucault, *Surveiller et punir* (Paris: Gallimard, 1975). From a different angle Klaus Theweleit has scrutinised practices of 'armouring' the male self and physique in his analysis of German 'Freikorps' and their efforts to wipe out the Bolshevik 'enemy' in 1919/20, *Male Phantasies: Psychoanalyzing the White Terror*, Vols 1, 2 (Cambridge: Polity Press, 1987, 1989). For further exploration of contemporary projections of maleness see

Claudia Bruns, *Politik des Eros. Der Männerbund in Wissenschaft, Politik und Jugendkultur (1880–1934)* (Cologne: Böhlau, 2008).
10. Eva Brücker, 'Und ich bin da heil "rausgekommen". Gewalt und Sexualität in einer Berliner Arbeiternachbarschaft zwischen 1916/17 und 1958', in Thomas Lindenberger and Alf Lüdtke (eds), *Physische Gewalt. Studien zur Geschichte der Neuzeit* (Frankfurt a.M.: Suhrkamp, 1995), pp. 337–65.
11. See Peter Weingart, J. Kroll and K. Bayertz, *Rasse, Blut und Gene: Geschichte der Eugenik und Rassenhygiene in Deutschland* (Frankfurt a.M.: Suhrkamp, 1988); Paul Weindling, *Health, Race, and Politics Between National Unification and Nazism: 1870–1945* (Cambridge: Cambridge University Press, 1989); cf. Stoff, *Ewige Jugend*. In these contexts, colonies both outside Europe but also within the European confines were used and even explicitly defined as laboratories; see Ann Laura Stoler, *Race and the Education of Desire: Foucault's History of Sexuality and the Colonial Order of Things* (Durham, NC: Duke University Press, 1996).
12. Ernst Friedrich, *Krieg dem Kriege* (Berlin: Verlag Freie Jugend, 1925); reprinted several times until 1926 but obviously still primarily circulating among pacifist circles.
13. Hans F. K. Günther, *Rassenkunde des deutschen Volkes*, 10th edn (München: Lehmanns, 1920); numerous further editions before and after 1933; 272.000 copies were printed until 1943.
14. Otto Schmeil and Paul Eichler, *Der Mensch: Menschenkunde, Gesundheitslehre, Vererbungslehre, Rassenhygiene, Familienkunde, Rassenkunde, Bevölkerungspolitik*, 88th edn (Leipzig: Quelle and Meyer, 1936, 96th edn 1938).
15. See on the range and rapid spread of this ideal Möhring, *Marmoleiber* and Stoff, *Ewige Jugend*.
16. On feature films and film stars in the 1930s and 1940s in Germany, see Erica Carter, *Dietrich's Ghosts: The Sublime and the Beautiful in Third Reich Film* (London: British Film Instiute, 2004); on the excluded 'other', see Frank Stern, 'Antijüdische Filmbilder vor 1945: verspotten, isolieren und vernichten', in *Sozialwissenschaftliche Informationen* 26 (1997), pp. 233–8.
17. Victor Klemperer was a professor of Romance languages at Dresden Technical University whom the Nazi laws rendered as 'Jew', his Protestant church membership notwithstanding. Klemperer in his diaries meticulously kept track of the methods of exclusion, violence and humiliation he and other 'Jews' had to stand every day and night from February 1933; see his book, *I Will Bear Witness: A Diary of the Nazi Years*, 2 vols (New York: The Modern Library, 1999; Munich, 1996). Hermann Stresau was a librarian with the Berlin Public Library. After his dismissal for political reasons in the spring of 1933 he tried to stay afloat as a freelance author and translator; see his book, *Von Jahr zu Jahr* (Berlin: Minerva, 1948).
18. *Der Große Brockhaus*, 15th edn, Vol. 13 (Leipzig: Brockhaus, 1932), p. 476. The entry cites H. F. K. Günther and Eugen Fischer, the latter being one of the leading physical anthropologists of the 1920s in Germany; both prominently furthered and engaged themselves with Nazism. This entry was not amended in the supplement volume of the *Große Brockhaus* (Leipzig, 1935) that otherwise introduced Nazi readings of a wide array of subjects.
19. Charlotte Beradt, *The Third Reich of Dreams* (Chicago, IL: Quadrangle, 1968; Munich, 1966). It remains to be seen to what extent discrepancies between

the ideal and the reality of the everyday enhanced the self-mobilisation among those who considered themselves as actual and legitimate members of the *'Volksgemeinschaft'*; see also Diehl, *Macht-Mythos-Utopie*, p. 128.

20. See Diehl, *Macht – Mythos – Utopie*, pp. 212ff., especially on marching, from its visual to its acoustic dimensions.

21. See on this *Deutschland-Berichte der SOPADE*, new edition by Klaus Behnken (Salzhausen: Nettelbeck, 1989; 1st edn 1980). For corroborating reports from the *SD*, the 'security service' of the *SS*, see Hans Boberach (ed.), *SS: Meldungen aus dem Reich, 1938–1945*, Vols 1–17 (Herrsching: Pawlak, 1984). For reports by *Regierungspräsidenten* and presidents of the courts of appeal, see Thomas Klein (ed.), *Der Regierungsbezirk Kassel 1933–1936: Die Berichte des Regierungspräsidenten und der Landräte*, Vols 1, 2 (Darmstadt: Historische Kommission für Hessen, 1985); Klaus Mlynek (ed.), *Gestapo Hannover meldet. . . .: Polizei- und Regierungsberichte für das mittlere und südliche Niedersachsen, zwischen 1933 und 1937* (Hildesheim: Lax, 1986); Hans Michelberger, *Berichte aus der Justiz des Dritten Reiches: Die Lageberichte der Obelandesgerichtspräsidenten von 1940–45, unter vergleichender Heranziehung der Berichte der Generalstaatsanwälte* (Pfaffenweiler: Centaurus, 1989).

22. On the encroaching restrictions of the regime and the administration on those defined as Jews, See Marion Kaplan, *Between Dignity and Despair: Jewish Life in Nazi Germany* (New York and Oxford: Oxford University Press, 1998).

23. See on the food shortage and its effects on health and mortality between 1933 and 1937 Jörg Baten and Andrea Wagner, 'Autarchy, Market Disintegration, and Health: The Mortality and Nutritional Crisis in Nazi Germany, 1933–1937', Munich, University Center for Economic Studies, Working Paper No. 800 (2002); cf. Winfried Süß, *Der 'Volkskörper' im Krieg: Gesundheitspolitk, Gesundheitsverhältnisse und Krieg im nationalsozialistischen Deutschland 1939–1945* (Munich: Oldenbourg, 2003), especially pp. 381–404, on the limits and deficiencies that Nazi health policies also entailed for the members of the 'master race', the *'Reichsdeutsche'*, particularly after 1942.

24. See Carter, *Dietrich's Ghost.*

25. To impose permanent hunger and push populations towards starvation had been a crucial element in German policies of extermination, from the confinement of German Jews to *'Judenhäuser'* to the ghettoes into which the European Jewry was brutally herded, primarily on territories that were occupied after 1939, especially in Poland and the USSR, and, then, the camps of extermination. For an overview, see Lea Rosh and Eberhard Jäckel, *'Der Tod ist ein Meister aus Deutschland': Deportation und Ermordung der Juden; Kollaboration und Verweigerung in Europa* (Hamburg: Hoffmann and Campe, 1990); more specifically, see Christian Gerlach, *Krieg, Ernährung, Völkermord: Forschungen zur deutschen Vernichtungspolitik im Zweiten Weltkrieg* (Hamburg: Hamburger Edition, 1998).

26. Rainer Gries, *Die Rationen-Gesellschaft: Versorgungskampf und Vergleichsmentalität. Leipzig, München und Köln nach dem Kriege* (Münster: Westfälisches Dampfboot, 1991). Of course, farmers and peasants had to comply with the rationing system too: their produce was confiscated prior to harvest.

Enforcement and policing of this rule ran, however, into widespread practices of withholding food and selling it on the black-market.

27. Michael Wildt, *Am Beginn der 'Konsumgesellschaft'*. *Mangelerfahrung, Lebenshaltung, Wohlstandshoffnungen Westdeutscher in den Fünfziger Jahren* (Hamburg: Ereignisse Verlag, 1994), pp. 20ff., especially p. 26 on a survey from 1942 on people's desires for the time 'after the war' which emphasised wishes to eat 'as much as you want'.

28. Due to the uprisings in the GDR from 16 to 18/19 June 1953, that film was never completed but just archived. Thus, *Baumeister des Sozialismus: Walter Ulbricht* (directed by Ella Ensink and Theo Grandy) was released only after the peaceful revolution and, hence, implosion of the GDR in 1989.

29. See the holdings of the *SED*, now in *SAPMO-Bundesarchiv Berlin*; here the files of the *Zentralkomitee* and the papers of Walter Ulbricht (ibid.).

30. For example, Franz Fühmann, *Kabelkran und Blauer Peter* (Rostock: Hinstorff, 1961). On DEFA films, see Peter Zimmermann, *Arbeit, Alltag und Geschichte im ost- und westdeutschen Film* (Konstanz: UVK, 2000).

31. André Steiner, *Von Plan zu Plan: eine Wirtschaftsgeschichte der DDR* (München: Beck, 2004).

32. Wildt, *Am Beginn der Konsumgesellschaft*, pp. 72–5, 107–8, 255–63.

33. Erik Neutsch, *Spur der Steine: Roman* (Halle: Mitteldeutscher Verlag, 1964).

34. It was one among half a dozen films banned in December 1965 by the XI. Plenum of the Central Committee of the *SED*. The main accusations focused on the possible effects such films would have on youth by showing serious conflicts and despair even among socialists; cf. Peter W. Jansen and Christa Maerker, *Verbannte Bilder. Verbotsfilme der DDR*, ARD-Video cassette (1991).

35. Dagmar Herzog, *Sex After Fascism. Memory and Morality in Twentieth Century Germany* (Princeton, NJ and Oxford: Princeton University Press, 2005), pp. 192–204.

36. The socialist male had carried this tool from the first organisational efforts in the nineteenth century; among the socialist left, to fight the ruling powers in a military struggle on the barricades of revolution had been a constant feature of imagery and political imagination alike. In biographical terms, many leading functionaries of the *SED* had been active members of the 'International Brigades' fighting Franco's *coup d'état* in the Spanish Civil War; see Walter Janka, *Spuren eines Lebens* (Berlin: Rowohlt, 1991), pp. 87–172.

37. The range became apparent as well in a popular novel by Erich Loest, *Es geht seinen Gang oder Mühen in unserer Ebene*, Gütersloh: Bertelsmann Verlag 1971 (Halle: Mitteldeutscher Verlag, 1978).

38. Mary Fulbrook, *Power and Society in the GDR: 1961–1979: The 'Normalization of Rule'?* (New York: Berghahn, 2009). For a partly different take, see Katherine Pence and Paul Betts (eds), *Socialist Modern: East Germans Everyday Culture and Politics* (Ann Arbor, MI: University of Michigan Press, 2008).

39. P. Piorkowski, 'Medizinische und ökonomische Aspekte der Fettsucht', *Das deutsche Gesundheitswesen* 25 (1970), pp. 1740–6, especially p. 1741. The basis here is the ideal weight; see M. Möhr, 'Epidemiologische Untersuchungen über die Adipositas und deren Risikofaktoren', *Das Deutsche Gesundheitswesen* 32(12) (1976), pp. 529–35; he also mentioned that since the 1970s, obesity rates in working-class households fell slightly.

Part III

Gender and Empire in Colonial Dictatorships

8
The State, Family and 'Womanhood' in Colonial Korea: 'Public' Women and the Contradictions of the Total Mobilisation Programme

Kyu Hyun Kim

This chapter explores the changing conceptions of the family and 'womanhood' during late colonial Korea, especially after 1937 when the Second Sino-Japanese War had escalated to bring about 'total mobilisation' as a mode of social management. The Japanese colonial government was faced with the task of making Korean women serve Japan's imperialist projects, including the conduct of an undeclared war in China (1937–45) and eventually the Pacific War (1941–45). The mainstream historiography generally concludes that the Korean women in this period became doubly bound by the obligations to the patriarchal system and to the colonial state, their collective political voice dwindling to virtual nothingness. Both nationalist and Marxist-socialist perspectives, when taken up by Korean historians, have largely chosen to define 'progress' for Korean women in terms of 'fighting alongside' the men against colonial oppression and discounted other types of activism on the part of the women as outcomes of being passively mobilised by the Japanese rulers or morally condemnable acts of collaboration with the enemy.[1] A typical assessment is that the colonial state 'endowed women's role in their homes with public meaning captured in the slogan "women in the rear, protecting the home (as opposed to men at the front, advancing the cause of the nation)". This slogan was in fact designed to isolate women inside the private domain and to effectively mobilise them for imperialist wars'.[2] But this immediately raises a question: how could the colonial state 'confine' women in the private sphere *and* effectively mobilise them for imperialistic wars at the same time? Is this not a contradiction in terms? How were these policies put into practice in reality and, more importantly, how were they interpreted and understood by women themselves?

By examining such historical sources as magazines catering to a female readership, especially those like *Yŏsŏng* (Female) that provided an important field of discourse for promoters of the total mobilisation campaign in the late 1930s and early 1940s, as well as state and civilian publications extolling the reconceptualisation of family as a social unit and an institution, this chapter attempts to address the above questions. At the heart of our concern is the possibly counter-intuitive and self-contradictory dynamics of social mobilisation by the Japanese colonial government and its ideologues, who might have inadvertently given an opening to Korean women for public participation and even empowerment, all the while trying to keep the latter confined in the domestic sphere. Finally, recognising this potentially self-contradictory nature of the colonial mobilisation compels us to question and rethink the very notion of the 'public/private' division as applied to modern Korean history, and the nature of colonial domination as understood in the existing historiography.

The problem of 'public' women in women's history and the history of the family

Women's appropriate public role is a difficult issue to tackle, and not just because there has been relative silence about it among theorists and historians until recently. As a rule, women were thought to have the biologically rooted social functions fundamentally different from those of men, namely the capacity for reproduction. It was thought to be natural that they were consigned to the domestic sphere of managing the household as a mother and a wife, severed from the 'men's' world of public policy making. And yet, the power holders, including the state, had to 'enfranchise' women and mobilise them for their own ends – religious, economic, political – and for that reason had to allow the latter to 'spill' into the public realm. Indeed, the difficulties encountered by the state or patriarchy to clearly demarcate the private and public realms and control women's places in one or the other without 'spillage' has been pointed out in numerous works of women's history and history of the family.

For instance, Philippe Aries, probably the most influential historian of the 'Western' family, notes in his pioneering work *Centuries of Children* that the family in Europe had always encompassed both domains of the private and public as we understand these categories from the twentieth century onward, although he sees the modern nuclear family as largely deprived of the rich resources available from civic engagement and extensive sociability in previous times.[3] Likewise, American historians of gender and family such as Mary Ryan and Nancy Grey Osterud have demonstrated that nineteenth-century American women and men led the lives that transcend or blur the boundaries of private and public realms, despite the efforts by the contemporary opinion makers and ideologues to consign women into the discrete 'women's sphere' characterised by 'domesticity'.[4] Adding her own research on Antebellum New England women in the nineteenth century to the achievements of her predecessors, Karen V. Hansen suggests that the distinct dimension of human activity that can only be defined as the 'social' and 'market economy' must be taken into account in addition to 'private' and 'public' activities.[5] Nonetheless, Hansen's own theoretical paradigm, while more refined and inclusive, appears to generate its own potential oscillations and tensions. She defines 'public', to cite one problematic example, as encompassing 'the state and all state-related activities, such as the law, the party system and local, state and national governments'.[6] This definition – too obviously anchored in the particularistic historical experience of the USA – could potentially exclude the kind of activities on the part of women that are obviously 'public' in orientation but might not exclusively pertain to legislation or matters of government – for instance, as we see below, the drive toward Korean rural women's education sponsored by the Japanese colonial authorities. Her argument is more convincing if we simply regard what she calls 'the social' as a realm of activities that flow in and out of both private and public realms, rather than as yet another distinct category.

It appears that women's public role, as investigated by European and American historians of family and gender, has always been constructed, contested and reconstructed in relation to the family as a field of social activity that could be both 'private' and 'public' in character. This ideological construction of a certain model of family has assumed the particular bourgeois, 'middle-class' character of a nuclear family based on a married couple in the industrial and post-industrial age. In modern times, the bourgeois ideal type of a couple-based family based on a formal marriage, rather than the strikingly diverse lived lives of women, became the model for the seemingly clear-cut demarcation between the private and public dimensions of women's lives.[7] Such demarcation served the power relations not only between the gendered selves (between the 'men who tell women what to do' and the 'women who listen to these men and agree with them') but also among the social bodies clustered into entities recognised as the state, civil society and family. But calling for such demarcation, or even instituting it in the name of law, did not automatically mean that it became material reality: nor did it mean that contradictions inherent in such a demarcation became naturally resolved.

John B. Thompson points out that ideology must function to 'sustain relations of domination', first by 'dissimulation', that is – as Marxists would argue – by hiding or blocking out some aspects of actual social relationships, by highlighting others or by calling these relationships something other than what they are, and then by 'reification', that is, making such relationships appear permanent and absolute when in fact they are subject to historical transience.[8] Seen in this way, it seems clear that the ideological construction of women's role by the ruling powers has not only been subject to criticism from the counter-discursive forces, for example, feminists, but also displayed tensions and contradictions between its function and substance: that is, even when women appear to be following the state's lead and being 'good mothers', they might in substance be doing something else entirely. This might be recognised as problematic by the agents of the state, but then again this could also force the latter to reckon with the very internal contradictions in their own ideological programmes. As we shall see below, the situation in colonial Korea involving women's public role was by no means any more 'clear-cut' than the one in modern Europe and the USA, despite the tendency to portray the Korean woman's plight with the monochromatic brush of oppression and exploitation. Let us first look at the history of Japanese women, as they supplied the model for modern Korean women to emulate in the early twentieth century, in conjunction with the outflow of modernity from the metropole to the colonised 'hinterland'.

The modern Japanese discourse on family and womanhood

Japan's rapid modernisation drive had by the late nineteenth century resulted in radical changes in the legal and social meaning of the family. The Japanese adopted civil codes modelled after the Napoleonic codes that redefined and reinforced patriarchal modes of organisation. They also separated the lineage-based, temporal 'family' (*kazoku*, 家族 *kajok* in Korean) from the marriage-based, spatial 'home' (*katei*, 家庭 *kajŏng* in Korean). The growth and consolidation of the Japanese empire between its two successful war campaigns in the international arena, the First Sino-Japanese War (1894–95) and the Russo-Japanese War (1904–05), was paralleled by the inculcation of a discourse on 'the good wife and wise mother' (*ryōsai kenbo* 良妻賢母), limiting women's social roles to those of supporting working men and raising sons. Around this time, 'housewife' (*shufu* 主婦) was introduced as a category and celebrated not only as a stable anchor that grounded Japanese society but also as the realisation of the feminine ideal. Finally, 'home' (*katei*) came to be firmly associated in some quarters with successful management and implementation of imperial wars. Male opinion makers in modern Japan expressed anxiety about the traditional, mother-dominated families 'feminising' Japanese boys and argued that modern 'housewives', well educated, patriotic and committed to social action, would effectively undermine such tendencies.[9]

In reality, the notion of 'the good wife and wise mother' was a continuously evolving construction that could mean different things to different constituents. Much of the discourse on *ryōsai kenbo* assumed surprisingly activist roles for women, especially in the field of education. The total war mobilisation showcased by World War I (1914–17) left an indelible mark on the minds of the Japanese state leaders and intellectual elite: but they were double-tongued in what they demanded from women, sometimes demonstrating a glaringly self-contradictory attitude toward Japanese women as a depository of 'Western modernity' and modern nationalism as well as of 'traditional values'.[10] Katō Chikako shows that men like Kikuchi Tairoku, the Education Minister during the Russo-Japanese War, and Shimoda Jirō, renowned education studies scholar, abhorred the 'Western' notions of equal rights of men and women and celebrated the superiority of the 'persevering spirit' and 'decorum' of Japanese women over European (most importantly British) women. In 1910, they even banned from bookstores a liberal feminist tome entitled *Fujo mondai* (The Problem of Woman) by Kawada Shirō, which used as its theoretical base John Stuart Mill's *On the Subjection of Women*. Still, in magazines and newspapers catering to a predominantly female readership such as *Fujo shinbun* (Woman's News), the state's and its ideologues' stringent argument for 'keeping women where they belong' was not only met with criticisms that it was old-fashioned and anti-modern but also, on some occasions, replaced by the image of a model woman far more actively engaged in public enterprises, especially education, charity and other social welfare programmes. Indeed, one eye-opening series of articles in *Fujo shinbun* strongly encouraged elite Japanese women to take on the task of 'educating Korean women' so as to facilitate the colonisation of Korea.[11]

The Japanese state had begun to claim its naturalised status as manager of social resources by the late 1910s. As Barbara Molony points out, even feminists and suffragists, often at the receiving end of the scorn and hostility of men like Shimoda, came to view the state as 'an established institution capable both of protecting rights against societal or civil oppression and of denying rights to groups or individuals who then would either resist the state or struggle for inclusion in it'.[12] It was not so much that the state became all-powerful but that it was increasingly able to offer a set of compromises to women in lieu of struggling for their enfranchisement. Typical of the positive response that such change in the perception of the playing field generated toward the state was the prominent feminist Hiratsuka Raichō's speech given to the All-Kansai Federation of Women's Organisations in 1919. In the speech, Hiratsuka deliberately distinguished between men's and women's rights and argued for a distinctive type of 'women's rights' (*joken* 女権) and 'mother's rights' (*boken* 母権), implicitly accepting the bio-social discrimination between the genders and moving away from the nineteenth-century liberal conception of equal rights.[13]

Sheldon Garon has illuminated the processes through which women's groups, including overtly feminist ones, came to collaborate closely with the state's social management policies by the 1930s. Since the late 1910s the state bureaucrats in Japan, spearheaded by the 'progressive' Bureau of Social Affairs in the Home Ministry, had spent much energy making women into dynamic social agents contributing to the national economy. They cooperated with the leaders of the women's groups to expand their roles in managing household economies, waging moral crusades against luxury, conspicuous consumption, vices such as alcoholism, 'Western-style' sexuality and excessive individualism. These 'daily life improvement' campaigns (*seikatsu kaizen undō* 生活改善運動) were generally supported by the feminist leaders. Garon points out that, by collaborating with the state in this manner, they condoned and aided the extension of state control over civil society and the expansion of the Japanese empire overseas, in exchange for their increased power in dealing with the social management and welfare issues, such as child-rearing, protection of mothers and reduction of poverty. This tendency became acute when political parties, their best allies in pushing for women's political rights, lost power following the Manchurian Incident (1931) and the rise of militarism. As he puts it: '[Women] leaders discovered that they most effectively influenced policymaking when they furthered causes that appeared to lie within the special domain of women'.[14]

However, we are not sure from reading Garon whether the state's incorporation of women into their social management policies and imperialist projects actually meant the decline of women's public role. He characterises the situations in the 1930s and 1940s as an 'expansion of the domestic sphere'. But should it be seen as such? Would it not be closer to the truth that many Japanese women chose to 'collaborate' with the state because the latter's policies had afforded an opening for them to punch holes in the bubble of the 'domestic sphere?' For example, Ichikawa Fusae, the noted feminist, continued to see the state-organised National Defence Women's Association and its local campaigns in the 1940s as a form of 'liberation' for rural women from the 'domestic oppression' they suffered under the hands of their husbands and traditional communities.[15] We cannot entirely dismiss her claim as self-justification. Not only feminists like Ichikawa, but also ordinary women might indeed have shared the view that total mobilisation allowed women to participate in the public realm that the state was ostensibly trying to shut them out from. In addition, we might ponder the fact that more than three million Japanese women had joined the workforce by 1945, although at comparatively lower wages than men, and that the groundwork for widespread participation of women in local civic activities and organisations in the post-war years was laid out largely due to war mobilisation policies. It is certainly a morally disturbing aspect of Japanese feminism that many of its leaders 'collaborated' with the state, especially in the latter's pursuit of brutal war campaigns in China and structural exploitation and denigration of the colonised population in Korea, Taiwan and South East Asia, but that does not negate the possibility that such actions might have contributed, in however twisted and ironic a manner, to the subsequent empowerment of Japanese women.

The colonial modernity, 'New Women' and domesticity in Korea, 1919–37

The Japanese colonial discourse on Korean women absorbed, with some time lag, the Japanese conceptions of family, home and womanhood in the late nineteenth and early twentieth centuries. The most noticeable changes came in the 1920s, and were connected to the shift in the Japanese colonial policy. Following the violent suppression of the March First Movement, a partly coordinated and partly spontaneous outbreak of massive anti-Japanese street demonstrations in 1919, the new Governor-General of Korea, Saitō Makoto, initiated 'cultural rule' (*bunka seiji* 文化政治). 'Cultural rule' involved the relaxation of administrative control, the granting of permission to Koreans to publish newspapers and books in the Korean language, as well as the abolition of official discrimination in the public service sector.[16] Even though there had been a pervasive interest since the 1910s in the 'new type of women', educated, literate and free from the shackles of arranged marriage, concubinage and other 'feudalistic customs', the term 'New Women' (*sin 'yŏsŏng* 新女性) and the public discourse on them were largely products of the 1920s.[17] By then the New Women, characterised not only by good educational backgrounds but also by 'bobbed' or short hair, 'Western-style' dresses, hats, heels and other modern clothing, and the kind of consumerist behaviour that defined the cutting edge of the mass culture of early twentieth-century capitalism – shopping at department stores, playing tennis or watching motion pictures with 'dates' – had ceased being a novelty.[18]

The emergence of these New Women was tied to the upward social mobility of non-*yangban* (literati) class women. The old *yangban* family looked askance at their daughters getting an education. Neither did they consider a working woman with income a desirable figure. In contrast, the biographical data regarding New Women suggests that their mothers sometimes expected their daughters to become the breadwinners of the family via 'modern education', in place of their economically incompetent husbands. The allure of becoming New Women was always tempered by realistic considerations of economic survival and the still-strong commitment to one's kinship network. Na Hye-sŏk, Korea's first Western-style woman painter, presents herself in the autobiographical 'Kyŏng-hŭi' (1918) as a New Woman, attempting to 'enlighten' other women whose values concerning the worth of women are defined by their ability to marry a rich or high-status husband and bear sons. However, Kyŏng-hŭi herself never rejects marriage and a happy family life as a choice for New Women. The strength of the novel actually comes from an honest depiction of the self-contradictory pull she feels toward the domestic stability of the 'old women's' lives and her desire to succeed in the world as men do.

New Women were certainly admired and envied, by both male and female Koreans. They were at the forefront of Korea's transition to modernity. On the other hand, these New Women, from the very beginning, were subject to male language that suppressed their right to sexual self-determination. Yi Sŏng-hwan's 1921 essay 'New Women's Seven

Virtues', for instance, claims that New Women should be able to converse intelligently with their husbands, should have a good sense of hygiene, should not follow superstitious customs, should raise children based on correct scientific knowledge, should be capable of writing letters and sending telegrams and, finally, should be good 'working companions' for their husbands ('Old Women know not what to do with a single sheet of newspaper. But New Women are capable of writing manuscripts, keeping household budgets and reading books to the husbands').[19] At the same time, there was a strong tendency to collapse the imagery of 'women in public', who had moved out of the domestic sphere, with that of courtesans, or *kisaeng*. The public nature of *kisaeng*'s social function was conflated with the newly public character of New Women's professional identities, and even the modernity represented by such bold forms of public visibility. Such conflation reminds one of a *yangban* woman's supposed response to a Christian missionary's statement that God loves all regardless of one's station, 'I don't want to love just anybody. That's what a whore does.'[20] As was the case in China, many Korean New Women became embroiled in triangular relationships, among the (desired) married New (modern) Men, their wives from arranged marriage, and themselves. Consequently, the New Women sometimes found themselves stuck in a glorified form of concubinage.

Male intellectuals, regardless of their left/right or nationalist/socialist affiliation, sought to define the New Women's body as the site in which the competing narratives of recovering patriarchies could be inscribed. Those women who resisted this and attempted to define their identities in their own terms were vilified or ignored, a steep price to be paid. Another tendency was to allow the New Women's subjectivity mainly in terms of their role as a consumer in the bourgeois, capitalist society, that is, as 'consuming subjects'. Their 'loose' morality and 'sexual freedom' were subtly and not so subtly linked in the mainstream Korean language media to consumption patterns of luxury goods and 'Western' fashion. The 'imported' (*hakurai* 舶來) and 'sophisticated in the Western manner' (*haikara*) commodities, associated with the metropolitan cultures of the West and Japan and sold in the Japanese shops, such as Hirata-ya and Jōjiya in Chingogae, and in major department stores, such as Mitsukoshi and Shinsegye, were identified in the minds of the Korean male elite with the New Women.[21] A fascinating analysis by film critic Paek Mun-im of the evolution of the iconography of Ch'unhyang and other 'suffering women' characters in Korean popular culture illustrates how colonial conditions were used by some Korean men to justify nostalgic invocation of 'traditional' patriarchal values. The ironic result was that the 'updated' Ch'unhyang in dime-store novels, melodramatic pastiches and early cinema became much less 'subversive' and 'active' than the versions of her presented in early modern literature. Paek extends her discussion to the heroines of popular melodramas in the colonial period, strongly characterised by the leitmotif of 'sold' daughters/younger sisters, usually eliciting an excessive outpouring of condemnatory rhetoric from the heroine's 'patriarchs'. What is troubling is the fact that the vicious and poisonous anger pouring out of Korean male lovers/fathers/'older brothers' is seldom directed at the colonisers/collaborators/or the 'wealthy but ugly oldsters' who violated the heroines' chastity, but at the victimised women themselves. The male anxiety about female sexual desire and subjectivity is thus sublimated under the 'shame of the Korean ethnos' (*minjok* 民族), which ultimately denies these women any form of agency and subjectivity.[22]

Yet, despite the barrage of critiques poured on New Women by both Korean men and the Japanese colonial state, harping on their lack of chastity and morality, their indifference to commitment, passion and loyalty, and their shallowness and fashion consciousness, the paradigm of modern womanhood established by the New Women in the 1920s was too powerful to be dismantled in the 1930s and 1940s. Even during the supposedly economically retrenched, socially conservative wartime, the notion of the New Women as embodiment of desirable modernity persisted and wielded great influence. Moreover, the Japanese colonial regime, rather than wanting Korean women to go back to their 'traditionalist' modes of livelihood, allowed various types of social movements geared toward 'reform' and 'rationalisation' of the family structure to thrive in the 1920s and 1930s. In their minds, many colonial bureaucrats saw themselves on the side of 'progress' toward modernity, whether their rhetorical subservience to the divinity of the Japanese emperor and his 'unbroken lineage' chafed against such a self-understanding or not.

The colonial state's modernisation drive also irrevocably transformed the Korean family in the 1920s. The colonial legal system in 1923 adopted the practice of the marriage license, removing older generation household patriarchs from their exclusive position as decision makers in marriage. The right to divorce had already been established legally in 1918, and officially acknowledged in a 1921 court case. The concept of the 'small family' based on the voluntary union of a man and a woman was idealised and pitted against the traditional 'extended family', associated in both the colonial and Korean nationalist discourses with 'feudalistic' oppressions of the past. The 'daily life improvement' campaign was also imported from Japan in the 1920s by the colonial government and promoted by elite civic associations, emphasising punctuality, financial savings, simplification of ceremonies and festivities and suppression of conspicuous consumption. In 1932, The Seoul Friends of the Housewife Society (*Keijō Shufu no Tomo no Kai*), consisting of the avid Korean readers of Japan's premier women's magazine *Shufu no tomo*, held a Home Life Rationalisation Exhibition at Kyŏngbok Palace.[23]

Nationalists, of course, had their own reasons for criticising the extended family system. As a *Tonga ilbo* editorial loftily pronounced:

> What was the ideology that Koreans, throughout the five-hundred-year history of Yi dynasty, have made their utmost priority to put into practice? What were the rituals that have always been perfectly prepared? The family ideology and family rituals, those are the answers…. [In the pre-modern period, Koreans] had no concept of public morality toward their national and ethnic community, but had an enormously developed concept of private morality toward their own lineages and family members.[24]

Male nationalist opinion makers in the 1920s agreed that the extended family system had to be reformed as part of a broad modernisation programme for strengthening the (forthcoming Korean) nation-state. Of course, few male writers and intellectuals had anything outright positive to say about women getting jobs and gaining 'economic independence'. Yi Ku-yŏng, writing in *Sin'yŏsŏng* magazine, asks his New Women readers: 'Can economic independence be the best method for obtaining freedom, nay, for raising your own status? This problem leaves much room for thought.' His answer, of course, is that women can (or should) remain perfectly satisfied with material achievements gained through their housework.[25] Significantly removed from such pompous displays of male arrogance was the noted children's rights advocate and writer Pang Chŏng-hwan's stirring denunciation of the extended family and a call for a better integration of 'livelihood' (*sallim* 살림) and 'enterprise' (*sa'ŏp* 事業). He advocated rearrangement of the priorities of Korean families so that they could devote their resources to raising children into happy, healthy adults. While Pang implicitly accepted the premise that women's premier role in a society is that of a mother-educator, he was unique among Korean men in his claim that privacy among family units (say, between a married couple and their parents-in-law) must be respected, and that children should be given their own rooms so that their autonomy and spirit of independence would be fostered.[26] Such a prescient expression of the championing of the individual rights of women and children within the family system was rare among male Korean intellectuals of the time.

Total mobilisation in the colonial Korea and women's response, 1937–45

With the Marco Polo Bridge Incident leading to a full-fledged war between Chinese Nationalists and the Japanese Army in 1937, state bureaucrats and the military pushed for 'total mobilisation' (*sōdōin* 總動員) programmes. A series of draconian measures, dubbed 'Imperial Subjectification policies' (*kōminka* 皇民化 or *hwangminhwa* in Korean), were implemented between 1938 and 1945. They were made up of four major components: religious reform, including obligatory worship at Shinto shrines; a national language movement through which Japanese would replace Korean as the 'national language' (*kokugo* 國語); adoption of Japanese family names (*kaiseimei* 改姓名 in Taiwan, *sōshi kaimei* or *ch'angssi kaemyŏng* 創氏改名 in Korea); and recruitment of voluntary soldiers (*shiganhei seido* 志願兵制度). Wartime rhetoric of guarding the 'home front' (*jūgo* 銃後), which practically constituted the entire population of the empire under the definition given in the Total Mobilisation Law, permeated the ideological statements directed at women by the colonial state. In addition to the continuation of life improvement campaigns, the colonial government gave women's organisations the tasks of saving monetary and material resources, inculcation of 'patriotism' for the Japanese empire and training regimens against potential enemy attacks, especially air raids. The Patriotic Women's Association, originally established in Japan in 1901, for the purpose of providing health and psychological care to the soldiers, had only 35,304 members in 1926 Korea with more than two-thirds of the members Japanese, but it had grown in size to 118,227 members in 1935, with more than 50 per cent of them Koreans. By 1940 its Japanese and Korean membership exceeded 430,000 (the statistical records stopped classifying the members' ethnic identities in 1938).[27]

The total mobilisation campaign was embraced by many major Korean language cultural media outlets, such as the *Chosŏn ilbo* company's comprehensive monthly magazine *Chogwang* (The Morning Light), its children's magazine *Sonyŏn* (The Youth) and the woman's magazine *Female*. *Female*, launched on 1 April 1936, and terminated in

December 1940, lavishly printed in colour and boasting frequent contributions and editorship by renowned literary figures including Ch'ae Man-sik, Kim Nam-ch'ŏn, Kim Tong-in, No Ch'ŏn-myŏng and Yun Sŏkchung, is particularly illustrative of the way that the social norms, class and status structures and everyday lives of Korean women interacted with the total mobilisation campaign of the late 1930s and early 1940s. In Korean language scholarship, Sin Chi-yŏn has extensively used *Female* magazine to explore the 'remodelling' of the 'home' and the female body by colonial modernity. Sin's treatise attempts to break new ground in the study of colonial-period women's history by exposing the essential continuity between 'Western' modernity and Japanese colonialism in their objective to regulate and discipline women's bodies and thereby their subjectivity.[28] However, her argument that the discourse on family and women in the late 1930s showed a rigorous drive toward 'abstractisation' and 'dichotomisation' of womanhood into 'New' and 'Old', and reproduced these distinctions in the separation of the state and the home is not quite convincing. In fact, judging from the actual contents of *Female* magazine, such efforts to regulate and discipline womanhood were themselves fraught with inner tensions and sometimes outright contradictions. Nor do I think, as she claims, that the boundaries of 'home' (*kajŏng*) were extended to 'apply to the society as a whole', in a way similar to the expansion of the domestic sphere that Sheldon Garon has noted for the Japanese case.[29]

To begin with, the invocation of 'motherhood' to justify the consignment of the women to the family was not always what it appeared to be. The male promoters of the total mobilisation programme sometimes sought to summon Japanese women as models for Korean women to emulate. Interestingly, despite their lip service to the sacredness of 'motherhood', they acknowledged that Japanese women are 'working outside the home' in various positions to aid the war efforts. Writer Kim Mun-jip, while exhorting Korean women to become more patriotic and grateful toward the Japanese empire, argues that they should be 'better educators' at home and more 'active' in public activities. He chides, '[if] there is a practice for preparing against air raids in a town, Japanese women work actively like a man wearing a *monpe*, while Korean women merely look on, keeping their hands in their sleeves and sporting indifferent expressions'.[30] Hyŏn Yŏng-sŏp, perhaps the ultimate Korean 'collaborator', summarises his anti-feminist position neatly in the following statement: 'The mistake of the feminist movement of the past was that it only knew individual women but it knew not the nation.' He actually praises Korean nationalist women for having a 'wider perspective' than 'thinking only about women', despite their critical mistake of not realising the greatness of the Japanese empire. According to Hyŏn, women under the total mobilisation campaign must first and foremost be 'mothers', who should avoid getting involved in public office or obtaining PhD degrees and, presumably as a result, living the rest of their lives in loneliness and dejection. In principle, women's happiness can only be found in the home but they should 'get rid of the narrow-minded notion that their own homes must be given priority at all times ... and never forget that their sons are not merely their children but young men needed by the state'. Having so self-satisfactorily laid out the ideal that Korean women have to measure up to, Hyŏn then backhandedly admits that the life improvement movement and other such campaigns must be led by 'New Women with girl's school education' and housewives from upper middle-class households. In his view, only these women could truly comprehend the significance of imperialist projects, and enlighten the ordinary Korean women still mired in 'barbaric' customs like spending money on shamanist rituals.[31] Ham Sang-hun takes a less flagrantly self-contradictory stance toward modern Korean women, acknowledging that many of them sought jobs outside the home because it was economically advantageous to do so, and that 'with some moral faculties cultivated, New Women will make incomparably superior beings than Old Women'.[32]

Women's own writings were even more pronounced in their ambivalent response to total mobilisation and the inculcation of 'motherhood' as the signature role for women. Hŏ Yŏng-sun's essay in *Female*, entitled 'The Female and Motherly Love' (1938), appears at first glance to typically praise women's maternal instincts and elevate them to the ultimate feminine virtue. But she soon turns the direction of her critique toward the continuing practice of concubinage and the abuse of children by stepmothers, openly pointing out that most Korean women still suffer from their status as men's playthings or 'home-bound slaves' (*kajŏng noye* 家庭奴隸). She even refers, without any logical connection to her ostensible praise of submissive motherhood, to Henryk Ibsen's *Doll's House*, managing some words of praise for Nora's quest for independence.[33]

And then there are the writings that seemingly buck the trend and essentially champion the New Women as the ideal image of Korean women in times of wartime mobilisation. Noted journalist Sŏ Ch'un, asked to contribute a piece on the wisdom of providing professional education for women, wrote a piece stringently attacking Korean society's refusal to acknowledge women's mental capacity. He even goes so far as to argue that in certain areas of military activity women might outperform men (for instance, female fighter pilots would concentrate on their jobs instead of drinking and smoking) and that, if a parent has to choose between a boy and a girl as a beneficiary of higher education, priority should be given to the girl.[34] What is interesting is that Sŏ draws upon not liberal theories of equal rights, but trendy 'scientific' ideas extolled by the imperialists, including eugenics, demography and theories of total war, to justify his views. In this way, Sŏ absolutely refuses to consider the reproduction and education of children as generic functions for women: both men and women can always relegate child-rearing to others for the purpose of making a greater contribution to society, and in any case, women's propensity for education allows them to be more effective disseminators of what they learned to the rest of the society. Similarly, No Chwa-gŭn goes further than Kim Mun-jip and Hyŏn Yŏng-sŏp in recognising Japanese women's participation in the total mobilisation campaigns as essentially 'liberating' in character and basically the extension of their political activism during the 'capitalist democracy' of a generation ago. No's criticism of Korean women as 'consuming subjects' actually derives from the quasi-feminist perspective of seeing these women as degrading themselves as 'playthings of men', beholden to fashion and physical appearance as defined by men. He concludes his piece by encouraging Korean women to come out into the streets, and live their lives in defiance of the stereotypical image of them as letter-writing romantics. This is hardly a ringing endorsement of a 'good wife and wise mother' demurely waiting for the husband and children to return home.[35]

Another interesting venue in which women's ambivalent response to the mobilisation campaigns can be read is the so-called round table talks on the pages of Korean magazines (*zadankai* or *jwadamhoe* 座談會). Many women invited to participate in these round table talks were not shy about voicing criticisms of the extended family system and patriarchy, using the rhetoric of 'rationalisation of the home' and an economically sound lifestyle to knock down the men and their wasteful, authoritarian behaviour. In one round table talk sponsored by *Female* magazine, Yu Og-gyŏng flatly states: 'The current social system is organised around men, so men generally have greater power, but inside the home women have power.... Men would be nothing without their rights to inheritance. But there is a point where we cannot tolerate any more oppression [from men]'. Kim Sŏn argues that one of the biggest threats to the health of the home economy is the fact that many men, with the exception of devoutly religious ones, keep concubines. Han So-je wonders if men saved all their money spent for social drinking how much help it would be for the home economy. Pak Maria puts it succinctly: 'You say women spend too much, but whatever we spend money on, we bring home. Can you say the same thing about men?'[36] The women also express objections against the rigidly uniform and impractical features of wartime colonial policies, such as the latter's insistence that the ties (*korŭm*) of the traditional costume be replaced by buttons ('This has no discernible economic advantage and only serves to ruin whatever aesthetic quality a Korean costume has'), Western-style socks be used instead of traditional foot covers (*pŏsŏn*) and traditional houses be replaced by so-called 'cultured dwellings' (*munhwa chutaek* 文化住宅). The participants, while appreciating the convenience and cleanliness of modern housing, also point out its problems, such as lack of air circulation.

It is noteworthy too that these round table discussions among the elite women make constant references to 'Western' (usually American) examples instead of Japanese practices of marriage and home life. As Kim Hye-gyŏng and Chŏng Chin-sŏng have shown, American theories of family relations, especially its 'cult of domesticity', had deeply penetrated Korea in the 1910s and 1920s, and continued to serve as a reference point for many Korean women, even after the notion of 'companionable marriage', centred on romantic love between husband and wife, came under criticism for its alleged tendency toward excessive individualism.[37] This situation is reflected, for instance, in the participants' scepticism toward the collective marriage ceremony ('it destroys the romantic spirit and mystery of the marriage'; 'Western couples in movies drag a Christian minister to a wide-open field, and bam, they get married without spending a single cent') as well as in their admiration of child-care policies in the USA (for instance, low infant death rates). The reference to American 'rationality' in home management as a model continues to appear in the women's discourse on family at least until the outbreak of the Pacific War in December 1941. Korean elite women also strongly demand that the colonial state build child-care centres on 'every street corner' of Seoul. The *Tonga ilbo* reporter Hwang Sin-dŏk argues that these child-care facilities should be available, with fees fixed at less than 20 *chŏn* per day, for working women of all classes, be they factory workers, shopkeepers, teachers or newspaper reporters. Ch'oe Ŭi-sun, wife of the former *Tonga ilbo* editor-in-chief, adds that housewives could most certainly use child-care facilities as well. Through their enthusiastic discussions, we find out that the Seoul Severance Hospital, the Salvation Army, the Tongdaemun Women's Medical Centre and the T'aehwa Women's Centre were equipped with day care centres.[38]

In late the 1930s, the colonial state implemented surname change, transforming the Korean lineage system with the wife and husband using different surnames and only recording the father's side of lineage, into a no less patriarchal Japanese one in which a married woman would have to adopt the husband's surname. While Korean nationalists have regarded the surname change as one of the greatest crimes Japanese colonisers committed (so much so that it had assumed the centrepiece position in the so-called Japanese 'ethnocidal' policies), women in the 1940s round table discussions express nonchalance and indifference to having to use their husband's surnames, Japanese-style. Hwang Sin-dŏk quips that her name can be Im-Hwang Sin-dŏk in Japanese-style four-character combination, combining her and her husband's surnames.[39] In fact, the round table participants are far more concerned about the protection of individual and professional identities established under their maiden names than keeping their family surnames. Writer Ch'oe Chŏng-hŭi raises the example of the Japanese writer Uno Chiyo and argues that she has remarried more than twice but has never changed her name to 'Kimura' Chiyo or 'Watanabe' Chiyo, following her husband's surnames.[40]

A 1941 round table discussion among young female students studying in Tokyo illustrates with greater honesty their balancing act between 'the demands of the state and society' and their personal desires to lead meaningful lives as women and as individuals. Participants admit that, as economic conditions get more difficult, many young, educated women increasingly opt for an early marriage, and as a result household economics and clothes-making are on the rise as preferred subjects of study. Yet, they all express a strong desire to work outside the home, even if temporarily. The main reason they cite for being 'working women' is not to become economically independent but to 'actively join and contribute to society' through their occupations (Nihon Joshi Daigaku student Chŏng Kwan-yŏng is one exception, insisting that building a happy home should be an absolute priority). They also are critical of the view that New Women are inherently wasteful. Tokyo YWCA officer Ch'oe Chik-sun points out that some Old Women, caught up in the feudalistic mentality that they must treat their guests to feasts beyond their means, take them to expensive restaurants, but New Women would consider it a true form of hospitality to cook meals for the guests. As for the best type of spouse, the discussants overwhelmingly vote for men with 'respectable personalities' (*ingyŏk* 人格), with the basic level of economic means, of course. The women students are shown to have retained the modernist outlook of the New Women, evincing a strong desire to move out of the confines of the domestic sphere and actively join the larger society. But we can also see that their desire for self-realisation has been tempered by the limitations imposed by the total mobilisation and couched in language privileging the 'greater society' and eschewing individualist orientations.[41]

In rural areas, the colonial state set up programmes to train young rural women to become 'core women leaders' (*chunggyŏn puin* 中堅婦人), who would lead rationalisation and regimentation of farm life. We have a fascinating report on a tour conducted at a state-sponsored 'rural core women education centre' set up in Tam'yang, South Chŏlla Province.[42] The centre in question was built in 1937 and had annually produced 30 graduates, among young women with basic elementary school education. The average age for freshmen was 17. The centre's explicit objective was moulding these Koreans girls into the image of the Japanese 'good wife and wise mother'. Its head (a Japanese gentleman referred to only as Mr Nakamura) claimed that it enjoyed a reputation as a form of preparatory school for brides (*hanayome gakko* 花嫁學校). But when the reporter interviewed one of its first graduates Yu Sŏk-rye, we find out that she, instead of happily raising children as a demure farmer's wife, had used the knowledge and expertise gained at the centre to become a woman instructor for Yŏsu County's Association for Agricultural Promotion, touring five counties and delivering popular lectures on farming technologies and household economics. She states, 'I want to continue this work [public lectures] but my parents are against it', indicating that the family was pressuring her to get married. Yu also divulges that she keeps regular correspondence with other alumni from the centre and has preserved the network of women committed to improving rural conditions.[43] This episode illustrates that rural young women incorporated into the colonial institutions of total mobilisation could use these institutions to assert their public identities as activists in mobilisation programmes against the expectations of the larger society.

Concluding thoughts

The colonial state's intervention into the lives of Korean women became more extensive and intrusive in the late 1930s and 1940s as the total mobilisation campaign went into full swing. And yet, the contradiction between women's public character as direct agents of the state and their roles as mothers and wives in the supposedly private realm of the family was never successfully resolved to everyone's satisfaction. This was partly due to the contradictions inherent in the ways the state mobilised women: the state claimed to 'protect' the family by separating it from society into a discreet realm, all the while attempting to infiltrate and regulate it. The fact that the Japanese colonial state, in its pursuit of a total war system, championed patriarchal and masculine values did not do much to stabilise the ambivalent status of women's public identity in modern Korea. As An T'ae-yun acknowledges, 'under the wartime regime elite women's opportunities for speaking out in public and social activism actually increased... the issues and concerns regarding everyday life and domestic labour were transferred from the private sphere into the domain of public discourse, as they were now considered a part of war efforts with national significance'.[44] As we have noted, this 'spillage' of women into the public realm was not confined to the case of the highly educated, metropolitan residents.

With minor exceptions, Korean men, whether nationalist or collaborator-imperialist, painted the New Women or working women in a negative light, insisting on the 'home' as women's natural domain and 'motherhood' as their natural inclination. However, by embracing modernity as mediated through the colonial empire, Korean men also trapped themselves in a series of self-contradictory positions. When they brought in the examples of patriotic Japanese women to parade before Korean women, they had to acknowledge that the former were not exactly confined in the domestic sphere. Neither could they eradicate the New Woman as a paradigm. Similar contradictions may be observed in the colonial state's stance, even though we are tempted to say that it, unlike Korean men, could afford to win Korean women's voluntary support more readily because it had more resources at its command and therefore had more to offer to the latter. Nonetheless, many Korean women, as much as we can ascertain from the primary sources, were not fooled by the colonial state's or Korean men's self-contradictory demands and sanctimonious injunctions. They continued to hold onto the paradigm of the New Woman and the ideals of self-determination and rationality as well as the desire to transcend the domestic sphere in defining the meaning of their lives. When the conditions of total mobilisation made it difficult for them to assert their desires, they opted for compromises, some through active participation in the state-sponsored mobilisation programmes, others by means of manipulating the rhetoric of being homemakers to resist patriarchal coercion.

Notes

1. Cf. Chŏn Kyŏng-ok, Yu Sang-nan, Yi Myŏng-sil and Sin Hŭi-sŏn, *Hanguk yŏsŏng chŏngch'i sahoesa* (Seoul: Sungmyŏng Yŏja Daehakkyo Ch'ulp'anguk, 2004).

2. Chŏn Kyŏng-ok, Pyŏn San-wŏn, Pak Chin-sŏk and Kim Ŭn-jŏng, *Hanguk yŏsŏng munhwasa* (Seoul: Sungmyŏng Yŏja Daehaggyo Asia Yŏsŏng Yŏnguso, 2004), p. 355.

3. Philippe Ariès, *Centuries of Childhood: A Social History of Family Life* (New York: Vintage, 1965); See also his essay 'The Family and the City in the Old World and the New', in Virginia Trufte and Barbara Meyerhoff (eds), *Changing Images of the Family* (New Haven: Yale University Press, 1979).

4. Mary P. Ryan, *Cradle of the Middle Class: The Family in Oneida County, New York, 1790–1865* (New York: Cambridge University Press, 1983); Nancy Grey Osterud, *Bonds of Community: The Lives of Farm Women in Nineteenth-Century New York* (Ithaca, NY: Cornell University Press, 1991).

5. Karen V. Hansen, 'Rediscovering the Social: Visiting Practices in Antebellum New England and the Limits of Private/Public Dichotomy', pp. 268–302, in Jeff Weintraub and Krishan Kumar (eds), *Public and Private in Thought and Practice* (Chicago, IL: University of Chicago Press, 1997).

6. Ibid., p. 295.

7. Mary P. Ryan, *The Empire of the Mother: American Writing About Domesticity, 1830–1860* (New York: Harrington Park Press, 1985); see also Martin Segalen, 'The Industrial Revolution: From Proletariat to Bourgeoisie', in André Burguière, pp. 377–415, Christiane Kapisch-Zuber, Martine Segalen, Francoise Zonabend (eds), *A History of the Family, Vol. 2: The Impact of Modernity* (Cambridge, MA: Belknap Press, 1996).

8. John P. Thompson, *Studies in the Theory of Ideology* (Berkeley, CA: University of California Press, 1984), pp. 126–32.

9. Muta Kazue, *Senryaku to shite no kazoku: kindai Nihon no kokumin kokka keisei to josei* (Tokyo: Shin 'yōsha, 1996), pp. 60–72; see also Ueno Chizuko, *Kindai kokka no seiritsu to shūgen* (Tokyo: Iwanami Shoten, 1994).

10. Koyama Shizuko, *Ryōsai kenbo to iu kihan* (Tokyo: Keisō shobō, 1991).

11. Katō Chikako, ' "Teikoku" Nihon ni okeru kihan-teki joseizō no keisei', in Hayakawa Noriyo et al. (eds), *Higashi Ajia no kokumin kokka keisei to jienda* (Tokyo: Aoki Shoten, 2007), pp. 66–73.

12. Barbara Molony, 'Women's Rights, Feminism and Suffragism in Japan, 1870–1925', *Pacific Historical Review* 69(4) (2000), p. 645.

13. Ibid., p. 646; also see Kathleen Uno, *Passages to Modernity: Motherhood, Child-hood, and Social Reform in Early Twentieth-Century Japan* (Honululu: University of Hawaii Press, 1999); Vera Mackie, *Creating Socialist Women in Japan: Gender, Labour, and Activism, 1900–1937* (Cambridge: Cambridge University Press, 1997). Such acceptance of women's proscribed role in exchange for the state protection is a phenomenon noted by Claudia Koonz in her path-breaking study of the German women under the Nazi regime: see her *Mothers in the Fatherland: Women, the Family and Nazi Politics* (New York: St Martin's Press, 1987).

14. Sheldon Garon, *Molding the Japanese Minds: The State in Everyday Life* (Princeton, NJ: Princeton University Press, 1997), p. 142. For the Japanese women leader's participation in the Japanese expansion into Manchuria, see Louise Young, *Japan's Total Empire: Manchuria and the Culture of Japanese Imperialism* (Berkeley, CA: University of California Press, 1999), pp. 161–80.

15. Garon, *Molding the Japanese Minds*, pp. 142–5.

16. However, in terms of social and political regulation, Saitō's administration in fact increased the number of policemen (employing many Koreans as 'surveillance police') and the numbers indicate that, despite making headway in some areas of public service (for instance, the number of Korean public school presidents), the proportion of Koreans in key administrative positions actually declined after 1919. (The proportion of Koreans among the members of the Governor-General's office was 39.5 per cent in 1918, 38.5 per cent in 1920 and 35.6 per cent in 1925.)

17. The term 'New Women' was said to be first used in the journal *Shinyŏja* 新女子 (founded in 1920 but surviving for only five issues), founded by the writer Kim Il-yŏp. In the 1920s, a series of magazines ostensibly geared toward female writers and consumers, including *Sinyŏsŏng* (New Women, founded in 1923), *Singajŏng* (New Family, founded in 1921), *Manguk puin* (Women of the World) and *Hyŏndae puin* (Contemporary Women), were published.

18. Cf. Theodore Jun Yoo, *The Politics of Gender in Colonial Korea: Education, Labor and Health, 1910–1945* (Berkeley, CA: University of California Press, 2008), Ch. 2. 'The "New Woman" and the Politics of Love, Marriage and Divorce in Colonial Korea'.

19. Yi Sŏng-hwan, 'Sin'yŏsŏng ŭn 7-dŏgi kubi', *Pyŏlkŏngon* (December 1921); quoted in Pak Yong-ok, 'Sinyŏsŏng e taehan sahoejŏk suyong kwa pip'an', pp. 51–82 in Mun Ok-p'yo, Yi Pae-yong, Pak Yong-ok, Song Yŏn-ok, Kim Kyŏng-il (eds), *Sinyŏsŏng: Hanguk kwa ilbon ŭi kŭndae yŏsŏngsang* (Seoul: Chŏngnyŏnsa, 2003).

20. Quoted in Kang Sŏn-mi, 'Chosŏn p'agyŏn yŏ-sŏngyosa wa kidok yŏsŏng ŭi yŏsŏng chuŭi ŭisik hyŏngsŏng', PhD Dissertation, Ewha Women's University (2003), p. 174.

21. Im Ok-hŭi, 'Pokchang ŭi chŏngch'ihak kwa singminji yŏsŏng ŭi sobi konggan', in T'ae Hye-suk et al. *Hanguk ŭi singminji kŭndae wa yŏsŏng konggan* (Seoul: Yŏiyŏn, 2004), pp. 261–71.

22. Paek Mun-im, *Ch'unhyang ŭi ttaldŭl, Hanguk yŏsŏng ŭi panjjokjjari kyebohak* (Seoul: Ch'aeksesang, 2001), pp. 54–65; see also Im U-gyŏng, 'Singminji yŏsŏng gwa minjok/kukka sangsang', in T'ae Hye-suk et al., *Hanguk ŭi singminji kŭndae wa yŏsŏng konggan*, pp. 48–76.

23. An T'ae-yun, 'Chŏnsi ch'eje wa kajŏngsŏng: Kajŏng saenghwal kwa chubu yŏkhar e kwanhan nonŭi rŭl chungsimuro, 1937–1945', *Yŏsŏng kwa yŏksa* 1 (December 2004), pp. 68–77.

24. *Tonga ilbo* (21 September 1926).

25. Yi Ku-yŏng, 'Kajŏng saenghwal kaejo wa kŭ silche', *Sin'yŏsŏng* 3(2) (February 1925), in Yi Hwa-hyŏng, Hŏ Tong-hyŏn, Yu Chin-wŏl, Maeng Mun-je, Yun Sŏn-ja, Yi Chŏng-hi (eds) *Hanguk kŭndae yŏsŏng ŭi ilsang munhwa*, vol. 7, *Kajŏng saenghwal* (Seoul: Kukhak Charyowŏn, 2004), pp. 64–67.

26. Pang Chŏng-hwan, 'Sallimsari taegŏmt'o: kajŏng saenghwal kang'ŭi', *Sin'yŏsŏng* 5(3) (March 1931), in *Kajŏng saenghwal*, pp. 64–110.

27. *Chōsen sōtokufu tōkei nenpō* (1935) (Keijō: Chōsen Sōtokufu, 1937); *Chōsen sōtokufu tōkei nenpō* (1940) (Keijō: Chōsen Sōtokufu, 1942).

28. Sin Chi-yŏn, ' "Kajŏng" kwa "yŏsŏngsŏng" ŭi ch'usanghwa wa kamgagŭi remodeling: 1930 nyŏndae chapchi "Yŏsŏng" ŭl chungsimŭro', pp. 235–257, in Hangukhak ŭi Segyehwa Saŏptan and Yŏnse Daehakkyo Kukhak Yŏnguwŏn (eds), *Ilche singminji sigi saero ikki* (Seoul: Hyean, 2007).

29. Ibid., p. 272.
30. Kim Mun-jip, 'Yŏja taun yŏja: Chosŏn punyŏ sahoe e koham', *Katei no tomo* 24 (September 1939), p. 25; see also P'o Hun, 'Pando puin ŭi kago', *Katei no tomo* 24 (September 1939), p. 4.
31. Hyŏn Yŏng-sŏp, 'Saeroun puin undong', *Katei no tomo* 25 (October 1939), p. 9.
32. Ham Sang-hun, 'Chosŏn kajŏng saenghwal chedo ŭi kŏmt'o', *Yŏsŏng* 3(9) (September 1939), pp. 30–2.
33. Hŏ Yŏng-sun, 'Yŏsŏng kwa mosŏngae', *Yŏsŏng* 3(9) (September 1938), pp. 36–9.
34. Sŏ Ch'un, 'Yŏja wa chŏnmun kyoyuk', *Yŏsŏng* 4(11) (November 1939), pp. 28–31.
35. No Chwa-gŭn, 'Kajŏng esŏ kaduro!', *Yŏsŏng* 5(1) (January 1940), pp. 23–5.
36. 'Kajŏng saenghwal kaesŏn: jwadamhoe', *Yŏsŏng* 4(2) (February 1939), pp. 18–23; 'Kajŏng puin jawadamhoe', *Yŏsŏng* 3(11) (November 1938), pp. 32–8.
37. Kim Hye-gyŏng and Chŏng Chin-sŏng, ' "Haeggajok" nonŭi wa "singminjijŏk kŭndae-sŏng:" Simgminji sigi saeroun kajok kaenyŏm ŭi toip kwa pyŏnhyŏng', *Hanguk sahoehak* 35(4) (2001), pp. 226–9.
38. 'Chŏnjaeng changgihwa "kajŏng saenghwal" chubu jwadamhoe', *Samch'ŏlli* (March 1940), pp. 233–6.
39. This is how some contemporary Korean women and men choose to spell their names, rejecting the practice of keeping women's surnames or adopting husband's surnames and regarding them equally patriarchal and oppressive.
40. Op. cit. (Note 38), pp. 236–7.
41. 'Tonggyŏng yŏja yuhaksaeng jwadamhoe', *Ch'unch'u* (May 1941), pp. 145–53.
42. Pak Wŏn-sik, 'Taechi ŭi yŏin pudae: chŏnnam nongch'on chunggyŏn puin yangsŏngso kŭp che il-hoe suryosaeng Yu Sŏk-rye pangmungi', *Katei no tomo* 32 (1940), pp. 7–11.
43. Ibid., p. 11.
44. An T'ae-yun, 'Chŏnsi ch'eje wa kajŏngsŏng', p. 98.

9
Mothers of the Empire: Military Conscription and Mobilisation in Late Colonial Korea

Michael Kim

Wars in the twentieth century have had a somewhat paradoxical effect on gender politics around the world. During periods of intense warfare, women are often thrust into new social roles as they increasingly assume public duties and enter the workforce to replace the men dispatched to the battlefront. The history of gender politics in colonial Korea (1910–45) after the outbreak of the Second Sino-Japanese War (1937–45) in many respects paralleled wartime developments found elsewhere. Korean women were called upon to display their loyalty to the Japanese Emperor by entering the workforce and fulfilling their obligations as mothers and wives of Korean soldiers drafted into the Imperial Japanese Army. Korean women were also encouraged to participate actively in local civil associations dedicated to supporting the home front while the men were away on military duty. The male-dominated public discourse of the late colonial period reinforced patriarchal gender roles, yet the women who participated in the wartime mobilisation were not necessarily acting in a passive manner. New venues for women to become active members of Korean society would emerge as a consequence of the war, and the numerous examples from the late colonial period of women addressing female audiences and discussing the importance of military conscription may be particularly revealing sources for understanding the significance of this shift in gender relations.

In some respects, Korean women who responded to the wartime mobilisation behaved in similar ways to Korean men with regard to their desire to achieve equality with the Japanese, almost to a point where the gender issues may seem less relevant. However, close attention to the women's discourse on military conscription can show that women did in fact define their roles and duties differently along gender lines, and this phenomenon cannot be properly understood without a consideration of the transformation of everyday life within the wartime mobilisation system. In particular, the local 'patriotic associations' introduced by the Japanese during the war would open new opportunity structures and space for women to become actively involved in Korean society. Thus, while the 'women's talk' on military conscription may be dismissed as mere propaganda, a careful explication of these texts intended for a female readership may provide a more comprehensive understanding of the gender politics during this period.

The question of agency and everyday life in colonial Korea

The role of women in wartime mobilisation raises a number of important questions about historical agency in colonial Korea. Koreans who openly supported the colonial order are rarely attributed agency, because most existing studies on the colonial period tend to emphasise the activities of either the Japanese colonisers or the victimised Koreans who resisted colonial rule. Considerable research has been conducted on how the Japanese formulated their colonial policies and how Koreans participated in independence movements, yet relatively little attention has been paid to collaborator Koreans who were active within the colonial system except to condemn their actions as traitors to the nationalist cause or rationalising their actions as having had no choice but to cooperate with an oppressive order. One early attempt to explore Korean agency during the colonial period, Carter Eckert's *Offspring of Empire*, has drawn considerable criticism for suggesting that Koreans played an active role in economic development under the colonial system.[1] Yet the controversies surrounding the work have largely overlooked the themes that Eckert raises of how colonised Koreans navigated and negotiated their way through the complexities of the colonial system. Instead of blindly condemning the collaboration, there is a need to examine the context under which colonial subjects choose to express their agency to accommodate rather than resist the demands of the colonisers and explore the space for social participation within the boundaries of the colonial order.

The complex dynamics of resistance and accommodation by colonial subjects can be seen readily in the gender politics of wartime mobilisation in colonial Korea. Women generated numerous new identities and struggled to define their social roles throughout the colonial era.[2] During much of the early colonial period, Korean women made only modest gains in this regard until the *sinyŏsŏng* or 'New Woman' emerged from the pages of fashionable women's magazines in the 1920s to carve out social liberation within a patriarchal colonial society. Newly established educational institutions and the advent of modern professional occupations for women created new opportunities for Korean women to break away from the existing gender confines. Yet by the late colonial period, the New Woman became the object of intense social criticism for her questionable morality and conspicuous consumption. Instead of the individualistic New Woman, the late colonial media offered an alternative identity for women to assume in the form of patriotic mothers and wives who selflessly guarded the home front and gladly sacrificed their husbands and sons for the nation.

On a basic level, this phenomenon of Korean women accepting patriarchal definitions of good mothers and obedient wives during times of war may be explained as male dominance over the definition of female roles. However, a nuanced understanding of why some Korean women actively identified with patriotic wives and mothers of Korean soldiers who fought on the side of the Japanese colonisers may be possible by combining insights from the history of everyday life with the history of gender.[3] An understanding of the complexities in the gender dynamics and an appreciation of the importance of the transformation of everyday life can be applied to a colonial situation to examine the position of women in colonial Korea. Therefore, while the everyday life of Korean women during the late colonial period is an area of Korean history that is rarely studied, an understanding of this issue may be critical for providing the proper 'thick descriptions' necessary to interpret the symbolic meaning of texts where women exhort other women to voluntarily submit themselves to traditional gender roles and sacrifice their sons and husbands to the oppressive colonisers.[4]

Gender politics and wartime mobilisation

In many respects, the history of Korean women in the late colonial period parallels developments found elsewhere with regard to the relationship between gender politics and warfare. As wars drag on, women are needed to participate in the workforce and contribute to the maintenance of the home front, which ultimately allows them greater space for economic and civic participation in wartime societies.[5] The literature on the wartime mobilisation of women also stress that traditional notions of motherhood are often reinforced, while they are simultaneously encouraged to work in new occupations on behalf of the war effort. Some research on women's mobilisation emphasises the importance of 'political opportunity structures' in explaining women's decision to participate in social movements.[6] Changes in access to power or shifts in the ruling alignment that encourage women to perceive an opportunity to improve their collective situation can determine the success and failure of women's movements.[7] Thus, the successful mobilisation of women for warfare often involves new social or political arrangements that can induce women to participate in mass movements to seek collective advantage.[8]

The fickleness of historical memory in recalling the role of women in past wars also applies to the case of Korean women during the Pacific War. Large numbers of Korean women had been mobilised by the colonial state, yet this phenomenon is one of the least appreciated aspects of modern Korean history. Korean women were brought into the workforce during the later stages of the war, and they were both encouraged and compelled to participate in civil associations that provided support for the war effort. Indeed, the fact that large numbers of women had been mobilised for wartime factory work has led to the conflation today in the Korean language of the term *chŏngsindae* (挺身隊) with *wianbu* (慰安婦), the latter referring to 'comfort women' or forced military prostitutes. The term *chŏngsindae* initially referred to both male and female workers, but after 1943 it referred to women who had been mobilised to work in the munitions factories because of a shortage of male labour.[9] Yet Koreans today generally confuse the two terms and there is little recollection of Korean women in the wartime labour force. Only the collective memories of the sexual slavery remain.

Korean women also contributed to the war effort by assuming the role of dutiful mothers and wives of Korean men who were conscripted into the Imperial Japanese Army. Korean women were entrusted with maintaining and defending the home front while the men went off to war. Kwŏn Myŏng-a and other researchers of the wartime period in colonial history have pointed out that the colonial media frequently deployed images of Korean women becoming *kukkun ŭi ŏmoni* (Mother of the National Army) and *ch'onghu puin* (Wives of the Home Front).[10] These recent studies on the late colonial period have shed considerable light on how the colonial state mobilised women and constructed new gender roles to encourage their participation. Yet one major aspect that remains missing from the existing studies of women's mobilisation is a nuanced understanding of the rationale of Korean women who became active in the wartime mobilisation system. Some scholars have raised the issue, but the overall opportunity structures and the dynamics of the social transformation that enabled women to participate in the wartime mobilisation is a topic that has yet to attract attention.[11]

However, before addressing the conditions under which Korean women participated in the war effort, it is first necessary to separate the gendered dimension from this issue from the overall logic of collaboration that induced cooperation with the Japanese. Foremost among the concerns of Korean collaborators was the desire to realise the slogan *naisen ittai* ('Japan and Korea are One').[12] By supporting the Japanese war effort Koreans hoped that an appreciative Japanese empire would reward them with equal treatment and give them a privileged place within the emerging Greater East Asia Co-prosperity Sphere.[13] The extent to which Koreans actually received equal treatment within the wartime period within the Japanese empire may be highly debatable, but Takashi Fujitani argues that the situation of Koreans under the Japanese empires may be compared to the situation of the Japanese in America who joined the military in their desire to achieve social and racial equality.[14] Even if few substantive gains towards achieving equality during the colonial period were apparent, there is little question that many Korean collaborators fully expected to be rewarded by the Japanese colonisers for their participation in the war effort. Korean women who collaborated with the Japanese also believed that they could achieve rapid equality through the war, but the areas in which they could contribute were few because of the patriarchal limitations on the range of female social and economic activity. The wartime mobilisation did, however, open up important venues for female participation through the establishment of women's organisations and through the formation of the neighbourhood *aegukban* (愛國班) or patriotic associations. The opening of new routes for social action through the restructuring of everyday life would be one of the unintended consequences of the total mobilisation effort on the Korean peninsula.

Patriotic associations and the total mobilisation system

The Japanese empire began its mobilisation of the Korean peninsula soon after the outbreak of the Second Sino-Japanese War on 7 July 1937. Despite considerable domestic controversy, the Japanese Diet passed the National Mobilisation Law (國家總動員法) in April 1938, which gave the state bureaucracy unprecedented powers to pass laws and enforce wartime controls of the economy.[15] The passage of the National Mobilisation Law would also introduce many significant changes in Japan's colonial policies in Korea.[16] The changes include the revision of the Korean Education Law (朝鮮教育令) in 1938, which made Japanese the official language of instruction and turned the Korean language into an optional rather than a required part of the elementary school curriculum. The later revision of the Korean Education Law in 1943 removed the Korean language altogether from the elementary school curriculum and initiated preparations for universal education to begin in 1946. Koreans were also compelled to change their names into Japanese ones with the revision of the Korean civil code in November 1939. These revisions of the colonial laws were all part of a broader effort to prepare the Koreans for military service. Koreans were admitted into the Japanese Army, first as volunteers in 1938 and later through a compulsory draft that was announced in May 1942 and implemented in 1944. Korean volunteers began to be accepted into the Japanese Army after 22 February 1938. By 1940 the number of applicants had grown to 84,443, but the number allowed to enlist started small and reached 9,223 by 1943.[17] The Japanese announced the start of military conscription of Koreans on 8 May 1942 and began to implement the system two years later in 1944. Because of the length of time required to train new recruits, Korean conscripts did not start to enter the Japanese Army until September 1944. Therefore, few conscripted Koreans were actually sent to the warfront before Japan's surrender in August 1945.[18]

The wartime mobilisation of the Korean peninsula that surrounded the entry of Korean soldiers into the Japanese Army would officially begin when Governor-General Minami Jiro (1874–1955) initiated the *Korean League for the Total Mobilisation of the National Spirit* (國民精神總動員朝鮮聯盟) on 7 July 1938, the one year anniversary of the Second Sino-Japanese War. In 1940, the League was later revamped into the *Korean League for National Total Mobilisation* (國民總力朝鮮聯盟), which became a more formal organisation that was both quasi-civil and quasi-governmental in character. The goal of the mobilisation effort was to place all Koreans within a voluntary grassroots organisation headed by the Governor-General, but its basic unit was the patriotic association composed of approximately ten households.[19] The Korean League published a Japanese-language journal titled *Ch'ongdongwŏn* (Total Mobilisation) as well as 350,000 copies a month of a vernacular Korean edition titled *Saebyŏk* or *Dawn*, which was distributed to the patriotic associations. A history of the movement published in 1945 claims that the 350,000 copies of the original publication run for *Saebyŏk* was a record for periodical publications in Korea at the time.[20] The tabloid was later renamed *Aegukban* in August 1940 and the circulation figures eventually grew to 470,000 per month.[21] *Ch'ongdongwŏn* was later renamed *Kungmin ch'ongryŏk* and maintained a monthly circulation in the tens of thousands throughout the war. These publications featured the activities of the various patriotic associations and often provided detailed information about household management, hygiene and medical knowledge in addition to the constant wartime propaganda.

As early as 1939, just two years after their inception, the number of patriotic associations had reached 318,924 and had 4,259,755 members, which effectively put a significant proportion of the Korean population under their organisational structure.[22] Women quickly assumed important roles within the patriotic associations as the head of these units. The patriotic associations held mandatory meetings each month, some met at the homes of the leaders, others on a rotating basis among the households in the unit. Each household was required to send a representative, but the regulations did not stipulate who was supposed to attend. So in many cases, the households sent the wives or female servants in the case of wealthier families. The compulsory yet undefined nature of who should serve as representatives often turned the meetings into gatherings of mostly women in the households and attending the meetings became linked with women's work. The high proportion of female attendance led to frequent cases of women becoming the *panjang* (班長) or leader of the units. The Seoul (Keijo) chapter of the National Mobilisation organisation noted in December 1942 that 70 percent of the patriotic associations in the city were headed by women, but they should be replaced by men because the rationing of fuel through the organisations was about to start.[23] The increase in the responsibilities of the patriotic association for air defence and rationing of necessities led to calls for more men to become involved as leaders, but the women continued to dominate leadership positions. The numerous journal articles that featured the leaders of the patriotic associations often held up female heads as model representatives.[24]

The patriotic associations ultimately became the basic unit for not only organising the households but they also became important for spreading guidelines on lifestyle improvement, labour mobilisation, rationing, fire-fighting and air defence.[25] Numerous guidelines were routinely promulgated to establish the goals for the patriotic associations. According to guidelines published in November 1941, each association was supposed to achieve the following goals for the month:

The *Korean League for National Total Mobilisation* has decided on the following guidelines for the goals that each patriotic association will realise for the month of November.

1. National Labour Service Movement
   Let us push ahead the National Labour Service Movement to another level.
2. Accommodate the National Food Policy
   Let us make a total effort to cooperate with the national food policy within each of our families.
3. Reform of Customs
   It is now the season for marriages. Let us thoroughly reform our customs.
4. Use of the National Language
   Let us strictly enforce the use of the national language in the schools, families and workplaces.
5. Encourage Savings
   Let us strictly enforce the early savings of proceeds from the common sales of rice.[26]

These instructions reflected both national efforts, such as the National Labour Service Movement which tried to spread the idea that labour service to the country was the duty of every Korean, as well as ongoing campaigns to transform the customs of Koreans such as marriage practices. Patriotic associations were without question an integral part of the colonial authorities attempt to reshape the everyday practices of Korean subjects.

While the goals were indeed ambitious, patriotic associations were at first poorly attended and the early discussions centred on how to increase the poor participation rates. However, when the patriotic associations become responsible for the wartime rationing of necessities such as rice between 1940 and 1941, their participation rates rose significantly.[27] Households could not purchase their rationed amounts without the stamp of the patriotic associations, which gave the unit heads the power to punish those who did not attend the regular meetings. The participation of Koreans in the patriotic associations may not be entirely accounted for because basic necessities for various sources from the period describe a story of personal empowerment through participation in the meetings. In a fictional broadcast story by the female author Ch'oe Chŏng-hŭi (1906–90) published in July 1942, the heroine Sŏng-hye decides that having a maid during times of war is an unnecessary luxury and takes charge of her household affairs. When she had a maid she would never go to the association meetings because she hated to meet strangers. Yet once her maid was gone she had to attend for the first time and gradually begins to participate actively:

Once she started attending the meetings, she realised that sending the maid until now was extremely wrong. Furthermore, she felt that there were many issues that had to be resolved among the district leaders, the head of the patriotic association and its members. Therefore, Sŏng-hye occasionally began to express her opinions at the association meetings. She hated to express her views in front of people, but she could not stand to view immature behavior and listen to immature words.[28]

The heroine is eventually asked to become the leader of the association because of her outspoken leadership in organising neighbourhood activities. While the above may be a fictional account, the theme of women who were initially reluctant to participant but gradually become active in the patriotic associations can be found in numerous other sources from this period. The journal *Sinsidae* (New Generation) published an article in February 1942 that spotlighted five female leaders of patriotic associations within Seoul. The testimonials relate the problems they first encountered in organising the meetings and how they used to hate going to the meetings but later enjoyed attending. One of the women observes how the associations gave her confidence as a leader and brought the entire neighbourhood together:

> I am embarrassed to admit, but when I first became the head of our patriotic association, all I could think about was what I was going to do. As I held the first association meeting, then the second and the third, I became friendlier with my neighbours and the meetings became increasingly fun. The members of our association have become even closer by saying to each other – let's buy ingredients for *kimchi* together, let's buy firewood together and let's buy pickled shrimp together. We also had many experiences helping each other with our actual household affairs. We used to be strangers, but now we have become close like a single family. It has only been five months of experience for me, but the patriotic association is not something that is necessarily because of current incident and the entire country must be mobilised for war. I believe it would be wonderful if we always had such regulations.[29]

This leader of this patriotic association closed her remarks with the observation that some wealthy households still sent their servants as representatives, which was highly regrettable. The fact that the wealthy and the poor were all a part of the same patriotic associations in certain units suggests that some degree of interaction was taking place among different social classes. While the published testimonials by patriotic association members were clearly intended for propaganda purposes, they reveal accounts of units that gathered daily for community activities such as listening to radio callisthenics programmes and exercising in the streets together. A guide published in November 1940 on how to hold patriotic association meetings suggests that once the formal business is over, members should listen together to Japanese music, watch movies, listen to the radio or hold talent shows and calligraphy demonstrations.[30] The positive changes that these community activities brought to the neighbourhoods would lead to the sentiments that Koreans should have formed patriotic associations at a much earlier period.[31]

Women's talk and military conscription

The changes in the everyday lives of colonial subjects introduced by the patriotic associations are difficult to measure, and there is no way to quantify their impact. However, there seem to be few doubts that the institution of patriotic associations led to the greater social participation of women in colonial society and created a space of female activity that reflected the broader transformation in everyday life. The significance of the local patriotic association in shaping the sphere of female activity during the wartime mobilisation period becomes apparent through an examination of the colonial discourse on women and military conscription. The acceptance of Korean volunteer soldiers into the Japanese Army in 1938 generated considerable discussion in the colonial media. Yet the flood of media interest in the military conscription announced on 7 May 1942 would far exceed the earlier focus on Korean volunteers. In the subsequent months following the announcement, numerous newspaper and journal articles were specifically directed towards Korean women and how they should prepare themselves for the implementation of the military draft that would begin in two years.[32] The patriarchic rhetoric mostly called upon Korean women to accept their domestic responsibilities and sacrifice their sons and husbands to the war effort.

On the surface, the discussions on the military draft encouraged women to accept their wartime duties and take responsibility for family affairs while the men were away. However, a careful reading of what the women were actually telling each other through the media reveals that they were being given entirely new responsibilities and exploring new ways to take social action. What may be an important point to keep in mind here is that the women were prepared to accept the challenge of becoming 'mothers of the national army' by expressing their agency within the newly expanded gender boundaries of wartime colonial society. The sight of large numbers of women gathered together for public rallies in colonial Korea was an extreme rarity before the outbreak of the war. However, the wartime mobilisation effort gave legitimacy and sanction to large public gatherings of women who clearly understood the historic significance of their unprecedented meetings. During a large public rally for women in March 1942, the famous female writer Mo Yun-suk (1910–90) observed:

> Ever since the Seoul Public Auditorium was built, this is the first time ever that we have seen such a large gathering of only the women of the peninsula. Whether you are a man or a woman, just by looking at this sight, it is without question true today that an unusual event is taking place. One can say that if a woman raises a child in the family and respects the in-laws well then she has done all that is expected of her. However, here we are in one location saying we should do this or that, and we keep producing new lifestyle guidelines that have never existed before. What in the world is going on here?[33]

The wonder expressed at the sight of so many women gathering together for the first time may be a landmark moment in the history of women's movements in Korea. However, the more important observation expressed by Mo Yun-suk may be that women were no longer expected to take care of only their family, but instead they were all expected to take an active role in Korean society. Women were encouraged to be politicised and increasingly entrusted to develop their own autonomous plans to contribute to the wartime mobilisation.

The wartime transformation of gender roles in Korean society is particularly evident in the transcript of a round table discussion by four prominent female activists on the newly announced military conscription published in the journal *Light of Korea* (朝光) in June 1942.[34] The women noted the importance of raising their sons to be responsible to the nation and for Koreans not to fear death in battle. The women expressed their sense of pride that Koreans would soon march off to war, but one confessed that she was ashamed that she could not contribute her share to the war effort, because she did not have a son.[35] The offering of sons and husbands to the war was only one of numerous duties expected of women during the war. The problem lay in educating all of the women of Korea on how to perform their new roles. When the topic moved to how they might educate Korean families on the importance of spreading Japan's martial spirit, which views death on the battlefield as the highest form of honour, various media campaigns through the radio and press were suggested at first. One of the women then points out that educated women could easily receive such media messages but the major challenge lay in reaching the uneducated women who could not read or have access to movies, journals and newspapers. The solution proposed to solve the problem of how to reach all Korean women was the patriotic association:

> In my opinion the Total Mobilisation League should make such a book and decide upon a method and then distribute it to all of the patriotic associations so that during each regular meeting they can hold a discussion. Furthermore, there are members of the leading class within the patriotic associations and this information can spread through their direction.[36]

The women all agree that this would be the best solution and the originator of this idea even notes that nothing ever gets done without the patriotic association. The effectiveness of their local patriotic association leads the women to conclude that a public awareness campaign could successfully overcome the problems of illiteracy and the lack of access to media by distributing a booklet with the necessary information.[37] Thus, this discussion on how to mobilise other women is informed by their familiarity with repetitive life-worlds of the patriotic associations.

The ultimate goal of these women who explored the newfound significance of the woman's life-worlds was the reinvention of the Korean family into a new kind of social unit that was capable of refashioning the colonial subject. One of the discussants observes that the best way to speed up the process of preparing for military conscription is to observe the lifestyles of Japanese families. The problem she notes is that:

> Although the *naisen ittai* movement has been introduced and many Japanese families live around us, we can't communicate with them and perhaps due to the lack of knowledge and sophistication, it is difficult for Korean families to unite with the Japanese families. Even if Japanese families live in your neighborhood, it is not uncommon to be completely in the dark about how they raise and educate their children, how they carry out their daily household affairs, or not even know their faces.[38]

One of the participants agreed that even though 30 years have passed since the annexation of Korea and much of Korean society had been merged with Japan, the families of the Japanese and Korean residents still remained far apart.[39] The Japanese and Korean residents tended to lived in isolation from each other even though so many of them occupied the same urban space. Yet despite living in such close proximity, Japanese and Korean women rarely interacted with each other except as household servants.[40] The participants in the discussion suggest that all Korean women must make an effort to visit Japanese households and invite Japanese neighbours to their homes to bring down the persistent barriers. The urgent calls for Korean women to visit neighbouring Japanese families and learn their way of managing the household was part of a much broader concern that all Korean women must play a pivotal role in the Japanisation of Korean identities. One leading activist Im Hyo-jŏng declared before an audience of women:

Our urgent task is then to become Japanese with a Japanese spirit. This means that the most important task is the awareness and realisation of becoming a subject of the Japanese Emperor. As a Korean, the longer this takes, the longer we remain unhappy.[41]

This Japanisation signified that Koreans had to contribute financially to the war effort, and they had to observe all of the national rituals that honoured the Japanese Emperor. A long list of patriotic acts such as participation in the Shinto shrines and the observation of national holidays usually followed such impassioned pleas to become members of the Japanese nation.

The site where all these important transformation had to take place was the everyday life of the family, which no longer served the function of rearing children for personal reasons, but was now entrusted with nothing less than the defence of the entire Japanese empire. The concept of *kukbang kajŏng* ('national defence family') was added to the numerous slogans designed to inject newfound significance to everyday housework.[42] Call for a 'New Order' in the family emphasised that every penny saved and every precious household resource diverted to the war effort was critical for the winning the war. As one professor of a woman's college declared at the time: 'The housewife must become the centre of family life, and she must establish a new order within the family.'[43] The housewives who could efficiently run the household were collectively imagined to play a critical role that was just as important as the soldier on the warfront. While these calls for the ordering of individual families emphasised the importance of every woman taking direct action to contribute to the war, the ever-present framework of the patriotic associations supported and enhanced their power to transform the Korean household. One article emphasised the importance of housework such as shaking the dust off the bedcovers every morning even if husbands wanted to sleep in late. The writer of the article recommends that if the husbands complain about the noise, then women could always invite the local leaders of the patriotic association to come into their households and shake the dust from the bedcovers in front of their husbands if they can't accomplish the job by themselves.[44] Even the task of taking care of garbage from the household was made more efficient by organisation of waste pick-up days through the patriotic associations.[45] The presence of such a ubiquitous support network gave newfound meaning to the importance of everyday housework and encouraged the women to view their everyday lives with newfound significance.

Conclusion

The spread of the patriotic associations and the transformation of everyday life by no means provide a complete explanation for what enabled wartime mobilisation in colonial Korea. The motivations of Korean women's participation in the war were inevitably multifaceted in nature. The Korean women who expressed their support for military conscription may have believed that their sacrifice would bring equality to all Koreans or perhaps they wished to elevate the general status of motherhood. Indeed, a wide range of speculation is possible about their motivations, yet one aspect that seems clear from the discussions on military conscription is that significant changes in the everyday life praxis had taken place during the wartime mobilisation. The range of actions available within the life-worlds of colonial subjects would greatly expand due to the establishment of a nationwide mobilisation network and by compelling Koreans to interact with each other and collectively organise their social lives. The problems reported in raising the participation levels of the patriotic associations suggest that many Koreans remained passively disengaged from the colonial order and found ways to avoid complying with the demands of the colonial state.

However, resistance to colonial authority cannot provide the complete picture because there were also Koreans who actively expressed their historical agency by participating in the patriotic associations and expressing support for the war. Those involved in the mobilisation effort may have been motivated by a myriad of daily concerns such as how to procure daily necessities and enjoying occasional community events. Yet, the end result of this dynamic between resistance and accommodation was that numerous Koreans were either willingly or unwillingly brought into the wartime mobilisation system, which allowed the colonisers to exercise unprecedented powers of control and surveillance. The participation of many prominent male and female activists in the wartime mobilisation would bequeath the contentious issue of collaboration for post-war Korean generations. What may be important to note is that even though women were in a highly disadvantaged position in colonial society, some of the most skilled at navigating the power grid of colonial society would emerge to social prominence. The important question to ponder here may be the conditions under which authoritarian regimes are able to mobilise individuals through coercive structures, yet still manage to achieve a certain degree of voluntary compliance, especially those who embraced the rapid social changes taking place during times of war.

Finally, we must factor in the colonial dimension of the issue at hand. For the binary narrative of perpetrators versus victims applied to colonial histories rarely yields satisfactory explanations, because by its nature colonialism requires considerable collaboration to be effective.[46] Finding collaboration within colonial circumstances may not be surprising, yet what may be unusual about the discourse of colonised Korean women is the powerful hope that they expressed of playing a critical role in equalising relations between Koreans and Japanese. Colonised Korean women who were dominated both by the patriarchal order and the fundamental inequalities of the colonial system arguably became active participants in perpetuating the system that oppressed them precisely because they faced the most social barriers and desired the most exhaustive change. Moreover, the redefinition of their roles as mothers and wives of soldiers and the elevation of the importance of their domestic lives as a space just as important as any warfront would bring newfound meaning to their individual lives. Such complex issues in Korean colonial history suggest important points of comparison with other examples around the world where the 'nameless multitude' did not always suffer and were not always dominated within authoritarian dictatorships.[47] The key to understanding this phenomenon may be to pay closer attention to the conditions of everyday life and the transformative impact of wartime mobilisation. Times of war can bring momentous developments, and the direct experiences with radical change within the life-worlds of individuals may serve as a powerful motivation for the marginalised elements of a society to hasten the processes that they believe will ultimately deliver their social liberation.

Notes

1. Carter J. Eckert, *Offspring of Empire: The Koch'ang Kims and the Origins of Korean Capitalism 1876–1945* (Seattle, WA: University of Washington Press, 1991).
2. For more on the gender politics of colonial Korea, see Theodore Jun Yoo, *The Politics of Gender in Colonial Korea: Education, Labor, and Health, 1910–1945* (Berkeley, CA: University of California Press, 2008).
3. Dorothee Wierling argues that simply viewing societies as patriarchic can rarely capture the full complexities of the gender dynamics, for there is a need for a differentiated description: 'one demonstrating that men and women certainly did not enter into any sort of a simple relation of dominance – but rather a set of relations that was a 'complex web of oppression, resistance, agreements, stagings, and rituals'. Dorothee Wierling, 'Everyday Life and Gender Relations', in Alf Lüdtke (ed.), *The History of Everyday Life: Reconstructing Historical Experiences and Ways of Life* (Princeton, NJ: Princeton University Press, 1995), p. 158.
4. For more on 'thick descriptions', see Clifford Geertz, ' "Deep play": Notes on the Balinese Cockfight', in *The Interpretation of Cultures: Selected Essays* (New York: Basic Books, 1973), pp. 3–30.
5. Harold L. Smith, *War and Social Change* (Manchester: Manchester University Press, 1986); Margaret Higonnet, Jane Jenson, Sonya Michel and Margaret Weitz, *Behind the Lines: Gender and the Two World Wars* (New Haven, CT: Yale University Press, 1987); Leila J. Rupp, *Mobilising Women for War: German and American Propaganda, 1939–1945* (Princeton, NJ: Princeton University Press, 1978); Susan Zeiger, 'She Didn't Raise Her Boy to be a Slacker: Motherhood, Conscription, and the Culture of the First World War', *Feminist Studies* 22 (Spring 1996), pp. 6–39.
6. R. Ray and A. C. Korteweg, 'Women's Movements in the Third World: Identity, Mobilisation, and Autonomy', *Annual Review of Sociology* 25 (1999), pp. 47–71.
7. One example of women taking advantage of wartime opportunity structures to advance social causes is the case of militant female suffrage activists who supported Great Britain's war effort to gain the vote for women. Nicoletta F. Gullace, *'The Blood of Our Sons': Men, Women, and the Renegotiation of British Citisenship during the Great War* (New York: Palgrave, 2002).
8. The many historical examples of women becoming actively involved in wars suggest that high levels of female participation can be achieved, yet this fact often recedes in our historical memories. As Mady Segal notes, 'In the aftermath of war, women's military activities are reconstructed as minor (or even non-existent), allowing the culture to maintain the myth of men in arms and women at home.' Mady Wechsler Segal, 'Women's Military Roles Cross-Nationally: Past, Present, and Future', *Gender and Society* 9 (December 1995), p. 761.

9. Kang Chŏng-suk, 'Wianbu, chŏngsindae, kongch'ang, sŏngnoye', *Yŏksa pipyŏng* (Spring 2006), p. 316.

10. For a comprehensive overview of women's identities as mothers and wives on the home front in late colonial Korea, see Kwŏn Myŏng-a, *Yŏksajŏk p'asijŭm: jegukŭi p'ant'ajiwa jendŏ jŏngch'i* (Seoul: Chaeksesang, 2005); see also An T'ae-yun, 'Ilchemalgi jŏnsich'ejewa mosŏngŭi singminhwa', *Han'gukyŏsŏnghak* 19(3) (2003); Yi Sang-kyŏng, 'Ilchemalgiŭi yŏsŏng dongwŏnkwa "gukkunŭi ŏmŏni" ', *P'eminisŭm yŏn'gu* 2 (2002).

11. Kawa Kaoru notes the high number of women participating in the war effort but largely rejects the argument that this phenomenon can be explained as a response by Korean women to opportunity structures. She points out that the colonial administration in Korea never implemented the vote for Koreans nor was there a realistic chance for female political participation unlike in the case of Japanese feminists such as Ichikawa Fusae (1893–1981). Kawa Kaoru, 'Ch'ongryŏkchŏn araeŭi chosŏn yŏsŏng', translated by Kim Miran, *Silch' ŏnmunhak* (Fall 2002), p. 311. Kawa's argument that the situation for Korean women was far different than Japanese women may be valid, but the possibility of eventually voting and eliminating the colonial inequalities through war participation was very much on the minds of Korean collaborators; The argument that Japanese women became involved in the war effort to achieve the voting franchise is much stronger because leading Japanese women's suffrage activists like Ichikawa Fusae became supporters of the war effort after the outbreak of the Second Sino-Japanese War. Dee Ann Vavich, 'The Japanese Woman's Movement: Ichikawa Fusae, A Pioneer in Woman's Suffrage', *Monumenta Nipponica* 22(3–4) (1967), pp. 402–36.

12. *Naisen ittai* is a difficult term to translate into English. The Chinese characters for the term means that '*nai*' (内) or 'inner' and '*sen*' (鮮) for Korea are 'one body' or '*ittai*' (一體). The term is used to suggest that the inner region of Japan is the same body as Korea.

13. The views of Korean collaborators may be comparable to the views expressed by W. E. B. Du Bois's statement in 1917, 'If the black man could fight to defeat the Kaiser…he could later present a bill for payment due to a grateful white America'. Stephen E. Ambrose, 'Blacks in the Army in Two World Wars', in Stephen E. Ambrose and James A. Barber, Jr (eds), *The Military in American Society* (New York: Free Press, 1972), pp. 178–9.

14. Takashi Fujitani points out that some Japanese continued to refer to an alien people. Colonial and military officials feared the consequence of employing a strategy of equality to mobilise Koreans would spin out of control. However, Fujitani also highlights the fact that colonial and military officials came to the conclusion that the mobilisation of Koreans would only be effective on an official stance of quality and spoke of the need to put genuine effort to put egalitarian policies into practice. Japanese military manuals reminded officers training Korean conscripts that the Koreans were members of the leading race of Greater East Asia. The Japanese promulgate two laws in April 1945 that would have eventually given Koreans over the age of 25 years and paid a minimum of 15 yen in direct taxes the right to vote in elections for the Lower House of the Imperial Diet. Takashi Fujitani, 'Right to Kill, Right to Make Live: Koreans as Japanese and Japanese as Americans During WWII', *Representations* (Summer 2007), pp. 18–19.

15. In Japan, the National Mobilisation Law was passed over the objections of the politicians and business leaders as an enabling measure that Prime Minister Konoe Fumimaro (1891–1945) promised to use only if the war in China expanded. Richard Rice, 'Economic Mobilisation in Wartime Japan: Business, Bureaucracy, and Military in Conflict', *Journal of Asian Studies* (August 1979), p. 695. The National Mobilisation Law was the precursor to the declaration of the New Order and the merging of all political parties into the Imperial Rule Assistance Association in December 1940. Japanese business and political parties still continued to function autonomously and the Meiji Constitution was not suspended as a consequence of the wartime measures.

16. Ch'oe Yu-ri, *Ilche malgi sikminji chibaejŏngch'aegyŏn'gu* (Seoul: Kukhakcharyowŏn, 1997). A discussion of the major social and economic transformations that took place in colonial Korea during the total mobilisation period can be found in Carter J. Eckert, 'Total War, Industrialisation, and Social Change in Late Colonial Korea', in Peter Duus, Ramon H. Myers and Mark R. Peattie (eds), *The Japanese Wartime Empire, 1931–1945* (Princeton, NJ: Princeton University Press, 1996), pp. 3–39.

17. Utsumi Aiko, 'Korean "Imperial Soldiers": Remembering Colonialism and Crimes against Allied POWs', in T. Fujitani Geoffrey M. White, and Lisa Yoneyama (eds), *Perilous Memories: The Asia-Pacific War(s)* (Durham, NC: Duke University Press, 2001), pp. 203–4.

18. Miyata Setsuko, *Chosŏnminjunggwa ⌈hwangminhwa⌋ chŏngch'aek,* translated by Yi Hyŏng-nam (Seoul: Ilchogak, 1997), pp. 42, 154–7.

19. The organisational structure at the neighbourhood level was introduced earlier in Korea than in Japan, where the wartime mobilisation system initially lacked a basic unit. In Japan, the *tonari gumi* or neighbourhood association was introduced in September 1940 and consisted of approximately 100 households. The leadership of each unit were either appointed by the local mayor or rotated among the households to share the burden. Ralph J. D. Braibanti, 'Neighborhood Associations in Japan and their Democratic Potentialities', *The Far Eastern Quarterly* (February 1948), pp. 136–64. The remnants of the patriotic associations still survive today in Korea in the form of the *pansanghoe* which still meet regularly in many parts of the country and may be understood as a lasting legacy of this period.

20. Kokumin sōryoku chōsen renmei, *Chōsen ni okeru kokumin sōryoku undōshi* (Seoul: Kokumin sōryoku chōsen renmei, 1945), p. 40.

21. Kokumin sōryoku chōsen renmei, *Kokumin sōryoku undō yōran* (Seoul: Kokumin sōryoku chōsen renmei, 1943), p. 65.

22. Yun Hae-dong, *Chibae wa chach'i* (Seoul: Yŏksa pip'yŏngsa, 2006), p. 376. The actual number of patriotic associations during the wartime period cannot be determined but by December 1942 the *Kyŏngsŏng ilbo* states that there were 11,000 in Seoul. *Kyŏngsŏng ilbo* (14 December 1942); cited in Yi Chongmin, 'Tosiŭi ilsangŭl t'onghae pon chumindongwŏngwa saenghwal t'ongje', in Pang Ki-jung (ed.), *Ilche p'asijŭm chibaejŏngch'aekkwa minjungsaenghwal* (Seoul: Hyean, 2004), p. 420.

23. Kawa Kaoru, 'Ch'ongryŏkchŏn araeŭi chosŏn yŏsŏng', p. 293.

24. 'Keijō no mohan aikoku hanchō san', *Kungmin ch'onryŏk* (January 1941), pp. 84–8; 'Mei aikoku hanchō hōmon ki', *Kungmin ch'onryŏk* (January 1942), pp. 110–4.

25. Yun Hae-dong, *Chibae wa chach'i*, p. 379.
26. 'Aegukbansilch' ŏnsahang', *Chogwang* (November 1941), p. 72.
27. *Kyŏngsŏng ilbo* (14 December 1942); cited in Yi Chong-min, 'Tosiŭi ilsangŭl t'onghae pon chumindongwŏngwa saenghwal t'ongje', p. 444.
28. Ch'oe Chŏng-hŭi, 'Changmi ŭi chip', *Taedonga* (July 1942), pp. 149–50.
29. 'Aegukbanŭn . . . charanda', *Sinsidae* (February 1941), p. 143.
30. Yi Chong-min, 'Tosiŭi ilsangŭl t'onghae pon chumindongwŏngwa saenghwal t'ongje', p. 439.
31. 'Uri Aegukbanŭi charang', *Pandojigwang* (July 1941), pp. 23–5. Holding community activities beyond the official business of the associations were generally encouraged.
32. Sangjeon Yongnam, 'Chingbyŏngjewa chosŏn ŏmŏniege', *Chogwang* (June 1942), pp. 34–7; 'Chingbyŏngryŏnggwa bandoŏmŏniŭi gyŏlŭi' (June 1942), pp. 38–44; 'Chingbyŏngjewa kajŏng ŭi tongwŏn! – Kukkun ŭi ŏmŏni chwadam', *Ch'unch'u* (June 1942), pp. 100–8; 'Kukkun ŭi ŏmŏni yŏlchŏn', *Maeil sinbo* (23–24 June 1942); 'Urido Kukkun ŭi ŏmŏni', *Pandojigwang* (July 1942), pp. 16–7.
33. Chosŏn imjŏnbodogukdan, 'Pandojidoch'ŭngpuinŭi kyŏlchŏn ŭi taesajaho', *Samchŏlli* (March 1942), p. 112.
34. 'Chingbyŏngryŏnggwa bandoŏmŏniŭi gyŏlŭi', *Chogwang* (June 1942), pp. 38–44. The discussants included two of the most prominent female educators in Korea after liberation in 1945: Pak Ma-ri-a (1906–60) and Pae Sang-myŏng (1906–86).
35. Ibid., p. 39.
36. Ibid., p. 43.
37. Several readers or *tokbon* designed to be circulated among patriotic associations were published during this period. Examples include a 1941 reader on how to deal with air-raids. Sinsidae pyŏnjipbu, *(Aegukbangajŏngyong) ŏnmunbanggongdokbon* (Seoul: Pakmunsŏgwan, 1941); Reprinted in Pang Ki-jung (ed.), *Ilche p'asijŭmgi han'guksahoe charyojip 6* (Seoul: Sŏnin, 2005). This reader suggests that the text be circulated among patriotic associations until the book falls apart to maximise the distribution of information.
38. Sangjeon Yongnam, 'Chingbyŏngryŏnggwa bandoŏmŏniŭi gyŏlŭi', p. 43.
39. Sources from the late colonial period often complain of the fact that Japanese women tended to view Korean women only as servants. The following example is from an article that encourages Korean women to socialise with their Japanese neighbours: 'However, Japanese women are not familiar with the Korean women. This is extremely regretful. The Japanese women residing in Korea were exposed only to the Korean housemaids or the "nannies" as it were, and as a result, they generally equate all Korean women with the identity of "nannies". I believe that this undermines the progress of the *naisen ittai* movement.' Yi Suk-chong, 'Naesŏnilch'ewa buin', *Yŏsŏng* (April 1940), p. 16.
40. By 1940, there were 154,687 Japanese residents and 775,162 Koreans living in Seoul. Seoul at the time had the largest population of Japanese in Korea. Sŏul sijŏnggaebalyŏn'guwon (ed.), *Sŏul 20segi saenghwal, munhwabyŏnch'ŏnsa* (Seoul: Sŏul sijŏnggaebalyŏn'guwon: Sŏulsiriptaehakkyo sŏulhakkyŏn'guso, 2001), p. 44.
41. Im Hyo-jŏng, 'Taejŏn kwa yŏsŏng ŭi kil', *Taedonga* (July 1942), p. 61.

42. Pak Sun-chŏn, 'Kukbang kajŏng', *Taedonga* (June 1942), pp. 104–7.
43. Im Suk-jae, 'Kajŏng ŭi sinjilsŏ', *Taedonga* (June 1942), pp. 102–3.
44. Pak Sun-chŏn, 'Kukbang kajŏng', p. 106.
45. Hŏ Ha-baek, 'Ch'onghubuin ŭi kako', *Taedonga* (June 1942), p. 110.
46. Empires are highly reluctant to expend resources on empire-building, which means that they rely heavily on the existence of collaborating native elites to expand their rule. As Cooper notes, the fact that 'strong imperial states should have found acceptable the exercise of relatively weak power in certain circumstances is so puzzling that many commentators prefer the myths of total exploitation or of modern governmentality to examining a more confusing reality'. Frederick Cooper, *Colonialism in Question: Theory, Knowledge, History* (Berkeley, CA: University of California Press, 2005), p. 157. For more on the logic of collaboration in colonial Korea, see Michael Kim, 'Regards sur la collaboration en Corée', *Vingtieme Siecle. Revue d'histoire* 94 (April–June 2007), pp. 35–43.
47. Alf Lüdtke has observed that 'Some – perhaps even a great many – of those who were "directly affected" turn out to be individuals who in fact did not suffer, were not dominated, not exploited. In particular, a difficult question has to be addressed: what is the significance of the recognition that "the many" during German fascism were at the same time perpetrators, accomplices and victims?' Alf Lüdtke, 'Introduction: What is the History of Everyday Life and Who are its practitioners?', in Lüdtke (ed.), *The History of Everyday Life*, p. 24. It may also be useful to keep in mind the mass dictatorship thesis that argues a fundamental characteristic of modern dictatorships is that they need massive backing from below to sustain themselves. Jie-Hyun Lim, 'Historiographical Perspectives on "Mass Dictatorship"', *Totalitarian Movements and Political Religions* (December 2005), pp. 325–31.

10
'Taming Soldiers': The Gender Politics of Japanese Soldiers in Total War

Yonson Ahn

The number of soldiers mobilised for the Japanese Imperial Army and Navy at the end of the Asia-Pacific War (1931–45) was around 6 million. This chapter is about those enlisted during the war[1] and the women euphemistically called 'comfort women' who were provided to the military men for sex. These women were forced into sexual servitude during the war, and were mainly Korean, and also Taiwanese, Chinese, Indonesian, East Timorese, Filipino, Burmese, Dutch, Australian and Japanese women. An extensive deployment of comfort stations for the exclusive use of the military started in 1937 following the Nanking Massacre in China.[2] After the invasion and occupation of large areas by Japan, especially after August 1942, the Ministry of War began to systematise policy regarding the comfort stations. As confirmed in a 1944 report by the US Office of War Information, 'the comfort girls were found wherever it was necessary for the Japanese military to fight'.[3] So far, evidence of comfort stations has been confirmed in China, Hong Kong, the Philippines, Malaysia, Singapore, Borneo, Indonesia, Thailand, Burma, New Guinea, Okinawa, Korea, Vietnam and numerous southern Pacific islands.[4] Military authorities issued permits to run comfort stations and collected taxes. The authorities drew up regulations for the use and running of comfort stations and distributed them to soldiers and comfort station managers. Regulations for soldiers included time allocation, cost, mandatory condom use, keeping military secrets and bans on drinking and fighting.[5]

In this chapter, I will investigate the ways in which the masculinity and sexuality of Japanese soldiers were reconstructed and controlled, in order to fit into the totalitarian war project during the Asia-Pacific War. More specifically, this chapter will explore the way in which military men were re-socialised as warriors to carry out total war. This investigation aims to show how gender, national identities and sexuality were used in the gender politics of the totalitarian regime. My primary focus will be on the hegemonic form of masculine and national identities in the Japanese Imperial Army and Navy, which were imposed on military men. The identities of Japanese military men were forged under the circumstances of totalitarian war and colonial expansion, in an overwhelmingly male-dominated institution.

My key tasks in this chapter are the following: firstly, the military forms of masculine and national identities, which were forged, reinforced and imposed on the Japanese soldiers, will be outlined. Secondly, I will show the ways in which military men were controlled and disciplined through daily practices in the Japanese military, including the Navy during wartime. Thirdly, I explore the paradox of the extremes of aggressiveness and submissiveness imposed on the soldiers, and how the comfort women system reconciled this contradiction by helping to make the soldiers both submissive to authorities and aggressive to enemies. This process illuminates how the extremes of feminisation and masculinisation in the military re-socialisation process were reconciled. Finally, I illustrate the ways in which soldiers positioned themselves in the face of totalitarian regimentation and inculcation drawing attention to the complex ways in which they dealt with everyday army life in the face of army re-socialisation reified in the reconstruction of masculinity and the regulation of sexuality.

This study draws on oral narrative material and historical and contemporary documents including those issued by the Japanese military. I rely most extensively on personal narratives, including testimonies and life histories of Japanese veterans and Korean comfort women obtained from interviews that I conducted as well as from previously published narratives.

Gender and national identities reinforced

Men are often thought to achieve their manhood through military service in the army, especially through combat, and this is by no means peculiar to Japan. Even plunder, rape and arson were utilised mostly to demonstrate their power or bravery.[6] In general, military masculine identity is sexualised in violent forms, and this was clearly the case in wartime Japan. While sexualisation of violence and violent sexuality were not unique to the Japanese military, it was essential to them. Former 'comfort women' report that they endured not only enforced sex, but sex routinely accompanied by violence. The construction of sexual intercourse as an assault is revealed in the name used for the condoms distributed to the soldiers by military authorities during the war: *totsugeki ichiban* (Attack, Number One).[7] Military metaphors abounded in the regulation of the encounters between the men and the comfort women. Yoshioka, a former officer, recalled his warning to the soldiers before they went to the comfort station: 'Wear a helmet when making an assault! Clean up your gun after a fight! Wearing a helmet means using a condom, and cleaning up one's gun means the disinfection of one's private parts after ejaculation' (I interviewed Yoshioka in 1996; he died in July 1998). In this warning, the behaviour and attitudes appropriate to the battlefield spilled over into the language of sexuality. If masculine identity in its military form in Japan at this period entailed the view of sex with females as a right to which they, as 'real men', were entitled, then a corollary was that women were merely sexual objects. Access to women was theirs by virtue of, and as evidence of, their status as 'real men'. A veteran, Wada, confirms this: 'Including me, there was a rampant feeling that it is really a shame not to have any chance to have sex with a woman before being killed, if one was born as a man. If not, one could not be a real man' (Wada, interviewed in 1996).

The sexualisation of violence is associated with misogyny. It repudiates the feminine, showing contempt for women. The coarse or sexual military vernacular served to amplify misogynist masculine identities. An example of such linguistic practice in the Japanese military was the use of the metaphor of 'tasting women'. Testimonies from Japanese veterans indicate that 'when new girls arrived at a comfort station, officers "tasted" them first'.[8] Women were represented as tasty objects to be eaten. Military language was accompanied with sexual words. These kinds of sexual metaphors circulating in the army devalued women and celebrated a violent, misogynistic form of masculinity anchored in the creation and perpetuation of female otherness. Furthermore, xenophobia and misogyny merged in the practice of routinised sexual violence against the comfort women who were from other Asian countries, mainly Korea. This abuse was a highly sexualised form of ethnic violence. Xenophobic sentiment was provoked and encouraged in everyday life in the army, for instance, through maltreatment of the comfort women and callous brutality against local people in the territories Japan occupied.

Soldiers' identity was accompanied by a sense of muscular patriotism. The rhetoric of Japanese 'ultra-nationalism' in wartime also recalls affective relations, bonding, familial loyalty and self-sacrificing behaviours.

The soldiers were taught to subordinate their own needs, desires and comfort, and even give their lives for the nation. A veteran, Yokota, reports that the search for a place to die for his country, thereby fulfilling a *Bushido* ideal, was his 'fervent desire and long-cherished dream'.[9] Here, being patriotic was virtually equivalent to being xenophobic. Urging patriotism on the Japanese people went hand in hand with disdain for other Asian and Western nations. Stressing the distinctiveness of Japanese national identity resulted in racist exclusions of others who were not Japanese. One of my informants stated how deeply xenophobia was ingrained in him from his early days: 'the sense of disdain of other Asian nations including Koreans, and the ideology of the Japanese Emperor system (*tennōsei*) were poured into me from my childhood through education' (Yuasa, interviewed in 1996). The military men's identity was rooted in a sense of racial superiority expressed through a heightened 'masculine' sexuality.

On the other hand, to be a soldier meant to be obedient and subservient. Military men in the Japanese Imperial Army and Navy were required to show absolute obedience to superiors in the military hierarchy. Military hierarchy was defined by pseudo-familial relationships in which filial piety was stressed: in the army barracks the company commander was specially designated as a surrogate father, the sub-officer as a surrogate mother and new conscripts as their children.[10] The hierarchical order was modelled on the parent-child relationship in the *ie* system, the Japanese family system, a principle of social organisation in Japan. Hierarchical relations between superiors and subordinates in the army were obscured or made more acceptable, in this pseudo-familial ideology. Relations of domination in the army were disguised under forms of voluntary filial piety.

Another ideological function of the family-state system[11] was providing an ethos of service to the nation. The family-state system placed special emphasis on the family as the foundation of the state and as the basic unit of the state's ruling order. The nation was imagined as a family, equating filial piety with loyalty to the Emperor, and exalting the Emperor as the father of all Japanese subjects in the family-state, *kazoku kokka*.[12] Iizuka Kōji argues that the inculcation of the two ideas, hierarchy and familialism, led the soldiers to internalise obedience to such an extent that the individuals would feel that they were acting on their own volition while in fact they acted under compulsion. The unequal relationships in the military hierarchy were naturalised by the two tropes. The extensive use of violence by superiors on their subordinates was justified on the pretext that it was an expression of the parents' 'benevolent feelings', *on jo*, and would do the children good.[13] Subsequently, the ideologies of hierarchy and familialism enhanced the creation of the submissive and sacrificial aspects of masculinity in the soldiers. Obedience and sacrifice, the feminine features of militaristic masculinity supported the trope of pseudo-family, and vice versa. The tropes provided the means whereby personal interests could be suppressed to obey hierarchical orders. The feminisation and infantilisation of military men in this figurative family were enacted through positioning the common soldiers in the inferior/dependent position of children while superiors were heads of the pseudo-family. Familialism was transformed into militarism.

These pseudo-familial hierarchies led to certain ways of understanding and structuring the comfort station system as well. The comfort women occupied subordinate positions within patriarchal families as daughters and wives. The model of the stern father disciplining wives and daughters 'for their own good', and feeling able to bully and maltreat them if they so chose, is very evident in the accounts of the comfort women. A former comfort woman Hwang Kūmju recollects that when any comfort women were rebellious, they were harshly beaten (interviewed in 1995). Violence was used by the soldiers and comfort station keepers to subdue the women. On the other hand, women in families also figure as powerful and loving mothers of sons. Later I will examine this aspect of women not only as sexual objects but also as maternal figures undertaking caring tasks.

Hierarchical relationships amongst the military men were sustained in the comfort stations through regulations such as time allocations, access to virgins, and to younger or to Japanese comfort women. Thus, for example, officers often had exclusive access to certain women. Forcible sexual initiation of virgins was frequently perpetrated by high-ranking officers.[14] Because almost magical properties were attributed to virgins, only officers were privileged to have sex with virgins when the women first arrived. There was a superstitious belief that having sex with a virgin brought good luck, and was, for example, a talisman for the avoidance of death in battle.[15] After this initiation, the women were forced to serve rank and file soldiers (testimony of Hwang Kūmju, interviewed in 1995). Sexual access was determined by power in the hierarchy, and this was a way of reproducing distance and superiority. Through these formal and informal practices in the comfort stations, hierarchical relationships between the enlisted men and officers, and between the soldiers and the comfort women were enacted and consolidated.

While noting stereotypical masculine aspects such as aggression, destruction, sexualisation and xenophobia, however, we also simultaneously observe stereotypical feminine aspects like obedience and sacrifice in the form of military masculine identity.[16] I argue that the military versions of gender identity during wartime were deeply contradictory, in that masculinisation and feminisation were enacted simultaneously. Extreme forms of machismo coexisted with features such as obedience, submission, self-sacrifice, compliance and discipline, which are more commonly associated with femininity. In summary, the military forms of masculine and national identities forged and reinforced in the Japanese forces in wartime were destructive, sexualised, misogynist, hierarchical, submissive and xenophobic.

Regulations and disciplines of military life

Next, I will further explore the strict control and discipline of military life in the Japanese forces during total war. Not all men are equally willing to engage in warfare, to kill or be killed. Surely social, political and educational conditions also shape the motivations of soldiers in war. Even though a close connection between masculinity and militarism exists, as Cynthia Enloe argues, masculinity is not inherently militaristic.[17] Her view of masculinity and militarism as not isomorphic provides an opportunity to examine the military authorities' regulation and disciplining of military life, in order to control and 'tame' the men. Military aggression always requires carefully controlled and systematic training and propaganda.[18] I will, therefore, examine how the military men were regulated through re-socialisation in their everyday practices in the Japanese Army. This re-socialisation of soldiers was required for the simultaneous processes of masculinisation and feminisation to produce both aggressive and submissive aspects of masculinity.

Japanese boys experienced military indoctrination in early childhood, long before they enlisted in the military. During the war, teachers gave semi-military instruction in primary schools when the pupils reached their eighth year. In middle and high schools, army officers gave military instruction, and similar programmes were conducted in colleges and universities.[19] In the Japanese Army, formal and informal training procedures were deployed to create or fortify masculinity in its military form. Discipline through military training played a very crucial role in the re-socialisation of fighting men, in order to promote or obtain consent or support for total war. During the war Japan had neither a firm industrial base, nor the industrial and technological resources to support the wars that Japan waged. Towards the end of the war there was even a lack of adequate food and medicine. Peter Duus describes this underdevelopment for war:

> Japanese industry lacked the productive capacities to support their far-flung forces in a war of attrition. Japan was economically outstripped to begin with, and steadily lost ground thereafter. Her military technology began to lag behind as the Americans developed and refined new tools of war.[20]

Morale was deemed the determining factor in combat. Army leaders clung to the notion that motivated troops willing to suffer high casualties could even overcome opponents with technological, industrial and logistical advantages.[21] Therefore, the conduct of war relied heavily on human resources to compensate for this lack of infrastructure and material resources. The fighting spirit was greatly emphasised and the readiness and willingness to die encouraged this spirit which was rooted in the tradition of *Bushido*, the way of the warrior, referring to 'the determined will to die', which before 1868 was monopolised by the samurai class.[22] Spiritual education was an essential resource for war in these circumstances. The wartime Infantry Drill Book stated that:

> On any battlefield we should steel ourselves to win glorious victory despite military forces and weapons inferior to the enemy's. Since we must be prepared for such a situation, it is self-evident that more spiritual education is necessary.[23]

Military training was designed to make men tough and brave, on the one hand, and to inculcate subservience and self-sacrifice on the other. The strategies used in military training – harsh treatment, humiliation, coercion and corporeal punishment – were achieved through violence to create obedience, compliance and aggressiveness in the Japanese masculine identity. The military leaders intensively inculcated an 'aggressive spirit' among the soldiers. The Japanese military put soldiering and violence together systematically. A peculiarity of the Japanese Army was that soldiers were frequently physically punished even for minor incidents, for example, arbitrary beating in the so-called *jigoku* (hell) style of military training. Drill sergeants and non-commissioned officers often carried out this kind of punishment on rank and file soldiers. Humiliation was part of the regime: 'new conscripts were humiliated until they felt less worthy than their horses'.[24] This treatment was designed to make the soldiers violent, aggressive and submissive. As a consequence of extensive violence, the men could become in turn more violent or brutal to their adversaries or non-Japanese civilians or to those who were lower in the hierarchy. The whole procedure of brutalising soldiers produced anger and frustration in the men. This led them to find somebody toward whom they could vent their emotions. Violence was instrumental and purposive. A Japanese veteran described army socialisation as a process designed to strip humanity away from the soldiers, so they became 'devils' in human form.[25] To produce goal-oriented collective identity as warriors, a totalitarian disciplinary regime was instituted, in which individuality, privacy, agency and humanity were denied.

The totalitarian hegemony infiltrated the private sphere in army life through surveillance and control of private life. For instance, conversations were overheard and reported, soldiers' diaries, memoirs and any other personal writings scrutinised, and their letters strictly censored. In addition, there was a taboo on the discussion of politics. Sociologist Kazuko Tsurumi analyses this process as infantilisation: 'the absence of privacy and the subjection to humiliation, terror and anxiety also helped to evoke childhood roles of dependence and obedience'.[26] The military men's visits to the comfort women were monitored. In Rule 1 of the appendix on discipline in the Serviceman's Club Regulations, set out by unit Yama 3475 stationed in Okinawa, executed in December 1944, it states that the concept of common possession of the 'female staff' is to be consistently applied throughout and the concept of special appropriation is strictly prohibited.[27] A regulation issued by the military administrators banned personal relationships with the comfort women. The authorities feared that soldiers might release military secrets such as movement of troops to their intimates. There was also the fear that these women would dilute the men's loyalty to the military, resulting in extreme cases in desertion together with the women. The number of visits to the same woman was reported and limited by the authorities.[28] This was another aspect of surveillance and control of private life.

An intensive level of control resulted in suicides in collective groups when Japan lost the war. Collective suicide shortly after the war, especially among officers, was widely reported.[29] A Japanese veteran recalled the moment of one group suicide: 'after shouting three times "Hurrah", loud and continuous sounds of firing rifles, "Bang, bang, bang", or the sound of an explosion of a bomb were heard'.[30] The Japanese, masculinist, military code of honour demanded victory or death: as the Field

Service Code of 15 January 1941 states, 'if alive, do not suffer the disgrace of becoming a prisoner; in death, do not leave behind a name soiled by misdeeds'.[31] Surrender was considered a great disgrace not only to the soldier, but also to his family and any defeat at the hands of the enemy was interpreted as loss of honour and masculinity. Death by suicide could be considered an honourable death for the sake of the Emperor (*tennō*) and wipe out the shame of defeat.

Promoting and regulating male sexuality was one of the most crucial instruments in control of soldiers by the totalitarian regime in wartime Japan. Sexuality was the centre of the regime of regulation to control the level of soldiers' aggression and to compensate for the practices of infantilisation or demasculinisation in the military hierarchy. Moreover, common bonds of masculine identity were promoted through sharing sexual domination of the women provided at the comfort stations. Male bonding as a member of the Japanese Imperial Army was created through sharing sexual experiences. On the other hand, having sex with the women was a form of pressure on the men to 'perform' sexually, as well as their right, regardless of whether they had a sexual need, emotional feelings or not. There was strong pressure to conform to the standards of 'masculine' behaviour through sexual activity. One of the veterans whom I interviewed confirms that: 'If I did not go the station even after I became a non-commissioned officer, I would have been left out and the rumour circulated that I did not enjoy being with a girl. I did not want to be excluded by others in the troop so I went for a girl' (Satō, pseudonym, interviewed in 1996). Sexual practice was one of the sites for the daily construction and reaffirmation of manhood in the Japanese military. Masculine identity as a member of the military became translated into sexual domination of the comfort women. Misogynist and sexualised aspects of masculinity were produced through the sexual domination of and contempt towards women.

Soldiers' sexuality was regulated through hygienic checks as well. There were medical checks for them in some areas. If the men were found to have caught a venereal disease, they and their superior might be punished. This was regarded as a great disgrace for a member of the forces.[32] Regulations and hygienic supervision of comfort stations were conducted by military authorities. The military authorities also regularly sent condoms to 'military brothels' in areas where soldiers were stationed and supported 'the brothels' financially.[33] This hygienic supervision of the comfort facilities by the authorities was primarily for the benefit of the soldiers or the military so that the military would not lose efficiency by infection with venereal diseases.[34] To some extent, the politics of military sex were camouflaged as merely the politics of soldiers' health.

Moreover, patriotism was instilled through the ritual of reciting the whole text of the Imperial Precept to Soldiers and Sailors (*Gunjin chokuyu*) at the start of each day. A veteran, Minoru Kawamoto, recounts that the text was difficult to read and understand, let alone memorise, because it was written in Imperial Court language. He recounts that if a soldier was not able to recite correctly, a meal was denied as penalty and corporeal punishments and humiliations were nothing compared to this.[35] In the text of the Imperial Precept to Soldiers and Sailors a heavy emphasis was placed on loyalty, propriety, valour, fidelity and simplicity. Among these five virtues, loyalty ranked first: 'fulfil your essential duty of loyalty, bearing in mind that duty is weightier than a mountain, while death is lighter than a feather'.[36] This text shows a one-sided loyalty from the bottom towards the top. This theme of loyalty was widely circulated and gained importance in identity formation practices. It provided a motif of commitment to the Emperor and the nation, especially during the national emergency of war. Indoctrination in the army included the word-for-word citation of the text. It was an ideological device which aimed to produce subjects ready to die for the sake of the Emperor, a key element in Japanese male identity: a national masculine ethos.

Through regular 'spiritual education' in the military, as in state propaganda, incessant claims were made that the sense of nation was perpetually in danger, never complete, or sharply on the decline.[37] The suicidal attacks of the *Kamikaze* (Divine Wind) and of the *Kaiten* (Turning of the Heaven), Japanese human torpedoes were the final outcome of the spiritual education of soldiers.[38] The Japanese forces took the suicide mission that had historically been expected of leading officers and extended it to all soldiers and then civilians towards the end of the war. The state destiny of Japan in danger was perpetually stressed to encourage a willingness for collective self-sacrifice. Kamikaze pilots were prompted endlessly to sing a Kamikaze anthem: 'You and I are cherry blossoms in season. . . . Every flower knows it must die. We will die gloriously, then, for our homeland.'[39] Emiko Ohnuki-Tierney explains that this song reveals the state's ability to 'aetheticise' the military to make student-pilots take the fragile cherry blossom as the soldier's symbol and thus idealise service to their country even when they had lost faith in the Emperor and his generals.[40]

Self-sacrifice for the sake of the nation was enshrined as 'the highest calling for any Japanese subject' or 'honourable service'.[41] 'The fighting spirit, the sentiments of blind and absolute loyalty, courage in the face of death, were prominent and highly prised.' Decorations and awards were given to military men to develop and maintain high standards of individual and unit morale.[42] Soldiers were told that 'they would become gods of the fatherland and would be worshipped in the Yasukuni shrine in Tokyo. To be made a Yasukuni god is a special honour bestowed only on national heroes.'[43] Tsurumi states that, in fact, the men must have had virtually no choice but to accept their fate.[44] In summary, in order to 'tame' the soldiers within the totalitarian frame of gender politics in the Japanese Imperial Army and Navy, formal and informal training accompanied by violence and humiliation, surveillance in everyday military life, the regulation and promotion of male sexuality and hygienic checks were carried out. The usefulness of sexual politics to the construction of national and gender identity can be clearly witnessed in this process.

Reconciling the paradox: aggressiveness and submissiveness

In this section, I would like to examine the way in which the extremes of feminisation and masculinisation in the military re-socialisation process were reconciled. The military re-socialisation of everyday practices produced and reinforced in the men both aggressiveness towards enemies and subservience towards superiors in the military hierarchy. Here the military administrators had some concerns about potential problems which might arise out of the extreme regimentation to which the soldiers were subjected. Both the physical and psychological health of the military was a great concern of the government and military authorities. War-related mental disorders were considered detrimental to service morale and public respect for the military.[45] Thus, it was declared that military training or education should not simply focus on strengthening the body but also had to be directed toward preserving the psychological fitness of recruits.[46] Furthermore, the superior mental fitness of the Japanese people as a whole figured prominently in government propaganda. The propaganda emphasised the unique qualities of the Japanese people that would help them withstand the hardships of war.[47] Soldiers were exhorted to control their anger and suppress private grudges on the grounds that military success depended to a great extent on harmonious relations within their unit. High standards of morality, according to training doctrine, must be maintained in the camp and on the battlefield.[48] However, Tsung-yi Lin, a Taiwan-born psychiatrist, points out that the enormous increase of war neuroses among soldiers, including 'shell shock' in battlefields far away from home, and neuroses and neurasthenia among civilians came as a shock to the Japanese in all walks of life.[49] Difficulties in enduring inhuman treatment in the barracks and the harsh realities of the battlefields led soldiers to frustration and even to mental disorder. The physically and psychologically bitter reality of the battlefield that the military men had to face can be witnessed in the diary of an officer: 'Today for the first time I lost two men under my command. Whether by luck, fate or my bad leadership, we neither tended to them nor looked back, just advanced; this is the true face of war. If you rest for one second and reflect, you're emotionally overwhelmed.'[50]

In this context, the comfort stations provided an environment where men could display their frustration and confirm the masculine features of their identities as aggressive, violent and sexualised warriors. First of all, the soldiers could retrieve their masculine power in the face of their enforced obedience and submission: the 'feminine' aspects of their military roles. At the comfort stations, the men could control the women. Having sex against the women's will displayed the men's power of self-assertion and control. The soldiers recovered a specifically masculine subjectivity through sexual objectification of the comfort women, and were returned to a masculine position again in their relations with the 'inferior' women. Maruyama plausibly underlines 'the transfer of oppression', in strict hierarchical systems, such as the armed forces, whereby soldiers' sense of oppression tends to be projected onto their inferiors, whose sense of oppression is in turn directed toward their inferiors and so on until the chain reaction reaches the very bottom.[51] The gendering of these hierarchies needs to be noted. Rank and file soldiers were not at the bottom of the punitive military hierarchy: the comfort women were a step further down in the hierarchy than the rank and file. The women could serve as inferiors onto whom oppression could be safely transferred. Japanese masculine superiority was exhibited by positioning the comfort women as promiscuous and inferior. The creation of the inferiorised, subjugated and powerless colonial identity of the women positioned the soldiers as superior and powerful. Colonial supremacy based on ethnic hierarchy and suppression of the Korean comfort women was naturalised in a circular way. Within the colonial context, re/production of superior Japanese identity could lead the Japanese soldiers, themselves often the victims of class domination, and serving as no more than 'cannon fodder', to share in colonial ideas of power and authority.

Secondly, the provision of the comfort women as quasi-maternal as well as sexual objects provided an emotional outlet for the military men in safe environments, enabling the men to release their own feelings of vulnerability and fear of death in war. The women could serve as sources of 'comfort', rather in the manner in which young children direct both rage and frustration and feelings of dependency and need towards their mothers. Former comfort women observed the vulnerability of some Japanese soldiers when facing the prospect of death in battle: 'they were so scared to go to fight and they wept with the women'.[52] Their vulnerability and fear of death was expressed by releasing their fragile emotions at the comfort station. The account by veteran Suzuki Yoshio shows the enlisted man seeking the 'comforts' of mothering. He reported that the men were even more desperate to go to the comfort stations and cling to the women toward the end of the war when the prospect of death was very close, since there seemed no hope.[53] In fact, diaries of the Kamikaze (*Tokkōtai*, Special Attack Forces), and other solders spoke much about their mothers.[54] The figure of the maternal woman was one of the images invoked in the relationship between the comfort women and the soldiers, in addition to the figure of the whore/slut/sexual woman.

This strategy to channel and release stress through the comfort women system was a deliberate one, considered as essential to keep the fighting spirit and morale on a fairly high level, as may be seen in the report of an army psychiatrist. 'It may well be said that there is nothing better than providing the soldiers with women to comfort the men on the battlefields.'[55] The Japanese military men during the war were mollified through their right of access to women's bodies as a tangible reward for their services. It was taken for granted that women were sexual objects and maternal figures whose purpose was to foster men's psychological security. The soldiers were displacing and projecting their own emotions onto the comfort women by simultaneously constructing the women as their 'comforters' and promiscuous 'whores'. Placing the comfort women in a dual feminine position as sexual objects and as 'maternal comforters' was integral to regulation and discipline in the army re-socialisation process. The women functioned as a buffer in the paradox between masculine aggressiveness and feminine submissiveness inculcated in the military. The comfort women thus offered a complex means of recovery from wounded masculinity and of regulating the aggressiveness of the men. The paradox of simultaneous masculinisation and feminisation in the military could be reconciled at the comfort stations.

Sexuality both regulated and expressed the aggressive aspects of masculinity and the aggressiveness of the soldiers. Their aggressiveness was regenerated before battle and tamed after combat through encounters with the comfort women at comfort stations. According to the narratives of the women, there was a pattern of violence before and after battles which seems to have produced and released military aggression. This pattern is elucidated by accounts of a former comfort woman, Hwang Kūmju: 'the men were even crueller than before; they were savage. Those who knew they were about to go into combat were even worse. It was simply unbearable' (interviewed in 1995). Here, the soldiers' vulnerability and fear of death was expressed in the form of violence at the comfort station. As Nishino Ryūmiko who has investigated the comfort women issue reports, the men were especially aggressive when their colleagues were killed in battle. The soldiers immediately killed any Chinese they saw on the way back to their camp. Their aggression and tension reached the limit. At this moment, sex with comfort women was provided to relieve their aggression.[56] It is interesting to note that the control of their sexuality served two entirely opposite functions: the relief and the reproduction of aggressiveness and cruelty.

A regime of sexual regulation was introduced by the Japanese through the comfort women programme. The provision of opportunities to have sex with the comfort women helped to self-regulate the Japanese armed forces, so that the soldiers could be sent back to the battlefields to fight again. Entertainment with sex was offered to offset tough soldiering during the war. One of my informants, a military physician Yuasa Ken, confirmed that 'sexual pleasure for soldiers is like gasoline for a car'. Japanese military documents also reveal that providing opportunities for sex was a means of relaxation and comfort, of reinforcing military discipline, of diverting soldiers' complaints and brutality, and an outlet for the fear and tension of war.[57] In addition, a former Japanese upper ranking officer I interviewed admitted the dependency of the military on the comfort women to help in the governance of subjugated people in Indonesia:

> The programme of comfort women was really wonderful in terms of two aspects; one is to keep the soldiers from rape and being imprisoned, the other is not to provoke local peoples' anti-Japanese reaction caused by the attempted rape of local women by the Japanese soldiers. If there were no 'Comfort Women', many soldiers would have been put into prisons, and the local population must have resisted the Japanese military government.... The women were among the most important in the Japanese forces. And owing to them, military governing of the local population could go on smoothly. Thus, I would like to thank the women very much.[58]

The fact that the comfort women system was considered an important component of the preparation for and carrying out of war reveals the military's dependency on women in maintaining and regulating the forces. The women were one of the mainstays of the military organisation. Cynthia Enloe draws attention to the notion that 'the military needs women as the gender "women" to provide men with masculinity – reinforcing incentives to endure all the hardships of soldiering'.[59] The comfort women provided a safety valve for the effects of the extreme regimentation to which the soldiers were subjected. However, on the other hand, precautions were advised by the military authority towards the women, who considered them, in a sense, possible symbols of treachery as well, so that the number of visits to the same woman was reported and limited. In summary, violence, on the one hand, and the comfort women, on the other, were two crucial axes of control of the men in order to carry out total war and to prepare the men to fight to the death on the battlefield.

A gender-specific identity was consolidated and imposed on the Japanese military man in relation to the femininity of the Korean comfort women. The masculinity of the military men was constructed or reinforced through its 'opposite'; the enforced femininity served to consolidate the military form of masculinity. Promiscuous or impure feminine identity fortified misogynistic masculine identity, and submissive feminine identity created a superior masculine Japanese national identity among military men. The Korean women's inferiorised ethnicity as 'uncivilised', sexualised and promiscuous served to enhance the Japanese men's ethnic identity as superior, patriotic, civilised and virile. These binary concepts of masculinity and femininity were mutually exclusive and interdependent.

Self-positioning of the soldiers

Finally, I will explore the self-positioning of the military men in the face of the army re-socialisation reified in the reconstruction of masculinity and the regulation of sexuality. The influx identities of the soldiers can be witnessed in the complex ways in which they dealt with everyday army life: the complex spectrum of compliance, consent, inaction and resistance. The soldiers' position in the Japanese totalitarian regime was also shifting. The soldiers played an important role as members of the Japanese Imperial Army or Navy which was at the 'core' of supporting the regime to wage total war for colonial expansionism. Tsurumi points out that, in particular, 'no peasant-soldier raised any doubt about why he had to die for the Emperor, any more than he questioned why he had to work to support his parents, wife and children. Both duties were simply taken for granted.'[60] A consequence of intensive military socialisation was the internalisation of compulsion to such an extent that the socialised individuals would feel that they were acting on their own. Among them, few showed their disapproval of the military system. In the Japanese Army, if the individual soldier refused to obey, he would certainly be tried for treason and condemned even to death. According to official statistics, toward the end of the total war in 1944, the number of soldiers who were court-martialled for rebellions, disobedience of orders and desertion from army barracks was 7994.[61] This was double the number court-martialled during the Russo-Japanese War, but still most soldiers, in a sense, consented and collaborated with the totalitarian regime, probably believing that their role as the 'core' of the regime gave them benefits, tangible or intangible rewards, or power. A student-soldier noted in his diary while at the front:

> Soldiers believe with extreme naiveté that they are heroes in the defence of their country. They are proud to be the saviours of their fatherland. That is an easy sentimentalism. But that is the anchor of their emotion. It is a kind of soldiers' mental masturbation for which they are willing to waste their youthful energy.... This is sad. They do not possess enough reason to be critical of their own state of mind. Moreover, should they deny this belief, they would have nothing left to sustain them in their hardships.[62]

This comment clearly shows the consequences of inculcating the values of self-sacrifice, subservience and loyalty in the soldiers for the expansionist project: their active support and enthusiasm for the totalitarian regime from below. Another narrative comes from a Kamikaze pilot. Hayashi Ichizo wrote his diary at Wonsan Air Base in Korea from 9 January to 21 March 1945. His final letter to his mother from Wonsan Air Base shows his strong patriotism: 'I am happy to go as a tokkotai pilot.... I will do a splendid job sinking an enemy aircraft carrier.'[63] There are substantial numbers of Japanese veterans who still, to the present day, believe that the war was fought for justice and liberation: that the aim of the war was the liberation of other Asian countries such as Indonesia, Vietnam and Burma from Western imperialism.[64] Yoshioka, a former officer whom I interviewed, says that there was no alternative for the soldiers but to support the war project to the death: 'whoever he was, if he was a Japanese man, he had to die for his country during the war. When I was conscripted, I was prepared myself to die. No other way to choose, if he was Japanese' (interviewed in 1996).

On the other hand, some military men showed scepticism about the war. According to Tsurumi there was stratification, a difference among student-soldiers and peasant-soldiers in the Japanese Imperial Army and Navy. He stresses that the students were more critical of the army and found more negative value in military experience than the peasants, and that the latter accepted the army ideology of death more willingly than the former.[65] There were also Kamikaze pilots who were sceptical about the war. Ohnuki-Tierney shows in Kamikaze diaries and correspondence that some student-soldiers wrote often heartbreaking private texts in which they poured out their anguish and fear, their reluctance to die, their yearning for family. They expressed profound ambivalence toward the war and articulated thoughtful opposition to their nation's imperialism. For example, at the end of World War II a Kamikaze pilot, Irokawa Daikichi, wrote: 'We tried to live with 120 percent intensity, rather than waiting for death. We read and read, trying to understand why we had to die in our early twenties. We felt the clock ticking away towards our death, every sound of the clock shortening our lives.'[66] Despite the regime's ambition to nationalise the masses, the soldiers held different attitudes that transformed them from the tailor-made subjects of a single identity to autonomous individuals, as Jie-Hyun Lim points out in the series Introduction in this volume. For example, some of the student-soldiers in the Japanese forces resisted being part of a uniform mass with a unitary will.

As already shown earlier, soldiers also disclosed fear of death and revealed the tensions of war, and some of them suffered from mental disorder. In a sense, Japanese military men were simultaneously invisible victims mobilised, controlled and victimised under the totalitarian regime through such means as violence, humiliation and propaganda. I am aware that the term 'men', and even 'soldiers', does not designate a unitary category. The costs and the benefits of the total war system were unevenly distributed. The former military doctor Yuasa Ken, whom I interviewed in Tokyo in June 1996, defended the soldiers:

> Some feminist scholars have blamed the soldiers, but they should consider the nature of war. It was a question of remaining alive or being killed on the battle field, rather than a gender issue. Seniors or officers gave orders to the rank and file, whatever they are, saying 'it is an order of the Emperor; it is a war for justice'. The problem was the war itself. The individual soldier was not that bad. The soldiers

never had any rights or opportunities to exercise their own will, or to refuse obedience during the war.

In his narrative, the soldiers were presented as forced or unwilling consenters rather than active supporters and/or collaborators, so that they appear as victims of war for the things they were ordered to do. Japanese historian Fujiwara also argues that the patriotic identity of the soldiers was forcibly imposed. He writes that 'the army was based on orders, force and coercion, by which the soldiers had to submit and became slaves, instead of voluntary involvement in the defence of their nation'.[67]

In fact, as Jie-Hyun Lim points out in the series Introduction, amongst consenters, consent itself is a multi-layered experience spanning internalised coercion, forced consent, passive conformity, consensus, self-mobilisation and forced participation. The Japanese soldiers might both be forced to fight on the battlefield and prepared to endure hardships and self-sacrifice on behalf of the nation even to the point of laying down their lives willingly. Fujiwara's argument begs the question of whether the soldiers managed to retain and exercise their own agency. For some, in particular for the Kamikaze groups, their active involvement in the 'Holy War' was from a rational calculation to make their death honourable: 'We were ready to die anyway, so to choose to die as a suicidal attacker was a genuine expression of our youthful pride to make our death most meaningful.'[68] Yuki Tanaka argues that the Kamikaze *Tokkōtai* forces fought out of a combination of loyalty to their country and family, solidarity with fellow pilots and a fear of being irresponsible or cowardly. He explains that to defend one's mother in one's hometown was thus the most basic, almost instinctive, element in rationalising a cadet's death as a Kamikaze pilot.[69] Sometimes, a person changed his view about the war as the war went on. For example, medical officer Taniguchi Kazuo, who was in Shanxi Province in China in 1937, initially strongly justified Japan's invasion of China, but later expressed remorse for some of his own actions as a representative of the Imperial Army.[70]

All these above accounts show that the self-positioning of the military men at war is not fixed but fluctuating amongst compliance, conformity, consent, inaction, calculation, resistance and opposition. It is difficult to draw a clear-cut line between 'forced' and 'voluntary' engagement with the totalitarian state programme too. It should be noted that soldiers' consent has a wide range from 'internalised coercion, forced consent and passive conformity to voluntary consensus'.[71] The complexity of soldiers' experiences in flux as perpetrators, beneficiaries and/or those who conformed to the totalitarian regime, as well as victims of the total war system, needs to be considered. Thus, monolithic, non-contradictory and unitary concepts of gender and national subjectivity cannot accommodate the complexity of self-subject positioning that took place within and against totalitarian contexts.

Notes

1. Among them, 1,130,000 armed forces of the Imperial Army were killed during the war. Hayashi Saburō, *Taiheiyō sensō likugun gaishi* (Tokyo: Iwanami, 1950), p. 295.
2. Senda Kakō, *Chonggunwianbu* (Seoul: Tamul, 1992); cited in Alice Yun Chai, 'Asian-Pacific Feminist Coalition Politics: The *Chōngsindae/Jūgunianfu* ("Comfort Women") Movement', *Korean Studies* 17 (1993), p. 69.
3. Inter-Ministerial Group on the 'Comfort Women' Issue, Republic of Korea, *Military 'Comfort Women' Under Japanese Colonial Rule*, Interim Report (July 1992), Seoul, Korea; cited in Chung Chin Sung, 'Ilbon kunwianbu jōngch'aekūi bonjil', in Hanguk sahoesa yōnkuhoe (ed.), *Hanmal iljehaūi sahoesasangkwa sahoeundong* (Seoul: Munhakkwa jisōng, 1994), p. 182.
4. See Yoshimi Yoshiaki, *Jūgunianfu* (Tokyo: Iwanami shoten, 1995).
5. Yoshimi Yoshiaki, *Jūgunianfu shiryoshu* (Tokyo: Ōtsuki shoten, 1992), pp. 217, 229, 262.
6. Nishino Ryumiko, *Moto heishitachi no shiyōgen: Jūgun ianfu* (Tokyo: Akashi shoten, 1992), p. 78.
7. Ibid., pp. 85, 88.
8. Jūgun ianfu hyakutōban henshuiinkai (ed.), *Jūgun Ianfu Hyakutōban* (Tokyo: Akashi shoten, 1992), p. 69.
9. Haruko Taya Cook and Theodore F. Cook, *Japan At War: An Oral History* (New York: The New Press, 1992), p. 309.
10. On familial ideology in Japanese society, see Dukutake Tadashi, *The Japanese Social Structure: Its Evolution in the Modern Century*, Second Edition (Tokyo: University of Tokyo Press, 1989) and Iizuka Kōji, *Nihon no guntai* (Tokyo: Todai Kyodo-kumiai Shuppanbu, 1950).
11. The family-state structure of the Meiji state first took shape in the 1880s, when family-state ideology advocated the merging of the individual stem family with state power and cast the Emperor as the great father of his subjects. This ideology was reflected in both the Meiji Constitution (1889), which defined Japanese people as subjects of the Emperor, and the Imperial Rescript on Education (1890), which taught schoolchildren filial piety and loyalty to the state (Miyake Yoshiko, 'Doubling Expectations: Motherhood and Women's Factory Work Under State Management in Japan in the 1930s and 1940s', in Gail Lee Bernstein (ed.), *Recreating Japanese Women, 1600–1945* (Berkeley, CA, Los Angeles, CA and Oxford: University of California Press, 1991), p. 270; Ryumiko, *Moto heishitachi no shiyōgen; Jūgun ianfu*, pp. 145–6.
12. The Emperor was simultaneously established as semi-divine father to the national community and head of state. Michael Weiner, 'Discourses of Race, Nation and Empire in Pre-1945 Japan', *Ethnic and Racial Studies* 18(3)

(July 1995), p. 449; Kathleen S. Uno, 'The Death of "Good Wife, Wise Mother?" ', in Andrew Gordon (ed.), *Post-War Japan as History* (Berkeley, CA and Oxford: University of California Press, 1993), p. 297.

13. Kōji, *Nihon no guntai*, pp. 43–5; cited in Kazuko Tsurumi, *Social Change and the Individual: Japan Before and After Defeat in World War II* (Princeton, NJ: Princeton University Press, 1970), p. 98.

14. Mun Pilgi, interviewed in 1992; Ustinia Dolgopol and Snehal Paranjape, *Comfort Women; An Unfinished Ordeal* (Geneva: International Commission of Jurists, 1994), p. 95.

15. George Hicks, *The Comfort Women; Sex Slaves of the Japanese Imperial Forces* (London: Souvenir Press, 1995).

16. I am aware that there are overlaps between traits of masculinities and femininities, and that gender stereotypes are too simplistic to encompass the complexities of constructions of masculinity and femininity in specific cultural contexts. However, at a theoretical level in my framework I am fixing the oppositions of stereotypical masculinity and femininity to show the interdependence and contrast of the two, and to show how gender is 'done' through the comfort women system.

17. Cynthia H. Enloe, 'Feminists Thinking About War, Militarism, and Peace', in Beth B. Hess (ed.), *Analyzing Gender: A Handbook of Social Science Research* (London: Sage, 1987), pp. 531–2.

18. Lynn Segal, *Is the Future Female?* (London: Virago, 1987), pp. 162–203; cited in Carolyn Steedman, *The Radical Soldier's Tale: John Pearman, 1819–1908* (London and New York: Routledge, 1988), p. 271.

19. Military Intelligence Service, 'Soldiers Guide to the Japanese Army' (Washington, DC: US Army Military History Institute, 1994), p. 3.

20. Peter Duus, *The Rise of Modern Japan* (Boston, MA: Houghton Mifflin Company, 1976), p. 230.

21. Saburō Ienaga, *The Pacific War, 1931–1945: A Critical Perspective on Japan's Role in World War II* (New York: Pantheon Books, 1978), pp. 48–9; Edward J. Drea, *In the Service of the Emperor: Essays on the Imperial Japanese Army* (Lincoln, NE: University of Nebraska Press, 1998).

22. Tsunetomo Yamamoto, *Hagakure* (Tokyo: Iwanami shoten, 1965), p. 23; cited in Tsurumi, *Social Change and the Individual*, p. 81.

23. Akira Fujiwara, *Gunjinshi: Nihon Gundaishi Taikei* (Tokyo: Tokyokeizai, 1961), pp. 111–4.

24. Tsurumi, *Social Change and the Individual*, p. 119.

25. Ryumiko, *Moto heishitachi no shiyōgen: Jūgun ianfu*, p. 63.

26. Tsurumi, *Social Change and the Individual*, pp. 96–7, 123, 124.

27. Fumiko Kawada, *Akagawara no ie: Chosen kara kita jūgunianfu* (Tokyo: Chikuma shobo, 1987), p. 81.

28. Dolgopol and Paranjape, *Comfort Women: An Unfinished Ordeal*, p. 125.

29. For example, the collective suicides have been reported in the testimony of Kang Soon-Ae in ibid., p. 89 and in the testimony of Yamaichi Takeo, in Cook and Cook, *Japan at War: An Oral History*, p. 289.

30. Ryumiko, *Moto heishitachi no shiyōgen: Jūgun ianfu*, p. 74.

31. Tojo Hideki and Army Minister, *Senjinkun* (Tokyo: The Army Ministry, 1941) (reprinted by Boei mondai kenkyukai, Tokyo, 1972); cited in Cook and Cook, *Japan at War: An Oral History*, p. 164.

32. Jūgun ianfu hyakutōban, p. 57; Ryumiko, *Moto heishitachi no shiyōgen: Jūgun ianfu*, pp. 96, 104.
33. Hayashi reports distribution of condoms by the Japanese military government in Malaysia during World War II (Hayashi Hirofumi, 'Mare hantoni okeru nihongunianjoni tsuite', in *Shisen, ningen, shakai* 15 (July 1993), pp. 75–6. For a discussion of Japanese military involvement in the comfort women system, see Yoshimi Yoshiaki, 'For Resolution of the Issue of the Military "Comfort Women" ', *Sekai* 626 (September 1996); Sensō sekinin shiryo centa (ed.), *Sensō sekinin kenkyū*, Vol. 1 (Autumn 1993), p. 34; cited in Chin Sung Chung, 'The Origin and Development of the Military Sexual Slavery Problem in Imperial Japan', *Positions* 5(1) (Spring 1997), p. 224.
34. Testimony of Ichikawa Ichiro in Dolgopol and Paranjape, *Comfort Women: An Unfinished Ordeal*, p. 125.
35. Minoru Kawamoto, 'Some Moments in the Barracks of a Japanese Army Recruit', http://www.star-games.com/exhibits/barracks/barracks.html (accessed 2 March 2009).
36. William T. de Bary and Donald Keene (comps), *Sources of Japanese Tradition* II (New York: Columbia University Press, 1958), pp. 198–200; cited in Tsurumi, *Social Change and the Individual*, pp. 122–3.
37. Carol Gluck, *Japan's Modern Myths: Ideology in the Late Meiji Period* (Princeton, NJ: Princeton University Press, 1985), p. 36.
38. This suicidal attack began with the organisation of a 'Divine Wind Special Attack Corps', the *Shimpu* or *Kamikaze Tokubetsu Kogekitai*, by the Imperial Navy during the Japanese defence of the Philippines. Escorted to their targets by fighters, the pilots were instructed to plunge their bomb-laden aircraft directly into enemy ships. Cook and Cook, *Japan at War: An Oral History*, p. 265.
39. James L. Huffman, 'Challenging Kamikaze Stereotypes: "Wings of Defeat" on the Silver Screen', *Japan Focus*, http://japanfocus.org/products/topdf/2910 (accessed 17 February 2009).
40. Emiko Ohnuki-Tierney, *Kamikaze, Cherry Blossoms, and Nationalisms* (Chicago, IL: University of Chicago Press, 2002), p. 300.
41. Leonard A. Humphreys, *The Way of the Heavenly Sword: The Japanese Army in the 1920's* (Stanford, CA: Stanford University Press, 1995), p. 49.
42. Military Intelligence Service, 'Soldiers Guide to the Japanese Army', pp. 7–8.
43. Tsurumi, *Social Change and the Individual*, p. 125.
44. Ibid., p. 133.
45. Janice Matsumura, 'State Propaganda and Mental Disorders: The Issue of Psychiatric Casualties among Japanese Soldiers during the Asia-Pacific War', *Bulletin of the History of Medicine* 78 (2004), p. 807.
46. Sakurai Tonano, 'Guntai ni okeru jusatsu nami ni jisatsu kito no igakuteki kōsatsu', in *Gun'idan zasshi* 316 (1939), pp. 941–2; cited in ibid., p. 821.
47. Ibid., pp. 808, 816.
48. Military Intelligence Service, 'Soldiers Guide to the Japanese Army', p. 7.
49. Tsung-yi Lin, 'Neurasthenia Revisited: Its Place in Modern Psychiatry', *Culture, Medicine and Psychiatry* 13(2) (1989), p. 110; Matsumura, 'State Propaganda and Mental Disorders', p. 815.

50. Tokyo: Boeicho boei kenkyūjo: Hamazaki Tomizo, 'Nisshi' (2 December 1937); cited in Aaron William Moore, 'Essential Ingredients of Truth: Soldiers' Diaries in the Asia Pacific War', *Japan Focus*, http://www.japanfocus. org/products/topdf/2506 (posted on 27 August 2007) (accessed 9 February 2009).

51. Masao Maruyama, *Thought and Behaviour in Modern Japanese Politics*, (London: Oxford University Press, 1963), p. 18; cited in Tsurumi, *Social Change and the Individual*, p. 95.

52. Hanguk chōngsindae yōn'guhoe and Hanguk chōngsindae munje taech'ek hyōpūihoe (eds), *Kangjero kkūllyōgan chosōnin kunwianbudūl* 1 (Seoul: Hanul, 1993), pp. 46, 75.

53. Dolgopol and Paranjape, *Comfort Women: An Unfinished Ordeal*, p. 128.

54. See Nihon Senbotsu Gakusei Kinen-Kai (Japan Memorial Society for the Students Killed in the War, Wadatsumi Society), *Listen to the Voices from the Sea: Writings of the Fallen Japanese Students* (Kike Wadatsumi no Koe), translated by Midori Yamanouchi and Joseph L. Quinn (Pennsylvania, PA: University of Scranton Press, 2005), pp. 215–8; Emiko Ohnuki-Tierney, *Kamikaze Diaries: Reflections of Japanese Student Soldiers* (Chicago, IL: University of Chicago Press, 2006).

55. Yoshiaki, *Jūgunianfu shiryoshu*, p. 216.

56. Ryumiko, *Moto heishitachi no shiyūgen; Jūgun ianfu*, p. 77.

57. Yoshiaki, *Jūgunianfu*, p. 53.

58. Miyamoto, interviewed in 1996.

59. Cynthia H. Enloe, *Does Khaki Become You? The Militarization of Women's Lives* (London: Pandora, 1988), p. 214.

60. Tsurumi, *Social Change and the Individual*, p. 133.

61. Ōoe Shinobu, *Chyōheisei* (Tokyo: Iwanami, 1981), pp. 155–6.

62. Wadatsumi-kai (ed.), *The Fifteen Years' War Seen Through the Messages of the Students Who Died in the War* (Senbotsu Gakusei no Isho ni Miru Jūgōnensensō) (Tokyo: Kōbunsha, 1963).

63. Nihon Senbotsu Gakusei Kinen-Kai, *Listen to the Voices from the Sea*, pp. 173–4, http://wgordon.web.wesleyan.edu/kamikaze/writings/books/ohnuki-tierney/index.htm (accessed 29 January 2009).

64. Senkyūhyakunanajūni Kyoto oshietakutasai ianfu jyoho denwa hokokushu henshu iinkai (ed.), *Sei to shinryaku: guntai ianjyo hachijuyon kasho motonihonheirano shogen* (Kyoto: Shakai hyoronsha, 1992), pp. 307–8.

65. Tsurumi, *Social Change and the Individual*, p. 126.

66. Ohnuki-Tierney, *Kamikaze Diaries: Reflections of Japanese Student Soldiers*.

67. Fujiwara Akira, *Tennōsei to Guntai* (Tokyo: Aokishoten, 1977), p. 28.

68. Shunpei Ueyama, *Dai Tōa Sensō no Imi* (Tokyo: Chūōkōronsha, 1964), pp. 2–3; cited in Tsurumi, *Social Change and the Individual*, p. 136.

69. Yuki Tanaka, 'Japan's Kamikaze Pilots and Contemporary Suicide Bombers: War and Terror', *Japan Focus* 25 (November 2005), http://www.japanfocus. org/products/topdf/1606 (accessed 12 January 2009).

70. Moore, 'Essential Ingredients of Truth'.

71. Jie-Hyun Lim, 'Historiographical Perspectives on "Mass Dictatorship"', paper presented at the RICH International Conference Mass Dictatorship Between Desire and Delusion, Hanyang University, Seoul, 17–19 June 2005.

Part IV
Post-War Authoritarianisms

11
Sex in Big-Character Posters from China's Cultural Revolution: Gendering the Class Enemy

Michael Schoenhals

> The big-character poster is...a powerful weapon for conducting debate and education in accordance with the broadest mass democracy. People write down their views, suggestions or exposures and criticisms of others in big characters on large sheets of paper and put them up in conspicuous places for people to read.
>
> Mao Zedong (1958)[1]

The medium of the 'big-character poster', as described by the Beijing publishers of Mao Zedong's Works in the epigraph above, may be thought of as a 1960s Chinese equivalent of the political blogosphere of the twenty-first century. Permitting a curious blend of superficial freedom and openness to coexist happily with stifling political correctness, it gave impetus to a campaign that brought down many a corrupt politician as well as traumatised and victimised no small number of innocent 'masses'. One way in which it did this was by not shying away from sex and gender, topics of considerable sensitivity hitherto taboo in Chinese Communist Party (CCP) political discourse. In this chapter, I attempt to illustrate this particular aspect of mass dictatorship in China by commenting on some recurring themes of gender and the male 'class enemy' and of sexuality and the revolutionary (or counter-revolutionary) woman.

Mass dictatorship

At the end of July 1965, police officers all over China were told that 'an issue of a fundamental nature' had been *the* subject of debate at

237

the recently concluded month-long 14th National Public Security Conference. As framed by CCP Chairman Mao Zedong himself, the issue had been 'how to rely on the masses in the exercise of dictatorship'. While some conference attendees apparently reasoned as if it were quite enough to 'let [the state's] political and legal organs handle dictatorship matters', the official post-conference communiqué in the periodical *People's Public Security* (classified 'for official use only') called such a view mistaken. 'In actuality', it explained, 'if [dictatorship] is to be exercised successfully, the entire Party and the masses all have to become involved.'[2]

The text of the communiqué, to which historians have recently gained access, affirms Jie-Hyun Lim's observation, 50 years later, that the socio-political engineers of the modern state system – in whose ranks the CCP Chairman no doubt belonged – were 'desperate to recruit and mobilise the masses' for their project and 'demanded their enthusiasm and voluntary participation'.[3] What this participation entailed to Mao Zedong was clarified in the months that followed. Little stories purporting to be quasi-journalistic accounts of actual events appeared in the Chinese media under headlines like 'The Might of the Dictatorship of the Masses Knows No Bounds: The Masses Restrict and Control an Arsonist' and 'A Serious Struggle: Relying on the Masses Transforms a Hooligan and Thief'.[4] At the start of 1966, a New Year editorial in *People's Public Security* proclaimed in bold-face that it was imperative for everyone concerned 'to continue the all-round implementation of the long-term policy of relying on the masses in the exercise of dictatorship'.[5] When the Cultural Revolution picked up steam in the weeks and months that followed, the stage was set for a bold Maoist experiment: on 10 June, an authoritative Top Secret *Notification* from the Ministry of Public Security ordered police officers all over China to lend the 'masses' their support.[6] Officers were still to take responsibility for the maintenance of public order, but when that task came into conflict with what historians would one day speak of as the 'mother of all mass movements',[7] a highly unusual provision would henceforth apply:

> If, in the course of the movement, incidents involving physical violence occur, [public security and police officers] should, while maintaining their own composure, seek to persuade [the violent party to desist]. When coming across instances of the leftist masses beating up counter-revolutionary elements or bad people after having been roused to righteous indignation, public security and police officers should first of all support the revolutionary acts of leftists.

After that, they should they seek to persuade the masses not to beat people up in the future.[8]

As envisaged by the Ministry of Public Security at the time, and arguably by Mao as well, this arrangement actually granted the 'masses' the right to creatively terrorise China's 'non-masses' in the name of the Cultural Revolution, while merely asking of the police that it stay informed:

> In the course of the movement, the public security organs should rely on the revolutionary masses, develop an acute sense of smell and remain able to sniff things out, ensure rapid access to information, stay on top of developments at all times, and quickly report what is happening to party committees and higher-level public security organs.[9]

On 28 July and 9 August 1966, the Ministry of Public Security's *Notification* was reclassified, first as secret and then 'for official use only', and given wider circulation.[10]

What was the outcome of this remarkable 'hands off' policy? 'Incidents involving physical violence' for sure, as was indeed anticipated, but also a precipitous decline in the authority of the police. For much of the rest of the 1960s, a chaotic situation prevailed in which self-styled, mostly young, members of the 'masses of the left' ruled China's streets. At first, they made life a misery for people who appeared on the basis of speech, appearance or demeanour to be 'bourgeois' or otherwise 'suspect'. Later, they became embroiled in their own internal gang wars that may have left the urban general public unscathed but which all the same claimed countless victims and casualties among the politically active. In due course, the initial violence in the autumn of 1966 was to be hailed as paving the way for the great victory of the Cultural Revolution.

Linguistic violence

In this chapter, my main concern is not with physical violence per se, but with linguistic violence – immaterial yet ever so capable of hurting the feelings and the soul, if not the body – in the most popular mass medium of the Cultural Revolution, the big-character poster.[11] In the posters, 'fighting words' often reigned supreme, the kind of words defined by the US Supreme Court as 'personally abusive epithets that, when addressed to the ordinary citizen, are, as a matter of common knowledge, inherently likely to inflict injury'.[12] As already noted, I will be looking specifically for examples of linguistic violence illustrating how the politically active 'masses' raised the sensitive subjects of sex and gender. In the past, these had been taboo; 'in the course of the movement', however, they came to be pointedly and publicly raised in something *called* a 'class struggle' which in actuality was but a politically driven 'brutal differentiation between inclusion and exclusion' that had little to do with the relationship of individuals to the means of production.[13]

As but one of many examples of what Mao Zedong would have regarded as the oppressive 'revisionism' to which his 'dictatorship of the masses' was to be a superior alternative, sexual relations had up to 1966 been deemed wholly unsuitable for discussion in big-character posters. In April 1963, the powerful mayor of Beijing and second highest ranking member of the CCP Central Secretariat Peng Zhen had reiterated this point after a factory visit that had convinced him of the positive role that posters could play in mass movement politics. Yet 'some things', he observed, 'have to be controlled. No big-character posters should be put up dealing with topics such as an individual's... private life'. Trying to be as clear as possible, Peng explained that this topic was off-limits and should be no part of 'our... mass line'. He added, though, that it 'may be raised in letters or in face-to-face conversation with the appropriate responsible cadre', and if this rule was observed 'no harm will come from the use of big-character posters'.[14]

In late May 1966, a more specific ban on keeping sexual relations and similar parts of the 'private life' of an individual out of the medium of big-character posters was issued by Peng's municipal party apparatus. But the ban, which asserted that 'illicit sexual liaisons' and 'moral depravity' were off-limits to big-character poster writers, was promptly made null and void by the 'dictatorship of the masses'.[15] Claiming in the typically aggressive language of the time to be writing and acting in the name of the Cultural Revolution, a group of 18 municipal government employees challenged their soon-to-be-former bosses in a big-character poster, asserting that

> [T]he important techniques used by the bourgeoisie to bring about peaceful evolution include morally depraved lifestyles and sexual entrapment. These are used to strike at the weak-willed for the sake of usurping political power.... This is a big issue of right and wrong. And yet the [municipal party committee] Study Office, for fear of seeing the masses reveal the decadent life of the black gang, has issued an order that states: 'Big-character posters should not have

as their subject illicit sexual relations and moral depravity'. What is the point of hastily issuing pointers like these – to tell the masses not to do this, and not to do that? What is it you're really trying to achieve?[16]

In the Cultural Revolution, allegations, claims and counter-claims about 'sexual relations and moral depravity' featured regularly in the linguistic violence that dominated big-character posters. To paraphrase and reverse the claim in the passage just quoted, they became prominent techniques used by self-styled 'mass representatives' in their effort to bring about change that was anything but 'peaceful'. Public forays into a previously taboo realm would contribute to a peculiarly 'gendered' style of discourse, as countless examples would show in the months that followed.

As increasingly substantial documentation begins to accumulate among social historians, linguistic violence centred broadly on the private sphere is emerging as an aspect of Mao's 'mass dictatorship' largely overlooked by past scholarship. Any attempt at describing and analysing what the CCP Centre insisted was 'a great revolution that touches people to their very souls' certainly needs to account for it.[17] What this chapter seeks to take, then, is a tentative first step in this direction and to bring to the surface a couple of discursive strands relating to sex in politics and revolution that proliferated in big-character posters from the Cultural Revolution.[18] Its first part quotes and contextualises stereotypical references to sex and the male 'class enemy' (his counterpart, the male class hero, as it were, was always a strangely asexual creature); its second part deals with politics, sexuality and the revolutionary and counter-revolutionary woman.

The male class enemy

If and when an attack on a political adversary of male gender included references to sex, the stereotypical account would usually depict the target as a debauched lecher intent on defiling the purity of any and all proletarian 'female comrades' who had the misfortune of crossing his path. In the less elaborate attacks, the accusation might well be a throwaway one. That, for example, was the case in a big-character poster that appeared on the premises of the State Science and Technology Commission, in Beijing, in which one Zhu XX was quoted in passing as calling Yu XX, a deposed senior propaganda official, 'a piece of shit who screwed my wife and whom I've hated ever since'.[19]

When the accusation was more elaborate, perhaps less immediately personal and more concerned with depravity in general, almost anything could be turned into a useful 'revelation'. In the Bureau of Foreign Affairs in China's Ministry of Higher Education, lower-level staff denounced their boss for his 'bourgeois lifestyle', alleging in a poster that during a visit to Paris he had 'let a car drive him around the nightclub district'.[20] In China's Ministry of Culture, a deputy minister (whose brief in an earlier posting had included, specifically, propaganda affairs) found some of his past unguarded admissions about non-socialist reading habits turned against him in big-character posters authored by disgruntled staff:

> Even more so, XX is a fan of erotic literature, and quite often late at night he can be found between the sheets reading erotic works like *Jin Ping Mei* and *Sex Histories*. He absolves himself from guilt by saying things like 'Well, as director of propaganda, one has to read all kinds of books, good and bad alike'.[21]

As an accusation, this one was on some level the most common one: it did not mean much on its own, but as a 'complement' to more substantial and serious allegations it served effectively to paint the target in a bad light. Typically, collections of big-character posters circulated in printed or stencilled form would put items of this kind at the very end, where they would back up those which raised allegations of a more purely political nature, for example, transgressions against the correct political line or distortions of Mao Zedong Thought. In this case, the depiction was of a hypocrite propaganda official who claimed the right to deny others the pleasure of reading whatever *they* might themselves have wanted, while all along himself indulging in reading habits altogether unbecoming a good communist. The cumulative effect of allegations and insinuations of this sort could be devastating, and responding to or deflecting them was notoriously difficult.

When a big-character poster writer's target was someone about whom nothing particularly salacious was known for certain, that person might all the same be attacked for conduct unbecoming if it turned out that he or she appeared to condone immoral behaviour in others. On university campuses, for example, this was an often easy charge to make against senior teachers or administrators. One vice-president of Tianjin University, for example, had the following charge levelled at him on 11 June 1966 in a poster signed by a group of engineering students:

During the Four Cleans campaign, when stuff happened between students, X applied tremendous pressure, reprimanded and cursed the people involved, calling them 'wicked', 'worthless', 'dog's shit', 'donkey balls' and so on. When students had affairs [all the same], he shamelessly said 'Oh well, young people, it's hard to prevent them from having affairs'. *This* is how seriously he took such matters![22]

The Four Cleans campaign (1963–66) referred to here, had seen the vice-president and many of his colleagues and students spend time in the Hebei countryside together. Here ostensibly, from dusk until dawn, they rooted out corruption and threw their weight behind the local poor and lower-middle peasants in the 'class struggle' against remnant land-lord elements – which is how China's central authorities had defined the purpose of the campaign. After sundown, however, judging from numerous big-character posters attacking the vice-president, it appears as if his administration had failed spectacularly to prevent the students from also enjoying themselves once their political chores and duties had been completed.[23]

Particularly vulnerable to charges of decadence were cadres in the sectors that regularly interacted with foreigners or with Chinese from overseas. The unstated assumption in their case was that the capital-ist world beyond China's borders was literally awash with smut and pornography, and that resistance to the 'sugar-coated bullets of the bourgeoisie' demanded super-human efforts only the most Maoist of Maoists were capable of. In the summer of 1967, a senior State Council official and long-time friend of Premier Zhou Enlai's found himself on the receiving end of charges similar to those levelled at the Deputy Minister of Culture above. He was accused by Shanghai Red Guards of 'discussing, in foreign languages, with foreign guests, the thoroughly obscene stories printed in pornographic bourgeois magazines'. Not only that: it was said that 'to him, looking at pictures of naked women in pornographic magazines was not enough. At home, he would show many Hong Kong and American movies, and even get hold of stuff like [the film] *Nude Heaven* with which he would corrupt cadres, sons and daughters.'[24] One of China's vice-premiers – a war hero and People's Liberation Army (PLA) Marshal described in an American biographical dictionary published in 1971 as the second 'most widely travelled mem-ber of the Chinese Communist military elite' – was also accused by Red Guards of indulging in the viewing of *Nude Heaven*, about which unfor-tunately nothing further is known.[25] It appears to have been equally popular with both sexes: after her death and posthumous vilification as an enemy of the revolution, the wife of CCP Vice-Chairman Marshal Lin Biao was also said to have enjoyed watching it in the company of some of her close (female) friends.[26]

That an event was well in the distant past mattered little: if it could be construed in such a way as to paint the target of a big-character poster in a bad light, it would be brought up even posthumously. The one-time CCP Politburo member Gao Gang, who had been purged and imprisoned in 1954 and soon thereafter died by his own hand, was denounced roundly on university campuses in 1967. In addition to being called a bourgeois representative who had wormed his way into the CCP to attempt to subvert China's revolution from within, Gao was denounced as a serial rapist and moral degenerate, such accusations 'substantiated' with stories about events that had taken place in the 1930s:

> Already back in his North Shaanxi days [in the 1930s], the big hooligan Gao Gang would often dance and indulge in all kinds of pleasures. He once spent 6,000,000 *taels* on having a dance floor made. At the dances he would always insist on picking the good looking girls and would violate them whenever he felt like it. During his eleven months in the North Shaanxi border region, he was removed from office twice because of his corrupt morals and the like. Gao Gang was a rotten egg who loved the new and loathed the old: nobody knows how many wives he abandoned along the way! He did not mend his bandit ways after he came to Northeast China [in the 1940s] where members of his clique such as XXX and XXX, in order to please their lord and master, would abuse their official positions to find women for him to insult and humiliate. When going away on official business trips, he would take his mistresses along and while recuperating he would insist on female company. ... He would trick female comrades into visiting him at home where he would seduce and rape them. Surely, he deserved to die ten thousand deaths![27]

In Gao's case, this particular aspect of his 'bandit' personality appears to have been embarrassingly close to the truth. Many years later, in response to a call for a reversal of the official verdict on Gao, an official CCP redress inquiry was launched to look into his past and 1954 purge. Unlike in the Cultural Revolution, critical voices were no longer raised concerning many of his political preferences or about the language he had used to express them, such as his likening of a stream-lined 'unified administration' to 'party, government, labour union and Youth League all pissing in the same pot' which in 1967 had been denounced as an attempt to downplay the overall leadership of the CCP.[28] But while all other charges against him were found to be in some sense open to reassessment, the evidence (depositions made at the time by the raped or abused 'female comrades') preserved in the central archives was that he had indeed engaged in sexual conduct altogether unbecoming and unworthy of a real communist. A complete and unqualified rehabilitation of his character is still judged by the CCP to be impossible.[29]

In the course of the Cultural Revolution, quite a few senior (living) military and public security officers became the subject of accusations similar to those directed at Gao. When their 'degenerate' sexual conduct was supposed to have manifested itself more recently, the accusations of the 'masses' were fleshed out with more details, though solely from the big-character posters themselves it is hard to tell whether those details were imagined or real. Here is an excerpt from an attack on General Chen Zaidao, the commander of the Wuhan Military Region in central China, signed on to by a number of organisations of factory workers in the city of Wuhan and published by students in one of Shanghai's engineering colleges in July 1967. In typical fashion, Chen's working-class attackers indulged in the use of 'fighting words' and abusive language, such as referring to the General simply as 'big pock-marked Chen':

> In the afternoon of a day in the month of x in the year nineteen-sixty-something, big pock-marked Chen had three young girls (none of them more than sixteen, seventeen years of age and working in different units within the armed forces stationed in Wuhan) come to his office. After telling his regular staff to take the rest of the day off, he 'ordered' (he habitually abuses his status as 'commander' in this way) the three girls to strip naked and then positioned himself on a sofa and started to give free reign to his bestial desires. Meanwhile, he insisted on having the other two girls assist him. These three girls alone were raped by big pock-marked Chen on no less than four successive occasions. Revolutionary worker-peasant-soldier comrades: that's how inhumanely and cruelly big pock-marked Chen – who deserves to die by ten thousand cuts inflicted by a thousand knives – abuses our class sisters!!![30]

In due course, news of this particular accusation against Chen Zaidao spread far and wide, sometimes with minor textual variations as in the case of one collection of big-character posters which included the caveat that the three girls 'had not dared to disobey the order to take all of their clothes off'.[31]

In big-character posters with titles like 'Licentious and Debauched!' and 'A Hooligan by Nature!', abusing the fine traditions of the Red Army by having one's way with nurses and maids and the occasional wife of a subordinate was the sexual trope of choice. In 'big pock-marked Chen's' case, in a printed collection put out by workers in the city of Wuhan's largest steel mill, the charge sheet included all of the above and more, though not always backed up with much in terms of hard evidence:

> In 1962, in the Sanzuomen guest house where he stayed during a conference in Beijing, he called the nurse XXX who was part of his entourage to his bedroom to give him an injection. He then proceeded to give reign to his bestial desires and raped her. She became emotionally very traumatised and cried her heart out afterwards...
>
> On one occasion he called the hospital nurse Sun XX to his room and told her to lock the door. It's not hard to imagine what they got up to.
>
> On another occasion, he lured the woman who headed the Kaifeng municipal Song and Dance Ensemble to [his room in] the Riverbank Hotel and raped her. In the summer of 1964, while attending a military exercise in Henan province, he gave watching an opera performance as his excuse for ordering the wife of the political commissar of the local artillery school to come to his premises. She came to his room and was in there for almost two hours. They never bothered to watch the performance, and eventually he sent her home. It goes without saying that they were up to all kinds of shady things.[32]

There is no record of the General either accepting or refuting these specific charges. In a self-criticism in which he addressed himself directly to Mao Zedong, on 1 December 1967, Chen did however acknowledge that 'gradually, my mind has become corrupted and my life has become one of debauchery. I behave like a gangster: I grope and fondle and attempt to take indecent liberties with every female comrade or nurse I meet.'[33]

Senior public security officers may not have had the same kind of access to 'nurses' and young women in uniform as did PLA commanders and commissars, but they were, on the other hand, able to enjoy the rare privilege of generous access to erotica. It was, after all, their professional duty to confiscate it when they or their subordinates stumbled across it and then scrutinise it in order to make an informed judgement on whether or not it was to be destroyed or locked away for safekeeping in a poison cabinet. Here is what one big-character poster writer with the Shanghai police had to say about one of the city's most senior public security officers:

> XXX is 'addicted' to obscene movies, dirty pictures, erotic literature and vulgar music. Citing professional oversight as his excuse, he regularly insists on watching confiscated thoroughly decadent American and French obscene movies. Now and then he even picks up no longer viewable scrap segments of film and sets out to scrutinise them under a light bulb. He loves to look at erotic magazines and books like *Jin Ping Mei* ... which he takes home with him. In his office, in his cabinet, he has a whole shelf full. Some of the dirty pictures are so rare, they're not even in the collection of the Forbidden City and he has a deputy section chief store them safely in one place exclusively for his own viewing pleasure.[34]

Many a hardened military or public security officer was able to shrug off accusations like these easily and some even took a certain perverse pride in the so-called 'crudeness' (*cu*) of their ways. Other targets of similarly worded big-character posters were not so thick-skinned, and to some, the smearing, the slurs and the malice and viciousness of allegations in this vein were simply too much to bear. In June 1966, when members of his staff in a highly public attack accused him of sexual misconduct, the 36-year-old head of propaganda in the Beijing Communist Youth League consumed a handful of sleeping pills and then attempted to electrocute himself. In August, his second suicide attempt succeeded.[35]

Revolutionary (and counter-revolutionary) females

The young women studying in the universities and schools at the heart of the Cultural Revolution sought to project an image of themselves in their big-character posters as tough, fearless and able to bear any hardship.[36] When the subject matter called for it, this self-image included the blanket denial of all forms of 'gendered' physical weakness. Four decades later, there is even an entry on these so-called 'Iron Girls' (*tie guniang*) in the People's Republic of China (PRC) equivalent of the Wikipedia, the *Baike Baidu*. 'Iron Girls was a Cultural Revolution term', the entry begins, 'describing girls who boasted a hard and staunch "iron" character. In the 1960s and 1970s, it was a term of praise that expressed the then prevalent de-gendering (alt. male gendering or gender-neutralisation) of the

Chinese woman, as well as the notion of sex appeal in an era opposing sex appeal.'[37]

Class discrimination on the part of state and party authorities was in this context regarded as entirely proper and called for; but *gender* discrimination – including of the positive kind – was as sure a sign as any of a creeping 'revisionism'. At Qinghua University, China's finest in the natural and engineering sciences, a poster by a woman in the Department of Mechanics in the summer of 1966 charged the university president and concurrent Minister of Higher Education of promoting 'revisionism' and 'peaceful evolution among female students' by discriminating in a most sinister fashion:

> Any female student who feels a bit queasy (Note: Some don't suffer from major illnesses at all), if she finds breakfast a bit too coarse, she will receive a special provision of milk and eggs. Regardless of her financial circumstances, she gets 1.5 yuan extra for food.... If she's on the factory floor [doing an assignment], if she has her period, she only has to work a maximum of four hours/day and no night shift. If she has to operate a lathe or welding equipment, she gets an extra two or three days off. She doesn't have to do any heavy labour at all, not even bend her back washing vegetables! Is this labour? It's bringing offerings to the Buddha! Nurturing revisionism![38]

At neighbouring Peking University, this 'if the men can take it, so can we' attitude was also common. Female students were aggressive big-character poster writers and excited participants in many other kinds of 'revolutionary activities'. On 18 June 1966, a chaotic rally at which selected teachers and staff were forcibly subjected to the 'righteous indignation' of the masses went rather further than some would have wanted and completely out of hand in the words of others. An official post-mortem spoke of how a student in the Department of Wireless Communications (a CCP member) had physically assaulted a female cadre, 'ripped her trousers, fondled her breasts and genital area. In the crowd, he also touched the private parts of two female students.'[39] While most of the people present are unlikely to have found a valid excuse for what the student did and agreed with the CCP organisation that promptly punished the student's 'hooliganism', some 'Iron Girls' did not. A second-year student in the Department of Economics even put up a big-character poster in mid July in which she claimed to be speaking on behalf of an unknown number of fellow students and announced that 'We were participants on "June 18" and it was with class hatred directed against the black gang that we shouted "Well struggled! Struggle is good! Let's have some more!"' Three of her fellow students in the same department insisted that the whole incident in fact had been a 'conscious act of revolution on the part of the masses' and 'It's like the Chairman says: those who were roughed up merely got what they deserved. To obsess about the violence to the point of censuring the revolutionary masses who, burning with bitter class hatred, beat these black gang elements, would be a very serious mistake indeed.'[40]

This one and other examples like it illustrate the extent to which women in the Cultural Revolution were by no means reduced to the passive status of mere objects. An even more aggressive attitude toward gender differences and their utility in politics was displayed by older, masculinised female Red Guards. They were not to be trifled with, as some men learned the hard way according to contemporary big-character poster revelations. During a confrontation in October 1966 between members of a Red Guard group in the Central Drama Academy (led by the daughter of a PLA marshal) and the guards of an archive to which the Red Guards insisted on being given access, two guards confronting the 'female hooligans' had their testicles squeezed so hard, according to a sympathetic contemporary account, that their 'future generations were put at risk' as they 'suffered such agony, drops the size of peas ran down their faces'. The guards were unable to prevent the women from looting the archive.[41]

Women of an older generation who, for whatever reason, ended up on the receiving end of denunciations no less virulent than those directed at General Chen Zaidao could never be certain they would be spared the humiliation of having their sexual past scrutinised and spoken ill of in public. Zhang XX was an 'old Bolshevik' (she had been a student at Sun Yat-sen University in Moscow between 1925–30) and already in her early sixties at the beginning of the Cultural Revolution and in her case, big-character posters touching upon the subject did everything possible to make her appear decadent and morally contemptible:

> Zhang XX was a hypocrite back in the 1930s, when her claim to fame among those who knew her was her immoderate and highly unconventional lifestyle. People gave her nicknames like the 'Red Modernity' and the 'Menage-a-trois and Swinger'. She murdered her baby boy, born out of wedlock, and saw to it that the bodyguard who knew about this ... was sent to the front to be slaughtered. The aim of this cunning and despicable act was to make sure that nobody ever found out about her scandalous behaviour.[42]

And as if denouncing her morals as a young girl was not enough, the author of this particular attack also made a point of depicting the mature Zhang in a no less favourable way as an 'over-sexed' older, bolder woman:

> Not only did Zhang XX cling madly to her bourgeois way of life and her licentiousness and corrupt morals in the past; as she approached the ripe age of half a century, in March 1951, she still wrote to her husband... (who was not in Beijing at the time) and asked him to purchase some hormone drugs to use as aphrodisiac. Don't scandalous things like these illustrate thoroughly enough how in her private world she is no different from what she was in the past and how filthy and shameless she is?[43]

A perfect illustration of the kind of 'punch-line' that invariably followed a smear of this kind was the following 'conclusion' with its proposed course of revolutionary action couched in the most explicitly violent language possible:

> Zhang XX is someone who loves a life of decadence and licentiousness and whose innermost soul is filthy to the core. She is a renegade with blood on her hands and a counter-revolutionary revisionist element through and through. On no condition can we allow her to continue to pretend to be an 'old revolutionary' and to continue to spread her vile bourgeois and revisionist odours. We must make sure we topple her, destroy her, discredit her, kick her until she's down, keep her down and make sure she will never be able to get up on her feet again![44]

This and the earlier quotes should not be read as evidence of sex as a central theme in big-character posters from China's Cultural Revolution. The main charge against Zhang was that of revisionism, just as the main charge against Chen Zaidao had been 'suppressing the Left'. But regardless, it seems, of whether the poster-writer or his/her subject was male or female, sex featured often and not very discreetly as something invoked *in addition to* the familiar Maoist themes of class struggle, proletarian revolution and bourgeois counter-revolution.

Conclusion

As a strategy, it was a revolution in *culture*: Mao's 'dictatorship of the masses' did away with the restraints that previously had succeeded in no small measure in keeping the most private of the private parts of people's lives out of the public arena. Had the Cultural Revolutionary experiment which the communist party chairman himself proudly described in February 1967 as 'a form, a method, to arouse the broad masses to expose our dark aspect openly, in all-round way and from below', been a fist-fight, his order to give creative play to the 'great spirit of fearing nothing' would have been tantamount to permitting strikes below the belt.[45] Not surprisingly, such strikes served their purpose well in the sense that some of the individuals struck, who saw their 'darkest aspects exposed openly', never recovered.

By the end of the 1970s, the Cultural Revolution had become history. In the words of Mao's successors, it had 'led to domestic turmoil and brought catastrophe to the party, the state and the whole people'.[46] Those who lived through it (be it as perpetrators or victims or both) have since sought to come to terms with what happened, and among them there are no small number who have commented on the whys and wherefores of the attacks on people's sexual morals and not merely their politics. Officially, the Cultural Revolution had been designed to 'touch people to their very souls'; but perhaps its *purely* political labels like 'ultra-leftist' or 'revisionist element' had been just so much meaningless verbiage, elusive and able at best to stir the intellect but not the emotions and the innermost? In a paper on fascist Italy, Robert Mallet quotes a 1937 report from an agent who warned that 'however charismatic and influential the figure of the *Duce* might be … there was no guarantee that his great doctrine would ever be understood and absorbed by Italy as a whole'.[47] In China, in the years leading up to the Cultural Revolution, the Ministry of Public Security had issued similar warnings about how even the most elementary ideas and concepts of Mao Zedong Thought were not well internalised and even less well understood. This was true, not merely of China 'as a whole', but even of state officialdom, as the following remarkable 1965 letter to the editors of *People's Public Security* from a public security office in Guizhou province illustrates:

Comrade Editor:

Recently, at a Bureau meeting to discuss relying on the masses in the exercise of dictatorship, one deputy police station chief actually said the following: 'Now, with respect to [the word] dictatorship (*zhuanzheng*): the first half of the word (*zhuan*) means to make headway (*zuan*) at any cost, while the second half (*zheng*) means that in order to be successful one must, oneself, first of all, be honest and upright ([homophone =] *zheng*)'. He even quoted the [Confucian] classics [in support], saying: 'When a prince's personal conduct is correct, his government is effective without the issuing of orders. If his personal conduct is not correct, he may issue orders, but they will not be followed'. At the time, I said that this explanation of his was utterly mistaken, but not only did he reject my criticism, he even gave me a dressing-down. To this very day, the matter has still not been resolved. In fact, nobody [here in the Bureau] takes an interest in who's right and who's wrong. Therefore, I decided to write to you and ask, hoping very much that you will be able to provide the answer.[48]

In their reply to this letter (the remarkable gist of which does not travel well in translation but which in any case revealed a total ignorance of what the word 'dictatorship' meant), the *People's Public Security* editors lamented the fact that 'some of our public security cadres, including the occasional leading cadre' did not take political study more seriously. Surely, they seemed to imply, the officer in question must have been totally alienated from the CCP discourse that assumed at least some ability to 'connect' with concepts like dictatorship (and/or 'democracy' for that matter)? 'If he is not even able to figure out what is meant by a dictatorship,' they asked, 'how can a public security cadre possibly manage to correctly carry out the policies of the Party?'[49] What this rhetorical question provokes in the historian is a follow-up question: was it perhaps because it was the only thing that actually made an impact, that nothing less than the most aggressive probing of the *private* sphere stood even the slightest chance of realising Mao's cultural revolutionary aims?

Wang Zhongfang, a one-time political secretary to the Minister of Public Security, removed from office and imprisoned for five years beginning in 1967, mulls over the subject of sex and the Cultural Revolution in his recently published memoirs:

In the 'Great Cultural Revolution', if you wanted to overthrow and *really* disgrace someone, the preferred way of going about it was to raise the subject of sexual relations. You'd take some tiny aspect of a person's private life, exaggerate it and blow it out of all proportion, even making things up altogether, all in order to tarnish his or her reputation. In the end that person might be too ashamed to face anyone, and might even attempt suicide. It was an utterly despicable and disgusting conduct. They tried it on me too ... [50]

Wang's observation was of course not a new one: it had been made by greater and lesser PRC political figures in the past, most notably a few years prior to the start of the Cultural Revolution by one of China's prominent 'rightists' Zhang Bojun. Commenting on what was happening to fellow 'rightist' Zhang Naiqi, he maintained that the CCP was only too happy to see Zhang Naiqi 'make a stinking spectacle of himself with all his womanising' because this would ruin his popular reputation far more effectively than anything the party might ever come up with about his politics. The Ministry of Public Security promptly reproduced Zhang Bojun's comment in its Top Secret *Public Security Intelligence*.[51]

Political campaigns in democracies, it has been said, can be 'long on sleaze and short on substance'. The raw, unfiltered and unfettered communication of opinion by the 'masses' in China's Cultural Revolution shared that quality. Unfettered from past constraints and mechanisms of self-censorship that had operated prior to their becoming fully 'involved in the exercise of dictatorship', they had turned the big-character poster into a powerful but blunt weapon that could hurt innocents as much as it was able to give 'class enemies' their due. The CCP Centre's programmatic August 1966 'Decision Concerning the Great Proletarian Cultural Revolution' had insisted that through the medium of the poster, the 'masses' would be able to 'raise their political consciousness in the course of the struggle, enhance their abilities and talents, distinguish right from wrong and draw a clear line between the enemy and ourselves'.[52] It proved to be a claim curiously at odds with reality. In an atmosphere shaped by the daily linguistic violence of slogans like 'revolution cannot be so very refined, so gentle, so temperate, kind, courteous, restrained and magnanimous', the Cultural Revolution instead distorted political consciousness, abused abilities and talents, and blurred whatever distinctions may previously have existed between right and wrong.

Notes

In this paper, I have anonymised those individuals whose identities and supposedly 'depraved lifestyles' and so on have not already for a long time been part of the public record.

1. Mao Zedong, 'Introducing a Cooperative', in *Selected Readings from the Works of Mao Tse-Tung* (Beijing: Foreign Languages Press, 1971), p. 404.
2. 'Gonganbu zhaokai di 14 ci quanguo gongan huiyi' (Ministry of Public Security Convenes 14th National Public Security Conference), *Renmin gongan* (*People's Public Security*) 15 (1965), pp. 4–6.
3. Jie-Hyun Lim, 'Historiographical Perspectives on "Mass Dictatorship"', paper presented at the RICH International Conference Mass Dictatorship Between Desire and Delusion, Hanyang University, 17–19 June 2005, p. 1.

4. 'Qunzhong zhuanzheng weili wuqiong: ji qunzhong zhifu yige zonghuo xianxingfan' (The Might of the Dictatorship of the Masses Knows No Bounds: The Masses Restrict and Control an Arsonist), *People's Public Security* 16 (1965), pp. 10–11; 'Yichang yanzhong de douzheng: Yikao qunzhong gaizao yige liumang daoqie fenzi de jingguo' (A Serious Struggle: Relying on the Masses Transforms a Hooligan and Thief), *People's Public Security* 21 (1965), pp. 10–11.

5. 'Henzhua tuchu zhengzhi yong Mao Zedong sixiang tongshuai yiqie' (Firmly Grasp Giving Prominence to Politics and Allowing Mao Zedong Thought to be in Overall Command of Everything), *People's Public Security* 1 (1966), p. 3.

6. *Jianguo yilai gongan gongzuo dashi yaolan* (Record of Crucial Events in Public Security Work since the Founding of the Nation) (Beijing: Masses Publishing House, 2003), p. 304.

7. Roderick MacFarquhar, *The Origins of the Cultural Revolution 3: The Coming of the Cataclysm 1961–1966* (Oxford: Oxford University Press, 1997), p. 465.

8. 'Gonganbu guanyu baowei wuchanjieji wenhua dageming yundong de tongzhi' (Ministry of Public Security Notification Concerning Safeguarding the Great Proletarian Cultural Revolution Movement), *People's Public Security* 9 (1966), p. 4.

9. Ibid.

10. 'Gonganbu an' (Ministry of Public Security Comment), *People's Public Security* 9 (1966), p. 3.

11. See David Jim-tat Poon, '*Tatzepao*: Its History and Significance as Communication Medium', in Godwin C. Chu (ed.), *Popular Media in China: Shaping New Cultural Patterns* (Honolulu: East-West Center, University of Hawaii, 1978), pp. 184–221.

12. Leon Hurwitz, *Historical Dictionary of Censorship in the United States* (Westport, CT: Greenwood Press, 1985), p. 109. See also Michael Schoenhals, 'Demonising Discourse in Mao Zedong's China: People vs. Non-People', *Totalitarian Movements and Political Religions* 8(3–4) (September 2007), pp. 465–82.

13. There are many unsettling similarities between the violent everyday practices of the Cultural Revolution and those in Nazi Germany of 'the people establishing its own homogeneity by separating all assumed heterogeneous elements' and in the process experiencing itself 'as the real political sovereign'. See Michael Wildt, '*Volksgemeinschaft* as Self-Empowerment', paper presented at the RICH International Conference Mass Dictatorship Between Desire and Delusion, Hanyang University, 17–19 June 2005, pp. 4, 7–9.

14. 'Peng Zhen tongzhi 4 yue 13 ri zai quanguo gongye jiaotong qiye kaizhan zengchan jieyue he "wufan" yundong zuotanhui shang de jianghua jiyao' (Minutes of Comrade Peng Zhen's Talk on 13 April at the National Meeting on Launching a 'Five Anti' Movement to Increase Production and Practice Economy in Industry and Transport Enterprises), in CCP Central Organization Department General Office (ed.), *Zuzhi gongzuo wenjian xuanbian 1963 nian* (Selected Organization Work Documents from 1963) (Beijing, 1980), pp. 104–6.

15. 'Xuexi bangongshi nimen we shei fuwu?' (Who Are the Study Office Serving?), big-character poster quoted in Roderick MacFarquhar and Michael

Schoenhals, *Mao's Last Revolution* (Cambridge, MA: Harvard University Press, 2006), p. 70.

16. 'Baohu de shenme huose?' (What Sort of Trash are They Protecting?), big-character poster quoted in MacFarquhar and Schoenhals, *Mao's Last Revolution*, p. 70.

17. 'Decision Concerning the Great Proletarian Cultural Revolution', in Michael Schoenhals (ed.), *China's Cultural Revolution, 1966–1969: Not a Dinner Party* (Armonk: M. E. Sharpe, 1996), p. 33.

18. On sex as a more wide-ranging subject in the Cultural Revolution, see Emily Honig, 'Socialist Sex: The Cultural Revolution Revisited', *Modern China* 29(2) (2003), pp. 143–75.

19. 'Jiefa Zhu Fengxi de fangeming yanlun' (Exposing Zhu Fengxi's Counter-Revolutionary Utterances), *Wuchanjieji wenhua dageming dazibao xuanbian* (Selected Big-Character Posters from the Great Proletarian Cultural Revolution) 9 (1968), p. 9.

20. Xu Guanglei, 'Kan, Li Tao pingshi fanmai de shenme huose' (Look at the Usual Trash Peddled by Li Tao), *Gaojiaobu wenhua dageming dazibao xuanji* (Selected Big-Character Posters from the Great Cultural Revolution in the Ministry of Higher Education) 13 (1966), p. 35.

21. *Jiefa fangeming xiuzhengzhuyi fenzi Li Qi fan dang fan shehuizhuyi fan Mao Zedong sixiang de taotian zuixing* (Expose the Counter-Revolutionary Revisionist Element Li Qi's Heinous Crimes of Opposing the Party, Opposing Socialism, and Opposing Mao Zedong Thought) (Beijing, 1967), p. 19. The English-language Wikipedia entry for the Ming-dynasty novel *Jin Ping Mei* describes it as the 'first full-length Chinese fictional work to depict sexuality in a graphically explicit manner, and as such has a notoriety in China akin to *Fanny Hill* or *Lady Chatterley's Lover* in English'. See http://en.wikipedia.org/wiki/Jin_ping_mei (accessed 1 September 2008). The Chinese work *Sex Histories* (*Xingshi*), which appeared in 1926, was the product of the sexologist Zhang Jingsheng (1888–1970), aka. 'Doctor Sex', on whom there is an informative entry in Fedwa Malti-Douglas (ed.), *Encyclopedia of Sex and Gender* (Detroit: Macmillan Reference USA, 2007).

22. *Cui Ximo dazibao zhaichao* (Excerpts from Big-Character Posters Attacking Cui Ximo), 2 vols (Tianjin: Tianjin University Cultural Revolution Office, 1966), Vol. 2, p. 20.

23. Ibid., pp. 3, 11–2.

24. Shanghai General Cultural Revolution Liaison Office of Returned Overseas Chinese (ed.), *Zalan Liao Chengzhi de 'xiao Guowuyuan'* (Smash Liao Chengzhi's 'Little State Council') (Shanghai, 1967), pp. 11, 44.

25. See the unofficial Cultural Revolution-era chronicle posted at http://www.s-tang.net/viewthread.php?tid=166555 (accessed 30 December 2007); Donald W. Klein and Anne B. Clark, *Biographic Dictionary of Chinese Communism 1921–1965*, 2 vols (Cambridge, MA: Harvard University Press, 1971), Vol. 1, p. 302.

26. See the excerpt from an unofficial biography posted at http://www.bookb2b.com/script/detail.php?id=4160 (accessed 30 December 2007).

27. *Ba fandang fenzi Gao Gang doudao douchou* (Struggle the Anti-Party Element Gao Gang until He is Overthrown and Stinks) (N.p.: East-is-Red University 8.3 Documentation Group, 1967), p. 9.

28. *Gao Gang wushi nian zuie shi* (History of Gao Gang's Fifty Years of Crimes) (Beijing: Beijing Institute of Electric Power, 1967), p. 24.
29. Interview with senior party historian with first-hand knowledge of the case, Beijing, January 2006.
30. *Liu Shaoqi He Long de sidang Chen Zaidao zuixinglu* (Record of the Crimes Committed by the Sworn Follower of Liu Shaoqi and He Long, Chen Zaidao) (Shanghai, 1967), p. 4.
31. *Qiandao wangua Chen Zaidao* (Death by Ten-Thousand Cuts Inflicted by a Thousand Knives to Chen Zaidao), 2 vols (Wuhan: Wuhan 2.4 Steel Organization, 1967), Vol. 1, p. 27.
32. Ibid.
33. Chen Zaidao, 'Chen Zaidao de jiancha jiaodai' (Chen Zaidao's Self-Critical Admission), in *Zhidian jiangshan* (We Pointed Our Finger at China) 54 (1967), p. 11.
34. Shanghai shi gonganju zhian huzheng chu dou-Lin xiaozu (ed.), *Lin Deming zuixing* (Lin Deming's Crimes) (Shanghai, 1967), p. 24.
35. *Beijing shi geming weiyuanhui di er xuexiban dangwei guanyu dui Wang XX de wenti fucha qingkuang* (Beijing Municipal Revolutionary Committee 2nd Study Class Party Committee Report on the Situation of the Reinvestigation of the Problems of Wang XX) (Beijing, 1973). Unpublished typescript, p. 1.
36. For a general overview of how the subject of women's sexuality had been discussed prior to the Cultural Revolution, see the study by Harriet Evans, *Women and Sexuality in China: Dominant Discourses of Female Sexuality and Gender Since 1949* (Cambridge: Polity Press, 1997).
37. Entry for '*tie guniang*', at http://baike.baidu.com/view/606861.htm (accessed 11 September 2008).
38. Li Baorong, 'Kan! Heibang dangwei shi ruhe zai nü tongxue zhong tuixing "heping yanbian" de!' (Look at How the Black Gang Party Committee is Promoting 'Peaceful Evolution' Among our the Girl Students!), big-character poster quoted in MacFarquhar and Schoenhals, *Mao's Last Revolution*, p. 68.
39. MacFarquhar and Schoenhals, *Mao's Last Revolution*, p. 74.
40. Ibid., p. 75.
41. Central Drama Academy Red Rebel Regiment (ed.), *Jiekai Zhongyang xiju xueyuan 'Maozedongzhuyi zhandoutuan' ouda wumie renmin jiefangjun de neimu* (Unveiling the Inside Story of How the 'Mao Zedong-ism Combat Regiment' in the Central Drama Academy Exchanged Blows With and Vilified the People's Liberation Army) (Beijing, 1967), pp. 4, 9–10.
42. *Fangeming xiuzhengzhuyi fenzi da pantu Zhang Qinqiu fan dang fan Mao zhuxi de zuixing* (Anti-Party and Anti-Chairman Mao Crimes of the Counter-Revolutionary Revisionist Element and Big Renegade Zhang Qinqiu) (Shanghai, 1967), Vol. 1, p. 35.
43. Ibid.
44. Ibid.
45. Quoted in *Important Documents on the Great Proletarian Cultural Revolution in China* (Beijing: Foreign Languages Press, 1970), p. 25.
46. Quoted in Schoenhals, *China's Cultural Revolution*, p. 299.
47. Robert Mallet, 'OVRA, the Political Police and Assessments of Public Opinion in Fascist Italy', paper presented at the RICH International Conference Mass

Dictatorship Between Desire and Delusion, Hanyang University, 17–19 June 2005, p. 16.

48. 'Shenme jiao zhuanzheng?' (What is Meant by Dictatorship?), *People's Public Security* 20 (1965), p. 16.

49. Ibid.

50. Wang Zhongfang, *Lianyu* (Purgatory) (Beijing: Masses Publishing House, 2004), p. 73.

51. 'Zhang Bojun quan Zhang Naiqi wu zuo choushi' (Zhang Bojun Urges Zhang Naiqi Not to Make a Spectacle of Himself), *Gongan qingbao* (*Public Security Intelligence*) 6 (11 January 1963), p. 6.

52. Schoenhals, *China's Cultural Revolution*, p. 36.

12
The Discourses of the Modernisation Project in South Korea and Its Gender Politics

Eun-shil Kim

The term modernisation (*hyeondaewha*) has been widely used for almost three decades both by the government and people at large in Korea. It refers to things and images such as 'new', 'Western', 'developed', 'scientific and technological', 'international' and so on. While the modernisation project was initiated by the Korean state, it has always been referred to as 'our' project in South Korea. Instead of individual terms such as 'I/me', collective ones of 'we/our' are commonly used to refer to the phenomenon of modernisation in the everyday language of Koreans. In this situation, words such as 'we/our' have normative connotations and shape people's ways of thinking and acting.[1]

In this chapter I seek to explore the way in which the Korean modernisation project becomes 'our' project through the construction of the identity, 'we, Koreans', which eliminates differences in the category, 'we/us.' In particular, I want to explore how women are incorporated into the modernisation project through the identity discourse of 'we/us.' I consider the Korean modernisation project, spanning the period 1961–87,[2] as a discursive framework for shaping contemporary Korean society by identifying who the Koreans are and how they came to be what they are today.

The main questions that I raise here relate to how the Korean modernisation project has worked as 'our' project, into which all Koreans have been merged together to form a social body. I also ask what kinds of power erase the differences and heterogeneity contained within the category, 'we/us' and how these powers achieve legitimacy in Korea. Finally, I ask how women are incorporated in the Korean modernisation project.

The modernisation project as an origin narrative of Korean history

The modernisation project was executed during the so-called 'regime of development dictatorship' from 1962 to 1980.[3] Notwithstanding a great deal of social and political resistance against President Park's regime, his modernisation project continued to convey a powerful and desirable message of strength for Korean society. The powerful and commonly used vocabulary of everyday life, and in a sense symbolising this period, included terms such as 'modern' (*'hyeondae'*) or 'modern style' (*'hyeondae sik'*). Although there are various ambiguities and contradictions in terms such as modern, it clearly manifests the need to move towards change in the future, while rejecting and extinguishing the past. Thus, the terms, 'modern', 'modern style', 'the modern way' and 'modernity', which were fused with the modernisation project, became linked with desires for, and images of, the 'new', 'developed', 'Western' and 'industrialised.' The new present has begun from this point onwards and the modern Korean came into being. In contrast, the era before the project came to be the past, as opposed to the modern.

The generation that underwent formal education during this period came to believe that the modern era was founded through the modernisation project. Thus the colonial generation of the past was imagined as a generation that had lived in feudal times of poverty and underwent great persecution at the hands of Japanese Imperialism, which they had resisted. The modern history of the colonial period, which has not been taught except in the way of so-called political history, has been denied during the past 40 years of the modernisation project. In addition, cultural representations made in Park's regime were strongly affected by state nationalism and the idea of building a new society. It relegated the modern history of the period before the modernisation project to a time of darkness, characterised by poverty and the absence of 'culture.'

Recently, new interest has emerged in the discussion of the formation of Korean modernity including the colonial-modern history of the country, along with cultural criticisms upon the outcome of the Korean modernisation project. This has led some feminist scholars in particular to reconsider the historicity and the power relations embedded in the discourse of the modernisation project.[4] Chungmoo Choi, for example, tries to unravel the aspect of capitalist hegemony present in the construction of Korean pre-modern/modern discourse by examining the process of decolonisation. Moon analyses the androcentric narrative of Korean modernisation and I have explored the power of scientific medicine in shaping the idea of the modern female body through Korean family planning policy. Cultural historians began investigating everyday experiences of colonialism and reconstructing the experience of the past, including the colonial era, which was represented as the 'dark-age' in the modernisation project. Jinsong Kim suggests a resemblance between material printed in the 1920s and 1930s in colonial Choson and today's modernisation discourse on the modern experience of everyday life.[5] Some scholars interested in the cultural products of the period prior to modernisation were surprised to find the time characterised by capitalist production, material fetishism and an inclination for Western culture. All of these aspects are illustrated in the people's lives shown in films such as *Madame Freedom* made in the 1950s.[6]

Keeping the above aspects in mind, in this chapter I ask how the modernisation project constructed the history of contemporary Korea and in what way it narrates modern Korean history. In order to explore these issues I have come to approach the modernisation project as a history-making discourse or an origin narrative of the new Korean identity. In this context, I see modernisation as a project for implementing a worldview in which an ideological system for modern Korea is created and an agenda for the future of Korean society is organised. Thus, I argue that Korean economic development has been a cultural process, which has transformed and organised the social and material reality of Korean society and its power relations in new ways. In this examination, I especially look at gender politics in the process of the Korean modernisation project.

Ways of looking at Korean modernisation as institutional change

South Korea has been introduced as the most rapidly industrialising country since its modernisation project was initiated in the 1960s. Today, the most important statement about the contemporary experience of Korean modernity starts with the remarkable economic development attributed to the modernisation project. Economic development is considered an achievement of the Park Chung-hee government, despite the many problems attributed to it and the criticisms leveled against its military administration from 1961 to 1979. President Park, who is seen as a dictator, is said to have liberated the people from poverty, which had dominated the Korean peninsula for thousands of years. In this process, Park created a 'new' Korean history, inspiring people with the idea of modernisation for economic productivity with slogans like 'let's live well' (*'Jal sal a bose'*) and 'we can do it' (*'Ha myeon doen da'*). As a consequence in less than 30 years South Korea attained international acknowledgment of having attained the status of a leading economic nation, raising itself up from the status of one of the most destitute countries in the world prior to the execution of its economic development policy in the 1960s. There has been an effort to explore the experience of modernisation and modernity as it appears in all areas of Korean society. However, the concepts of modernisation and modernity differ depending on the ways in which they have been used in different disciplines. Ways of deploying meanings and disseminating some of these terms have also differed among various scholars. In some cases modernity has been used as a marker for a particular period and has thus become an important topic in the debate on when the modernisation began. Modernity has also been used to explain the spirit of the era termed the modern. However, in Korean society a large number of these ongoing discussions explain modernisation as the process through which modern institutions have emerged.

Most discussions concerning the modernisation of Korea from the 1960s to the mid 1980s have been led by economists, political scientists and sociologists. The main debates have largely focused on how to explain 'the failure of democracy in politics' and 'successful economic growth' simultaneously during this period that has been christened 'the regime of development dictatorship.' Most analysts engaged in these discussions have agreed that modernisation means overall changes in all social domains and these changes are understood as 'development' or 'progress', which are essentially positive value laden concepts. They were asking how modernisation brought institutional and systematic changes.

The most popular ways of exploring the modernisation process are as follows: economist Daehwan Kim understands the Korean modernisation project as led by modernisation theory and has called this period 'the age of development.'[7] He appraises this period of modernisation as characterised by export-led economic growth, achieved through industrialisation strategies and made possible by the government through its exercise of coercive political power. Kim suggests that the basic conditions of modernisation comprise three levels: continuous growth and industrialisation under economic standards; the expansion of political participation and democratisation at political levels; and the introduction and diffusion of a rational value system. However, Kim's concluding appraisal is that Korean modernisation was focused on only

one goal for economic development: although it gained social consent, modernisation here can only be implied in the economic sense,
while in the spheres of social and political development, he considers
it to have failed. He attributed this failure to the discrepancy between
economic and political and ideological developments and to the mis-
takes of Korean development experts who misunderstood the processes
of Western modernisation that they imported; Kim argues that they
mistakenly thought that rational values and political democracy would
automatically follow economic development and industrialisation.[8]

Political scientist Changchip Choi described the modernisation
project as an integral effort comprising three aspects: the construction of
a modern nation, industrialisation through capitalism and democratisation.[9] Among these he considers the formation of a modern nation
and the project of industrialisation to have been accomplished in the
Korean modernisation process under the political leadership of President Park Chung-hee. Choi considers industrialisation to have been
possible because of Park's political power, which combined militarism
and developmentalism. This militarism, a product of the Cold War, was
blended with developmentalism, keeping the rivalry between North and
South Korea in focus, and leading to a dynamic process of industrialisation.[10] Choi concludes that in this period all arenas of Korean society
underwent revolutionary change in both negative and positive ways.

Park's political power effectively utilised the existence of North Korea
as an adversary in the Cold War. It used memories of the Korean War to
bind the citizenry into a single united collective. Using nationalist sentiment stemming from the destruction caused by the Korean War and the
concomitant antagonism towards North Korea, Park was able efficiently
to accomplish his aim of national integration for export-oriented economic development and thereby generate great solidarity, putting the
country virtually on a war footing. By promoting the value of 'all united'
(*'Chong wha dan gyel'*), no difference or disruption was permitted within
a collective that viewed dissent as an impediment to the achievement
of economic growth. According to Choi, Park's militarism and developmentalism, which sought to liberate people from the desperate poverty
of the past, can be understood as an outcome of the collective will,
expressed in the slogan of 'Let's Live Well.' Choi considers Park's success
as having been able to combine the dire economic need for modernisation from the top with mass sentiment based on memories of poverty
and war.[11] Thus, Choi notes that Korean people's memories of poverty
and war were strong factors that led President Park to execute his modernisation project. However, Choi does not pay attention to how these

sentiments were socially produced, maintained and mobilised to shape people's idea of Korea.

On the other hand, sociologist Hoki Kim's institutional analysis of modernisation differs somewhat from the analyses of the aforementioned economist and political scientist. Kim proposes approaching modernity through changes in the experience of individuals' life worlds. Kim stresses the dual nature of the experience of modernity as essentially the simultaneous occurrence of liberation and oppression, joy and sorrow. However, he explains the era of the Park administration as one of prominent institutional contradictions and tensions about modernity. In the process, he highlights the contentious issues of democratisation and economic development that are distinctive features of this era.[12] He also points to the controversial points of Park Chung-hee's modernisation strategy by presenting the issues of nationalism and statism and by drawing attention to a colonisation of personal life worlds. However, he fails to address the ways in which nationalism, statism and the colonisation of personal life worlds have produced contradictions and tensions among the Korean people.

Many Korean social scientists assert that the Korean modernisation project did not bring democracy as it dealt with poverty. They are of the view that no nation in the world has been able to avoid modernisation and the cost of transformation into a modern society is inevitable. Choi discusses how best to mitigate negative effects of modernisation such as the power of the *chaebol* (conglomerate), the authoritarian means of labour control, regional discrimination and the colonisation of people's private lives. These social scientists point out the negative effects or the 'dark side' of Korean modernisation. They acknowledge that some achievements were possible thanks to the sacrifices of workers and farmers. Thus, on the one hand, in the arguments of most male scholars, modernity is approached from an institutional perspective and they evaluate the extent of its success or failure. They do not consider significant the cultural processes operating in the design and execution of the modernisation project.

Contradictions of modernity and the formation of self-identity

Economic development and the failure of democratisation do not in themselves create the contradictions in people's experience of everyday life. Although most social scientists have presented critical viewpoints of the developmentalism promoted by Park Chung-hee and his suppression of democracy, there is virtually no analysis of what made this kind of modernisation project possible in Korea. Here I want to ask what kind of discursive and cultural politics in Korean society made Korean modernisation possible. There are commentaries that see developmental dictatorship as carried out in sequence, while the modernisation project absorbed contradictions through its patriarchal culture, the memories of the war and fear of the Cold War order. Nonetheless, there are few empirical studies regarding the concrete operation of the meanings of that social order.

Usually, the term of modernity or modernisation in Korean scholarship on modernisation refers to a period constituting a homogeneous time that started at a particular moment in history. Modernisation repudiates the past and pursues change for the future. However, I would like to approach the concept of the modern or modernisation as constituting temporal and spatial experiences comprising a collection of interlocking institutional, cultural and philosophical strands as they emerged and developed in different times and spaces. The 'modern' or modernisation refers not to a substantive range of socio-historical phenomena such as capitalist development, Westernisation, bureaucracy, industrial development and so on, but to particular though often contradictory experiences of temporality and historical consciousness.[13] Thus, if we look at the internal structure of modernisation discourse, it encompasses not only concrete and empirical time but also ambiguous, various and multidimensional concepts of time. In addition, there is a cultural and ideological device that mediates these diverse discontinuous times and puts them in a coherent ideological framework. Then, we must ask, what kinds of temporality and spatiality are conceptualised in the Korean modernisation project?

People who attended school in Korea during the Park Chung-hee modernisation period in the 1960s and 1970s remember repetitive images painted by elementary students of the smokestacks of factories, a divided Korean peninsula with the northern half painted in red and images of proud soldiers representing 'our' national army, for example.[14] Many people also recall being provided with images of General Lee Sunshin, portrayed as the most esteemed of Korean ancestor, whose bronze replica was placed right in the heart of Seoul on Sejong Boulevard. Many girls also learned of the model of desirable womanhood, Shin Saimdang, whose womanly virtues were disseminated as a foundation for girls' education in many girls' middle and high schools.

To foreigners 'we' frequently recounted the story about the worthy turtle boat of General Lee as a legacy of our civilisation, while proclaiming the splendour of the clear, blue autumn sky as a symbol of 'our' land. In national ethics classes, Koreans learned of their mission to ceaselessly build a strong nation, mindful of the history of being vulnerable to outside invasions.

The desire for a strong country and the remembrance of a nation that had suffered many injuries in the past were part of everyday rituals during the modernisation period in all public institutions, including schools. Children stood in salute, with their right hands placed on their hearts, and watched the fluttering national flag while singing the national anthem. These everyday practices unconsciously evoked strong emotions for the nation and virtually transmitted a sense of 'us', while the development and wellbeing of the nation, as an object of love, became 'our' task. 'We', as the nation were given a sense of mission to build a rich and powerful nation. 'We' were responsible for taking it forward and away from its past of poverty and colonial subjugation. Through this process 'we' came to learn that the most 'proud Korean' was the one who contributed to the growth of 'our' nation and society.

Modernisation became an integral part of the Korean's everyday life experience and memory through many symbolic images and messages: industrialisation was represented by the smokestacks of factories; the Cold War was symbolised by the red colour of North Korea; militarism and patriotism were represented by General Lee Sunshin and the other men of 'our' army; and femininity as motherhood was represented by the image of Shin Saimdang. Patriotism was portrayed through the territory of 'our' beautiful country and its blue autumnal skies that 'we' must seek to protect. The images of modernisation were a chaotic mixture of the various ideological systems of Western-oriented industrialisation, militarism, recurring tradition, nationalism and patriarchal gender relations. How can we come to understand these cultural images of Korean modernisation represented in such a chaotic fashion? What kind of relationship do these images have with modernisation as institutional change through economic development and democratisation?

The modernisation project, from an institutional perspective, meant Western style institutional development in the context of industrialisation, scientific and technological innovation, urbanisation and the building of a modern nation-state and so on. However, these institutional changes were not part of a value-free process because modernisation was essentially Western in its orientation. Therefore, right from the beginning there were conflicts and tensions surrounding meanings, values and norms embedded in the modernisation project. Modernisation means the extinction of the past and thus it cannot but imply loss of an essential self in losing the past. This brings with it tensions and conflicts in existing social relations, leading to debates about Korean/us versus Western/others. As the ideology of the modernisation project developed, the conflicts and tensions were organised and signified through more paradigmatic oppositions, such as West and East/Korea, modernity and tradition, and men and women.

The direction of militarist Park Chung-hee's Korean modernisation was 'national reconstruction', which had three main goals: capitalist industrialisation, defence against North Korea through military might and the establishment of a national identity.[15] Among these, the establishment of a national identity, and the label 'proud Korean' was a most important ideology for driving industrialisation and establishing a military self-defence. At the same time, this national identity provided a means of resolving conflicts and tensions produced in Korean society due to the Western-oriented modernisation process.

Like the images of modernisation represented in the elementary school students' paintings described earlier, there were contradictory and contesting images of the past and present, spiritual and material, and the roles of women and men. Modernisation modelled on Western development was a kind of threat to existing social relations.[16] But the Korean project sought to resolve this problem by associating modernisation with the material/economic Western and institutional aspects of life and separating it from the spiritual, Eastern, Korean or cultural aspects of life. In this scheme, the characteristics of material/modern/West/men and spiritual/past/East/women are divided. The Korean modernisation project, however, sought to simultaneously pursue the material wealth of the West and the spiritual and cultural values of Korea. Thus, modernisation discourse is full of a number of dilemmas, most importantly between the acceptance of wealth that comes with modernisation and a rejection of Western liberal democracy based on laissez-faire individualism.

In Korea's modernisation process, only material and institutional modernity was accepted and in this acceptance only the experiences of men, of rationality, productivity and the desire for endless growth were considered relevant. On the contrary, the spiritual/consumption/feminine side of Western modernisation, which is associated with Western spirit, pleasure and individuality, was suppressed, marginalised and portrayed as deviant. Moreover, economic development programs, targeting export as opposed to domestic consumption, exhorted Korean people to suppress capitalist consumption and the related experiences of freedom, pleasure and imagination[17] that are usually associated with the modernised/Western/feminine/'negative' aspect of modernity. Instead in the Korean modernisation project, traditional Korean feminine values were adopted and formalised into official nationalism. In this sense, the temporal and spatial orientation of modernisation is anachronistic.

There were two major elements enabling the Korean modernisation process: industrialisation and 'Korean style democracy' that translated into official state nationalism based on patriarchal social relations. Thereafter, existing social relations based on nepotistic networks, gender and region were reproduced. Using the strong coercive powers of its administration, the state constructed the subject of the Korean nation, created an ideology of homogeneity and suppressed any heterogeneity within the category 'we/us.'

The modernisation project and its gender politics

The institutional arrangements of the Korean modernisation project included its orientation towards the West/the present/the modern and thereby implied material technological achievement. At the same time, it culturally stressed preservation of the Korean/the past/tradition as its Korean spirit. These aspects of modernisation were part of the process of organising official state nationalism based on the Korean way of organising familial and gender relations, wherein men and women had distinct roles and experiences. The modernisation sought by Korea considered production and development desirable. This masculine aspect was represented as part of the public sphere. Other aspects of modernity, however, such as freedom of consumption, pleasure and imagination were denied and repressed in Korean modernity as private and feminine affairs. Women in the modernisation process were represented as opposites of the masculine and were ignored. The subjects of social agency were represented as male by state nationalism and traditional patriarchy and thus women became passive assistants to nation building. I briefly explain below how women were mobilised by the nation and how their bodies, images and roles were produced by the state.

Industrialisation, which was one of the most important factors in Korean modernisation, began by promoting a 'labour-centred' and 'export-oriented' manufacturing industry, mainly using young unmarried women's labour. Manufacturing industries that employed many women workers drew upon the major population of industrial workers in Korea.[18] Nationalism and patriarchy, which were significant cultural components of the Korean modernisation project, mobilised young women's labour and integrated them into national development. Moreover, they ignored and subordinated the interests of these women labourers for the so-called larger national interest.[19]

Therefore, women's labour and work in the modernisation project was defined in terms of the cultural norms of gender relations and the ideological meanings of social and national development. Unmarried women workers' labour was signified as making a contribution to the economy of their families and nation, and their social role included 'fostering prosperity and developing' the society. In the modernisation process, women workers stepped out from private spaces into public arenas in industrialisation. However, in these public spaces the women were not treated as rational and individual workers, but rather as 'unmarried young women/girls' working for their parents, the firm and the nation. This signifies how women's labour was incorporated into a cultural and ethical relationship with the family and the nation. So, even if at a personal level they were referred to in disparaging terms such as *kongsunyi* (factory girl), at a social level they were recognised as industrial warriors fighting for the growth and welfare of the nation and as dutiful daughters supporting their family members, especially brothers.[20]

These women, called in to meet the needs of the family and the nation, were deemed as having the protection of the family, the firm and the nation. But at the same time they were to justify their existence by continuing to work. The nation's attitude towards these women was one of encouragement for being conscious of and fulfilling 'responsibilities', to the nation, their parents and the economy, and thus it adequately compensated their sacrifice. This was understood as the unmarried women's 'role' in labour, that is, their responsibility to the nation, company and family, rather than their economic right to work. The right of labour implies the idea that having a job for an individual is not only a means of obtaining a livelihood but is also a means of gaining a position in society. Working women, therefore, could go out of patriarchal familial relations and into public spaces. However these unmarried women workers who went to factories were in the custody of the firm and the nation. In this situation, these working women did not define their identities as workers. Unmarried women, who were included in the nation's construction via their labour, could only visualise their role as labourers in transition, before they proceeded to take on the permanent identity of 'woman/mother' that came through marriage.[21] The worker's right to labour and compensation has been understood as a crucial factor for the development of the capitalist economy. In the process of Korean modernisation, however, work was always viewed within the context of building the nation-state, emphasising the consequences of labour, and excluding the individual experience of work or intention to work. Therefore, in being confronted with the historical duty of constructing the modern nation, unmarried women internalised the nationalist consciousness based on patriarchal social relations and thought they could achieve citizenship by contributing to the nation.[22] Of course in order to secure their rights as workers there were several resistance struggles initiated by unmarried factory women workers in the 1970s such as among the Dong-il textile women workers, the YH women workers and others. However all these struggles by women workers were repressed severely by various forms of violence including sexual control and sometimes very extreme measures such as putting urine mixed with excrement on striking women workers.[23] Women were strictly controlled as the female members of family, factory and nation-state.

The Family Planning Policy (FP), which extended modern contraceptive technologies widely, was introduced as a program for economic development and modernisation by the state.[24] FP for economic development was a means of limiting population growth for underdeveloped nations after World War II. In Korea, this was adopted, following the advice and recommendations of economists and international development agencies that viewed population growth as a serious threat to the security, progress and economic development of individual countries and the world.[25] The rationale underlying the implementation of FP was that without any control over population growth, economic development projects could not be executed efficiently. Accordingly, women as a social group, whose fertility rate was 6.3 in the early 1960s, were regarded as impediments in the development planning and economic growth of the nation.[26] It was therefore considered necessary to curb the high birth rate by controlling the bodies of Korean women. As the initiator of modernisation, the state provided various contraceptive methods with the aim of controlling women's reproduction. The government also mobilised major national resources to perform this task such as provision and dissemination of medical technologies, administrative support and ideological campaigns.

The FP initiative not only became a means of controlling the bodies of women and their reproductive practices, but also reorganised the everyday experience of women. The discourse of FP[27] began to affect people's consciousness through campaigns that spread the message that rapid population increase would impede the quality of individuals' lives and the modernisation of the nation. In the early 1960s, when the reproductive rate was very high, the program focused on presenting an image of family welfare, happiness and modernity that could be acquired by controlling reproductive capacities through contraception. Some of the widely disseminated and popularised slogans of the FP campaigns were as follows: 'Bear few (children) and raise them well'; 'Our family's wealth starts with Family Planning'; 'Don't bear many (children) and don't suffer much, bear few and raise them well'; 'Bearing children without thinking leads to poverty'; 'Three in a row with three years in between and finish at the age of 35'; and 'Bearing few and raising them well is good for parents and good for children.' In these slogans, having children became linked with the burden of family, thus transforming the earlier association of children with prosperity into an association with the capacity to consume and parental responsibility for child-rearing and education. These campaigns disseminated an idea of children that was very different from the idea of the traditional Korean family, where children were seen as a source of wealth and familial wellbeing. The slogans also directly connected women's contraception with familial happiness and national development.

The introduction of FP was basically an effort to establish a new family model, which most desirably integrated with modernisation. This social and political discourse viewed and projected low birth rates as most efficiently able to reduce the number of mouths so that the per capita share of economic growth would become larger. The family in the modernisation process was no longer a place to merely produce children, but an integral unit of a nation for producing proper nationals. As the state's campaigns of FP positioned the family in the role of bearing and rearing children for the social and economic processes of modernisation, the feminine role of reproducing children became part of social and economic productivity.

With the onset of the 1970s, FP became more institutionalised, with several incentive programs put into place.[28] The idea of a small-sized family became a social norm. New programs were introduced offering government assistance to families that adopted the new model. In the late 1970s, population education became part of the formal education curriculum from elementary school to high school, in government training courses and those of other social organisations. Television conveyed strong social and cultural messages; for example, couples appearing in television series and soap operas were always shown to have less than two children and a number of programs were especially produced about the population explosion and its disadvantages. In this way, mass media was used for social education on population control. The government entered people's everyday spaces in order to disseminate negative views and images about population increase and posted material on buses, the subway, taxis and trains. Advertisements were placed on cigarette packets, postage stamps, bank passbooks, housing lotto tickets and so on. In the big cities, population towers were established for passers-by to monitor the increasing population of Korea on an everyday basis.

In the 1980s, new campaigns emerged to encourage the implementation of sterilisation operations after the birth of only one child. New slogans were coined such as 'Two is too many. Bear one and raise it well'; 'Have one happy and loving child'; and 'Take the short cut to family planning – vasectomy or sterilization.' FP campaigns produced a political discourse that projected women with fewer children as more modern. They promoted goals such as 'Let's restrict women's reproductivity with a limit of two children' and 'Let's realise ideally qualified modern motherhood through the birth of fewer children.'

From the 1970s until the mid 1980s, FP was the most visible public health service associated with local health centres and sub-centres,[29] and many people in the provinces considered public health service centres to be family planning clinics. Thus, when people saw health service workers in the villages, they immediately thought they were there to proffer advice about having fewer babies. They were also considered agents of the government in search of potential cases for sterilisation surgeries. For people who lived in provincial areas in the 1970s and early 1980s, public health facilities signified projects that prohibited having children. State control treated women as a social body generally characterised by fertility. The reproductive/sexual discourses of FP transformed the natural and biological functions of women into a social force for organising quantitative national development. Gradually, women's reproductivity/sexuality, which had previously been kept hidden and secret, as per the Confucian tradition, became a social and political issue in the period of modernisation.

Since the 1960s, through FP, the government was able to construct the image of the small-sized family, associated with the discourse of modernity, wealth, happiness, efficiency and welfare. Women were motivated to have fewer children through the offer of contraceptives, as endorsed by the government. This process signified new perspectives about the body, produced by the state, that were integrated with women's own desire to control their reproductive capacity. Furthermore, the enforcement of FP was not seen as state intervention into the private lives of individuals, but as a necessary means of adapting women to a new social environment.

A new modern motherhood was created by the intervention of the state, as new reproductive practices came to be institutionalised. At the same time, the discourse of FP had another effect: it separated sex for pleasure from sex for reproduction, even though this was only applicable to married women. It also established the idea that sex was an integral part of married women's lives, while issues about unmarried women's sexual/reproductive lives were never mentioned in the FP discourse. The practice of FP emphasised reproductive control rather than reproductive rights or sexual freedom for women. As a result, it led to the essentialisation of all women as a category of reproductive beings. By making women's fertility and reproductive practices a focus of its social and political consideration, the state initiated and executed a policy for serving the social and economic interests of the nation. Thus, married women, as reproductive beings, came to be instrumentalised and judged for their propriety and normalcy according to the needs of the state.

Conclusion

In this chapter I have examined the discourse of the Korean modernisation project, an important matrix in determining present Korean identity. I have assessed how this discourse has transformed the relations of men and women into an ideological system of the state and how men and women have been integrated within the idea of Korean culture. I also examined how the modern experience of Korean society has been produced by the modernisation discourse and have asked how family planning policies operating within modernisation discourse have constructed the idea of modern women who are controlling their production. Using the slogan, 'the personal is political' since the early 1990s, Korean feminist scholars assert that the domestic/private domain is a space for women's oppression. Thus, the family, marriage and heterosexual relations, which belong to the domestic realm, are seen as sites in which male power is reproduced. They also have shown that in modern society the domestic/private sphere is neither autonomous from nor organically linked to the public sphere. Instead, the division between the public and the private is a political construction.[30] Therefore, in order to understand women's status, gender relations and agency, it is important to take the gendered nature of the public sphere into account, especially as it is represented by the state, a critical domain. It is also important to read gender politics as they are embodied in the language, law and policies of the state. The state is not a gender-neutral institution at all. Instead, it reorganises gender relations though its discourse on policies, the law and so on.

In the modernisation project of Korea, which was accomplished through coercive state power, the productivity and reproductivity of women's bodies were transformed into state productivity. While unmarried women were used by the state as factory labour, the married ones were directed to curb their fertility as per the new norms propagated by the FP program. Thus, through unmarried and married women's productive and reproductive capacities, the state incorporated women within its newly constructed concept of productivity. Here women's bodies were identified as functional for the development of the nation and for preserving the life of the state organism.

The modern or modernisation is always discussed in terms of Westernisation, Western systems and relations with the West. Thus, the question of what Korean identity is in the modernising process inevitably arises as there are tensions, contradictions and conflicts in the orientation towards the West and in the process of self-identification of Koreanness. The solution to this contradictory problem in the Korean modernisation project is the cultural reformation of state nationalism and Confucian family ideology as the foundational logic of material and institutional modernisation. Here woman as a signifier has been mobilised to comprise the core element of the cultural discourse of the modernisation project and to mediate these tensions, contradictions and conflicts.

Differences among women have been cast aside and suppressed through the dictatorship of development that directed the nation as a single collective subject, signified by the terminology of 'we/us.' The gendered meanings of women's bodies in the modernisation project are neither a natural product, reflecting the biology of women, nor a function of women's bodily practices. These are, instead, a serial effect or meaning produced in social relations on the body and behaviour through complex social and political apparatuses.[31] In this context, gender relations and the gender of women, which have been incorporated within the Korean modernisation project, have been produced by the state power that regulates the gender system.

Interestingly women's bodies, which became socially visible through the FP program within the modernisation project, were approached as a biological species even though state policy transformed women's reproduction/sexuality into economic productivity. Through this process, women were incorporated into the new gender system of the modern Korean state. However, women were not considered rational, independent, autonomous individuals, like modern men. Thus, gender relations in Korean modernisation discourse, once of the private realm, were transferred into the public domain. Women, who lived in the patriarchal family, came to be envisaged as a single collective: women of the state/nation/society. That is, women's relations with their fathers and husbands were extended to or replaced by the impersonalised power of men in the labour market and the welfare state system. This situated women's identity within a set of multiple social relations.

Through this study I address the problem of cultural power in the gender system by showing how it worked in the Korean modernisation project. In Korean society men are identified through their social relations, social achievement and the positions they occupy. Women, however, despite occupying various social positions, are forced to identify themselves with the category of female, which is homogeneous and ahistorical. This is caused by the homogenising power of cultural norms that define and control what women are and what they can do. Cultural power was neither recognised seriously nor raised as part of the agenda of feminist activism in Korea, except by the Alternative Culture Group (*Tto hana eu mun hwa*) in the 1980s. However, since the mid 1990s young feminists, in particular, started to problematise the issue of cultural power, which shapes the idea of Korean women and the notions of femininity. Thus young feminist cultural activists became visible in challenging the Korean nationalist and family based patriarchal culture.[32]

Notes

1. In my previous paper, 'Women and Discourses of Nationalism: Critical Readings of Culture, Power and Subject', which is published first in Korean *Korean Women's Studies* 10 (1994), pp. 18–52 and later in English [*Women's Experiences and Feminist Practices in South Korea*, Pilwha Chang and Eun-shil Kim (eds), Seoul: Ewha Womans University, 2005], I dealt with how nationalist discourse is dominant in shaping the everyday sentiments of Koreans and provides a lens for interpreting well-known cultural texts. A prominent example of the dissemination of the idea of 'we/our' during the modernisation period in Korea can be found in *The Charter of National Education* (*Gukmin Kyoyuk Heonjang*) promulgated by President Park in 1968 and abolished in 1994. This started with the following sentence: 'We are born in this land with a historical mission for national restoration . . .'

2. In this chapter, I define the period of modernisation as starting in 1961 with Park's military revolution and a strong state-initiated economic development plan. The period ends with the achievement of political democratisation against the military dictatorship and the conclusion of national territory-based development. In addition, a shift to a globalisation policy occurred

in 1988 when it was formally announced that Korea was joining the World Trade Organization (WTO) system.

3. Here I focus mainly on President Park's modernisation project based on economic development plans; the first economic development plan started in 1962 and President Park was assassinated in 1979.

4. Sengnai Kim, 'Min sok jeon tong eu dam ron bun sok' ('The Discourse Analysis on the Tradition of Shamanism') *Korean Cultural Anthropology* 22 (1990): pp. 211–43; Eun-shil Kim, 'The Making of the Modern Female Gender: The Politics of Gender in Reproductive Practices in Korea', PhD Dissertation, University of California, San Francisco, 1993; Chungmoo Choi, Sorcery and Modernity', paper presented at the Kwangju Biennale International Academic Symposium, 1996; Chungmoo Choi, 'Nationalism and Construction of Gender in Korea', in Elaine Kim and Chungmoo Choi (eds), 9–32 (New York and London: Routledge, 1997); Seungsook Moon, 'Economic Development and Gender Politics in South Korea 1963–1992', PhD Dissertation, Brandeis University, 1994.

5. Jinsong Kim, *Seoul e dancehall eul heo ha ra* (Permit the Opening of a Dancehall in Seoul) (Seoul: Hyeonshil munwha yeon gu, 1999). The Korean Peninsula was called Choson, after its last ruling dynasty, before emancipation from Japanese colonial rule (1910–45).

6. Soyoung Kim, 'Questions of Woman's Film: The Maid, Madame Freedom and Women', in the *Proceedings of the Conference on Post-Colonial Classics of Korean Cinema*, University of California, Irvine (1988), pp. 13–21, Irvine California, USA.

7. Daewhan Kim, 'Kae bal yeon daw wa hanguk sa hoe eu ji sik in' ('Korean Society and Intellectuals During the Developmental Period'), paper presented at the Commemoration Conference for the Seventh Year of the Establishment of the Professors' Newspaper (1999), p. 2, Seoul, Korea.

8. Ibid., pp. 3–4.

9. Changchip Choi, 'Park Chonghee jeong geon gwa hanguk hyeondae sa' ('Park Chung-hee's Regime and Korean Contemporary History'), *Dialogue Quarterly* 5 (1995), p. 143.

10. Ibid., p. 150.

11. Ibid., p. 151.

12. Hoki Kim, 'Park Chonghee si dae wa geun daesong eu myeong am' ('Park Chung-hee's Era and the Duality of Modernity'), *Chang jak gwa bi pyeong* (Spring 1988), pp. 93–111.

13. Rita Pelski, *The Gender of Modernity* (Cambridge, MA: Harvard University Press, 1995), pp. 12–13.

14. Much of the information in this and subsequent paragraphs is based on my own memories and the personal accounts of my peers and colleagues.

15. Moon, 'Economic Development and Gender Politics in South Korea 1963–1992', p. 36.

16. Usually, in the discussion of the modern the chronological order of pre-modern-modern-post-modern is not dissociated from the geopolitical configuration of the world. Historically, modernity has primarily been compared to what came historically before it. Geopolitically, it has been contrasted to the non-modern or, more specifically to the non-West. The historico-geopolitical pairing of the pre-modern and the modern has been a major

organising principle in academic discourse. However, the validity of this pairing has been challenged and the Korean modernisation project also challenges the pairing of the pre-modern and modern. Naoki Sakai, *Translation and Subjectivity* (Minneapolis, MN and London: University of Minnesota Press, 1997), pp. 153–4.

17. During the 1970s state censorship was strongly enforced to ensure propriety in popular culture, a propriety that was supposed to contribute to achieving the goals of state policy. A well-known example of this kind of censorship was the arrest of young long-haired men and/or the cutting off of their hair. Long hair was associated with the hippie culture, Western liberalism and individual resistance.

18. Seungkyung Kim, 'Productivity, Militancy, and Femininity: Gendered Images of South Korean Women Factory Workers', *Asian Journal of Women's Studies* 3 (1997), pp. 8–44.

19. Using oral history and interview methods, Won Kim tries to reveal their voices in his book *Yeogong* (women factory workers). He tries to criticise the dominant discourses on *Yeogong* that were male and national development centred. Won Kim, *Yeokong 1970: Their Counter-History* (Seoul: Imagine, 2005).

20. Hyun-mee Kim, 'Modernity and Women's Labor Rights in South Korea', *Journal of Korean Women's Studies* 16(1) (2000), pp. 37–64.

21. Seungkyung Kim, 'Productivity, Militancy, and Femininity'; Eun-shil Kim, 'The Making of the Modern Female Gender'.

22. Hyun-mee Kim, The Formation of Subjectivities among Korean Women Workers: A Historical Review,' in *Women's Experiences and Feminist Practices in South Korea*, Pilwha Chang and Eun-shil Kim (eds.) (2005), pp. 177–204.

23. Won Kim, *Yeokong 1970*, p. 346.

24. Bang Sook, 'Korea's Family Planning Policies and Program: A Quarter Century Quest – Past, Present and Future', in Department of Preventive Medicine and Institute of Population and Community Medicine (ed.), *Collected Research Papers of Professor Bang Sook and His Co-workers on the Occasion of His Retirement*, 29 February 1988, reprint (Onyang: Soonchunhyang University, 1986/1988), pp. 495–547.

25. Betsy Hartmann, *Reproductive Rights and Wrongs: The Global Politics of Population Control and Contraceptive Choice* (New York: Harper and Row Publishers, 1987).

26. Korean Institute of Health and Social Affairs, *The National Fertility and Family Health Survey Report* (Seoul: Author, 1990), p. 11.

27. I collected many of these family planning slogans as they circulated via the magazine *Gajong eu Beot* (Friends of the Family), published by the Department of the Ministry of Health in the 1970s. These slogans were also referred to in the work of Bang Sook, 'Korea's Family Planning Policies and Program', and Mee Kyung Lee, 'A Case Study on Determining Factors of Women's Contraceptive Practice in Rural Korea', MA Thesis, Ewha Woman's University, Seoul, 1988.

28. For example, after 1976, reductions in income tax and priority allocation of public housing were given to two-child households. Other financial benefits included medical benefits to households where one or both spouses had undergone sterilisation surgery. Cash payments were also made to people of

lower socio-economic status to undergo sterilisation. While abortion was and still continues to be illegal in Korea, women were allowed to have abortions if contraception had failed.

29. Bang Sook, 'Korea's Family Planning Policies and Program'.
30. Jane Collier, Michelle Rosaldo and Sylvia Yanagisako, 'Is There Family?: New Anthropological Views', pp. 25–39, in Barrie Thorne and Marilyn Yalom (eds), *Rethinking the Family: Some Feminist Questions* (New York: Longman, 1982).
31. Teresa De Lauretis, *Technologies of Gender* (Basingstoke: Macmillan, 1987).
32. Notable examples of these include young women activists working on university campuses. These women have begun to raise issues about gender and sexual harassment as it affects social activism, which is predominantly influenced by nationalist, male-centered and ageist ideas. Another aspect of the activism of such young women is its focus on womens' right to work for their livelihood. This challenges the assumption that all women get married and are taken care of by their husbands.

13

From Welfare State to Self-Welfare: Everyday Opposition among Female Textile Workers in Łódź, 1971–81

Małgorzata Mazurek

Introduction: forgotten protagonists

Recently, '*Solidarność*' hunger marches of female workers, and more generally, women's resistance in Communist Poland, have begun to attract scholars' attention.[1] An article by Padraic Kenney entitled 'The Gender of Resistance' revealed how powerful and subversive were the ways that women workers linked their ascribed roles as breadwinners, consumers and mothers during strike actions.[2] However, when looking at the public commemoration of '*Solidarność*', or remembrances published by former trade union activists, women suddenly become invisible. While celebrating the anniversaries of national struggles against the Communist party-state, one forgets, for example, that the claims of female workers during mass strikes in 1971 changed party-state social policy to a much greater extent than the famous upheaval of shipyard workers in December 1970.[3] A chronicler of Łódź '*Solidarność*' pointed even at a natural predisposition of men to strike actions and self-organisation: 'In the case of a long-term sit-down strike, men usually show more determination and are more resistant to attempts at intimidation (than women)'.[4]

This gendered narrative has led to the marginalisation of women textile strikers in the public discourse and social memory of the Communist period in Poland. Not only have women been forgotten as heroes of '*Solidarność*', but they have also been discriminated against during the post-socialist transformation of Poland. After 1989, women were shifted from the working class to the enclaves of unemployment and poverty as about 100,000 textile workers were made redundant. At that time,

Illustration 13.1 Photo No. 1, 30 July 1981: A mass 'hunger march' of Łódź female textile workers through the main streets of the city was not only a protest against the provision crisis and the party-state politics of food distribution, but a highly gendered manifestation of '*Solidarność*' strike actions. In the photo, a group of women, guarded by the '*Solidarność*' security members, carry a banner '35 years of party leadership. We are hungry ... we will be naked'. Instytut Pamięci Narodowej, IPN BU 024/80/1.

the government decided not to provide the Łódź textile industry with retraining or development programmes. Instead, such social schemes were dedicated to strategic sectors of heavy industry such as mining.[5] Therefore, the cultural and social disadvantages of female textile workers tended to accumulate over time and expand into different spheres of life. Their low stature made women textile workers more vulnerable both to the shortages of the socialist economy and to the challenges of the free-market system (Illustrations 13.1 and 13.2).

Questioning the protectiveness of the Polish Communist dictatorship

This chapter aims not only at indicating the scope of deprivation and difficult living conditions that constituted the background of female worker upheavals in Łódź. Nor am I concerned with the development of events or the dynamics of women's protest in 1971 and 1980–81 in Łódź. The narrative based on the classic scheme of poor living conditions leading to social discontent, leading to strikes has already been

Illustration 13.2   Photo No. 16, 30 July 1981: The culmination of the 'hunger march' at Freedom Square in Łódź. The demonstration gathered 20,000–50,000 people (according to state security police and '*Solidarność*' trade union, respectively). Instytut Pamięci Narodowej, IPN BU 024/80/16.

embraced by historians. Padraic Kenney and Klaus Pumberger have also noted the gender dynamics of the strikes, namely, that the symbolic representations of women textile workers as 'mothers of the nation' were included both in the language of the party-state and '*Solidarność*'.[6] Instead, or additionally, I would like to go beyond an interpretive scheme of popular protest that would potentially lead us straight from economic crisis or bad conditions of work and pay, to the outburst of social anger and discontent. Therefore, I would like to combine the sociology of work, a 'gender of survival' along with a 'gender of resistance' in order to present the *function* of the division of labour within the feminised shop floor, and the *role* of the double identity of women as breadwinners and consumers in transforming the sphere of production into a sphere of consumption. I argue that this powerful transformation, apart from the dynamics of social discontent, also contributed to the delegitimisation of 'really existing socialism' in Poland, because it put the socialist 'welfare-state' to the test.

The combination of care and coercion with which the communist system has been associated, became almost a cliché in Polish research on post-war state-socialism. In the ongoing public debates, the socialist 'welfare-state'[7] is understood through the prism of the 1980s, when the distributive functions of industrial plants had been vastly extended. However, many students of 'really existing socialism' do not realise that part of the working class in post-war Poland, especially in underfunded industries such as Łódź's cotton and wool industries, had been deprived of social protection. These industrial areas were more like the poverty-filled, capitalist Łódź at the turn of nineteenth and twentieth centuries than over-bureaucratised 'factory-offices' (*fabryki-urzędy*).[8] Therefore, the claims of Łódź female textile workers formulated in the early 1970s and 1980s should be analysed not only as a call for a better politics of consumption, but more broadly, as a demand for implementation of the socialist 'welfare-state' in their private and professional lives. Eventually, this became a public appeal to party-state officials for better collective consumption: a model of provision that had been systematically neglected in post-war Poland compared to other countries of the Soviet Bloc.

In the hunger marches in Łódź and other Polish centres of light industry, women textile workers spoke the language of 'waiting in line', a language of consumption and motherhood, for this was their ascribed sphere of knowledge and expertise. In this context, hunger marches differed greatly from modern food riots by housewives against speculation: women consumers setting prices in eighteenth-century England[9] or World War I Berlin[10] took place directly in the public sphere of the street, whereas public protests in late socialist Łódź reflected the social organisation and hierarchy of the socialist enterprise. A shop floor dominated by women demonstrates very clearly how the roles of consumer and producer were closely intertwined and how women themselves were well aware of these linkages. Moreover, as a social space per se an industrial plant made the individual consumer's concerns public and collective action possible. I argue, then, that one of the most specific features of women's experience under 'really existing socialism' was the effort of constant translation of work experience into a language of distribution and consumption, and the other way around. A powerful fusion of producer and consumer identity caused women textile workers to perceive the industrial plant as a place determining their status in a 'queuing society'.[11] They saw it as an extension of their household, rather than as a potential space of individual 'self-fulfilment' or 'women's rights'.

Women's Day, or the strike for half of a chocolate bar

In 1971, Women's Day in Łódź – three weeks after mass strikes in which 55,000 female textile workers protested against price hikes[12] – was celebrated according to a long-standing scenario.[13] Workers' councils and women's committees distributed a little something for female employees: chocolate, flower-scented eau de cologne, small towels and handkerchiefs. Nobody from the male staff, including the foremen who supervised the women's work, came to the shop floor to offer wishes and greetings. Undoubtedly, this would have been a significant gesture toward the women as the mass strikes one month earlier, in February 1971, had disclosed bad relations between male management and female workers. On 8 March 1971, in the Cotton Industry Works 'Champions of Peace', a solemn concert was organised. However, of nearly 7000 women employees, only 150 were invited to the event. Similar ceremonies took place in other textile plants, though official celebrations were organised just for the first shift. Second and night shifts never received any thanks from the factory management. Observers from the Central Committee of the Polish United Workers' Party (PZPR), sent to Łódź in March 1971 in order to monitor the post-strike situation in the city, heavily criticised the inertia of local and factory party organisations.[14]

The fact that Women's Day was considered by female workers as a sign of respect and attention – and not only an empty socialist ritual – was shown through a strike action in the Cotton Industry Works 'Watra' in the Silesian town of Lubawka that also took place on 8 March 1971. Textile workers from 'Watra' brought their machines to a standstill in the early morning, because they were 'discontented with the inappropriate form of the Women's Day celebration in the factory'.[15] Why were 'Watra' female workers so insulted? Firstly, a majority of women had not received Women's Day greetings. Secondly, women workers felt offended by the gifts presented to them by the party committee and the council of trade unions: strangely enough, rank and file textile workers were given only half of a chocolate bar, whereas each official woman activist in the Women's League (*Liga Kobiet*, a regime organisation representing women) got the whole chocolate bar.[16] In response, women in the 'Watra' factory organised a one-day strike, demanding equal treatment and basic respect for all women. This short protest demonstrates that the first Communist Party Secretary Edward Gierek's promises of social, political and economic improvement were immediately confronted by the everyday habits of the local party-state apparatus. In Lubawka, like in Łódź, attempts to meet women's demands with far-reaching promises and economic decisions were not seriously able to improve relations between female shop floor workers and male management, or to weaken deeply rooted hierarchies within the industrial social system.

The strike of the 'Watra' textile workers against their symbolic humiliation proved how great was the social distance between social organisations and the social world of the women employed in production. Women's Day protests against humiliation, caused by an odd distribution of small gifts, suggested that spectacular mass strikes did not automatically make a difference for workers in need; the institution of the industrial plant constituted a social space in which habits and embedded relations of power overwhelmed people's agency. More precisely, the acceptance of women textile workers' claims meant an important political change as well as a shift in the politics of consumption. Indeed, mass strikes in Łódź contributed to the development of a pro-consumer policy in Communist Poland. However, these political decisions were not able to transform hierarchies within the industrial social system.

'Light' industry

In the economic system of Communist Poland, the place of the textile industry, which was part of so-called light industry, was clearly defined. Light industry had the task of supporting investments in the key sectors of heavy industrial production. As a result, on the one hand, light industry received meagre financial means both for modernisation of machinery and for social services for the employees.[17] On the other hand, it made the most of its output capacity by sustaining three shifts of work and the exploitation of a cheap labour force. In that regard, postwar practices continued nineteenth-century forms of exploitation. They made the traditional seperation into a badly paid textile industry and a privileged better-paying heavy industry even wide than before. This distinction, historically embedded and supported by Communist ideology, was closely linked to the gender segregation of labour, which embraced a division of work within socialist enterprises as well. During all decades of Communist Poland, women were employed almost exclusively as machinery operators, even if their qualifications made them eligible for supervisory posts, whereas men less qualified than female textile workers frequently landed in managerial positions. This kind of professional career was de facto inaccessible for women.[18] Even at the end of the 1970s, when a significant percentage of women had obtained secondary school professional qualifications, textile plants' management did not take this into consideration and sent women directly to the hard physical work at looms.

Strikes in 1971 unmasked the scale of the disadvantage of light industry as well as the exploitation of its labour force. The latter was marked by a high intensity of physical work that compensated for the low productivity of old machinery.[19] In Łódź textile plants, the rate of piece-work[20] and shift work was the highest in the country. Despite women workers' protests, state employers maintained the night shift, which had been lifted at the end of nineteenth century[21] but then restored under communism. The first concessions were made only under pressure of '*Solidarność*', when some enterprises in Łódź, by way of experiment, ended night shift work.[22]

Meal breaks were also liquidated in the post-war Łódź textile industry. As a result, work at the machines lasted eight hours without a stop. Therefore, it is not surprising that the introduction of meal breaks was one of the main demands of female textile workers in February 1971. Characteristically, socialist enterprises seemed not very eager to fulfil this demand and did it quite tardily.[23] A lack of a statutory break until the year 1971 was all the more shocking because nearly half of the female workforce started the first shift with an empty stomach.[24] Another widespread aspect of exploitation in light industry was low wages.[25] Workers experienced a sharply growing disparity between the global rise of their productivity and their incomes. Workers remained constantly underpaid. The complicated and obscure system of calculating workers' wages helped to hide the scale of embezzlement.[26] Additionally, a majority of female textile workers were not able to work overtime in order to earn money on the side, a regular practice in other sectors of industry.[27]

Indeed, earnings in the textile industry reached only 80 per cent of the average pay in the national economy. Many women workers in Łódź thus lived on the verge of subsistence level as 40–50 per cent of them received subsistence allowances for low-income persons. If one adds the fluctuating level of pay in the textile industry caused by frequent downtimes and shortages of materials,[28] it is easy to imagine that every fall of monthly income meant serious financial trouble for women's household budgets. Lack of equivalence between workers' productivity and their purchasing power as well as the embezzlement of social funds in many textile plants made Łódź weavers feel robbed, if not simply exploited: 'We fulfil the plan every year, but our annual bonus decreases. Where is our money that was stolen from us? Workers are beaten on the ass!' – one of the women strikers exclaimed in 1971.[29] Another said, 'We don't need comrade Gierek, let them give us back what belongs to us!'[30]

Weavers had serious doubts about political promises concerning the improvement of their branch of industry, so low in the industry 'queue', and about the notion that textile workers would be treated equally to male workers from heavy industry.[31] Unfortunately, they were right to feel so. As long as the burdensome, three-shift work of textile workers was being defined in the political distribution list as 'light', employees in heavy industry would always win out in informal bargaining over pay. Also in the 1970s, the predominance of heavy industry pushed light industry back to a remote place in the industry 'queue'. It happened partly against the will of the highest party officials, who were not able to provide textile plants with money and resources, although the programme to modernise Łódź light industry was ready for implementation.[32] For the average cotton or wool workers, the overall balance of the Gierek decade (1971–80) was as negative as the times of his predecessor, the First Party Secretary Władysław Gomułka (1956–70) when considering these years in view of the relative disadvantage of light industry vis-à-vis other sectors of production. The only industries in a worse position in terms of investments and the level of social service were the printing and fodder industries. According to the Institute of Labour and Social Affairs, the secondary position of textile work prevailed until the end of the 1980s.[33] The work of the weaver and the spinner remained badly paid and hard to perform. Even in the last decade of Communist Poland, in spite of the protests and demands of '*Solidarność*', the textile industry was still defined and perceived as 'light'.

Collective consumption in Łódź

In the winter of 1971 (under the new government and the freshly reorganised Central Committee of the PZPR), textile workers sent nearly 13,000 petitions to the Ministry of Light Industry.[34] Demands submitted by women weavers embraced a wide range of issues, reaching from food supply in the local shops to detailed claims concerning the system of rewards in the workplace. The characteristic feature of the demands was a close interdependence between the sphere of production and consumption. This connection was reflected clearly in the demands for the development of collective consumption: canteens, buffets and food supply kiosks. The strike demands pointed to the low level of state-sponsored consumption within industrial plants. This was definitely the consequence of the regression of post-war food supply schemes that took place between 1957 and 1970.[35] Despite socialist rhetoric, textile plants in Łódź provided collective consumption – in the form of cafeterias and buffets – only to a very limited extent.

Social, collective consumption – designed as one of the foundations of the socialist order – was to guarantee more free time for the 'working woman' (*kobieta pracująca*), to increase productivity, and to create ties between members of the shop floor and the state employer. Optimally, it meant that workers' lives would concentrate on public institutions at the expense of the private sphere. Or, at least, the aim was to alleviate women from the burden of domestic tasks such as cooking. However, the case of Łódź demonstrates very explicitly that the post-Stalinist state employer had retreated from the role of social protector by reducing the social infrastructure and had focused entirely on the control over production and productivity. The outcomes of this process were twofold. On the one hand, the lack of industrial social consumption helped to preserve traditional ways of cooking and eating at home. On the other, this absence put the whole burden of family nutrition on women's shoulders, prolonging the time dedicated to shopping and supplying family members with food. Moreover, it made women particularly vulnerable to food shortages as nearly 92.7 per cent of individual food expenses were spent on eating at home. Nutrition depended invariably on the individual efforts of shopping and queuing.[36]

If there was something like a model of enterprise consumption, then it was a very reduced one, run on a scale proportionate to the place of the textile industry in the industry 'waiting line' for social services. Nevertheless, the number of eating facilities in the factories stagnated at a very low level in the whole country. Even after the accelerated development of the factory canteens in the first half of the 1970s, in 1975 only 7 per cent of those employed in state-owned enterprises ate lunch at the workplace.[37] In other socialist countries this percentage was much higher: in the German Democratic Republic (GDR) 40 per cent of employees consumed meals in the enterprises, in Czechoslovakia and Hungary 30 per cent and in the Soviet Union nearly 70 per cent.[38] The Polish post-war model of consumption remained then a domain of individual households. It was based on the time and financial resources of individual families, which led to a strict separation of production from the fulfilment of consumer needs. In Łódź industry only 3 per cent of employees took advantage of the factory canteens while many shop floor staffs, even those numbering more than 2000 persons, were completely deprived of access to such facilities.[39]

Looking at the social cross-section of workers frequenting enterprise canteens shows that women textile workers were practically excluded from this form of welfare, or at best they made use of it only rarely. In the textile plants' cafeterias one usually met only men, singles as well as white-collar workers and management personnel. One of the principal factors determining this situation was the price of meals. Although the enterprises covered the cost of maintenance of the canteens – charging employees only for the cost of food – eating at the workplace was still more expensive than eating at home. Surveys conducted among female textile workers did not confirm that there was any correlation between the price of meals and frequenting the canteen. However, a closer look at the home budgets of women textile workers suggests that the female members of the shop floor felt ashamed to say that they did not have enough money to pay for lunch in their enterprise.[40]

What was the weavers' opinion about the factory canteens? The sociological research from the 1970s does not really offer a precise answer, because its results diverge depending on the methodology of the questionnaire. However, one can risk a statement that women preferred eating meals with their families, though not necessarily at home. For that reason, they rejected the strictly worker's type of collective provisioning and hoped for the enlargement of access to canteen services for their relatives.[41] Unfortunately, the state employer did not take this request into account. Since the factory cafeterias 'only for employees' were not popular among female textile workers, the management stated bluntly that the collective form of provisioning did not meet the expectations of workers, so there was no need to extend them.

In fact, this simple diagnosis did not reflect the complex interplay of cultural and economic factors relating to social consumption in Łódź. Firstly, a deficit of public dining services in town, in other state enterprises, but most of all at schools[42] forced women to cook at home in any case; the female workers were not able to pay for their individual meals at the workplace and, additionally, cover the expenses of preparing domestic meals in their own households. Secondly, Polish families in general preferred domestic meals, which were said to be cheaper, tastier and served more quickly than public meals.[43] But according to surveys, if the latter changed for the better, nearly 63 per cent of Łódź families would take advantage of them.[44] And thirdly, the slow development of factory food services in the 1970s intensified an impression that lunches at work did not 'catch on' and, in the end, women had no choice but to cook traditionally at home.

At the end of the Gierek decade, female weavers no longer expected that the state employer would relieve them of cooking at home. Trying to negotiate a minimum model of collective consumption, they did expect, however, that the socialist enterprise would save them the trouble of queuing and waiting. A possible modus vivendi included small buffets and kiosks that did not require much space, expenditure or technical infrastructure. Those facilities could play a double role. On the one hand, they enabled workers to buy a breakfast or a small snack at work. On the other hand, they created an additional distribution system, which privileged the working class over those not employed in national industry. Meal breaks, introduced in February '71 in Łódź under pressure of the mass strikes, inclined party officials to develop this form of food supply. On the whole, such a model of social consumption cost less than a network of big canteens. Moreover, this gave the state employer a feeling that he had done his duty well. In the 1970s, factory kiosks and buffets became common and popular, especially when one could buy scare goods such as meat there. Because they alleviated the burden of everyday shopping, it was mostly women who took advantage of them[45] – as opposed to the case of factory canteens frequented mostly by single white-collar male employees.[46]

The factory as a sphere of consumption and the 'extension' of the household

In the 1970s, the factory kiosks and buffets, an industrial network for the distribution of scarce goods, became a central space where the needs of worker-consumers could be expressed. This sphere of consumption also offered a space for informal communication about provision problems. While these industrial institutions integrated women consumers, the everyday shopping outside the factories antagonised them. In the everyday life of the shortage-stricken economy, women consumers competed against one another for scarce goods. Conflicts with the shop clerks, who were women as well, were commonplace. Thus the shop counter as well as queuing divided women rather than allowing them to sympathise with one another. For example, the most characteristic distributive conflicts in which women were involved were those between privileged waiting lines, consisting of elderly and handicapped people, pregnant women and women with babies, and the unprivileged queues. Distributive conflicts in front of the shops tended to divide women into privileged and unprivileged ones. Socialist enterprise, on the contrary, was a social and integrative space per se, especially when workers shared the same occupation, the same position in the enterprise hierarchy and the same living conditions.

This community based on trust was inhabited predominantly by workers with a primary education: the female weavers.[47] Female weavers took up jobs in the factory and accepted poor working conditions at the expense of their free time and health to better the lives of their families.[48] Women workers in Lódź, making up 80–90 per cent of the shop floor in each big textile mill, perceived themselves primarily not as producers participating creatively in the work process, but rather as family suppliers. They treated their low-wage and low-skill occupation as a secondary activity vis-à-vis family obligations. According to the sociological surveys conducted in the Łódź industrial plants, women workers discussed their family troubles at the workplace much more intensively than male workers.[49] They also declared themselves to be passive observers of industrial life rather than active participants in the work process.[50]

The feminised shop floor did not struggle against the highly gendered division of work in the textile mills. Women workers did not directly address the fact that they earned 20 per cent less then male workers or were systematically ignored for promotion. They did not complain about their status as a cheap input of production that was to be mobilised when tight production planning required it. However, they expressed their opinions when the issues of production translated into consumer privileges and entitlements. Since they saw the industrial plant as the extension of work for the household, female textile workers actively took advantage of the sphere of production in order to fulfil their ascribed role as providers for their households. In such cases, they did not hesitate to oppose local party officials, state employers and party-state organisations.

Women's interests crystallised through informal contacts, far from official institutions. Answering the question 'which organisations should solve the workers' most important problems', only 1 per cent of female textile workers chose the PZPR and the party-state trade unions.[51] They believed that political organisations did not adequately represent workers' interests. Thus, women weavers showed no confidence toward formal socio-political institutions, though the latter still remained the main recipients of the workers' petitions and claims. Apart from a short period of social and political activism just after the 1971 strikes, the situation of distrust and social distance persisted well into the next decade. One can envision it better when recalling the celebration of Women's Day in March 1971.

In the 1970s, the newly arranged meal corners and kiosks were a main space of communication among women, where they talked about the everyday experiences of shortages. On the walls of the meal corners, one could find 'inscriptions with hostile content' referring to waiting in lines and food deficits. Undoubtedly, the introduction of the meal breaks in 1971 gave women an opportunity and time to share information about work, food provisions, price policy or the quality of goods.

The secret service and the police closely observed small gatherings and conversations that took place around the meal corners and the factory kiosks, from which they collected opinions and hearsay evidence on the atmosphere on the shop floor. The kiosks served also as a meeting point, where the workers gathered to demand a better distribution of goods.

Female textile workers managed to transform the industrial network of food distribution into an effective tool of power. The party informer from Łódź noted in 1977: 'In the Thread Works "Ariadna" women workers prolonged their meal breaks in order to purchase food products in the factory kiosk. Reprimanded by the male foremen, they answered: "give us and our families better supply, then we will keep working." '[52] Female weavers also sent anonymous letters to the enterprise party committees: 'to work one needs to be satiated, how can we work in such a system (that does not guarantee this)?' or 'Shall we work and be hungry?'[53] Perceiving the workplace as an extension of work for the household created a specific language and code of behaviour that enabled women workers to translate their consumption concerns into attitudes towards work. The gatherings and queues in front of the factory food kiosks reflected both economic instability as well as the emergence of self-organised groups of workers who exerted pressure on local party-state officials. The queues on the factory grounds were something more than a spatial manifestation of shortages. They also demonstrated how the workers made their individual productivity dependent on the sphere of social consumption.

For the enterprise management the factory kiosks and buffets were a double-edged sword. On the one hand, additional supplies of food for the industry allowed local authorities to influence the mood of workers, especially women workers. In 1976 in the Łódź textile plants, informal rationing of sugar had been introduced before the national programme of rationing was officially announced.[54] Therefore, ration cards 'only for employees' circulated independently from the national food schemes.[55] For example, neutralising workers' unrest by local deliveries of meat became a typical practice of the late 1970s, including during the big strikes of industrial workers in 1980. On the other hand, if the provision of factory kiosks was worsening, this had an immediate impact on the productivity of workers and their attitudes toward work. And because the industrial plants were already involved in the sphere of consumption, female textile workers expressed their opinions about food shortages, waiting in lines or market speculation at work. Socialist enterprises constituted a main location where consumer discourse 'from below' was shaped and reported further up to the top party officials.

'Solidarność' in Łódź and distribution conflicts

Amidst the deep economic crisis of 1980–81, enterprises tended to transform themselves into vast networks of food distribution including their own rationing schemes, suppliers in the countryside and even separate food processing facilities.[56] Therefore, from the very start, 'Solidarność' had to confront these distributive privileges and the pressure exerted by the worker-consumers. Indeed, the situation of the independent trade unions vis-à-vis distribution was quite troublesome. They were expected to continue the distributive function of the old trade unions but the logic of the shortage economy led to the escalation of distributive conflicts, putting the spirit of national community and solidarity into danger. Moreover, the introduction of a rationing system in the whole country did not fully compensate for these centrifugal tendencies. A massive mobilisation of 'Solidarność' members did not neutralise the growth of distributive particularisms. The local activists of 'Solidarność' had then to conciliate the conflicting claims of the egalitarian politics of consumption, on the one hand, and local distributive particularism, on the other. To strike a balance between the earlier privileges determined by industrial hierarchies and the new rhetoric of distributive justice was, indeed, a mission impossible.

For female textile workers, the enterprise committees of 'Solidarność' were the natural audience for questions both of production and consumption. However, the responses of the regional activists were cautious and sceptical: 'our members will "fix" up workers with scarce goods, the society will get divided and it will not even notice when we lose a chance of carrying out profound economic reforms and getting the national economy out of the crisis. We will not notice, when the government passes laws on self-government, the subsistence level, family allowances or the price hikes. And even if we notice, we will be too antagonised to stand up for our rights together.'[57]

The words of the warning made no particular impression on the Łódź female shop floor. On the contrary, the striking workers accused the 'Solidarność' leaders of a lack of efficiency in procuring goods in short supply and turned away from the goals of the hunger marches. This violent exchange of views made clear that the modest representation of women in 'Solidarność''s higher ranks, and their total absence in the closed circle of trade union leaders, resulted in a lack of knowledge of what women 'down there' were experiencing during the food crisis. The determination on the part of female textile workers forced male activists to confront the radical language of weavers' protests and the mundane reality of chronic shortages. Not surprisingly, a call for the liquidation of buffets in the Łódź factories in a radio announcement of the regional '*Solidarność*' fell on stony ground. All in all, the local '*Solidarność*' units – having opposed the appeals of the higher ranks of the trade unions together with the enterprise administration – continued to distribute scarce goods among the workers,[58] again linking the role of producer with consumer.

Conclusion: the sphere of production and consumption intermingled

The industrial plant was a space of intersection for two contradictory social phenomena: the integration of workers' interests on the issues of production and consumption, on the one hand, and the creation of social privileges antagonising various professional groups, on the other. A metaphor of 'waiting in line' seems to depict the two-way processes rather well. The enterprises and their shop floors can be defined as social actors participating in the contest for funds, investments and social services. They might be described as collective petitioners who were trying to obtain a hearing from the top party-state decision makers. This struggle for the means of production and social infrastructure, though informal and deregulated, had its proper, hierarchical structure – a stable hierarchy of access to the key political and economic resources. This 'branch' or industrial 'queue' demonstrates that for the various parts of the working class the access to the socialist 'welfare-state' was uneven.

Just like other goods in the economy of shortage, state social welfare was subjected to rationing and selective distribution, creating, in turn, islands of relative social preference as well as deprivation. To enjoy party-state protection, the socialist enterprises, branches and industrial concerns mobilised all accessible resources: political patronage, arguments of social justice voiced by striking workers and the discourse of welfare the Communist Party promised to put into practice. But still, social protection remained a deficit good. A big part of it had been rationed in the form of paternalistic control and surveillance; another, smaller part had been attained in response to workers' unrest. Until now the problem was that historians confused party-state care and coercion within factories with a guarantee of social welfare. Historians have too seldom considered how unevenly the socio-economic resources were distributed, mostly under pressure of strikes and protests.

Undoubtedly, during the decade 1971–81, and even up to the end of Communist Poland, in socialist enterprises there were increasing intersections between the spheres of production and consumption. Due to the economic crisis and workers' demands, which culminated in the birth of 'Solidarność', industrial plants had to take over responsibility for control of the production process as well as for the welfare of the workers. This happened because enterprises constituted a natural social, and therefore integrating, space. Moreover, they had facilities that could be easily transformed into a separate system of distribution. In the years 1980–83, amidst the deepest economic crisis, the number of factory buffets increased from 4552 to 6394. However, they functioned as small shops for individual worker-consumers rather than as a chain of collective cafeterias, as was the case in other socialist countries. At that time, the transformation of the enterprises into centres of food provision was welcomed by three-quarters of Polish workers. Only a minority of them preferred to be rewarded for their work with money.[59]

Further, the socialist enterprise was a platform of self-organisation, which translated the feelings of deprivation and social injustice into an egalitarian discourse. The social movement of 'Solidarność' opposed the atomising logic of competition between people and economic units. However, when accepting the role of food supplier, the industrial plants witnessed the outburst of distributive conflicts, occurring usually in the public sphere of consumption. For 'Solidarność', this inflation and diffusion of distributive conflicts was a big challenge, especially when the new trade unions took over the provisioning tasks of party-state social organisations. Precisely for that reason, the 'Solidarność' higher level activists stood against any food supply actions organised by rank and file trade unionists. But for the latter, consisting mostly of female textile workers, the workplace still offered an extremely valuable opportunity to 'jump the line'; to give their entitlements away and condemn themselves to a nightmare of food crisis chaos did not really make sense.

Indeed, with its egalitarian rhetoric 'Solidarność' gained legitimacy among female textile workers, whose work had been arbitrarily regarded as 'light' and badly paid. The central coordinating bodies of 'Solidarność' stated soon after the August 1980 strikes that 'the situation in light industry is particularly unjust and needs to be changed without delay'.[60] This diagnosis of the trade union leaders demonstrated, in fact, how limited were the effects of the high-sounding politics of consumption in the 1970s. 'Light' industry remained underprivileged and the living conditions of women textile workers again became a paradigmatic example of deprivation in both the spheres of production and consumption. In reality, the interventionism of the Łódź socialist 'welfare-state' boiled down to the development of factory kiosks and buffets and the organisation of seasonal trips to the countryside for cheap fruit and vegetables. Thus this kind of paternalism was unlike modern social consumption, as it did not interfere with the traditional status of woman in the family and preserved the extent of her home obligations.

Similarly, the significance of the hunger marches in Łódź also strengthened the traditional image of women, categorising them as mothers and breadwinners dedicated to family and domestic tasks. The regional leaders of '*Solidarność*', in order to neutralise radical moods among workers and shake up the party-state authorities, encouraged women textile workers with the announcement, 'if you are hungry, come with your child to the hunger march'.[61] I argue that the words of male trade unionists reduced women's identity to their traditional, reproductive roles.[62] But at the same time, Łódź female textile workers defined themselves both through the domestic and professional spheres. When analysing the women's boycott of reduced ration cards in the summer of 1981, one sees clearly that female proletarians referred to their work effort and their professional problems. It does not mean that they rejected traditional roles. Rather, they identified themselves with all dimensions of their lives – including those concerning the workplace. For example, they compared themselves with male occupational groups such as miners and steelworkers, and not only with other mothers, with whom they shared the burden of shopping and supplying the family with food.[63] The category of gender served to politicise the issues of everyday consumption. Moreover, this gendered discourse enabled women also to voice their deprivation in the sphere of production. In this way, the circle of interconnecting spheres of production and consumption closed.

Notes

1. Małgorzata Fidelis, *Women, Communism and Industrialisation in Postwar Poland* (New York: Cambridge University Press, 2010); Krzysztof Lesiakowski and Grzegorz Nawrot, 'Marsz głodowych kobiet' (Women's hunger march), *Biuletyn Instytutu Pamięci Narodowej* (Bulletin of the Institute of National Remembrance) 12 (2002), pp. 28–30; Stefania Dzięcielska-Machnikowska and Grzegorz Matuszak, *Czternaście łódzkich miesięcy: studia socjologiczne, sierpień 1980-wrzesień 1981* (Fourteen months in Łódź: sociological studies, August 1980–September 1981) (Łódź: Wydawnictwo Łódzkie, 1984); Klaus Pumberger, *Solidarität im Streik: politische Krise, sozialer Protest und Machtfrage in Polen 1980/1981* (Frankfurt am Main: Campus, 1989); Zbigniew M. Kowalewski, *Rendez-nous nos usines!: Solidarnosc dans le combat pour l'autogestion ouvrière*, translated by Jacqueline Allio (Montreuil: PEC, 1985); Adam Leszczyński, *Anatomia protestu: strajki robotnicze w Olsztynie, Sosnowcu i*

Żyrardowie, sierpień-listopad 1981 (The anatomy of protest: worker strikes in Olsztyn, Sosnowiec and Żyrardów, August–November 1981) (Warszawa: Wydawnictwo Trio, 2006).

2. Padraic Kenney, 'The Gender of Resistance in Communist Poland', *American Historical Review* 104 (1999), pp. 399–425.

3. Krzysztof Lesiakowski, 'Strajki robotnicze w Łodzi w latach 1957–1980' (Workers' strikes in Łódź in the years 1957–1980), in Krzysztof Lesiakowski (ed.), *Opozycja i opór społeczny w Łodzi, 1956–1981* (Opposition and social resistance in Łódź, 1956–1981) (Warszawa: Warszawa Instytut Pamięci Narodowej, 2003), pp. 30–41.

4. Włodzimierz Domagalski, *Kartki Trautmana, Strajk w MPK i powstanie łódzkiej Solidarności, Miejskie Przedsiębiorstwo Komunikacyjne w Łodzi* (Trautman's cards. Strike and the birth of Łódź 'Solidarność' in the City Transport Enterprise) (Łódź: Archiwum Opozycji Niepodległościowej, 2005).

5. In comparison to Upper Silesia, where male mining workers constituted a majority, Łódź received 20 times less financial support for the restructuring of local industry and for job training schemes for the unemployed. Wielisława Warzywoda-Kruszyńska, 'Koncentracja i gettyzacja ludności biednej w Łodzi – porównania międzydzielnicowe' (Exclusion and concentration of the poor population in Łódź: comparative studies), in Wielisława Warzywoda-Kruszyńska and Jolanta Grotowska-Leder (eds), *Ryzyka transformacji systemowej (na przykładzie Łodzi)* [The risks of systems transformation (the case of Łódź)] (Łódź: Absolwent, 2000), pp. 201–28; here p. 203.

6. Padraic Kenney, 'The Gender of Resistance', Pumberger, *Solidarität im Streik*.

7. The term was coined by a Polish sociologist Winicjusz Narojek. See Winicjusz Narojek, *Socjalistyczne 'welfare-state': stadium z psychologii społecznej Polski Ludowej* (A socialist 'welfare-state': study in the social psychology of People's Poland) (Warszawa: Państwowe Wydawnictwo Naukowe, 1991).

8. Tomasz Żukowski, 'Fabryki-urzędy. Rozważania o ładzie społeczno-gospodarczym w polskich zakładach przemysłowych w latach realnego socjalizmu' (Factory-offices. Reflections on the socio-economic order in the Polish industrial plants in the years of 'really existing socialism'), in Witold Morawski (ed.), *Zmierzch socjalizmu państwowego. Szkice z socjologii ekonomicznej* (The waning of state socialism. Sketches in economic sociology) (Warszawa: Wydawnictwo Naukowe PWN, 1994), pp. 160–174.

9. Edward Palmer Thompson, *The Making of the English Working Class* (London: Penguin Books, 1980); Edward Palmer Thompson, *Customs in Common* (London: Penguin Books, 1993).

10. Belinda Davis, *Home Fires Burning: Food, Politics, and Everyday Life in World War I Berlin* (Chapel Hill, NC: University of Carolina Press, 2000); Belinda Davis, 'Food Scarcity and the Empowerment of the Female Consumer in World War I Berlin', in Victoria de Grazia (ed.), *The Sex of Things: Gender and Consumption in Historical Perspective* (Berkeley, CA: University of California Press, 1996), pp. 287–310; Victoria de Grazia, 'Geschlecht und Konsum. Rolle und Bild der Konsumentin in den Verbrauchprotesten des Ersten Weltkrieges', *Archiv für Sozialgeschichte* 38 (1998), pp. 119–39.

11. The notion of 'queuing society' stems from my PhD thesis on the social experience of shortages in Communist Poland. See Małgorzata Mazurek,

Społeczeństwo kolejki. O doświadczeniach niedoboru 1945–1989 (Society waiting in lines. On social experiences of shortages 1945–1989) (Warszawa: Wydawnictwo Trio, 2010).

12. Lesiakowski, 'Strajki robotnicze w Łodzi' (Workers' strikes in Łódź), p. 34; Tomasz Balbus and Łukasz Kamiński, *Grudzień '70 poza Wybrzeżem w dokumentach aparatu władzy* (December '70 outside of the Coast in the documents of the state apparatus) (Instytut Pamięci Narodowej, Wrocław, 2000), p. 68.

13. Archiwum Akt Nowych (AAN), 926/59 KC PZPR. Wydział Organizacyjny, Notatka na temat pracy wśród kobiet pracujących w Łodzi (March 1971) (A notice on political work among working women in Łódź), unpaged.

14. Ibid.

15. Archiwum Akt Nowych (AAN), 926/60 (KC PZPR). Wydział Organizacyjny, Informacja nr 47/K/1971 o przerwach w pracy. Zakłady Przemysłu Dziewiarskiego 'Watra' w Lubawce, pow. Kamienna Góra (woj. wrocławskie) (Information no. 47/K/1971 about strikes. Cotton Industry Works 'Watra' in Lubawka, district Kamienna Góra), 10 March 1971, unpaged.

16. Ibid.

17. On the regional, sector and branch differentiation of social services funds, see Kazimierz Szwemberg, 'Poziom świadczeń socjalnych w przemyśle lekkim' (The level of social provisioning in light industry), in Jolanta Kulpińska (ed.), *Włókniarze w procesie zmian* (Textile workers in the process of changes) (Warszawa: Instytut Wydawniczy CRZZ, 1975), pp. 243–60.

18. Stefania Dzięcielska-Machnikowska, 'Struktura społeczna załóg a modernizacja przemysłu lekkiego' (Social structure of shop floor and modernisation of the light industry), *Przegląd Ekonomiczno-Społeczny m. Łodzi* 2 (1975), pp. 39–55; Barbara Nowakowska and Zofia Zarzycka, 'Aktywność zawodowa kobiet a ich wykształcenie' (Professional activity of women and their educational training), *Acta Universitatis Lodziensis. Zeszyty Naukowe Uniwersytetu Łódzkiego. Nauki Ekonomiczne i Socjologiczne* 3(44) (1979), pp. 23–42.

19. In 1971 only 50 per cent of all textile plants qualified to further exploitation and adaptation of new production technologies. See Fundacja Dokumentacji PRL (Foundation of Documentation of Communist Poland), non-classified acts, Sprawozdanie zespołu badającego problemy społeczno-ekonomiczne m. Łodzi, raport dla członków Biura Politycznego i Komitetu Centralnego PZPR, 8 kwietnia 1971 (Report of the expert group on socio-economic conditions in Łódź for the Central Committee and Political Bureau of PZPR), manuscript, p. 2.

20. Ibid., p. 3.

21. Marta Sikorska-Kowalska, *Wizerunek kobiety łódzkiej przełomu XIX i XX wieku* (An image of Łódź woman at the turn of the nineteenth and twentieth century) (Łódź: Wydawnictwo Ibidem, 2001), pp. 46–7.

22. Henryka Maj, 'Zmniejszenie stanu zatrudnienia przy pracach ręcznych, uciążliwych i szkodliwych dla zdrowia (Wyniki badań w przemyśle bawełnianym) [The reduction of handwork and workplaces dangerous to health (Results of the examination in the cotton industry)], część II', *Studia i materiały Instytutu Pracy i Spraw Socjalnych* 8 (1982), p. 19.

23. Archiwum Państwowe m. Łodzi (APŁ), 140, Komitet Łódzki PZPR. Posiedzenia plenarne, Protokół stenograficzny Plenum KŁ PZPR odbytego w dniu 26.06.1971 r. Stan realizacji zakładowych programów poprawy

warunków pracy w świetle listu Sekretariatu KC ze stycznia br (dyskusja) [Łódź Committe of PZPR. Plenary session. Protocol from the session of Łódź Committee of PZPR, 26 June 1971. A State of affairs of factory programmes on the improvement of working conditions in the light of Central Committee letter from January 1971 (discussion)], p. 132; Irena Dryll, 'Kierunki zmian w sytuacji społeczno-zawodowej włókniarzy' (Socio-professional situation of textile workers: directions of change), in Kulpińska (ed.), *Włókniarze w procesie zmian* (Textile workers in the process of change), pp. 209–10.

24. Czesław Kos, Remigiusz Krzyżewski and Krystyna Szymańska-Piotrowska, 'Wypoczynek, ochrona zdrowia i żywienie pracowników przemysłu lekkiego' (Recreation, health protection and nutrition of textile workers), in Kulpińska (ed.), *Włókniarze w procesie zmian*, pp. 261–75; here p. 271.

25. Sprawozdanie zespołu badającego problemy społeczno-ekonomiczne m. Łodzi (Report of the expert group...), p. 4.

26. Ibid., pp. 3–4.

27. Ibid., p. 3.

28. Archiwum Akt Nowych (AAN), 926/59, KC PZPR. Wydział Organizacyjny, Notatka dotycząca analizy pracy KD PZPR Łódź-Górna i KZ PZPR przy ZPB im. Armii Ludowej i przyczyn wydarzeń lutowych w Łodzi sporządzona przez instruktora CKKP Z. Kosteckiego za okres pobytu w Łodzi w dniach 1–6 marca 1971 r. (A notice concerning the functioning of District Committee of PZPR Łódź-Górna and Factory Committee of PZPR at the People's Army Cotton Works prepared by the party instructor Z. Kostecki during his stay in Łódź, 1–6 March 1971), unpaged.

29. APŁ, 1892, Komitet Łódzki PZPR. Wydział Organizacyjny, Sytuacja w ZPB im. J. Marchlewskiego dnia 12.02.1971 (Situation in the J. Marchlewski Cotton Works on 12 February 1971), p. 115.

30. Ibid., p. 119.

31. APŁ, 1892, Komitet Łódzki PZPR. Wydział Organizacyjny, Próba oceny przyczyn politycznych, ekonomicznych i społecznych lutowych wydarzeń w przemyśle włókienniczym i innym m. Łodzi (An attempt to evaluate political, economic and social causes of the February event in the Łódź textile industry) (March 1971), unpaged.

32. For more about the programme of modernisation launched in the years 1971–72, see Kulpińska (ed.), *Włókniarze w procesie zmian*.

33. Maj, 'Zmniejszenie stanu zatrudnienia', p. 18.

34. Dryll, 'Kierunki zmian w sytuacji', p. 203.

35. Jerzy Dietl and Teresa Jaworska, 'Kierunki rozwoju i usprawnienia gastronomii (w świetle doświadczeń w kraju i za granicą)' [The venues of development and improvement of local gastronomy (in the light of Polish and foreign experiences)], *Acta Universitatis Lodzensis. Zeszyty Naukowe Uniwersytetu Łódzkiego. Folia Oeconomica* 34 (1978), p. 56.

36. Archiwum Ruchu Zawodowego (ARZ), not classified files, Centralna Rada Związków Zawodowych, Wydział Socjalny, Tezy Komitetu Gospodarstwa Domowego dotyczące szerszego rozwoju usług żywienia zbiorowego na rzecz rodziny pracowniczej (17 February 1971) (Central Council of Trade Unions. Department of Social Affairs, Thesis of the Household Committee concerning the development of social consumption for workers' families), unpaged.

37. Dietl and Jaworska, 'Kierunki rozwoju i usprawnienia gastronomii', p. 54.
38. Ibid.
39. Józef Marczak, *Z pracy i życia włókniarzy* (From work and life of textile workers) (Warszawa: Instytut Wydawniczy CRZZ, 1976), p. 169. Zob. też Józef Marczak, Władysław Cieloch and Leon Polanowski, *Z badań nad budżetami domowymi i warunkami socjalno-bytowymi 4-osobowych rodzin łódzkich włókniarzy* (From the research on household budgets and social conditions of 4-person Łódź textile workers' families) (Łódź: Ośrodek Badawczy Zarządu Głównego Związku Zawodowego Pracowników Przemysłu Włókienniczego, Odzieżowego i Skórzanego, 1967); *Ośródek Badawczy ZG Pracowników Przemysłu Włókienniczego, Odzieżowego i Skórzanego, Usługi w opinii włókniarek łódzkich* (Łódź, 1977).
40. Archiwum Ruchu Zawodowego (ARZ), files not classified, CRZZ. Wydział Socjalny, Dobrosław Żuk. Recenzja opracowania pt. 'Żywienie przyzakładowe pracowników przemysłu lekkiego' (Social consumption in the textile plants), 1974, not paged.
41. APŁ, 148, KŁ PZPR. Protokoły posiedzeń plenarnych Komitetu Łódzkiego PZPR, Protokół plenarnego posiedzenia KŁ PZPR odbytego dnia 21 kwietnia 1975 r. Przemówienie wprowadzające o pomocy kobiecie pracującej (Plenary session protocols of the Łódź Committee of PZPR. An introductory speech on support for the working women) (21 April 1975), p. 101.
42. At the beginning of the 1970s only 8000 children among 90.000 pupils in Łódź primary schools had access to hot meals at school. Archiwum Akt Nowych (AAN), 926/59, KC PZPR. Wydział Organizacyjny, Notatka na temat pracy wśród kobiet pracujących w Łodzi, March 1971, unpaged. See also Wacława Starzyńska, 'Rynek usług gastronomicznych w opinii mieszkańców Łodzi' (Local gastronomy in the opinion of Łódź inhabitants), *Acta Universitatis Lodziensis. Zeszyty Naukowe Uniwersytetu Łódzkiego. Nauki Ekonomiczne i Socjologiczne* 3(31) (1978), pp. 71–80.
43. Dietl and Jaworska, 'Kierunki rozwoju i usprawnienia gastronomii', p. 67.
44. Stanisława Kacprzak-Wilmańska, 'Gastronomia w osiedlu mieszkaniowym w świetle preferencji jego mieszkańców' (Gastronomy in the housing: projects and preferences of their inhabitants), *Acta Universitatis Lodziensis. Zeszyty Naukowe Uniwersytetu Łódzkiego. Nauki Ekonomiczne i Socjologiczne* 3(12) (1977), pp. 81–100.
45. In the middle of the 1970s nearly 60 per cent of Łódź female workers shopped there.
46. Cz. Kos and R. Krzyżewski, *Żywienie w zakładach pracy jako element świadczeń socjalnych* (Collective nutrition in industrial plants as a part of the social provision system) (Warszawa: Dział Wydawnictw i Upowszechniania Instytutu Handlu Wewnętrznego i Usług, 1976), p. 39.
47. Stefania Dzięcielska-Machnikowska and Danuta Duraj, 'Rola kobiet w klasie robotniczej' (Role of women in the working class), *Acta Universitatis Lodziensis. Zeszyty Naukowe Uniwersytetu Łódzkiego. Folia Sociologica* 10 (1984), pp. 1–154.
48. Jolanta Kulpińska, 'Niektóre problemy stosunków społecznych w zakładach pracy przemysłu włókienniczego' (Some problems concerning social relations in the textile plants), in J. Kulpińska (ed.), *Włókniarze łódzcy. Monografia* (Łódź: Wydawnictwo Łódzkie, 1966), pp. 390–402; here pp. 398–401.

49. Dzięcielska-Machnikowska and Duraj, 'Rola kobiet', p. 134.
50. Kulpińska, 'Niektóre problemy stosunków społecznych', p. 398.
51. Dzięcielska-Machnikowska and Duraj, 'Rola kobiet', p. 139.
52. Archive of the Instytut Pamięci Narodowej, Łódź Division (AIPN Ld), IPN Ld Pf 10/980, t. 1, Informacja dotycząca nastrojów wśród załóg zakładów pracy na tle aktualnej sytuacji rynkowej (Information on the situation among industrial plants' crews vis-à-vis actual market provision) (8 August 1977), p. 78.
53. APŁ, 1418, Komitet Łódzki PZPR. Wydział Organizacyjny, Informacja nr 76/76 nt. sytuacji społeczno-gospodarczej oraz nastrojów w województwie (Information no. 76/76 on the socio-economic situation in the Łódź district), July 1976, p. 182.
54. Sugar rationing introduced in the summer of 1976 in Poland was the first rationing scheme after Stalinist austerity. Within the next few years, in 1980–81 in particular, food rationing schemes became commonplace. APŁ, 1418, Komitet Łódzki PZPR. Wydział Organizacyjny, Informacja nr 76/76 nt. sytuacji społeczno-gospodarczej oraz nastrojów w województwie, July 1976, p. 182.
55. APŁ, 1418, Komitet Łódzki PZPR. Wydział Organizacyjny, Informacja nr 78/76 dot. działań polityczno-organizacyjnych instancji oraz społecznego odbioru decyzji rządowych w sprawie zasad sprzedaży cukru (Information no. 78/76 concerning activities of political authorities and social reactions to the new regulations on the sugar supply), not dated, p. 188.
56. APŁ, 156, Komitet Dzielnicowy PZPR Łódź-Bałuty, Informacja z życia wewnątrzpartyjnego, spraw produkcyjnych i nastrojów wśród załogi ZTK 'Teofilów' (Information on local party activities, production issues and moods among the shop floor of 'Teofilów' works), 10 June 1980, p. 88.
57. According to sociological surveys from the autumn of 1981, 86.6 per cent of Polish society agreed that food grievances led to the conflicts between various social groups and individuals. See Elżbieta Skotnicka-Illasiewicz and Edmund Wnuk-Lipiński, 'Socjalne podłoże konfliktów' (Social background of conflicts), in Władysław Adamski (ed.), Polacy '81. Postrzeganie kryzysu i konfliktu (Poles '81. The perception of crisis and social conflict) (Warszawa: Instytut Filozofii i Socjologii PAN, 1982), pp. 71–92.
58. APŁ, 241, Komitet Dzielnicowy PZPR Łódź-Śródmieście, Informacja tygodniowa o sytuacji politycznej w w dzielnicy Łódź-Śródmieście (Weekly information on political situation of Łódź-Śródmieście district) (2 October 1981), p. 134.
59. Andrzej Wiśniewski, 'Sprzedaż towarów konsumpcyjnych w zakładach pracy' (Purchase of consumer goods in industrial plants), Handel Wewnętrzny 4–5 (1986), pp. 51–4.
60. 'Włókniarze nareszcie' (Textile workers, finally!), Solidarność Ziemi Łódzkiej 8 (20 November 1980), p. 3.
61. APŁ, 1440, Komitet Łódzki PZPR. Wydział Organizacyjny, Informacja nr 245/81 dot. sytuacji łódzkich zakładach pracy.
62. See also 'Postawy: dlaczego w "Solidarności"? Rozmowa z przewodniczącym Komitetu Zakładowego NSZZ "Solidarność" przy ZPO im. A. Próchnika' (Attitudes: why in 'Solidarność' trade union? An interview with a leader of the factory committee of 'Solidarność' in the A. Próchnik Textile

Works), *Solidarność z Gdańskiem. Pismo współpracujące z niezależnym ruchem związkowym* 15 (5 January 1981), p. 2.

63. Archiwum Akt Nowych (AAN), 38/4, Urząd Rady Ministrów, Oświadczenie załogi Łódzkich Zakładów Przemysłu Bawełnianego im. Obrońców Pokoju 'Uniontex' w Łodzi w sprawie reglamentacji mięsa (A communication of Uniontex Cotton Works on the meat distribution), 24 July 1981, p. 148.

Index

Lightning Source UK Ltd.
Milton Keynes UK
UKOW06n0622260216

269166UK00018B/226/P